# Biology, Medicine and Society 1840–1940

*Edited by*
CHARLES WEBSTER

CAMBRIDGE UNIVERSITY PRESS

Cambridge
London   New York   New Rochelle
Melbourne   Sydney

Published by the Press Syndicate of the University of Cambridge
The Pitt Building, Trumpington Street, Cambridge CB2 1RP
32 East 57th Street, New York, NY 10022, USA
296 Beaconsfield Parade, Middle Park, Melbourne 3206, Australia

First published 1981

Printed in Malta by Interprint Ltd

*British Library Cataloguing in Publication Data*
Biology, medicine and society 1840–1940.
–(Past and present publications).
1. Medicine – History
I. Webster, Charles, *b. 1936*   II. Series
610′ 9′034   RC131   80–41752
ISBN 0 521 23770 X

# Contents

# Contributors

John R. Durant is a Staff Tutor in biology in the Department of Extramural Studies, University College of Swansea. His chief interests are the history and social relations of late-nineteenth- and twentieth-century biology; he is currently engaged in research into the influence of ethology theory on the sciences of man in this period.

Carol Dyhouse teaches social history and education at the University of Sussex. She is particularly interested in the history of women in nineteenth- and twentieth-century England and is currently working on a history of girls' socialization.

Brian Harrison is a Fellow and Tutor in Politics and History at Corpus Christi College, Oxford. Among his publications are *Drink and the Victorians* (1971) and *Separate Spheres. The Opposition to Women's Suffrage in Britain* (1978).

Daniel J. Kevles is Professor of History at the California Institute of Technology and the author of *The Physicists: The History of a Scientific Community in Modern America* (Knopf, 1978). He is currently at work on the history of genetics and eugenics in the United States and Britain.

Donald Mackenzie is Lecturer in Sociology at the University of Edinburgh. He is completing a study of the development of statistical theory in Britain between the 1860s and 1920s.

B. Norton teaches history and social relations of science at Leicester University. He is interested in the roles played by modern psychology in British and American culture.

G. R. Searle is Lecturer in History at the University of East Anglia. His previous publications include *The Quest for National Efficiency* (1971) and *Eugenics and Politics in Britain 1900–1914* (1976). He has recently completed a study of the Radical Right in early twentieth-century Britain. At present he is working on the theme of corruption in the Edwardian political system.

Gillian Sutherland is Fellow, Lecturer and Director of Studies in History at Newnham College, Cambridge. Her publications include *Policy-Making in Elementary Education 1870–1895* (1973). She is a member of the editorial board of *Social History*. The paper published here forms part of a larger study, *Ability, Merit and Measurement: Mental Testing and English Education*, to go to press in 1981.

Paul Weindling is Research Officer at the Wellcome Unit for the History of Medicine, Oxford. He has contributed to three collaborative volumes on the history of scientific organizations, and is completing a dissertation on Oscar Hertwig. His main research is on the social history of medicine in Imperial Germany.

# Preface and Acknowledgements

This volume has its origin in the conference on 'The Roots of Socio-biology', held by the Past and Present Society in conjunction with the British Society for the History of Science on 29 September 1978. The volume comprises revised texts of the four main papers delivered at the conference by Harrison, Mackenzie, Searle and Norton, together with additional contributions by other partici-pants in the conference: Durant, Dyhouse, Kevles, Sutherland and Weindling. The editor is particularly grateful to John Durant and Paul Weindling for preparing full-length contributions at relatively short notice. The brief Introduction is designed to provide a con-text, without in any way duplicating the contents of the volume.

As might be expected the conference was heavily subscribed and included much lively debate on controversial issues. The organizers were grateful to Professor J. Maynard Smith for representing the biologist position, and to Dr R. M. Young and members of the Radical Science Collective for their contribution and criticisms. Dr W. H. Bynum and Mr G. L'E. Turner from the British Society assisted with the organization of the meeting.

The essays by Kevles and Sutherland are to appear separately in *Isis* and D. Hamilton and J. V. Smith (eds.), *The Meritocratic Intel-lect: Studies in the History of Educational Research* (Aberdeen: Aberdeen University Press, 1980) respectively. The editor and the Past and Present Society would like to thank the editor of *The Journal of Social History* for permission to reprint the essay by Dyhouse.

The index has been prepared by Penelope M. Gouk.

*Corpus Christi College, Oxford*                    Charles Webster

ix

# Introduction

CHARLES WEBSTER

Modern biology and medicine are inescapably involved with questions of policy and politics. The essays comprising the present volume explore major dimensions of this interrelationship. The authors demonstrate convincingly that cross-currents between the arenas of biological and social thought have persisted into the present century, notwithstanding the apparent greater isolation, sophistication and objectivity of the modern experimental sciences. The current sociobiology debate is merely the most recent manifestation of this interaction. It is by no means lost on participants in the many-sided controversy surrounding sociobiology, that generic sources for their respective views may be located at various points within the modern scientific movement, Darwinian evolutionary theory being outstandingly important. When, in an isolated and intentionally inscrutable remark in the *Origin of Species* (1859), Darwin conceded that 'light will be thrown on the origin of man and his history' he was inaugurating a new phase in the continuing debate concerning the relationship between the biological and social sciences.[1] The novelty of evolutionary language failed to obscure the deeper historical roots of ideas concerning the relevance of evolution to social thought. Indeed the programme for deducing political principles from the experimental sciences is virtually concomitant with the scientific movement.

Problems of population have provided an important occasion for the transference of ideas between the scientific and political areas. The whole rise into industrialization of Western Europe has been accompanied by theorizing concerning the relationship, between wealth and population. The sciences provided a stimulus for data gathering in the fields of economics and population and they evolved tools for mathematical analysis of these data. Natural philosophers contributed freely to economic and population theory; their speculation and analysis periodically questioned the ability of western

[1] Charles Darwin, *On the Origin of Species* (London, 1859), p. 488.

1

society to sustain economic growth and population expansion without commitment to radical redirections of policy.

Major initiatives in social theory and policy characteristic of Britain in the 1840s such as Chadwick's sanitarianism, Farr's vital statistics, or Spencer's social statics, were conceived with explicit reference to biological and physical principles. The principal evolutionists Charles Darwin and Alfred Russel Wallace, as well as Spencer, derived fundamental insights concerning the mechanism of evolution from their reading of Malthus on population. Farr's independent conclusions concerning evolutionary trends in human society were founded upon his negative reaction to Malthus.[2] Since the theory of natural selection emerged with reference to Malthusianism and against a background of experience conditioned by *laissez-faire* utilitarianism, it comes as no surprise that the evolutionists should fuel the fires of economic individualism in the later nineteenth century. Evolutionary theory, from its outset, provided a ready means for the free transference of ideas between the biological and political 'sciences'. The two have existed in symbiotic relationship, the interplay of ideas extending through the behavioural sciences even into cell biology and physiology, as indicated by the essays by Weindling and others in this volume. Darwinism came to the aid of a variety of social causes, including the obstruction of state interference in the field of social welfare, opposition to feminism, defence of imperialism and subjugation of inferior races, and support for the traditional industrial order and free trade. Evolutionary theory rivalled the scriptures in the degree to which it could pronounce on specific cases of conscience. Like the scriptures it could justify mutually incompatible objectives.

Before the publication of G. E. Moore's *Principia Ethica* (1903), contributions to naturalistic ethics by Spencer, Stephen, and Alexander seemed to provide a definitive application of natural

[2] J. R. Poynter, *Society and Pauperism: English Ideas on Poor Relief, 1795–1834* (London, 1969); J. M. Eyler, *Victorian Social Medicine. The Ideas and Methods of William Farr* (Baltimore, 1979); D. E. C. Eversley, *Social Theories of Fertility and the Malthusian Debate* (London, 1959); A. Chase, *The Legacy of Malthus* (New York, 1977); R. M. Young, 'Malthus and the Evolutionists: the Common Context of Biological and Social Theory', *Past and Present*, no. 43 (1969), pp. 109–45; S. Herbert, 'The Place of Man in the Development of Darwin's Theory of Transmutation', *Journal of the History of Biology*, vii (1974), pp. 249–57; *ibid.*, x(1977), pp. 155–227; H. E. Gruber, *Darwin on Man* (New York, 1974).

selection. After Moore's book it was more difficult in philosophical circles to make the equation between 'better' and 'more evolved'. but the advent of modern sociobiology indicates that biologists are inclined to ignore the problems raised by this 'fallacy'. Organic evolution played a central role in naturalistic ethics by virtue of the ready analogies offered between animal and human societies, and because it provided a convenient means whereby metaphysical principles such as Spencer's 'differentiation and integration', or Driesch's 'entelechy', could be implanted in the social sciences.

John Durant's essay on the origins of ethology illustrates the dialectic between the biological and social sciences, by indicating the transference of ideas about human society to the animal order, and then their return to provide a biological rationale for behaviour within the human family. The essential emphasis of pioneer animal behaviourists from Heinroth to Lorenz was to locate the maximum component of behaviour in innate characteristics of long-standing evolutionary origin, so paving the way for identification of a strong racial component in human character. This line of argument was implicit in Darwin's *Descent of Man* and *Expression of the Emotions in Man and Animals*. 'Survival of the fittest' came to be interpreted with respect to the preservation of the kinship group of animals or primitive man, or in more advanced societies in terms of subservience to the interests of the state or economic system. Darwinists would have recognized their kinship with modern sociobiologists, whose fusion of elements from ethology, ecology and genetics has been used to undermine the 'ultra-environmentalism' of modern anthropology and sociology, in the interests of establishing that 'the more stereotyped forms of human behaviour are mammalian, and even more specifically primate in character, as predicted on the basis of general evolutionary theory'.[3]

[3] E. O. Wilson, *On Human Nature* (Cambridge, Mass., 1978), pp. 16–20, 32. See also the final chapter 'Man: From Sociobiology to Sociology' in E. O. Wilson, *Sociobiology: The New Synthesis* (Cambridge, Mass., 1975). For a contrary view see C. Geertz, *The Interpretation of Cultures* (New York, 1973); R. C. Lewontin, *The Genetic Basis of Evolutionary Change* (New York, 1974). For Darwinism and sociobiology, see especially M. Sahlins, *The Use and Abuse of Biology* (London, 1977) and R. C. Lewontin, 'Sociobiology – A Caricature of Darwinism' in P. Asquith and F. Suppe (eds.), *PSA 1976*, ii (E. Lansing, Michigan, 1977), pp. 22–31. For a philosophical presentation see M. Ruse, *Sociobiology: Sense or Nonsense* (Dordrecht, 1979). For collections of papers

The introduction of the civil registration of births, marriages and deaths in England and Wales, and William Farr's appointment as Compiler of Abstracts to the Registrar General in 1837 provided the first firm foundation for the study of population trends in Britain. Darwin's first notebook on the transmutation of species dates from the same year. The *Annual Reports* of the Registrar General which Farr transformed into demographic classics contain copious data confirming the fears of sanitarians concerning excessive mortality, and of the Malthusians about excessive fertility among the lower orders. Evolutionists took these phenomena as a sign of the operation of natural selection within societies which had reached the level of industrialization – the highest plane of evolution. Few Darwinians shared Spencer's confidence in the adaptability of modern populations. Most saw sanitarianism and social welfare as the route to the preservation of the unfit, thereby contributing to the prevailing mood of pessimism concerning the future of the nation and the race. These fears seemed to be amply confirmed by the condition of the Boer War recruits as exposed by the *Report of the Inter-departmental Committee on Physical Deterioration* (1904), and similar reports on the physical condition of conscripts during the first World War. Creation of the Ministry of Health in 1919 further extended the data-gathering process concerning ill-health.

Charles Darwin's son, Major Leonard Darwin, gloomily pronounced that the nation as a whole was slowly and steadily deteriorating as regards its average inborn qualities, and would not be able to fight another major war.[4] Even technical experts like J. B. S. Haldane concluded that owing to the overfertility of the unskilled classes the national intelligence quotient was declining at the rate of 1–2 per cent per generation. The Wood Committee (1929) accepted that mental deficiency had doubled within twenty years. R. B. Cattell predicted that mental deficiency was increasing

representing various points of view on sociobiology, see *The Sociobiology Debate*, ed. A. L. Caplan (New York, 1978); *Readings in Sociobiology*, eds. T. H. Clutton Brock and P. H. Harvey (Cambridge, 1978); *Sociobiology and Human Nature*, eds. M. S. Gregory, A. Silvers and D. Sutch (San Francisco, 1978); 'The Evolution of Adaptation by Natural Selection', *Proceedings of the Royal Society (B)*, ccv (1979), pp. 433–604; V. Reynolds, 'Sociobiology and the Idea of Primordial Discrimination', *Ethnic and Racial Studies*, iii (1980), pp. 303–15, with exchange between Reynolds and P. L. van den Berghe, pp. 475–83.
[4] L. Darwin, *The Need for Eugenic Reform* (London, 1926).

at such a rate that the western nations were degenerating into races of 'sub-men'.[5] Between the wars, writers on social policy frequently echoed the refrain of Lloyd George that the nation was courting disaster by attempting to run an A1 Empire equipped with only C3 health.

The reaction of evolutionists to the above situation was not uniform with respect to theory or practice. One faction believed that social reform was an indispensable protection against racial decline, whereas its opponents argued that degeneration was exacerbated by social amelioration. At the theoretical level there was disagreement concerning the degree to which the evolutionary mechanism applied to animals could also be effective in man. Alfred Russel Wallace adopted a dualist position, admitting that man's body was developed by natural selection, but rejecting the view that his intellectual and moral faculties were so developed.[6] The evolution of man's moral sense, as well as his mathematical, artistic and metaphysical qualities were thought to belong to the 'unseen universe of Spirit'. Other Darwinists were dismayed by this concession, which was seen as opening the way to the further erosion of the theory of natural selection. Like their modern counterparts in the field of sociobiology, the Darwinists took up the challenge to apply natural selection to all aspects of human behaviour, including the moral sense, regarding this as the 'best initial test of the adequacy or inadequacy of the theory of natural selection outside the merely biological domain'.[7]

More thoroughgoing natural selectionists were divided in their loyalties with respect to 'hard' and 'soft' theories of heredity. Decision on this issue profoundly affected social ideas, although it would be erroneous to make a simple equation between Lamarckian inheritance and reformist environmentalism. Characteristically, Darwin vacillated over the relative importance of the selection of hereditary characteristics and the inheritance of acquired characteristics. Spencer was responsible for deflecting

[5] J. B. S. Haldane, *Possible Worlds and other Essays* (London, 1927), p. 206; *idem, Heredity and Politics* (London, 1938), p. 186; R. B. Cattell, *The Fight for National Intelligence* (London, 1937). Also on the theme of 'sub-man', see R. Austin Freeman, *Social Decay and Regeneration* (London, 1921).
[6] A. R. Wallace, *Darwinism* (London, 1889), pp. 476–8.
[7] A. D. Richie, *Darwinism and Politics*, 2nd edn. (London, 1891), p. 96.

Darwin in the 'Lamarckian' direction.[8] Ultimately a significant body of evolutionary opinion in England inclined to this Lamarckian standpoint, which tended to highlight the flexibility of human societies to adapt to the needs of the changing environment. Departure from a strict selectionist account of evolution tended to be associated with the introduction of obscure directional influences, or holistic forces, to account for trends in organic or social evolution. 'Neo-Lamarckism' received its greatest formal expression in America at the turn of the century.[9] In Germany the inheritance of acquired characteristics was embodied into Haeckel's monism. The contribution to this volume by Paul Weindling draws attention to the strength of the non-Darwinist position in Germany, and to the complexity of the debate regarding evolutionary theory in German scientific circles. The widely used theory of the cell state is used to illustrate the broader social and institutional ramifications of biological theory.

At one stage it seemed that the selectionist position was becoming seriously undermined, particularly with respect to human evolution.[10] The selectionist position was strengthened by the hypothesis founded on a marriage of the ideas on heredity and the cytological basis of inheritance of August Weismann and Francis Galton, the latter being inclined to a more consistently hereditarian view of natural selection than his cousin Charles Darwin. Galton's ideas concerning human heredity and his prevailing concern to protect the hereditary endowment of his own class crystallized into the science of 'eugenics', first announced in his *Inheritance of Human Faculties* (1883). The degree to which the ground was prepared for Galton's eugenics is indicated by the extent to which he was anticipated in the writings of William Farr. The two joined

[8] The relationship between Darwin and Spencer is discussed in detail in a series of contributions to *Current Anthropology*, xv (Sept. 1974), pp. 211–37. For a broader consideration of Darwin's contemporaries, see J. W. Burrow, *Evolution and Society: A Study in Victorian Social Theory* (Cambridge, 1966).

[9] G. Stocking, 'Lamarckism in American Social Science, 1890–1915', *Journal of the History of Ideas*, xxiii (1962), pp. 239–56; for recent reappraisals of the relationship between the biological and social sciences see R. N. Soffer, *Ethics and Society in England: the Revolution in the Social Sciences 1870–1914* (Berkeley, Cal., 1978) and R. C. Bannister, *Social Darwinism: Science and Myth in Anglo-American Thought* (Philadelphia, 1979).

[10] P. Geddes and J. A. Thomson, *The Evolution of Sex* (London, 1889), pp. 303–6 for a lucid statement of the debate as it stood in the year of publication of Wallace's *Darwinism*.

forces on the Anthropometric Committee of the British Association for the Advancement of Science in the 1870s.[11]

Eugenics made its impact through the colourful work of Galton. The original researches were consolidated into the science of biometrics by Galton's aggressive lieutenant, Karl Pearson. Paradoxically, neither Pearson nor his Mendelian rival William Bateson, joined the Eugenics Education Society, although both were leading advocates of eugenics. Regardless of the reticence of some experts, the eccentric gospel of eugenics became a major force in middle-class opinion in the period before the second World War. Genetics, anthropometry and psychometry advanced the science of eugenics, and eugenics was a spur to the professionalization of genetics and psychology. Eugenics could scarcely advance without lay support, but the extent of this support surprised and in certain cases dismayed the experts. Eugenic societies spread throughout the western world, and they became the spearhead for the protection of entrenched middle-class interests, which seemed fortuitously to coincide with the proper workings of the laws of evolution. The historical importance of the eugenics movement in Britain and America in both its professional and lay dimensions is recognized by its detailed consideration in the contributions to this volume by Kevles, Mackenzie, Norton and Searle.

Although the British eugenics movement attracted influential supporters, and on many points represented a coalition of diverse interests, it was slow to make an impact on social policy. Negative eugenics made more unimpeded headway in many American states and in Hitler's Germany, finding extreme expression in sterilization laws.[12] Compulsory sterilization of various classes of the unfit and voluntary euthanasia were under continuous discussion in Britain until about 1939, but parliament resisted action on either front.

[11] R. S. Cowan, 'Nature and Nurture: The Interplay of Biology and Politics in the Work of Francis Galton', *Studies in the History of Biology,* i (1977), pp. 133–208; J. M. Eyler, *Victorian Social Medicine,* pp. 28–9.

[12] K. M. Ludmerer, *Genetics and American Society: A Historical Appraisal* (Baltimore, 1972); G. E. Allen, 'Genetics, Eugenics and Class Struggle', *Genetics,* lxxix, supplement (1975), pp. 29–45; H. Ehrhardt, *Euthanasie und Vernichtung 'Lebensunwerten' Lebens* (Stuttgart, 1965); B. Schreiber, *The Men Behind Hitler* (London, 1975). For the background biological controversies, see *Heredity and Society: Readings in Social Genetics,* ed. A. S. Baer, 2nd edn (London, 1977); H. Cravens, *The Triumph of Evolution: American Scientists and the Heredity-Environment Controversy 1900–1941* (Philadelphia, 1978); *Eugenics: Then and Now,* ed. C. J. Bajema (New York, 1976).

Compulsory birth control for the lower classes was a potent measure in negative eugenics; but in this case middle-class fears of the adverse moral consequences of birth control confronted their delusions concerning racial decline. It was not until the 1920s that the Eugenics Society came to terms with the birth-control movement. Even then R. B. Cattell found few supporters in calling for compulsory contraception for the lower classes. In the absence of a more positive lead from the Eugenics Society, eugenist Marie Stopes formed the Society for Constructive Birth Control and Racial Progress (1921) as a means of disseminating birth control among the lower classes.[13]

Leading members of the Eugenics Society such as Cyril Burt and Lord Horder were also active in such pressure groups as the Malthusian League, the National Birth Control Association, the National Association for the Care of the Feeble-Minded and the National Council for Mental Hygiene. The eugenist impulse was accordingly important in the movements for birth-control, sterilization, euthanasia, and the control of deviant groups ranging from the blind to the mentally handicapped. All of these policies found keen advocates within the medical profession into the 1930s in Britain as well as Germany and the U.S.A. Advocates of birth control were slow to disentangle their movement from more extreme eugenic policies. The German sterilization law of 1933 was looked upon as an important medical experiment. Pressure for similar legislation in Britain led to a departmental investigation conducted under the Chairman of the Board of Control which reported in 1934, as well as unsuccessful bills within parliament.[14] As Searle points out, eugenists encountered vigorous medical and

[13] J. A. Banks, *Prosperity and Parenthood: A Study of Family Planning Among the Victorian Middle Classes* (London, 1954); *Population, Evolution and Birth Control*, ed. G. Hardin, 2nd edn (San Francisco, 1969); P. Branca, *Silent Sisterhood, Middle Class Women in the Victorian Home* (London, 1975); Geddes and Thomson, *The Evolution of Sex* (note 10), pp. 292–8, were exceptional among biologists in their open support for birth control.

[14] Sterilization was keenly advocated by such influential figures as Lord Dawson of Penn, Leonard Darwin and E. W. Macbride. For representative British pronouncements on sterilization from medical experts, see J. Gifford, 'Sterilization of the Mentally Defective', *Medical Officer*, xlix (1933), pp. 85–6; *Public Health*, xlvii (1934), pp. 245–7 (editorial). For a leading medical advocate of euthanasia, see C. Killick Millard, 'The Legislation of Voluntary Euthanasia', *Public Health*, xlv (1931), pp. 39–47 (presidential address to the Society of Medical Officers of Health). K. Jones, *Mental Health and Social Policy, 1845–1959* (London, 1960), pp. 50–6, 87–90.

lay opposition in their campaign for negative eugenic measures. Such minor gains of the eugenists as the Mental Deficiency Acts of 1913 and 1927, left their major objectives in the field of negative eugenics only incompletely accomplished.

The major impact of the eugenists came in the area of intelligence testing, a eugenist priority since the time of Galton's original work on the heredity of genius. Contributions to this volume by Norton and Sutherland are concerned with the theory and practice of intelligence testing. The elaboration of objective tests of intelligence, and their application in state education, emerged as the means whereby the eugenists could exercise a major social influence, without provoking widespread resistance. All political groups were likely to see the advantages of the application of a rational calculus to the placement of children in schools according to their natural aptitudes. Leading educationists such as Sir Percy Nunn were rapidly converted to intelligence testing by the work of Burt and his associates. Little impact was made by the findings of objectors, whether pointing to the adverse effect of the environment in the expression of aptitudes of working-class children, or to the great extent of educational waste caused by social deprivation.[15] It is only recently that the intelligence testing of the 1930s has become subject to critical scrutiny.[16]

Despite its major success in the field of education, during the 1930s the eugenics movement was largely overtaken by events. The example of Germany gradually created a distaste for negative eugenics. The Registrar General's statistics confirmed that the birth rate among the poor sections of the community had been steadily declining since before the turn of the century, while those classes were still affected by high rates of infant mortality, thought necessary by many eugenists to provide a check on the unfit.[17] The social impact of the depression emphasized the degree to which the lower classes were at the mercy of vagaries in the economic system. Since this plight affected skilled artisans as indifferently as the meanest labourers, it could scarcely be attributable to genetic

[15] Summarized in R. M. Titmuss, *Birth, Poverty and Wealth* (London, 1943), pp. 62–6.

[16] L. Kamin, *The Science and Politics of I.Q.* (New York, 1974); *The I.Q. Controversy*, ed. N. J. Block and G. Dworkin (New York, 1976).

[17] J. W. Innes, *Class Fertility Trends in England and Wales 1887–1934* (London, 1938; Sir Robert Hutchinson (President of the Royal College of Physicians), 'Paediatrics, Past, Present and Prospective', *Lancet*, (1940), ii, p. 799.

incompetence, or long-term racial decline. Increasingly the Eugenics Society was able to mitigate its emphasis on negative eugenics, and support the general application of positive inducements to family welfare, such as child allowances. Massive evidence accumulated during the depression to support the position of environmentalists within the eugenics movement who claimed that the greater part of the difference in physique and intelligence between the social classes was based on environmental rather than genetic factors. Since the environment was the more easily controlled, it was advocated that policy should be directed towards the production of a 'single equalised environment in which the inherited qualities of the race can develop under the most favourable conditions'.[18] As a reversion from his earlier tolerance of negative eugenics, these views were adopted by the American Nobel Prize-winning geneticist, Thomas Hunt Morgan, in both his *Embryology and Genetics* (1934) and his Nobel lecture delivered in the same year.[19]

This reformist environmentalism guided such movements as the Campaign Against Malnutrition, and the writings of Sir John Boyd Orr, the major spokesman on the question of the debilitating influence of dietary deficiency, which was increasingly recognized as endemic among the lower social groups. R. M. Titmuss used the Eugenics Society as a platform to draw attention, by an analysis of the Registrar General's statistics, to the persisting inequalities of health between the social classes and between the more prosperous and poorer regions, which in his view were patently associated with economic factors and which rendered premature any conclusions regarding hereditary differences between the classes.[20] Thus by 1940 the Eugenics Society was at least partly won over to the views of such leading outside critics of eugenics as Lancelot Hogben.

[18] J. Huxley, 'Eugenics and Society', *Eugenics Review*, xxviii (1936), p. 11 (Galton Lecture). Huxley withdrew from a more conservative eugenic position into line with other biologists favouring environmentalism. See G. Wersky, *The Visible College* (London, 1978), pp. 241–3.
[19] G. E. Allen, *Thomas Henry Morgan: The Man and his Science* (Princeton, 1978), p. 233. For a more severe assessment of Morgan and American eugenics, see Allen, 'Genetics, Eugenics and Class Struggle' (note 12); B. Mehler and G. E. Allen, 'Sources in the Study of Eugenics. Inventory of the American Eugenics Society Papers', *The Mendel Newsletter*, no. 14 (1977), pp. 9–15; see also *ibid.*, no. 16 (1978), pp. 6–11 and no. 17 (1979), pp. 5–10.
[20] R. M. Titmuss, *Poverty and Population* (London, 1938); *idem, Birth, Poverty and Wealth* (note 15).

As indicated in the essays by Harrison and Weindling, the Darwinists and eugenists provided scientific strength to the arguments of the anti-feminists. Building on the obvious biological differences between male and female thought to be occasioned by sexual selection, they tended to emphasize the physical inferiority of women, their lower mental capacity with respect to the creative arts and sciences, and their adaptivity to the domestic role to which they were destined by biological and social evolution. In the case of lower classes, persistently high rates of infant mortality were thought to be indicative of some kind of racial degeneration of child-rearing instincts among their women.[21]

Harrison and Dyhouse, in the opening essays in this volume, examine the social context of population change with respect to mortality rates and standards of health among women and infants. It is agreed that both groups experienced a major improvement in health, but there is less agreement concerning the explanation of this trend, and about the relative importance of a variety of medical and social factors. The demographic changes are clearcut and striking. They constitute one of the major features in the modern demographic history of western Europe. The crude mortality rate declined steadily from 1871 to 1931, during which period it was reduced by some 50 per cent. The downturn in infant mortality rates began only at the turn of the century, but here also the decline was rapid, the rate being halved by 1940.[22] Harrison swims against the tide of feminist history, to marshal evidence pointing to the limited feminist involvement in the movement for the improvement of women's health, while conceding some role for women's organizations in general.

Dr Harrison's paper raises the broader question of the involvement of women in the health movement, whether in a lay or professional capacity, and irrespective of their subscription to militant feminism. Organizations of nurses, midwives and health visitors unquestionably contributed to the improvement in the professional standing of their groups, by improving the quality of their training and service, and by acting as pressure groups where

[21] For a summary of the views of major evolutionists who commented on this issue, see Susan Sleeth Mosedale, 'Science Corrupted: Victorian Biologists Consider "The Woman Question"', *Journal of the History of Biology*, xi (1978), pp. 1–55.
[22] For the most recent detailed survey of demographic trends, see *Scottish Population History from the 17th century to the 1930s*, ed. M. Flinn (Cambridge, 1977).

legislation was involved. Women formed or contributed to innumerable health-orientated societies such as the Charity Organization Society and many minor provincial variants often called Ladies' Sanitary Societies, the Ladies' Association for the Diffusion of Sanitary Knowledge, and the Women's Imperial Health Association. More recently women have worked in the Association of Infant Welfare and Maternity Centres, the National Society of Day Nurseries, the Women's Cooperative Guild, and the National Council for Social Service. Many of these organizations rose to a position of importance during the interwar years. The appointment of Dr Janet Campbell to oversee maternal and child welfare in the newly formed Ministry of Health confirmed the extent of effective female participation in this field.

The effectiveness of the above groups is signified by such indices as the expansion of maternity and child welfare agencies. Infant welfare centres, first established in 1907, reached nearly four thousand in number by 1940; ante-natal clinics began in 1915 and grew to nearly two thousand by 1940. By this date 60 per cent of expectant mothers were attending ante-natal clinics. As Carol Dyhouse appreciates, we are currently unable to judge the degree to which the infant welfare centres contributed to the decline in infant mortality, especially in the early years of the century. If these centres performed an educational function, it is not clear whether their effect was primarily to improve infant feeding, or to prevent diseases of infancy.[23]

The continuing rise in standards of health, even during the depression, is variously taken as a tribute to the increasingly comprehensive edifice of public health and social services, as a reflection of the impact of advances in the medical sciences, or as a sign that there was a general improvement in standards of living, notwithstanding hard times temporarily experienced in certain areas. We need to be reminded that many informed contemporary observers, whether of environmentalist or selectionist persuasion, tended to adopt a more pessimistic estimate of achievements in the field of health. In infancy wide discrepancies persisted between the levels of mortality of rich and poor, and there was serious concern about the standards of health and physique of children from the lower classes. Maternal mortality actually increased until 1936, and

[23] F. B. Smith, *The People's Health 1830–1910* (London, 1979), pp. 65–135.

there are clear indicators of a high level of maternal disablement associated with childbirth. Reliable indices of morbidity considerably qualify the initial optimistic impressions derived from our initial reference to trends in mortality. Observers like Titmuss pointed to a decline of standards of health in Britain by comparison with other western nations. Notwithstanding the great fall in the crude death rate before 1940, it was felt that advances in nutritional science, medicine, sanitation, hygiene and housing had failed to bring proportionate benefits to the mass of the population.[24]

[24] R. M. Titmuss, *Birth, Poverty and Wealth* (note 15), p. 33.

# 1. Women's Health and the Women's Movement in Britain: 1840–1940

## BRIAN HARRISON

The statistics for improvements in women's health since the 1840s are impressive. Between 1840–9 and 1960–5 the death-rate of women between the ages of twenty-five and thirty-four in England and Wales fell continuously from 10.6 to 1.8 per thousand. The ratio of male to female mortality in England and Wales (adjusted for age differences) was simultaneously rising – from 1.096 in 1841–5 to 1.276 in 1931–5. Maternal deaths per thousand live births in the United Kingdom fell from 4.71 in 1900–2 to 0.17 in 1972–4. These trends continue: for example, perinatal mortality per thousand births in Great Britain fell from 37.7 in 1949 to 34.6 in 1959, to 23.6 in 1969, to 19.5 in 1975. Female deaths due to pregnancy, childbirth or abortion fell strikingly between 1968 and 1975. There are no comparable statistics for levels of morbidity, whose relationship to levels of mortality is complex; but the improvement in mortality rates is impressive enough in itself, and the continuous fall in the age of menarche – by three to four months per decade during the last century – reflects an improved nutrition which can hardly have left morbidity levels unaffected.[1]

Many factors apart from improved nutrition have combined to produce this improvement: improved standards of public health, a reduced birth-rate which has the advantage of concentrating births at physiologically the most suitable time, and the dramatic decline in puerperal sepsis. The period has also seen major improvements in the diagnosis of pregnancy, in the understanding of

I am most grateful to Mrs Jenifer Hart, of St Anne's College, Oxford, for commenting on an earlier draft of this essay; I alone am to blame for any mistakes which remain.
[1] B. R. Mitchell and P. Deane, *Abstract of British Historical Statistics* (Cambridge, 1962), pp. 40–1; B. R. Mitchell and H. G. Jones, *Second Abstract of British Historical Statistics* (Cambridge, 1971), p. 26; Central Statistical Office, *Annual Abstract of Statistics, 1976* (London, n.d.), p. 48; Department of Health and Social Security, *Health and Personal Services Statistics for England, 1977* (London, 1977), pp. 13, 16; W. J. Martin, 'A Comparison of the Trends of Male and Female Mortality', *Journal of the Royal Statistical Society*, ser. A, cxiv (1951), p. 296; W. A. Marshall and J. M. Tanner, 'Puberty', in J. A. Davis and J. Dobbing (eds.), *Scientific Foundations of Paediatrics* (London, 1974), p. 146.

menstruation, in the provision of ante-natal care and in surgical obstetrics and gynaecology.[2] All this amounts to a major liberation of women and perhaps deserves more attention than the legal, educational and political dimensions of women's emancipation which have hitherto dominated the textbooks. So complex a change can be explained only by breaking down the inquiry into manageable dimensions. The prominence of twentieth-century doctors in combating disease suggests that a beginning can usefully be made by analysing their impact on women's health over a longer time-span. But scientists respond, in the questions they ask and the answers they provide, to their environment, and that environment has in no respect changed more dramatically between 1840 and 1940 in Britain than in the transformation of attitudes to women. Here, then, is a second way of controlling the inquiry: women's health is now rightly seen by feminists as central to women's emancipation, and feminists' direct or indirect impact on doctors therefore seems worth investigating before wider inquiries are pursued by others.

Yet the doctor's impact on the health of both sexes is itself controversial during this period. Furthermore, the relationship between doctor and patient is confidential – a difficulty compounded by a British reticence on sexual matters which has only recently been overcome. Two incidents illustrate how profoundly the doctor could affect the lives of individual women. In 1852 Sir James Clark broke the last of the ties between Florence Nightingale and her family by telling her that her sister Parthe, who was psychologically devouring her, could recover her health only if Florence left home. And in 1894, when Bertrand Russell proposed to marry Alys, of whom his family disapproved, doctors were primed to inform him that his children would probably be mad, and 'a thick atmosphere of sighs, tears, groans, and morbid horror was produced in which it was scarcely possible to breathe'.[3] Few indeed are the documents likely to survive from incidents of

---

[2] D. M. Potts, 'Which is the Weaker Sex?', *Journal of Biosocial Science*, suppl. II (1970), p. 151; P. Branca, *Silent Sisterhood. Middle Class Women in the Victorian Home* (London, 1975), p. 83; *Historical Review of British Obstetrics and Gynaecology 1800–1850*, ed. J. M. Munro Kerr, R. W. Johnstone and M. H. Phillips (London, 1954), pp. 86, 89, 92, 121, 129, 152–3.
[3] C. Woodham-Smith, *Florence Nightingale 1820–1910* (London, 1953 edn.), pp. 103–4; Bertrand Russell, *Autobiography 1872–1914* (London, 1967), p. 84; cf. J. Harris, *William Beveridge. A Biography* (Oxford, 1977), pp. 69–70.

this kind and difficult indeed would it be to measure the overall impact on women of such consultations.

Problems are also posed by the secondary sources. Many historians of medicine adopt an unduly biographical approach and their perspectives are often excessively internal – neglecting the impact of social conditions and contemporary lay attitudes upon medical research, the impact of patient upon doctor. Ricci's *One Hundred Years of Gynaecology*, for instance, claims to be 'an historical document',[4] but virtually no historical context sullies its mood of professional self-congratulation. Fletcher Shaw's history of the Royal College of Obstetricians and Gynaecologists is entirely institutional and biographical in approach, and breathes an air of complacent male clubbery. The historians of British feminism are unhelpful from a different direction: they show surprisingly little interest in the medical dimension of so many feminist careers, despite the centrality of improvements in women's health to women's emancipation. The three leading biographers of Florence Nightingale, for instance, say all too little about her attitude to disease and her relationship to the attack on the Contagious Diseases (C.D.) Acts; nor does Sophia Jex-Blake's biographer relate her career adequately to the structure and outlook of the mid-Victorian medical profession. Some recent writings on nineteenth-century women have even ascribed to anti-feminism treatments which were then applied to all patients, whether male or female.[5] In view of these difficulties, this essay cannot do more than raise questions for discussion; this will be done through considering three hypotheses about the relationship between women's health and the women's movement.

I

The first hypothesis for consideration is that, insofar as advances in women's health result from medical research and treatment at all, they were assisted by the feminist inclinations of the male doctors and medical researchers. Some male doctors did indeed support

---

[4] J. V. Ricci, *One Hundred Years of Gynaecology 1800–1900* (Philadelphia, 1945), p. vii (preface); see also *Health Care and Popular Medicine in Nineteenth-Century England*, ed. J. Woodward and D. Richards (London, 1977), pp. 12, 17.

[5] See R. Morantz, in M. S. Hartman and L. Banner (eds.), *Clio's Consciousness Raised. New Perspectives on the History of Women* (New York, 1974), pp. 39, 47–8. 51.

nineteenth-century feminists, as the careers of Josephine Butler, Florence Nightingale and Sophia Jex-Blake testify. The nineteenth-century medical profession was never monolithic, and embraced several competing professional bodies, schools of thought, regional groupings and status loyalties. Nonetheless the doctors' day-to-day experience repeatedly seemed to reinforce that central plank of the anti-feminist case, the 'physical force argument': the belief that the two sexes should occupy separate spheres in life because woman's physical weakness must disqualify her for political power. Doctors were frequently being required to treat men for injuries received in war, fighting and dangerous trades: whereas their female patients were involved in a recurrent childbearing which was then far more dangerous than it is now. Furthermore doctors, as an overwhelmingly male profession, were continuously reinforced in their consciousness of male superiority by the deference they received from a predominantly female nursing profession. Even in 1971, men accounted for 80.0 per cent of the qualified medical practitioners in Great Britain, but for only 8.6 per cent of the nurses.[6]

Self-interest no doubt sometimes reinforced the doctor's prejudice as to women's weakness, so that he actually exaggerated the problem in hand. He certainly needed to cultivate a female clientele, and was often advised to treat his female patients with care: to cultivate the social graces and gain a reputation for tact and sympathy. Through this curious combination of adulation and depreciation of women – widespread in the anti-feminist world – invalids were created. In the presence of the doctor, however considerate and polite, women patients were confirmed in their subordination by always seeming at a disadvantage as a sex – whether because of childbirth, or because they sought abortions, or because they had damaged their health by procuring abortions illegally, or because they were suffering from a 'hysteria' which itself often merely reflected social deprivation.[7] Dora Russell's doctor in

[6] Census 1971, Great Britain, *Economic Activity, Part 2* (London, 1975), p. 55 (10 per cent sample), 5257 male doctors, 1314 female doctors, 3795 male nurses, 40,103 female nurses. For the situation in 1901, see B. Abel-Smith, *A History of the Nursing Profession* (London, 1960), p. 52.
[7] C. Smith-Rosenberg, 'The Hysterical Woman: Sex Roles and Role Conflict in Nineteenth-Century America', *Social Research* (Winter, 1972), p. 663, and cf. K. J. and R. J. Lennane, 'Alleged Psychogenic Disorders in Women – A Possible Manifestation of Sexual Prejudice', *New England Journal of Medicine*, cclxxxviii (1973), p. 291. See also M. J. Peterson, *The Medical Profession in Mid-Victorian London* (Berkeley, 1978), p. 129.

1922 insisted that she was well able to feed her baby herself: 'doctors were still in those days very dictatorial towards women', she recalls, 'especially to mothers, as I was soon to find out in some of our political campaigns'.[8]

British feminism suffered by the doctor's tendency to generalize about women from those he encountered in his daily practice. When Sir Almroth Wright in 1912 attacked the suffragettes with generalizations of this kind, R. Douglas Powell rightly stressed 'the impropriety of deductions from the experience of the medical consulting room being exploited in the public Press'.[9] Women's recurrent childbearing combined with the continuous fear of criminal or class violence at home and of war overseas to render anti-suffragist arguments more plausible: they increased the credibility of Belfort Bax's claim that 'the whole female organism is subservient to the functions of child-bearing and lactation, which explains the inferior development of those organs and faculties which are not specially connected with this supreme end of Woman'.[10] Only in recent times has the typical mother found herself with half her life-span still to run after completing her cycle of motherhood.

The doctors might have responded otherwise to this situation. They could have pointed out, with the pioneer woman doctor Elizabeth Garrett Anderson, how curious it was that the alleged weakness of women did not apparently extend to women servants: and with Sophia Jex-Blake the oddity of the fact that medicine should be too indelicate an activity for women, whereas nursing was not.[11] They could have recognized, with Joseph Cowen the radical M.P. in 1884, that much of woman's weakness stemmed from society's warped expectations of her: 'the enervating habits we have imposed on her have impaired her physical powers', he said, 'and then we cite to her detriment the weakness which our customs have created'. Perhaps the most striking instance of this was the much smaller diet allocated to the female members of Victorian working class families by comparison with the male – in the belief

[8] D. Russell, *The Tamarisk Tree* (London, 1977 edn.), p. 157.
[9] *The Times* (1 Apr. 1912), p. 6.
[10] B. Bax, *The Fraud of Feminism* (London, 1913), p. 32.
[11] For Anderson, see Esperance in Woodward and Richards (note 4), p. 117; S. Jex-Blake, *Medical Woman. A Thesis and a History*, 2nd edn. (Edinburgh, 1886), p. 40; cf. Lady F. Bell, *At the Works. A Study of a Manufacturing Town* (London, 1911 edn), p. 312.

that 'the husband wins the bread, and must have the best food'.[12] Doctors could even have retained their preoccupation with women's weakness, but have pointed out – with Olive Schreiner – that owing to technological developments, 'crude muscular force, whether in man or beast, sinks continually in its value in the world of human toil'.[13] They could have shared the view of several suffragists that differences between the sexes constitute an actual qualification for the vote, which exists for self-protection and to reflect the diverse characteristics of the population.[14]

But like the women, the doctors were fighting their own battle for recognition; their professional status was too insecure to allow any vigorous dissent from prevailing attitudes. Rejecting J. S. Mill's proposal for woman suffrage in 1867, *The Lancet* pointed out that woman's place is in the home; women's 'organization shows a comparative delicacy; the conformation of structures and organs is less developed; there is less strength and vigour, and less fitness to encounter the obstacles of intercourse with the world'.[15] It even seemed necessary to enhance the mysteries of the doctor's art by maintaining secrecy on medical matters which it was in women's interest to discuss publicly. This reticence owed something to ignorance; the extent and timing of the menstrual 'safe period', for instance, was not precisely defined till the 1930s.[16] Women's ignorance, nurtured by the doctors, helps to explain the long survival of that semi-superstitious manual, *Aristotle's Masterpiece*: women are so ignorant of sexual matters, it claims, that they are unable to remedy their illnesses, 'and such is their modesty also that they are unwilling to ask in order to be informed'.[17] But women's reticence owed more to contemporary attitudes widespread among their own sex; 'respectability sank deep through working-class womanhood',

[12] Quotations from House of Commons Debates (12 June 1884), col. 165; T. C. Barker, D. J. Oddy and J. Yudkin, *The Dietary Surveys of Dr Edward Smith 1862–3. A New Assessment* (Queen Elizabeth College Department of Nutrition, Occasional Paper no. 1, 1970), p. 32. See also *ibid.*, p. 46 and D. J. Oddy, 'Working-class Diets in Late Nineteenth-century Britain', *Economic History Review* (Aug. 1970), p. 320.
[13] O. Schreiner, *Woman and Labour* (London, 1911), p. 42, cf. pp. 41, 209.
[14] E.g. Sir Alfred Mond, House of Commons Debates (5 May 1913), col. 1793; Willoughby de Broke, House of Lords Debates (6 May 1914), col. 90.
[15] *Lancet* (30 Mar. 1867), p. 401.
[16] R. Ledbetter, *A History of the Malthusian League 1877–1927* (Columbus, 1976), pp. 16, 22, 43, 83.
[17] *The Works of Aristotle the Famous Philosopher* (complete edn, Camden Publishing Co., n.d. [c. 1890]), p. 9. See also Blackman, in Woodward and Richards (eds), *Health Care and Popular Medicine* (see note 4), p. 81, cf pp. 60, 83, 90.

writes Robert Roberts of the slums in Edwardian Salford.[18] Even feminists displayed this reticence. If Henry Maudsley felt coy in 1874 about discussing the physiological basis of anti-feminism in the *Fortnightly Review*, so also did his feminist antagonist Elizabeth Garrett Anderson, who saw 'grave reason for doubting whether such a subject can be fully and with propriety discussed except in a professional journal'.[19]

A demure reticence therefore obstructed British feminism in several of its dimensions. The alleged need to shield women from indecency was one of the major arguments used by opponents of equal opportunity for women in medical education. Victorian advocates of state-regulated prostitution, like Edwardian opponents of woman suffrage, repeatedly argued that it was impossible publicly to discuss the full range of their objections to the proposed reform. That ardent anti-suffragist Loulou Harcourt told an anti-suffrage meeting in 1912 that

There are certain physiological facts which, though unfitted for discussion on the platform, cannot be neglected or rejected in the assumption of sex equality. They are facts so immutable, carrying with them consequences so immense and results so indisputable, that, at the proper time and in the proper place, they must be discussed and considered – even, if need be, at the cost of delicacy. But the time is not now and the place is not here.[20]

The feminist movement therefore became a campaign for free speech in a double sense: not merely to propagate woman suffrage or repeal of the C.D. Acts at public meetings, but to widen the range of the topics which women could discuss in public. Only through breaching the taboos could the full strength of the feminist case be revealed. A frighteningly suppressed underworld of pain, ignorance, fear and helplessness – even among relatively educated working women – emerges from the comments collected by the Women's Co-operative Guild into its *Maternity* in 1915.[21] Several

[18] R. Roberts, *The Classic Slum. Salford Life in the First Quarter of the Century* (Harmondsworth, Pelican edn, 1973), p. 57.

[19] *Fortnightly Review*, n.s., xv (1874), p. 582, cf. H. Maudsley, p. 466.

[20] *Anti-Suffrage Review* (Mar. 1912), p. 9; cf. *Votes for Women* (2 Feb. 1912), p. 276; *Anti-Suffrage Review* (May 1909), p. 4 and B. Harrison, *Separate Spheres. The Opposition to Women's Suffrage in Britain* (London, 1978), pp. 60, 111–12.

[21] See, e.g., *Maternity. Letters from Working-Women collected by the Women's Co-operative Guild*, ed. M. Llewelyn Davies (Virago edn, 1978), pp. 50, 56, 58, 64, 102, 157, 187–8.

contributors breathed sighs of relief at being free at last to ventilate their hidden sufferings, and urged the Guild to promote lectures on sex and hygiene.[22] Nor was ignorance current only among working women, as the single instance of Marie Stopes must suffice to illustrate. She was brought up by her mother to believe that ignorance was synonymous with innocence and failed to understand why she did not get pregnant by her impotent first husband. Her family doctor failed to enlighten her when she consulted him and the disastrous experience of her first marriage became her lifelong justification for promoting sex education.[23]

Josephine Butler's was the most vigorous and sustained protest against this suffocating mystification, but as she herself admitted in 1871, 'for women ... to come forward in public on such a matter cost them more than tongue could tell'.[24] This did not prevent her from persisting with her campaign, at great social cost to herself and her family, or from attaching particular importance to a distinctive female agitation on the subject through her Ladies' National Association. She knew that discussion on sexual questions was remarkably free among men in their London clubs and medical lecture-rooms, and saw publicity and open discussion as her major weapons. But the medical press was disgusted that her propaganda should introduce innocent women for the first time to the very existence of prostitution:[25] and in 1872 that a doctor should actually get up at a meeting and describe an inspection of the female sexual organs.[26] 'The only really *vicious* and *unfair* and *stupid* opposition I have met with in all the meetings abroad', she told Mr Edmondson in 1875, 'has been from *English doctors* who came to the meetings with large bundles of the *Lancet* under their arms. Stupid geese!'[27]

The public discussion of sexual matters re-entered British feminist crusading with Christabel Pankhurst's articles in the militant periodical, *The Suffragette*, in autumn 1913. Whereas Josephine Butler had always founded her movement on collaboration between the sexes, Christabel's tone was more strident and

[22] *Ibid.*, pp. 81, 97, 157, 167.
[23] R. Hall, *Marie Stopes. A Biography* (London, 1977), pp. 89, 95–6, 109.
[24] *Sheffield and Rotherham Independent* (13 Apr. 1871), p. 3.
[25] *Lancet* (21 May 1870), p. 740.
[26] *British Medical Journal* (27 Jan. 1872), p. 111.
[27] Josephine Butler Papers: Josephine Butler to Mr Edmondson, 13 Feb. 1875 (copy at City of London Polytechnic).

anti-male. Her articles on venereal diseases capitalized on the West End male immorality exposed by the Piccadilly Flat case. Like Josephine Butler, she argued that prostitution could best be attacked through raising male standards of morality; otherwise marriage would remain 'intensely dangerous,' especially as doctors were acting on 'an established and admitted rule' to keep the wife ignorant if infected by her husband with venereal diseases.[28] Her articles aroused widespread disgust, but she was unrepentant: 'the important point about the articles', she wrote in October, '... is not whether they are decent or indecent, but whether they are *true*'. Her paper in November condemned the decision of the royal commission on venereal disease to take its evidence in private as part of an 'evil conspiracy of silence'.[29] Her *The Great Scourge and How to End It* (1913) brought her articles a wider readership, but was attacked by *The British Medical Journal* for exaggeration and distortion: 'the cause of social progress', it pronounced, 'is not served by rhetorical statements which ignore half the facts'.[30]

We shall probably never know how justified were feminist fears of a medical conspiracy against women. *The Lancet* in 1870 admitted in passing that some doctors recommended the male resort to prostitutes as a 'cure' for nocturnal emissions, and if the anonymous author of the erotic autobiography *My Secret Life* is to be trusted – either as recording his own actions, or actions which his readers would find plausible – the West End libertine frequently made his doctor his confidant in the course of his amours. Havelock Ellis felt it necessary, in his *Sexual Inversion*, to reject recommendations to the brothel as an effective cure for homosexuality: such 'treatment' seldom succeeded, he claimed, and he saw 'the acquisition of the normal instinct by an invert' as 'very much on a level with the acquisition of a vice'.[31] Rare indeed was the doctor who, like Sir Victor Horsley in 1914, publicly linked the existence of prostitution with the depreciation of women widespread in anti-suffrage circles;[32] most doctors accepted the stereotyping of women into those antithetical pure and impure roles

[28] *Suffragette* (12 Sept. 1913), p. 829; also (8 Aug. 1913), p. 737.
[29] *Ibid.* (10 Oct. 1913), p. 991; (14 Nov. 1913), p. 95.
[30] *British Medical Journal* (4 Apr. 1914), p. 768.
[31] Havelock Ellis, *Sexual Inversion* (Studies in the Psychology of Sex), 2nd edn (Philadelphia, 1908), p. 197; see also *Lancet* (23 July 1870), p. 125; Anon. (Walter), *My Secret Life*, 2 vols. (Amsterdam, n.d., British Library copy), i, p. 257; ii, pp. 8, 61.
[32] *Anti-Suffrage Review* (Aug. 1914), p. 141.

which lay at the foundation of anti-suffragism. Still less did doctors attack that closer delimitation of sex-roles which the anti-suffragist regarded as ordained by God and/or Nature. It was left to a literary man, J. A. Symonds, cautiously to point out in 1891 that 'the line of division between the sexes, even in adult life, is a subtle one';[33] and it was the literary men Edward Carpenter and Havelock Ellis (a trained, but non-practising, doctor) who pioneered the systematic study of sex psychology.

In general, then, doctors tacitly acquiesced in those aspects of the anti-suffrage philosophy which impinged on their sphere. *The British Medical Journal* on 9 July 1870 adduced the average weight of the male and female brain against women's entry into the medical profession, and – like *The Lancet* in 1883 – pointed out that the female psychology was better adapted to domestic than to professional life.[34] Havelock Ellis's calmly argued and firmly empirical *Man and Woman* (1894) effectively discredited brain weight as a guide to women's intelligence, and dismissed Herbert Spencer's notion that man had evolved further along the evolutionary line than women. Ellis's candid admission that so little was then known about intellectual differences between the sexes[35] contrasts refreshingly with the confident pronouncements of Sir Almroth Wright eighteen years later. Any student of parliamentary debates on woman suffrage between 1867 and 1914 will share Ellis's view that 'the history of opinion regarding cerebral sexual difference forms a painful page in scientific annals. It is full of prejudices, assumptions, fallacies, over-hasty generalisations'.[36]

The doctors were not merely passive in their anti-feminism: their conduct and attitudes actively reinforced the male assault on movements for women's emancipation. If doctors before 1914 lagged behind many feminists in their view of woman's potential, they could still have encouraged women to realize that potential by helping to open up the professions and the universities to them. They might even have promoted women's health by doing so, for as Florence Nightingale's *Cassandra* pointed out, the mid-Victorian physician's excessive prestige required him to remedy the phy-

[33] J. A. Symonds, *A Problem in Modern Ethics* (London, 1896 edn), p. 91.
[34] *British Medical Journal* (9 July 1870), p. 42; *Lancet* (3 Nov. 1883), p. 780.
[35] For example, in his *Man and Woman: A Study of Human Secondary Sexual Characters* (London, 4th edn, 1904), pp. 218, 441.
[36] *Ibid.*, p. 102.

siological symptoms whose roots lay in intellectual starvation.[37] Yet the doctors emphasized the conflicting claims of intellect and motherhood; stressing the competing demands of academic study and menstruation on the female physique, Henry Maudsley pointed out in 1874 that 'when Nature spends in one direction, she must economize in another direction'.[38]

Harriet Martineau's writing career was successfully conducted against a continuous and insidious susurration of warnings against overwork, and required great courage and determination. Miss Buss told Miss Davies in 1874 that Girton 'suffers largely ... from the determined opposition of medical men, and as for me, I scarcely expect anything else if a medical opinion be asked, in the case of any girl. The smallest ailment always proceeds from overbrain-work!!! never from neglected conditions of health, from too many parties, etc. etc.'.[39] Medical objections of this kind were thought sufficiently serious by the women's colleges at Oxford and Cambridge in 1887 to justify organizing an elaborate survey of former students in order to discover the impact made by university education on their health. The favourable outcome vindicated Elizabeth Garrett Anderson's rejoinder to Maudsley in 1874: 'there is no tonic in the pharmacopoeia to be compared with happiness. and happiness worth calling such is not known where the days drag along filled with make-believe occupations and dreary sham amusements".[40] But Auberon Herbert could still argue, in his protest of 1888 against examinations, that women's delicate health rendered examinations even more damaging to their education than to men's.[41] It is against this background that the sporting preoccupations of mid-Victorian girls' schools and colleges must be seen.

Doctors reinforced the claims of politicians and eugenists that

[37] Reproduced in Ray Strachey, *'The Cause'. A Short History of the Women's Movement in Great Britain* (London, 1928), pp. 405–6.
[38] *Fortnightly Review*, N.S., xv (1874), p. 467.
[39] Quoted in B. Stephen, *Emily Davies and Girton College* (London, 1927), p. 292; see also H. Martineau, *Autobiography*, 2nd edn (London, 1877), i, pp. 187–8.
[40] *Fortnightly Review*, N.S., xv (London, 1874), p. 590. See also Mrs. H. Sidgwick, *Health Statistics of Women Students of Cambridge and Oxford and of their Sisters* (Cambridge, 1890); for American precedents, see M. R. Walsh, *'Doctors Wanted: No Women Need Apply': Sexual Barriers in the Medical Profession, 1835–1975* (New Haven, 1977), p. 131.
[41] A. Herbert, 'The Sacrifice of Education to Examination. A Protest', *Nineteenth Century* (Nov. 1888), p. 622.

women rarely attain the rank of genius, and that those who do are 'exceptional' and provide no index to women's overall capacities. In vain did Havelock Ellis point out that this testified – not to women's lack of intelligence as a sex – but to the relative variability of the male intelligence, which produces lunatics and geniuses with relative abundance.[42] And it was left to the feminists, most notably Virginia Woolf and C. P. Gilman, to emphasize the immense social obstacles which the woman genius had to overcome. Masterpieces grow out of a creative tradition, and require a degree of specialization which was impossible for Victorian women. 'What makes the difference between man and woman?', Florence Nightingale asked herself on the death of the Belgian statistician she so greatly admired: 'Quetelet did his work and I am so disturbed by my family that I can't do mine'. Extensive reading before breakfast was one way out – for Florence herself in the 1840s, for instance, or for Beatrix Potter in the 1870s.[43] Invalidism was a second – one of the few respects in which the china doll ideal of women actually assisted women's achievement. Explaining in her *Cassandra* why women's artistic achievement was so limited, Florence Nightingale described the frittering away of women's time by social convention: 'dinner is ... the great sacrament. To be absent from dinner is equivalent to being ill. Nothing else will excuse us from it. Bodily incapacity is the only apology valid'.[44] After 1857 Florence herself followed Harriet Martineau in taking this escape-route.[45] But these were single women; for married women, escape was more difficult, even when catered for by an abundance of servants.

Not content with reinforcing anti-feminist argument, doctors used their votes and influence to exclude women from Oxford, Cambridge, Edinburgh and other universities. Discouraging Sophia Jex-Blake from campaigning at Cambridge in 1869, Henry Sidgwick pointed out that the university was in the last resort governed by convocation, 'an assembly got together by agitation

[42] H. Ellis, *Man & Woman* (note 35), p. 420; cf. M. H. Thomas, Viscountess Rhondda, *This Was My World* (London, 1933), p. 235.
[43] Woodham-Smith, *Florence Nightingale* (note 3), p. 529; cf. B. Webb, *My Apprenticeship*, 2nd edn. (London, n.d.), pp. 101–11; B. Stephen, *Emily Davies* (note 39), p. 30.
[44] R. Strachey, *The Cause* (note 37), p. 399.
[45] G. Pickering, *Creative Malady* (London, 1974), p. 167; Woodham-Smith, *Florence Nightingale* (note 3) p. 303; T. Bosanquet, *Harriet Martineau. An Essay in Comprehension* (London, 1927), p. 132; R. K. Webb, *Harriet Martineau. A Radical Victorian* (London, 1960), pp. 198, 200.

among all graduates of a certain standard, and in which the influence of the London doctors is practically preponderant';[46] this assembly rejected a proposal to admit women to medical degrees in 1868. Again in 1920, in the controversy over women's full admission to the university, the London doctors reinforced local anti-feminists in the one major setback to women which Cambridge has administered; as late as 1921, Mrs Sidgwick could still describe 'the selfish trades-union opposition of the medicals' as a major obstacle to women's full acceptance there.[47] At Oxford in 1896, one commentator bracketed doctors with the clergy among the non-tutorial element who helped exclude women from the B.A. degree, and a similar alignment reappears in other universities.[48] As for Edinburgh, the resistance faced by Sophia Jex-Blake is notorious, and was always allegedly founded on the medical students' strong distaste for admitting women to their profession; 'Scottish Universities, without endowments', Lyon Playfair told her in 1869, 'cannot go in face of the Constituency by which they are supported'.[49]

Doctors offered vigorous intellectual resistance to the campaign for women's suffrage. When militant feminists adopted unorthodox political methods, there were doctors who argued that psychological instability was typical of their sex when under strain. One of the recurring themes in medical anti-feminism is the inevitability of illness for women: it is integral to the womanly ideal, yet inevitable if women repudiate that ideal.[50] It was true that feminist activity – like all political activity, male or female – sometimes assuaged psychological ills; but insofar as these resulted from women's deprivation, as they sometimes did, such motivation might now be thought actually to reinforce the feminist case. We would now echo

[46] M. Todd, *The Life of Sophia Jex-Blake* (London, 1918), pp. 219–20.
[47] E. Sidgwick, *Mrs Henry Sidgwick. A Memoir* (London, 1938), p. 228; R. McWilliams-Tullberg, *Women at Cambridge. A Men's University – Though of a Mixed Type* (London, 1975), pp. 180, 224; *Woman's Leader* (17 Dec. 1920), p. 981; (28 Jan. 1921), p. 1095.
[48] *Manchester Guardian* (11 Mar. 1896), p. 387; see also J. N. Burstyn, 'Education and Sex: The Medical Case against Higher Education for Women in England, 1870–1900', *Proceedings of the American Philosophical Society*, cxvii, no. 2 (10 Apr. 1973), pp. 88–9.
[49] M. Todd, *The Life of Sophia Jex-Blake* (note 46), p. 251; cf. pp. 249, 256, 291, and E. M. Bell, *Storming the Citadel. The Rise of the Woman Doctor* (London, 1953), pp. 54, 76.
[50] S. Delamont and L. Duffin, *The Nineteenth-century Woman. Her Cultural and Physical World* (London, 1978), p. 31.

Florence Nightingale's *Cassandra* in recognizing the relationship between mental instability and social deprivation; 'the accumulation of nervous energy', she wrote, 'which has had nothing to do during the day, makes them [women] feel every night, when they go to bed, as if they were going mad'.[51] Yet no such awareness deterred the Emeritus Lecturer in Psychological Medicine at Bart's in 1908, T. Claye Shaw, from likening suffragettes' interruption of political meetings – adopted for purely tactical reasons, however mistaken – to 'the explosive fury of epileptics'.[52] Ideas of this type re-emerged in the extraordinary attack on the suffragettes mounted in *The Times* by Sir Almroth Wright on 28 March 1912, where he alleged that 'there is mixed up with the woman's movement much mental disorder'. His views were echoed in *Times* leaders, notably in that of 16 March which, under the heading 'Insurgent Hysteria', described the 'regrettable by-products of our civilisation' whose lack of mental balance provided the suffragettes with their recruits. Despite Wright's distinction as a bacteriologist, for which he had been knighted in 1906, *The British Medical Journal* and *Lancet* saw fit to ignore the outburst entirely; no doubt his views were too embarrassingly forceful an expression of arguments widely accepted by doctors.

No claim is being made here that anti-feminism was peculiar to the medical profession, or that British anti-feminism would have withered and died without its medical fertilizer. Curzon no doubt spoke for many non-medical British people, male and female, when he told the anti-suffragists' annual meeting in June 1914 that the suffragettes 'have rendered us the service of showing how easily disturbed the mental balance of some women, at any rate, can be'. The same instinctive suspicion of politically active women surfaces (in a quite different context) in the diary of John Burns, ex-docker and President of the Local Government Board between 1906 and 1914, watching a protest against vivisection on 10 July 1909; he saw 'a well dressed crowd of breastless Amazons who make up for their love of children by an inordinate love of cats and dogs'. Ridicule from street urchins was one of the crosses which Hannah Mitchell had to bear in her suffrage days and it was many years before

[51] Ray Strachey, '*The Cause*' (note 37), p. 408.
[52] *Times* (31 Dec. 1908), p. 13; cf. (19 Dec. 1908), p. 10 (A. E. Shipley); (26 Dec. 1908), p. 9 ('Physiologist').

Salford slum children ceased to regard even non-political spinsters past middle age as fair game for practical jokes.[53] The doctors' arguments merely reinforced a preconception which – in public and in private – was usually formulated in an unscientific manner. All that is claimed here is that doctors were prominent, in their persons and in their arguments, for upholding the anti-feminist case before 1914, and that from an educated group of men whose profession rendered them more aware of women's sufferings than most – something different might have been expected. Yet it was precisely those sufferings which were turned against women for political purposes.

Nor did doctors confine themselves to argument; they also resorted to a violence which can be understood only in the context of that complex of exclusive nineteenth-century clubs so prominent for their anti-feminism in Victorian Britain. The London medical schools developed tight corporate loyalties; H. E. Counsell, a medical student of the 1880s, recalled that he and his fellow-students were as proud of being at Guy's as was any guardsman of his regiment; he once told Jowett that he was as proud of his institution as any Balliol man.[54] With the London hospitals, as with the colleges in Oxford and Cambridge, male clubbery often resulted in a violence which advertised women's weakness from a new direction. In view of doctors' diagnosis of suffragette militancy, it is perhaps ironic that medical students often used violence against the feminist movement. This was partly because violence has always attracted young men at a loose end in a town: medical students were active in London's jingo agitation of 1877–8 and in student riots in Paris during 1908, for example. 'No class or profession of young men ... come more frequently into collision with the authorities', wrote William Gilbert of medical students in 1879, 'or exhibit more frequent instances of ungentlemanly behaviour'. But feminists do seem to have been a regular target of the medical students, who were disrupting feminist meetings as early as 1867, when 'an uproarious mob of medical students, whose conduct

---

[53] Curzon, *Anti-Suffrage Review* (July 1914), p. 108; British Library, Add. MSS 46327 (John Burns's diary), entry for 10 July 1909; H. Mitchell, in C. Mitchell (ed.) *The Hard Way Up* (London, 1968), pp. 153–5; R. Roberts, *A Ragged Schooling* (London, 1978 edn), p. 81.
[54] M. J. Peterson, *The Medical Profession* (note 7), p. 88; cf. B. Harrison, *Separate Spheres* (note 20), ch. 5.

was simply disgraceful' filled the galleries at a lecture on Bloomerism by the American woman doctor Mary Walker.[55] Josephine Butler's movement encountered hostility from medical students and by 1912 London medical students were using violence against suffragette meetings and making life very difficult for Miss Seruya in her International Suffrage Book-shop in Adam Street.[56]

In her attack of 1881 on the medical profession, Frances Power Cobbe damagingly contrasted Bob Sawyer in youth and maturity. He begins as 'a rowdy and dissipated youth, with linen of questionable purity, and a pipe and foul language alternately in his mouth; the *bête-noire* of every modest girl, and the unfailing nuisance of every public meeting, where he may stamp and crow and misbehave himself'. Suddenly a transformation occurs – far more dramatic than that of lawyer, soldier or parson – into the physician who 'emerges ... to flit evermore softly through shaded boudoirs, murmuring soothing suggestions to ladies suffering from headaches'. Not surprisingly, there were cautious footnotes from the editor and sharp rejoinders from doctors in later numbers. Miss Cobbe was no doubt exaggerating; but feminists entering the medical profession were as convinced as feminists everywhere else that theirs was the cause of moral elevation. Elizabeth Blackwell deliberately rejected the option of easing her way into medical training by disguising herself as a male student because 'it was to my mind a moral crusade on which I had entered ... and it must be pursued in the light of day, and with public sanction, in order to accomplish its end'. She was soon to observe her own refining influence on her fellow medical students,[57] but many years were to elapse before women's health could profit from the prevalence of feminist ideas among the doctors.

---

[55] W. Gilbert, 'The London Medical Schools', *Fortnightly Review* (1 Jan. 1879), p. 47; *Englishwoman's Review* (Jan. 1867), p. 111; see also H. Cunningham, 'Jingoism in 1877–78', *Victorian Studies* (June 1971), pp. 450–1; *Times* (25 Dec. 1908), p. 9.
[56] J. Butler, *Personal Reminiscences of a Great Crusade* (London, 1896), p. 36; Public Record Office, *Mepol 2/1560* (memorandum by Supt. Sutherland, 29 July 1913); *Daily News and Leader* (4 Mar. 1913), p. 1; H. M. Swanwick, *I Have Been Young* (London, 1935), p. 221; E. Pethick-Lawrence, *My Part in a Changing World* (London, 1938), pp. 163, 196.
[57] F. P. Cobbe, *Modern Review* (Apr. 1881), p. 305; E. Blackwell, *Pioneer Work in Opening the Medical Profession to Women* (Schocken Books, New York, 1977), pp. 62, 257.

II

There is a second possibility: that a medical profession initially indifferent or hostile to feminism could be induced to focus on questions of women's health by feminist pressure from without. One might at first sight expect such pressure to succeed. There was, after all, extensive common ground between doctors and feminists: both challenged the assignment of status by birth rather than by merit: both were extensively recruited among the middle class, championed the ideal of work against that of idleness, and saw themselves as in the van of progress. Both were therefore natural recruits for Liberalism. Yet it is often between those who have much in common that the bitterest disagreements occur, and this was certainly true for British feminists and doctors between the 1860s and 1914. Disagreement stemmed firstly from the doctor's concern to protect his professional status, and secondly from a series of specific disagreements between doctors and feminist organizations.

Feminists seemed to threaten the doctor's professional status for three reasons: their support for the woman doctor threatened to dilute a profession only recently and precariously established, they often moved in circles hostile to the medical profession and their methods offended the professional style of conduct. Each of these sources of friction must now be discussed in turn. Feminists had more reason than the doctors to share the Liberals' distaste for monopoly. Josephine Butler in 1869 was surprised to learn from Sophia Jex-Blake how recently the male medical monopoly had been established, and in 1875 Sophia concluded her defence of women's entry into the medical profession with a quotation from J. S. Mill: 'the proper sphere for all human beings is the largest and highest which they are able to attain to. What this is, cannot be ascertained without complete liberty of choice'.[58]

Whereas feminists were fighting for increased opportunity, nineteenth-century doctors were using techniques of exclusion as weapons in their resistance to quacks, heretics and intruders of every kind. Professional self-interest reinforced their club-like world of male sociability and led doctors to resist women in search of new careers. From the late eighteenth century, male doctors had been

[58] Quoted from *Fortnightly Review* (Mar. 1875), p. 407, cf. p. 392; see also M. Todd (note 46), p. 254.

encroaching on the midwife's preserve[59] and made it difficult for her to acquire professional qualifications.[60] The doctors' late-Victorian attack on abortion was aimed partly at reinforcing their position as against chemists, herbalists and midwives.[61] And although *The Lancet* might fulsomely welcome Florence Nightingale's admission to the freedom of the City of London in 1908,[62] it had virtually ignored her activities during the Crimean War, and her schemes for elevating the nurse's professional skills encountered much resistance from doctors.[63] Professional self-interest (not always incompatible with the public interest) lay behind much of the doctors' resistance to the spread of birth control between the wars;[64], the Drysdales' heroic efforts within the Malthusian League were not typical of medical attitudes.[65] Not only were doctors slow to interest themselves in any aspect of preventive medicine; they feared the lay influences which pioneered the new movement, and on scientific grounds they rightly contested many of Marie Stopes's assertions.

Doctors' suspicions were reinforced by the feminists' personal connections. The medical dissenters and anti-vivisectionist, anti-vaccinationist laymen, whose interference the doctors so feared, were as ready to associate with feminists as with any other type of reformer. Temperance reformers dabbled in hydropathy and phrenology: anti-vivisectionists hobnobbed with homoeopaths:[66] and the anti-vivisectionist doctor tended to be a Chadwickian pioneer of public health[67] who expected medical progress to arise only from sanitary measures which would bring man into closer harmony with the divine order – not from grovelling in the entrails of

[59] J. Donnison, *Midwives and Medical Men. A History of Inter-Professional Rivalries and Women's Rights* (London, 1977), pp. 20–2; J. M. M. Kerr *et al.*, *Historical Review* (note 2), pp. 5, 332.
[60] J. Donnison, *op. cit.*, pp. 134, 176–7; J. M. M. Kerr *et al.*, *Historical Review* (note 2), p. 339.
[61] A. McLaren, 'Abortion in England, 1890–1914', *Victorian Studies* (1977), p. 390.
[62] *Lancet* (21 Mar. 1908), p. 868.
[63] E. Cook, *Life of Florence Nightingale*, 2 vols. (London 1913), i, p. 467.
[64] Cf. with A. McLaren, *Birth Control in Nineteenth-century England* (London, 1978), p. 118.
[65] R. Ledbetter, *A History* (note 16), pp. 121–2.
[66] For example, *The Dunlop Papers*, ed. J. G. Dunlop, 2 vols. (London, 1939), ii, p. 229; R. D. French, 'Medical Science and Victorian Society: the Anti-Vivisection Movement' (Univ. of Oxford D. Phil. thesis, 1972), p. 292.
[67] L. G. Stevenson, 'Science Down the Drain. On the Histility of Certain Sanitarians to Animal Experimentation, Bacteriology and Immunology', *Bulletin of the History of Medicine* (Jan–Feb. 1955), pp. 2, 25; R. D. French (see note 66), pp. 318, 344.

animals. He was also likely (as in Josephine Butler's movement) to be a provincial Lydgate who 'would keep away from the range of London intrigues, jealousies, and social truckling, and win celebrity'.[68] Josephine Butler at Kirkdale in 1872 said she was not surprised to find the fashionable London doctors upholding the C. D. Acts because

> fashionable life, wealth, and honours, and the atmosphere of courts, are as injurious to the moral judgment and the spiritual life of doctors, as of other men ... but in our great provincial cities there is, I think, more manly independence of character, and so it happens that there are vast numbers of doctors here, and in other towns, who refuse to bow the knee to King Jenner.

Her gratitude to sympathetic provincial doctors – most notably to Dr Birkbeck Nevins of Liverpool – was generously expressed. These movements ventilated the provincial man's grievance against the metropolis, the individualist's protest against the state. P. A. Taylor told the House of Commons in 1883 that compulsory vaccination was 'the most absolute invasion of the sacred right of the parent, of the right of individual liberty, at the bidding of medical supervision, that this country knows', and Joseph Arch's autobiography proudly recounts his success in resisting the compulsory vaccination of his children.[69]

All these movements – for religious, libertarian, feminist and/or intellectual reasons – undermined the doctor's prestige,[70] and forced him to explain himself before a parliamentary arena whose culture, as Darwin often complained, was uncongenial: 'the governing classes are thoroughly unscientific', he told Huxley in 1858, 'and the men of art and of archaeology have much greater weight with Government than we have'.[71] For our purpose, he might have

---

[68] George Eliot, *Middlemarch*, ed. W. J. Harvey (Penguin Books, 1970), p. 174; for anti-vivisection, see R. D. French (note 66) p. 346; *Zoophilist* (1 Dec. 1884), p. 149.
[69] *The Shield* (29 June 1872), p. 990; House of Commons Debates (19 June 1883), col. 990; *Joseph Arch. The Story of his Life Told by Himself*, ed. Countess of Warwick, 2nd edn (London, 1898), p. 54. See the memoirs of Nevins in *The Storm-Bell* (Oct. 1898), pp. 83, 90 and *The Dawn* (1 Oct. 1890), p. 11, and the comment in J. Butler, *Recollections of George Butler*, 2nd edn (Bristol, n.d.), p. 222.
[70] *The Shield* (25 May 1872), p. 951; R. D. French (see note 66), p. 379. See also B. Harrison, 'State Intervention and Moral Reform in Nineteenth-century England' in P. Hollis (ed.), *Pressure From Without in Early Victorian England* (London, 1974), pp. 312–16, 319.
[71] *More Letters of Charles Darwin*, ed. F. Darwin and A. C. Seward (London, 1903), i, p. 110, cf. p. 113; *The Life and Letters of Charles Darwin*, ed. F. Darwin (London, 1887), iii, p. 203; E. Cook, *Florence Nightingale* (note 63), ii, p. 396.

added the religious humanitarians, who by the 1870s had become restive at the pretensions of science and active in the constituencies; convinced that moral progress ought to spring from material progress, they expected the intelligentsia to pioneer progressive causes and saw the doctors as traitors in their midst.

But there were perhaps deeper reasons why doctors were unlikely to heed lay pressure, whether from feminists or from any other type of reformer. A profession of any kind is in some respects antithetical to the popular pressure group, for it is by definition concerned with exclusion, whereas the popular agitator seeks comprehensiveness. The profession fears the layman, who is the agitator's major asset: the profession fraternizes with those in authority, whose unpopularity fuels the reformer's fire: the profession defends an interest, whereas altruism is the popular agitator's proudest boast. Doctors felt uncomfortable in the presence of a lay audience, for the scientist needs to distance himself from the layman if he is to acquire the concentration of attention needed for rapidly advancing his research. 'The subject is one which it is impossible to treat fairly in all its bearings before a mixed and uninstructed audience in the compass of a speech', said the Association for Promoting the Extension of the C. D. Acts in 1872, 'and we have felt that opinions, founded on the superficial statements which a public meeting alone allows of, are not to be relied on'.[72] Most doctors saw Josephine Butler's movement as emotional, irrational and ignorant, and were alarmed when Liberal politicians responded to its cries. *The Lancet* in March 1872 felt that ministers should distinguish 'between public opinion and the agitation of noisy nobodies', and emphasized that 'the respectable middle classes cannot agitate, and they look to statesmen to protect them against the results of agitation'.[73] Among the reasons for H. S. Maine's gloom about popular government in 1886 was the unpopularity of Malthusian and Darwinian ideas, which revealed the 'marked antagonism between democratic opinion and scientific truth as applied to human societies'.[74] For some doctors, as for

[72] Association for Promoting the Extension of the C. D. Acts, *4th Annual Report, 1872* (London, n.d.), p. 9; see also T. S. Kuhn, *The Structure of Scientific Revolutions*, 2nd edn (London, 1970), p. 164.
[73] *Lancet* (2 Mar. 1872), p. 298; cf. (13 Mar. 1886), p. 498; *British Medical Journal* (18 May 1872), p. 529; (28 Apr. 1883), p. 824.
[74] H. S. Maine, *Popular Government. Four Essays*, 2nd edn (London, 1886), p. 37.

other groups within the intelligentsia, Irish home rule in 1886 may well have provided the pretext for a move towards Conservatism which originated partly elsewhere. At Liverpool in June 1886 Gladstone noted that the more privileged the profession, the more likely it was to oppose the Liberal Party, and in July the 200 doctors who attended the Medical Benevolent Fund's jubilee dinner cheered 'lustily and unanimously' a post-prandial sentiment that the Union should be preserved.[75]

Effective feminist pressure on the medical profession was rendered still less likely by the sequence of more specific disagreements between doctors and feminist organizations between the 1860s and 1914, culminating in the actual physical combat which the forcible feeding of suffragettes entailed between 1909 and 1914. Victorian feminism shared that faith in self-help, thrift, individual moral progress, reason, personal liberty and letting well alone which was central to the outlook of the Victorian radical, who had no desire to be as dependent on the doctor as earlier generations had been upon the chinless aristocrat or the canting clergyman. 'Pain, sickness and anguish are his harvest', wrote William Godwin of the doctor, '. . . He looks blank and disconsolate, when all men are at their ease . . . He pretends to be most wise, when he is most ignorant'. Welcoming the success of a water-cure in 1856, Richard Cobden explicitly linked the attack on doctors with that staple radical belief in leaving the natural order undisturbed: '*Laissez faire*', he told Bright, 'seems as applicable to the medical profession as to trade'.[76] The self-help element in Victorian feminism caused British feminists to clash with doctors at several points: at the level of individual liberty, public morality and personal health-care.

A rationalistic and libertarian scepticism about the doctor's art ran through the many popular movements which feminists tended to join. The idea that each individual is the best guardian of his own health runs through the temperance movement, whose Canon Basil Wilberforce once infuriated the medical profession by saying that 'some doctors, if they went down inside you with a lighted

[75] Gladstone quoted in *The Nineteenth-Century Constitution 1815–1914* ed. H. J. Hanham (Cambridge, 1969), p. 205; J. C. Macdonnell, *The Life and Correspondence of William Connor Magee*, 2 vols. (London, 1896), ii pp. 235–6.
[76] W. Godwin, *The Inquirer. Reflections on Education, Manners, and Literature* (London, 1797), p. 227; Cobden Papers, f. 197: Cobden to Bright, 21 Mar. 1856; British Library, Additional MSS 43650.

candle, could not tell what was the matter with you'. The belief in cleanliness, sobriety and good order was integral to the public health movement; Chadwick and Florence Nightingale in the late 1850s conspired to render the medical profession redundant. For Chadwick, curative medicine was 'nothing but *consolatio animi* . . . pretending to alleviate disease which if they [the doctors] had the will they had not the skill to *prevent*'.[77] Florence Nightingale's *Notes on Nursing* (1860) – commonsensical, empirical, and popular in tone – was written at Chadwick's suggestion, and quietly circumscribed the doctor's curative role.[78] She despised inoculation and the germ theory of disease, and was apparently uninfluenced by Lister; 'instead of wishing to see more Doctors made by women joining what there are', she told Mill in 1860, 'I wish to see as few Doctors, either male or female, as possible'.[79]

Radicals feared the doctor's cavalier approach towards the community's moral values: indeed, they believed that his attack on disease could succeed only through a strategy which respected them. It is her pursuit of moral progress which helps to explain Frances Power Cobbe's recurrent attacks on doctors. 'There is . . . a great and ever-present temptation to a physician to view things from the material or . . . carnal side', she wrote in *The Modern Review* for 1881 – a tendency to exaggerate the influence of body on mind, to neglect the influence of mind on body. At a Gloucester meeting held in 1872 to protest against the C. D. Acts, Dr Peacock's argument that 'it was the duty of the medical man to alleviate human suffering irrespective of moral considerations' encountered 'Loud shouts of "oh, oh", and "Stop, stop"'.[80] Josephine Butler's attack on the C. D. Acts assumed that the state should not protect the individual from diseases consciously risked in the course of committing immoral acts. Her movement's conviction

[77] Quoted in G. W. E. Russell, *Basil Wilberforce. A Memoir* (London, 1917), p. 55; cf. B. Harrison, *Drink and the Victorians* (London, 1971), pp. 161–2, 185; S. E. Finer, *The Life and Times of Sir Edwin Chadwick* (London, 1952), p. 158.
[78] See Nightingale Papers: Chadwick to Nightingale, 14 Jan. [1860]; Chadwick to Nightingale, 9 June 1860 (draft), British Library, additional MSS 45770, ff. 116, 118; F. Nightingale, *Notes on Nursing: What it is, and What it is Not* (London, 1860), pp. 5, 74.
[79] Nightingale Papers, British Library, Additional MSS 45787, f. 11 see also Z. Cope, *Florence Nightingale and the Doctors* (London, 1958), pp. 16, 20; E. Cook, (note 63), i, p. 393.
[80] F. P. Cobbe, *The Modern Review* (Apr. 1881), p. 309; *The Shield* (4 Jan. 1873), p. 6.

that 'health will follow upon morality, and only upon morality'[81] could attract nonconformist and atheist radicals alike; venereal disease could best be curbed, it was argued, by encouraging a healthy recreational and married life in the rank-and-file of the armed services.[82] James Stansfeld, the parliamentary leader of the attack on the Acts, frequently repudiated any specialization which left medicine to the doctors and morality to the church; for him, the laws of science and morality could never conflict, and the lay public were as competent as any expert to pronounce on questions of morality.[83] These movements constitute a major dimension of religion's mid-Victorian counter-attack upon science. As George Russell put it, in the House of Commons debate on vivisection in 1883, 'we ought not to permit affairs of conscience and morals to be ruled by the arbitrary edicts of the scientific priesthood'.[84]

A powerful combination of libertarian and moralistic sentiment lay behind Josephine Butler's Ladies' National Association, which maintained a distinct existence partly because it saw its members as 'a special power from the very fact of their sex'[85] in maintaining the highest tone of argument against the Acts. By encouraging women to speak publicly on sexual matters, the Association made its contribution to the growth of British feminism. The C. D. Acts seemed yet another demonstration of the iniquities which could emerge from an exclusively male parliament, and reinforced the case for women's suffrage. Legislation of this type seemed surreptitiously imposed on laymen by a conspiracy of London-based medical experts;[86] citizens could and should take care of their own health, without any need for an inflated bureaucracy which threatened their liberties and humane values generally. Samuel Whitbread expressed the idea in the C. D. Acts debate of 1883: 'one

[81] Quoted in C. Rover, *Love, Morals and the Feminists* (London, 1970), p. 79, cf Royal Commission on the ... C. D. Acts, *Parliamentary Papers* 1871 (408) xix, Q. 13104; Select Committee of the House of Commons on the Contagious Diseases Acts, *Parliamentary Papers* 1882 (340) ix, Q.5418; J. S. Mill. *Liberty*, Everyman edn (London, 1960), pp. 75–6.
[82] C. Woodham-Smith (see note 3), p. 401; Beales in *The Shield* (11 July 1870), p. 157; Howell, *ibid.* (11 Mar. 1871), p. 416; see also *The Shield* (1 Oct. 1870), p. 236.
[83] See, e.g., his speech in Social Purity Alliance, *Annual Report 1883–4* (London, n.d.), p. 17.
[84] House of Commons Debates, 4 Apr. 1883, col. 1447; cf. R. D. French (note 66), pp. 310–11.
[85] Ladies' National Association, *Report ... for the Year Ending November 14, 1871* (London, 1871), p. 5; cf. *7th Annual Report, 1876* (London, n.d.), p. 21.
[86] See, e.g., P. A. Taylor, House of Commons Debates, 19 June 1883 cols. 994–6.

of the things which Parliament ought to be most watchful about was when doctors asked to have policemen at their backs'.[87] Whereas the anti-vivisectionists favoured state interference to eliminate cruelty, therefore, their overall presumption lay against state action; the doctors, on the other hand, were increasingly permeating official circles and recognizing the virtues of government intervention. Condemning Josephine Butler's advocacy of free trade in vice, *The Lancet* on 21 May 1870 saw her outcry as 'similar, in its morality and in its regard for truth and right, to the arguments that are used to defend the adulteration of food, or any like abuse with which commercial interests are bound up'.

But it is at the level of personal health-care that the feminist threat to the Victorian doctor's livelihood was at its most direct. British feminism eroded the doctor's role in four respects: by undermining the psychological causes of illness in so far as it extended women's opportunities for a career, by encouraging women to live in a more healthy manner, by encouraging preventive medicine (in the widest sense) within the home and by promoting the open discussion of sexual matters. Many feminists aimed to emancipate themselves from the male doctor, and perhaps from doctors altogether. For Frances Power Cobbe, recommending women to pursue the healthy life in 1878, the medical profession occupied 'with strangely close analogy, the position of the priesthood of former times, assumes the same airs of authority ... and enters every family with a latch-key of private information'.[88] The same priestly analogy was drawn by Helen Taylor, addressing the annual meeting of the Vigilance Association for the Defence of Personal Rights (closely allied to Josephine Butler's movement) in 1878; she condemned the tendency towards state intervention 'which has very much taken the form of the old clerical meddling – the legal meddling, and the modern medical meddling which threatens to interfere with every branch of life'.[89]

The attack on what Alfred Mond described in 1912 as 'woman as a sort of china doll on a sacred hearth to be worshipped from afar' was integral to the feminist movement.[90] Florence Nightingale's

[87] House of Commons Debates, 20 Apr. 1883, col. 841.
[88] 'The Little Health of Ladies', *Contemporary Review* (Jan. 1878), p. 292.
[89] Vigilance Association for the Defence of Personal Rights, *8th Annual Report, 1878* (London, n.d.), p. 22.
[90] House of Commons Debates, 28 Mar. 1912, col. 620.

career was founded upon repudiating the middle class ideal of female idleness.[91] Frances Power Cobbe, dismissing the ladylike ideal of ill-health in 1878, argued that male chivalry to women actually created idleness, just as indiscriminate charity to the poor created beggary.[92] 'Women are not healthy', wrote Emily Davies in 1866: 'it is a rare thing to meet with a lady, of any age, who does not suffer from headaches, languor, hysteria, or some ailment showing a want of stamina'.[93] Her campaign for women's higher education showed the way towards an effective cure. Invalidism might provide an escape-route for individual women in certain circumstances, but the essence of the feminist movement consisted in convincing women that good health was not only feasible but necessary to real achievement.

It is difficult now to imagine the cramped, frustrating and even stultifying lives which so many women were once required to lead, and which – as Elizabeth Garrett Anderson pointed out in 1871 – must have been 'one of the very greatest hindrances that women have to being really vigorous and healthy'. Dorothea Beale quoted to a Royal Commission in 1869 the view of Mr Solly, F.R.S., who was '*quite certain* that there would be less illness amongst the Upper Classes if their brains were more regularly and systematically worked'. It was intensely irritating for an intelligent young woman like Mrs Swanwick to be denied the opportunity for intellectual concentration she craved. 'Early in life', she recalled, 'I grasped the immense part which the conscious direction of attention plays in achievement of any sort and I suffered acutely from the efforts to distract my attention which endured for the whole of my girlhood'.[94]

It was not only intellectual frustration which lay behind so many illnesses (mental and physical) of nineteenth-century women: it was frustration at the lack of any worthwhile social role. One prominent suffragette recalled in old age an interaction between health and political activity reminiscent of Josephine Butler's strange alternations between ill-health and vigorous campaigning.

I always realized that there was something or other that I'd got

[91] F. Nightingale, *Notes on Nursing* (note 78), p. 59.
[92] *Contemporary Review* (Jan. 1878), p. 282.
[93] B. Stephen, *Emily Davies* (note 39), p. 95.
[94] Quotations from *Women's Suffrage Journal* (1 May 1871), p. 47; A. K. Clarke, *History of Cheltenham Ladies' College 1853–1953* (London, 1953), p. 55; H. M. Swanwick, *I Have Been Young* (note 56), p. 16.

to do, and I didn't know what it *was*, and ... before I actually
touched the movement, I remember I used to get very, very
hot in my hands and my forehead and every day I used to get
very keyed up because there was something or other I'd got to
do but I didn't know what it was. I wasn't the only one who got
like that, because I found out afterwards that a great many
women, after the movement started ... *rose up* out of bath chairs
and did the most marvellous work, and they were *burning up*
because they felt there was something in them they had to do
and they didn't know what it was.[95]
For the limited number of women who joined it, the feminist
movement itself contributed directly towards improving women's
health.

But feminists promoted women's health in other ways. As early
as 1860, *The English Woman's Journal* reprinted an article by
Chadwick on 'physical training' deploring restrictions on young
girls' freedom of movement and recommending Ling's Swedish
system of gymnastics. The London Association of Schoolmistresses'
first lecture in 1868 was Elizabeth Garrett Anderson's on 'The
Physical Training of Girls'. After recommending walking, dancing,
sports and gymnastics, she declared that 'what we wanted from the
body was, that it should be a strong and willing slave, instead of a
tyrannical and capricious master'. *The English Woman's Review* in
1872 pointed out how exercise came naturally to boys whereas
gymnastics were necessary to a girl's education if she was to reach
the same standard of health. The hygienic motive for dress reform
was a significant, if minor, theme in the British feminist movement
in the 1880s. An undercurrent of feminist distaste for the fashion-
designer occasionally erupts between the wars, often through the
brisk, almost martial, tones of Mary Stocks – though less frequently than the importance of the subject might lead one to
expect. 'The designing of fashions for women, like all trades, is
largely in the hands of men', complained Dr Christine Murrell,
recommending sensible clothes and physical exercise for women in
1923. When the prominent feminist Ray Strachey made contact, as
founder of the Women's Employment Federation, with prominent
fashion designers in the late 1930s, she felt she had entered a totally
unfamiliar world; given her own carelessness about dress, she was

[95] Author's tape-recorded interview with Miss Grace Roe, 23 Sept. 1974.

regarded by them as (in her own words) 'their pet oddity'. But although feminist unorthodoxy about dress sometimes resulted from preoccupation with health, it more often stemmed from indifference to the whole subject: from a feeling that other things were more important.[96]

The triumph of Swedish gymnastics over Prussian drill in the 1880s – largely due to the feminist Mme Bergman-Österberg – assisted women's emancipation in at least two ways: by improving the health of pupils in the many girls' schools which adopted this new approach to physical education: and by providing a new career for women. Seventy-one of the British College of Physical Education's 114 members in 1903 were women.[97] Physical education was a cause taken up by many suffragists, most notably by Mary Bagot Stack who – with that distrust of doctors which will now be familiar – founded the Women's League of Health and Beauty in 1930, and died in 1935 after refusing a second operation to remove a swelling in her neck.[98] 'Keeping Fit' was also a minor theme running through the history of the Townswomen's Guilds in the 1930s.[99] 'The beauty of perfect health and of high spirits', wrote Lecky in 1896, 'has been steadily replacing, as the ideal type, the beauty of a sickly delicacy and of weak and tremulous nerves which in the eighteenth century was so much admired'.[100]

But feminists' enthusiasm for preventive medicine was more ambitious than this; they saw women as crusaders for better health within the community at large. Improvement in women's diet and knowledge of family health questions was one of the hopes held out by advocates of women's entry into the medical profession in the 1860s.[101] For Florence Nightingale in 1860, women were potential

[96] E. G. Anderson quotation from *Englishwoman's Review* (Oct. 1868), p. 12; see also *English Woman's Journal* (1 Dec. 1860), p. 264; *Englishwoman's Review* (July 1872). pp. 179–81. C. Murrell, *Womanhood and Health* (London, 1923), p. 115; Ray Strachey Papers (in the care of her daughter, Mrs Barbara Halpern); Ray Starchey to her mother, 28 Jan., 13 May 1936, 25 Nov. 1937.
[97] P. C. McIntosh, *Physical Education in England since 1800*, 2nd edn (London, 1968), pp. 113–17, 136–40.
[98] *Suffragette* (5 Dec. 1913), p. 169; Prunella Stack, *Movement is Life; The Autobiography* (London, 1973).
[99] *The Townswoman* (Nov. 1935), p. 176; National Union of Townswomen's Guilds, *Annual Report, 1937* (London, n.d.), p. 15.
[100] W. E. H. Lecky, *Democracy and Liberty*, 2 vols. (London, 1899 edn), ii, p. 531.
[101] See Drs Elizabeth and Emily Blackwell, 'Medicine as a Profession for Women', *English Woman's Journal* (1 May 1860), p. 153; Sophia Jex-Blake, *Medical Women* (note 11), pp. 50–1.

missionaries of health throughout the community.[102] Feminists like Charlotte Gilman wanted to take this development further.[103] They wanted to encourage expertise in food preparation and baby care through professionalizing housekeeping, which would in turn entail communal catering. Only thus would expertise cumulate; 'as a science', said Mrs Gilman, cooking 'verges on preventive medicine', whereas at present 'it is the lowest of amateur handicrafts'. Likewise with child-rearing: 'our children', she said, 'pass under the well-meaning experiments of an endless succession of amateurs'.[104] Both writers were influential among Edwardian British feminists and ideas on co-operative housekeeping sometimes appear in suffragette and suffragist periodicals.[105] Under the existing system, wrote Christabel Pankhurst in 1913, 'every woman has to be a Jill of all trades. Every woman her own laundress, cook, housemaid, marketer, and so on means that too many tasks are undertaken and none are done well enough ... Co-operative housekeeping is the hope of married women!'[106]

The scale of feminist preoccupation with these matters, and of its influence in society at large, should not be exaggerated. In view of the importance of the subject to women's emancipation, it is surprising that domestic economy was not a major concern of feminist periodicals before 1914, and that it remained only a minor theme thereafter. Part of the explanation is that until the second World War, British feminism – which recruited so heavily within the middle class – rested upon a substructure of cheap domestic service. Peace, family endowment, professional opportunity, handicrafts and the minutiae of housekeeping were the topics really prominent in women's organizations between the wars – witness the history of bodies like the Women's International League, the London Society for Women's Service, the Townswomen's Guilds and the Women's Institutes. Christabel Pankhurst might recom-

[102] F. Nightingale, *Notes on Nursing* (note 78), p. 79.
[103] C. P. Gilman in C. N. Degler (ed.) *Women and Economics. A Study of the Economic Relation Between Men and Women as a Factor in Social Evolution* (Harper Torchbooks, New York, 1966), pp. 239–43, 288; cf. T. Denno, *The Communist Millennium. The Soviet View* (The Hague, 1964), p. 47; Bernard Shaw *et al.*, *Fabian Essays*, Jubilee edn (London, 1948), p. 144.
[104] C. P. Gilman, *op. cit.*, pp. 230, 293.
[105] For example *Common Cause* (17 June 1909), p. 126; *Votes for Women* (7 Apr. 1911), p. 442; Ebenezer Howard in *Suffragette* (29 Aug. 1913), p. 799; (5 Sept. 1913), p. 815.
[106] *Suffragette* (5 Dec. 1913), p. 169; cf. (26 Dec. 1913), p. 245.

mend central heating, bulk purchase of food, central kitchens and laundries and co-operative dwellings as the platform of her Woman's Party in 1917 (echoed by the Women's Freedom League in the following year)[107] – but no subsequent feminist organization or political party took up the programme. The mechanization of the home and the spread of pre-packed foods are later developments which have to some extent realized the dreams of the Besants and the Gilmans, but by an entirely unexpected and non-feminist route.

The Women's Electrical Association after 1924 encouraged women to use the new electric aids and, together with the Women's Gas Council, received some publicity from the Townswomen's Guilds in the 1930s. At their Council meeting in 1935, Townswomen's Guilds were urged 'to study the application of modern science to the daily life of the home and the city, including the recent developments in transport and communications; lighting, heating and ventilation; hygiene and cleanliness; the prevention of illness; and the preservation of food';[108] but the Guilds' major role was to provide recreation, intellectual stimulus, companionship and household hints for women who readily accepted the role of housewife and mother while the breadwinner was away. Townswomen's Guilds and Women's Institutes in the 1930s co-operated with, and even supplied information to, a government which had independently recognized the importance of improved nutrition, ante-natal care and public utilities.[109] Organization women were going along with a tide which they were no more responsible than the anti-suffragists for creating. Even Eleanor Rathbone – whose efforts for children's nutrition and family endowment were relatively single-minded, original and independent – could do little more than ginger the government into activity and wait for opportunities spontaneously to open up. Women's organizations even as late as the 1930s were only an ancillary influence on improving women's health.

[107] A. Rosen, *Rise Up, Women! The Militant Campaign of the Women's Social and Political Union 1903–1914* (London, 1974), p. 267; cf. *The Vote* (1 Mar. 1918), p. 162.
[108] National Union of Townswomen's Guilds, *Annual Report, 1934* (London, n.d.), p. 32; cf. Mrs Corbett-Ashby in *Woman's Leader* (7 Mar. 1930), p. 35. See also *The Townswoman* (Mar. 1935), p. 241; (Nov. 1936), p. 178.
[109] See, e.g., *The Townswoman* (May 1935), p. 45; National Union of Townswomen's Guilds, *Annual Report, 1937* (London, n.d.), p. 10; National Federation of Women's Institutes, *22nd Annual Report, 1938* (London, n.d.), p. 13.

Not content with doing the doctor out of business, feminists began shedding light on the whole area of sexuality, whose mystery had hitherto proved so lucrative to him. British feminists were cautious in this area by international standards, so that women were often left to fend for themselves without explicit feminist guidance. The female complement of Victorian male clubbery and pubbery was always the informal discussion-group and family or street relationship between women (sometimes frowned upon by husbands) where mutual and informal help could provide protection against a male-dominated world.[110] The double standard of sexual morality ensured that access to abortion would be a major preoccupation of these female gatherings, if only in self-defence. It was not a form of self-help which the feminist movement could then publicly espouse, but it was integral to women's welfare, as the shocking blackmail attempts by the Chrimes Brothers in 1896–8 vividly illustrate.[111] The nineteenth-century medical profession, in distancing itself from quackery and in pursuing respectability, felt unable to give women precise information on birth control technique, and sometimes even posed as guardian of female health and virtue in opposing coitus interruptus and the sheath.[112] This did not prevent nineteenth-century women of all social classes from employing abortion as one among a range of birth control techniques; the extension of mechanical methods of birth control from the 1870s seems to be far less important in the spread of contraception than was once supposed.[113] But abortion was not a safe form of contraception: in Yorkshire mining towns even during the 1950s, many female illnesses resulted from self-induced miscarriages.[114] These could send women on visits to the doctor which were even more humiliating than usual.

Yet some feminists did venture to grapple with these problems,

[110] See B. Harrison, *Separate Spheres* (note 20), pp. 98–9; D. Gittins, 'Women's Work and Family Size between the Wars', *Oral History*, v, no. 2 (Autumn, 1977), pp. 88–9, 97–8; R. Roberts, *Ragged Schooling* (note 53), pp. 20, 22.
[111] A. McLaren (note 61), pp. 383–6.
[112] J. Woodward and D. Richards (note 4), pp. 94–6; R. Ledbetter (note 16), pp. 122, 141; A. McLaren, *Birth Control* (note 64), p. 120; M. Simms, 'Gynaecologists, Contraception and Abortion – From Birkett to Lane', *World Medicine* (23 Oct. 1974), p. 49.
[113] See A McLaren, *Birth Control* (note 64), pp. 14, 135; A. McLaren (note 61), pp. 389–92.
[114] N. Dennis, F. Henriques and C. Slaughter, *Coal is Our Life. An Analysis of a Yorkshire Mining Community* (London, 1956), p. 208.

though rather indirectly. Woman's desire for control over her own body was probably important in the campaign for women to enter the medical profession in the 1860s. This was far more than a campaign merely for widened professional opportunity, just as Josephine Butler's movement involved far more than the mere repudiation of immoral legislation; a pronounced concern for the privacy of the female person inspired both movements. In 1869, Sophia Jex-Blake told the pioneer American woman doctor Lucy Sewall, who inspired her own assault on the British medical profession, that she was 'more and more amazed how women *can* go to men for uterine treatment. I think that, sooner than go to any, I would come across the Atlantic again to you'.[115] Disgust at the C. D. Acts' compulsory inspection of prostitutes for venereal disease was a major influence on Josephine Butler. 'It is coming to be more and more a deadly fight on the part of us women for *our bodies*', she told Mr Edmondson in 1872: 'if these doctors could be forced to keep their hateful hands off us, there would be *an end* to laws which protect vice and to many other evils'.[116] She told the 1882 select committee that 'every woman has a right, a Divine right, to protect the secrets of her own person'. Her lifelong fear of the 'great net of medical tyranny ... craftily planned, and cautiously begun' referred not only to the danger of centralized bureaucracy, but also to male doctors' infringement of female privacy and liberty.[117]

Josephine Butler's 'fanatical crusade, preached chiefly amongst the least educated classes, and carried on by an unscrupulous use of all the arts of agitation, upon a subject which admits easily of shocking misrepresentations and inflammatory appeals'[118] – to use *The British Medical Journal's* words of 1872 – disgusted doctors partly because of its presumption in claiming to purge the medical profession of its materialism and amorality. The attack on the C. D. Acts is perhaps the most sustained example of feminist hostility to the doctor, but the antagonism reappears later. The non-militant suffragist leader Mrs Fawcett greatly admired Josephine Butler, whose influence on the non-militant National Union of Women's

[115] M. Todd (note 46), p. 247.
[116] Josephine Butler Papers: Josephine Butler to Mr Edmondson, 28 Mar. 1872 (deposited at City of London Polytechnic).
[117] *Parliamentary Papers* 1882 (340) ix, Q. 5379; *Storm-Bell* (Feb. 1898), p. 19.
[118] *British Medical Journal* (18 May 1872), p. 529.

Suffrage Societies was unobtrusive but considerable; Mrs Fawcett also opposed vaccination and vivisection.[119] The anti-vaccination theme reappears in the remarks of Mrs Parsons during the deputation from Sylvia Pankhurst's adult suffragist East London Federation to Asquith in June 1914; she had informed a magistrate that she did not wish her child to be vaccinated, but to her disgust the magistrate replied that in the eyes of the law she was not the parent. 'We feel that it is an insult to us', she declared, 'when we bring children into the world we at least should be able to say what is good for them'.[120]

But it was in the area of sexuality that feminists in the generation after Josephine Butler's crusade concentrated their most powerful fire against the doctors. In her most militant phase between 1912 and 1914, Sylvia's mother Emmeline referred more than once to the infant deaths from syphilis which she had encountered as registrar of births and deaths in Manchester. In a speech of 1913 she explained that this was 'one of the things that made me a militant Suffragist', and that

> whenever a woman came to register her baby's death, and brought the certificate in a sealed envelope, before I opened that envelope, and read that certificate, I knew what her baby had died of – inherited syphilis. Sometimes the name was put; sometimes other names were given. The father knew, or did not care to inquire, because there was a sort of conspiracy in those days between the medical man and the husband, so that the woman did not know what her baby died of.[121]

The Women's Social and Political Union's petition to the King, of February 1914, mentions the 'white slaves, outraged children, and innocent mothers and their babes stricked [sic] by horrible disease'.[122] Mrs Pankhurst later claimed that much of the government's hostility to her movement at this time stemmed from resentment at her daughter Christabel's exposé of male immorality in *The Great Scourge*.[123] Suspicion of doctors influenced one of her

---

[119] See Miss Lucas's memoir of Mrs Fawcett in *Woman's Leader* (15 Nov. 1929), p. 316.
[120] F. Primrose Stevenson's notes of the deputation ... 20 June 1914, Bodleian Library, Oxford, MS Asquith 89 f. 143.
[121] *Suffragette* (8 Aug. 1913), p. 738.
[122] Public Record Office, HO 45/249187. File 1 (Box No. 10720), petition dated 25 Feb. 1914.
[123] E. Pankhurst, *My Own Story* (London, 1914), p. 268, cf. pp. 291, 293.

disciples who was to become perhaps even more famous, Marie Stopes. As a true hypochondriac, she placed her faith as a young woman in self-medication; she later blamed the doctors for the fact that her first child was stillborn, because they failed to act on her advice about her positioning during its birth. Her subsequent conflicts with doctors were numerous, and ended tragically at the end of her life when her contempt for their diagnosis of cancer caused her to delay treatment until too late.[124]

In conclusion, the battle between 1909 and 1914 over forcible feeding can perhaps be taken to illustrate the difficulties involved in mounting effective feminist pressure on the medical profession: it constitutes a dramatic denouement to this long-standing mutual antagonism. The psychological torture involved in hearing warders gradually approaching one's cell with their tubes and jugs, accompanied by the mounting cries of agony from the prisoners they fed – almost exceeded the physical horror of forcible feeding itself, with all its threats to health, appearance and dignity. To those who experienced it, forcible feeding must have seemed an invasion of female dignity even more humiliating than the compulsory inspection of prostitutes which had so stirred Josephine Butler a generation earlier: a form of rape the more horrible for being committed by doctors at the insistence of government. It was, as one prisoner recalled, 'like hell with the lid off'[125] – an aspect of modern British history too unpleasant to have received subsequent discussion except in the most general terms, a set of incidents the more tragic for its inevitability in the face of the leadership which both suffragettes and Liberal government received. By September 1909, Labour backbenchers were expressing their horror at the brutality involved. Keir Hardie spared his fellow M.P.s no details, offered them no circumlocutions: his whole aim was to make them imagine themselves into the situation of the imprisoned suffragettes – to make them feel for themselves what he described as this 'horrible outrage, beastly outrage'.[126] M.P.s were not spared the vomiting, the bleeding gums and other horrors, which culminated in Hardie's detailed account on 27 June 1912 of Mrs Sadd Brown's

[124] R. Hall (note 23), pp. 74, 153–4, 323.
[125] *Arncliffe-Sennett Collection*, xviii, f. 86: Ada Wright's phrase, British Library.
[126] House of Commons Debates, 27 Sept. 1909, col. 924; for Hardie's other protests, see *ibid.* col. 1262 (29 Sept. 1909); col. 1637 (1 Oct. 1909); cols. 1652–4 (4 Oct. 1909); cols. 1999–2001 (6 Oct. 1909); also *ibid.* 18 Mar. 1913, cols. 919–20.

forcible feeding despite having warned the doctor of a previous nose fracture.[127]

In their periodical *The Suffragette*, the suffragettes tried to capitalize on the physical force which their militancy had evoked from the government; through tactics of provocation which have since become familiar, their indictment of government proved self-fulfilling. The paper announced on 24 October 1913 that 'the medical profession has now become a police force whose task is to break the spirit of the Suffragist women by injuring their bodies'.[128] Forcible feeding would have been less nasty if the prisoner had acquiesced in it, and Asquith correctly explained on 25 June 1912 that imprisonment would immediately cease for suffragettes who undertook to refrain from violent tactics; but as Lansbury pointed out in his celebrated protest-scene, 'you know they cannot'.[129] Nor could the government possibly allow violent tactics to bring the law into contempt – least of all a Liberal government faced by an agitation which campaigned in effect for a property-based female franchise. Militant tactics had placed both sides in an impossible position. One might have expected the correspondence-columns of the medical press to be buzzing with these events, yet *The Lancet* and *British Medical Journal* gave surprisingly little space either to woman suffrage or to forcible feeding. On 2 October 1909 *The British Medical Journal* accused Keir Hardie of exaggerating: 'the only force introduced into the procedure is that supplied by the persons fed, in resisting ...'. There were protests in the next issue from Louisa Garrett Anderson, but doctors continued forcibly feeding suffragettes right up to the first World War.

Still, the medical profession was not unanimous. Dr Forbes Winslow drew on his experience of insanity cases when enlarging upon the injuries which the stomach-pump could inflict and C. Mansell-Moullin objected in *The Times* to C. F. G. Masterman's term 'hospital treatment' (for forcible feeding) as a 'foul libel', because 'violence and brutality have no place in hospitals'. As early as October 1909 Sir Victor Horsley and 116 other doctors informed the government of the dangers involved in forcible feeding.[130]

[127] House of Commons Debates 27 June 1912, col. 500, cf. Lord Robert Cecil, *ibid.* 28 June 1912, col. 648.

[128] *Suffragette* (24 Oct. 1913), p. 33; cf. (6 Feb 1914), p. 369 and (24 Apr. 1914), p. 33.

[129] House of Commons Debates, 25 June 1912, col. 217.

[130] E. S. Pankhurst, *The Suffragette* (London, 1911), pp. 432–5; House of Commons Debates, 6 Oct. 1909, cols. 1999–2002.

Mansell-Moullin was a distinguished surgeon whose wife remained a suffragette till 1913; Horsley was a distinguished brain surgeon, teetotaller and enthusiastic suffragist. In August 1912 Horsley collaborated with Dr Agnes Savill and Mansell-Moullin in preparing a memorandum on the subject, which mentioned the mental torture and the nightmares involved; it was discussed by Hardie in Parliament, and was sufficient to alert the Liberal journalist H. W. Massingham to the full horror of the process.[131] In November 1913, at a meeting of about twenty doctors, mostly women, in the rooms of the Medical Society of London, the chairman Dr W. Hugh Fenton said that prison doctors, far from preserving the patient's life and health, were being required to act 'in a way that was not consonant with the best traditions of the profession'.[132] As a Harley Street doctor, he was in a position to give valuable but unobtrusive help to several hunger-striking suffragettes on their release from prison. Dr Flora Murray did the same, and later became a distinguished army surgeon.[133] Her resolution called on the Home Office to cease requiring prison doctors to engage in forcible feeding: 'the medical profession was esteemed by the public not only because it was scientific and humane, but because it put the interest of the patient before everything else, and the relations between the two were confidential'. Nonetheless the suffragettes – here as elsewhere – were battling against a hostile majority which was continuously recruited by their own actions. By June 1914, Mansell-Moullin could tell H. W. Nevinson that almost all the doctors were hostile and that he and Horsley were cut by nearly everyone.[134]

The fact that the suffragettes failed to advance the cause of woman suffrage after about 1908, and perhaps even retarded it after 1912, does not detract from their courage. The memory of it has done more than anything else to ensure that whenever woman suffrage is mentioned, the name Pankhurst immediately springs to mind, however unfair this may be to the non-militant suffragists in

[131] Memorandum in *British Medical Journal* (31 Aug. 1912), p. 507; see also S. Paget, *Sir Victor Horsley* (London, 1919), pp. 203–11; K. Hardie, House of Commons Debates, 28 June 1912, col. 659; for Massingham, see H. W. Nevinson's Diary, 2 Sept. 1912, Bodleian Library, Oxford, MS Eng. Misc. e 617/2.
[132] *British Medical Journal* (22 Nov. 1913), p. 1393.
[133] See memoir in *The Vote* (10 Aug. 1923), pp. 249–50.
[134] F. Murray, *British Medical Journal* (22 Nov. 1913), p. 1393; cf. H. B. Hanson, *British Medical Journal* (28 Sept. 1912), p. 822; *Nevinson Diary*, 8 June 1914, Bodleian Library, MS Eng. Misc. c 618/2.

the impression it conveys of how and why the vote was won. Lord
Curzon told an anti-suffrage meeting in June 1914 that suffragette
outrages 'are little by little breaking down that sense of chivalry
and respect which has hitherto existed like a shield in front of
women to defend them from outrage and insult in the world'.[135]
But he drew the wrong conclusion, for it was precisely that
dependent role in women which the feminist movement aimed to
erode. The suffragettes, as Lady Rhondda later recalled, 'broke
more than windows with their stones; they broke the crust and
conventions of a whole era'.[136] The cramping of women's abilities,
and even of their health, by prevailing social conventions has
already been emphasized. Christabel Pankhurst knew this, and
however much her militant tactics may in the short term have
obstructed the narrowly political cause by arousing the hostility of
a male Parliament – in the long term the Pankhursts gave British
women a myth and a legend which have inspired feminists ever
since. Yet the immediate impact of militancy was simply to advert-
ise male superiority in muscle-power, whether in confrontations
with the police during Westminster demonstrations or in obstruct-
ing the doctors who were forcing food upon them. The militants
were increasing the credibility of the anti-feminists' 'physical force
argument' with their every action, as the shrewder feminists observed at the time. They thereby lent a new twist to the feminists'
failure – or even lack of desire – to bring effective pressure on the
medical profession.


III


There is a third possibility – that the major advances in women's
health during the nineteenth and twentieth centuries were accele-
rated neither by feminist male doctors nor by feminist pressure
upon the medical profession, but by the women doctors whose
advent was one of the British feminists' proudest and earliest
achievements. Women were far keener to become doctors than
to enter any other profession: as late as 1911, the census records
no woman lawyer or engineer, and only a handful of women
accountants and architects. The growing professionalization of

---

[135] Anti-Suffrage Review (July 1914), p. 109.
[136] Viscountess Rhondda, This Was My World (note 42), p. 162; cf. Christabel
Pankhurst's leader in Suffragette (7 Nov. 1913), p. 78.

medicine may have obstructed feminists in some areas, but it did at least have the advantage of clarifying the qualifications for entry.[137]

Many of the pioneer women doctors were decidedly feminist. Both Elizabeth Garrett Anderson and Sophia Jex-Blake spoke out for woman suffrage at crucial moments, and reinforced the case for it with their medical expertise and prestige.[138] Twelve of the forty-five British medical women registered in 1885 signed the suffragists' letter to the House of Lords in that year.[139] The category 'medical and nursing' in the list of representative signatories to *The Fortnightly Review*'s woman suffrage declaration of July 1889 included twenty-three doctors – including Sophia Jex-Blake, Elizabeth Garrett Anderson, Mrs. Scharlieb and Elizabeth Blackwell – and claimed support from twenty-six medical students. Twenty-five of the seventy-three registered British medical women had now openly declared themselves for woman suffrage, whereas none of the seventy-three signed *The Nineteenth Century*'s protest against women's suffrage of that year. The leading medical women also signed the suffragist appeal to Parliament of 1893–4, and when registered medical women were polled for their views on woman suffrage in 1908, 538 were in favour and only fifteen against. The woman suffrage petition in November 1910 attracted signatures from 407 medical women,[140] and woman doctors were active in the suffrage movement at several levels – from the militancy of Helen Hanson and Louisa Garrett Anderson to the tax-resistance of Jessie Murray, to the heroic and politically influential work done by woman doctors like Marion Wilson, Elsie Inglis and Flora Murray in hospitals during the first World War.

For several reasons, though, it would be surprising if these doctors made much impact on women's health. To begin with, there were so few of them: twenty-five in England and Wales in 1881 (0.17 per cent of the total), 495 in 1911 (1.98 per cent).[141] In

---

[137] W. J. Reader, *Professional Men* (London, 1966), p. 181; M. R. Walsh, '*Doctors Wanted*', note 40, *pp.* 14–15.
[138] E. G. Anderson, *Women's Suffrage Journal* (1 May 1871), p. 47; (1 July 1884), pp. 183–4; Sophia Jex-Blake, *ibid.* (2 Feb. 1880), p. 23; (2 June 1884), p. 132; *Englishwoman's Review* (15 Sept. 1885), pp. 408–9.
[139] The signatures are in *Women's Suffrage Journal* (1 June 1885), pp. 98ff.; cf. the list of registered medical women in *Englishwoman's Review* (15 Feb. 1889), pp. 65–8.
[140] *Englishwoman's Review* (16 July 1894), p. 171; *Times* (14 Dec. 1908), p. 6; *Lancet* (19 Nov. 1910), p. 1506.
[141] Census of Great Britain, *Parliamentary Papers* 1913 (Cd. 7018) lxxviii, p. 552.

absolute terms, the late-Victorian growth in the number of woman doctors was impressive, but much less impressive when seen as a proportion of the medical profession as a whole. The number of women whose United Kingdom diplomas licensed them to practise as doctors reached 434 in the United Kingdom in 1900 and doubled between then and 1909; in 1910 *The Englishwoman's Year-Book* discontinued listing women doctors individually 'owing to the great increase in the number of qualified medical women'. But their influence on British society was diluted in several ways. Of the seventy women with British medical qualifications and still alive in February 1880 whose location can be traced, sixteen had gone to India (nine as medical missionaries), sixteen more were overseas, three were in Edinburgh, twenty-three in London – leaving twelve for the rest of the United Kingdom. In 1900 one-third of the total (434) were overseas, and those who remained in Britain tended to congregate in London (ninety-two), Edinburgh (twenty-seven), Glasgow (seventeen) and in provincial towns where a sizeable female clientele could be anticipated.[142]

Regional variegation was compounded in its diluting impact by family distractions. Even Sophia Jex-Blake admitted that, on marriage, family claims must take priority over medical careers,[143] and it is perhaps significant that in 1911, 80 per cent of the woman doctors in England and Wales were unmarried;[144] but even unmarried daughters have parents and in those days the obligations of the unmarried daughter to them were considerable. As time went on, women doctors were more prone to marry, and to marry earlier. Of the twenty-eight woman B.M.s emerging from Oxford between 1922 and 1930, 60 per cent remained single: of the eighteen between 1931 and 1940 only 27 per cent: and of the ninety-three between 1941 and 1950, only 19 per cent. Whether marriage resulted in children or not, it was followed by a sharp fall in the time committed to medical work, partly because the female emancipation which brought women into medicine took them out of domestic service. The twentieth-century qualified woman doctor has therefore found help in the home impossible to obtain, or – given the narrowing differential between professional and other

---

[142] *Englishwoman's Review* (15 Feb. 1889), pp. 65–8; *Englishwoman's Yearbook* (1900), pp. 132f.; (1910), p. 108.
[143] M. Todd (note 46), p. 503.
[144] Census of Great Britain, *Parliamentary Papers* 1913 (Cd. 7018) lxxviii, p. 2.

salaries – impossible to afford.[145] If she had children, modern theories of child-rearing told her that they required her undivided attention in early years. Her consequent opting for part-time medical work made it difficult to get the range of experience or consistency of career which leads to the top. Although the percentage of general practitioners in England and Wales who were female rose from 10 per cent in 1963 to 14 per cent in 1974, the percentage of qualified woman doctors who were inactive in 1975 was much larger (30 per cent) than the male (12 per cent);[146] it has recently been calculated that a woman doctor during her career may give as little as 60 per cent of the male person-years of work.[147] For all these and other reasons, women were underrepresented at the higher levels of medicine; in 1975, males accounted for 97 per cent of the councils of the Royal Colleges, central policy committees and General Medical Council, females for only 3 per cent.[148]

The woman doctor's impact on women's health was further circumscribed by the fact that she did not specialize in problems peculiar to women. Surprisingly little has been written on the careers of woman doctors; the triumphant story of their entry into the profession is enthusiastically chronicled, but nobody analyses their achievements on arrival. In the 1860s it was argued that woman doctors would uncover a host of female illnesses which female reticence had hitherto concealed from male doctors. Such an argument had the advantage of reassuring male doctors who feared losing their custom to female rivals; woman doctors would not then be competing for a fixed clientele, but would actually be enlarging

[145] A. H. T. Robb-Smith, 'The Fate of Oxford Medical Women', *Lancet* (1 Dec. 1962), p. 1158; see also R. Henryk-Gutt and R. Silverstone, 'Career Problems of Women Doctors', *British Medical Journal*, (1976), ii pp. 574–5; C. A. Flynn and F. Gardner, 'The Careers of Women Graduates from the Royal Free Hospital School of Medicine, London', *British Journal of Medical Education*, iii (1969), pp. 31–2, 41; L. A. Aird and P. H. S. Silver, 'Women Doctors from the Middlesex Hospital Medical School (University of London) 1947–67', *British Journal of Medical Education*, v (1971), p. 240.
[146] Office of Health Economics, *Compendium of Health Statistics*, 2nd edn (London, 1977), section 4, pp. 4–5; *Women in Medicine: Proceedings of a Conference Organised by the Department of Health and Social Security, 4–5 July 1975* (background paper), n.d., n.p.l.
[147] Editorial in *Journal of the Royal College of General Practitioners* (Apr. 1979), p. 195.
[148] *Women in Medicine*, Dr Pamela Ashurst (n.p.); cf. *Lancet* (8 July 1978), p. 89.

it.[149] The advent of the woman doctor was certainly welcome to some women; Elizabeth Blackwell was encouraged towards medical study by a woman dying of a painful disease who told her that 'if I could have been treated by a lady doctor, my worst sufferings would have been spared me'.[150] Josephine Butler reported to a friend on her consultation with Elizabeth Garrett in 1868 as follows: 'I was able to *tell* her so much more than I ever could or would tell to any *man* ... O, if men knew what women have to endure, and how every good woman has prayed for the coming of a change, a change in this ... I pray God that many Miss Garrett's may arise'.[151] In the long term, the laws of supply and demand – which Sophia Jex-Blake thought should be trusted here as elsewhere[152]– vindicated the change, and discredited *The Times*'s belief in 1873 that the doctor's qualities 'are not such as would be described by the adjective "feminine"'.[153]

Furthermore, *The British Medical Journal*'s prediction of 1870 that women would specialize in the diseases of their own sex or of children[154] proved accurate in some instances: Olive Claydon in Oldham and Mary Murdoch in Hull spring to mind. Women doctors were valuable to the feminist movement as a continuous restraint, actual or potential, on the anti-feminism of so many male doctors. They could be relied upon to come forward when necessary to defend women against medical attack – as did Elizabeth Garrett Anderson against Maudsley in *The Fortnightly Review* of 1874 or Agnes Savill against forcible feeding in 1912. There were also some hints of a distinct feminist perspective on medicine. Christine Murrell's *Womanhood and Health* (1923), published with financial aid from the suffragist Marie Lawson, challenged the idea that man is the physiological norm and woman the deviation; 'it is of the first importance', she wrote, 'that women should recognize that they no less than men are normal healthy individuals'.[155]

Yet it is surprising that after two generations of woman doctors,

---

[149] See, e.g., Sophia Jex-Blake in J. E. Butler (ed.), *Woman's Work and Woman's Culture* (London, 1869), pp. 101, 107.
[150] E. Blackwell (note 57), p. 27; cf. *English Woman's Journal* (1 Sept. 1862), p. 69.
[151] Josephine Butler Papers: Josephine Butler to unidentified friend, 22 Feb. 1868 (typescript copy, at City of London Polytechnic).
[152] *Fortnightly Review* (Mar. 1875), p. 407.
[153] *Times* (23 Aug. 1873), p. 9; cf. *Lancet* (3 Nov. 1883), p. 780.
[154] *British Medical Journal* (30 Apr. 1870), p. 444.
[155] *Womanhood and Health* (London, 1923), p. 89.

this should still need to be said. Furthermore, Dr Murrell's insights were accompanied by several dubious ideas on the psychological dimension of menstrual pain and the existence of a male monthly cycle. Women have never been prominent in the world of gynaecology and obstetrics. The British College of Obstetricians and Gynaecologists was set up in 1929 under officers and an executive committee whose composition was entirely male. So masculine was the College's ethos that its historian sees the election of its one woman president (Hilda Lloyd) among the sixteen appointed between 1929 and 1978 as 'a revolutionary step' which evoked doubts from some of the fellows; but, he goes on, 'there was no need for fear ...'.[156] Only four of the eighty-nine British and overseas fellows whose Christian names reveal their sex in 1931 were female (5 per cent): twenty-seven of the 242 in 1945 (11 per cent): seventy-two of the 520 in 1960 (14 per cent): 200 of the 1590 in 1978 (13 per cent).[157] Far from transforming the ideas and methods of the medical profession, the American and British woman doctor seems to have accommodated herself quickly to the ethos of her male-dominated profession.[158]

Woman doctors could of course have improved women's health through their overall excellence in medicine. Yet here too their impact seems to have been small. Even Elizabeth Garrett Anderson's biographer admits that 'if one regards medicine as a pure science, her claims to distinction are not high', and Margaret Todd comes near to saying the same of Sophia Jex-Blake.[159] Florence Nightingale told J. S. Mill in 1860 that woman doctors 'have made no improvement: they have only tried to be "men", and they have only succeeded in being third rate men'.[160] Mill rightly rejoined that it was too early to gauge women's potential as doctors and denied that their claim to enter the profession rested on their capacity for reforming it.[161] Yet it would have been

[156] F. Shaw, *Twenty-Five Years. The Story of the Royal College of Obstetricians and Gynaecologists 1929–1954* (London, 1954), p. 159.

[157] Statistics calculated from British [later Royal] College of Obstetricians and Gynaecologists, *2nd Annual Report (1930–1)* (London, n.d.); *17th Annual Report 1945* (London, n.d.); *32nd Annual Report 1960* (London, n.d.); *Register of Fellows and Members, 1978* (London, n.d.)

[158] Cf. Morantz, in M. Hartman & L. Banner (note 5), pp. 48, 50, also cf. Wood, *ibid.*, p. 13.

[159] J. Manton, *Elizabeth Garrett Anderson* (London, 1965), p. 266.

[160] Nightingale Papers: Florence Nightingale to J. S. Mill, 12 Sept. 1860 (copy), British Library, Additional MSS, 45787.

[161] *Ibid.*, ff. 17–18. Mill to Nightingale, 23 Sept. 1860.

surprising if the early woman doctors had achieved major advances in medical research. Just as the doctor's insecurity of status in the wider society made it difficult for him to espouse feminist ideals, so the insecurity of women inside the medical profession made it difficult for them to do anything unorthodox – yet it is only through iconoclasm that science advances. Innovation in science is in practice less welcome within the scientific community than its public face might lead one to expect; the early woman doctors would have been still less popular with their colleagues if they had vigorously exposed the falsity of their theories. They had successfully breached one of the major obstacles to women's achievement: they could not simultaneously breach them all.

The early woman doctors had to be on their best behaviour, and this limited not only their scientific adventurousness, but even the scale of the direct aid they could give to feminist organizations. Elizabeth Garrett Anderson kept very much in the background when it came to feminist work and behaved in many respects as conventionally as possible, if only because she believed that this would increase her influence.[162] The comments of a woman factory inspector many years later illuminate the plight of the pioneer professional woman: 'I do not believe that people in general have the slightest idea of the enormous strain under which the pioneer women in the professions have to work', she said. She then explained how factory inspectors had to attend court when a charge was brought under the Factory Act:

> when the inspector is a man, it is merely a matter of routine for him and everyone else concerned. As soon as a case of mine comes on, I am acutely aware of a change in the atmosphere. When I stand up in court, my appearance, my dress, my manner of speech – all are criticised ... I, too, am on trial. In addition to proving my legal case, I am also required to prove my right to be a factory inspector.[163]

If the early woman doctors had to be prudent in their feminism, they also sometimes diverged from the feminists, for the doctor's psychological distance from the pressure group applied to female doctors as well as to male. Nor does a woman's personal success necessarily lead her to sympathize with women who are less successful than herself: she may prefer to accept the suggestion,

---

[162] Manton (note 159), p. 311.
[163] *The Vote* (2 Aug. 1929), p. 245.

frequently preferred by anti-feminist males, that her talents are 'exceptional'. Women doctors of this type came to resemble the anti-suffragist woman whose wealth and influence so often led her to diverge from a feminist movement which catered for the less privileged members of her sex. They may, in other words, have grown into some of the anti-feminist attitudes so widespread in the profession they joined. Josephine Butler greatly regretted the failure of Miss Pechey and Miss Jex-Blake to support her attack on the C. D. Acts. As for Elizabeth Garrett Anderson, she publicized her view that 'degradation cannot be taken by storm, and the animal side of human nature will outlive crusades'.[164] She had much in common with Florence Nightingale, both in her outwardly conventional conduct and in her coolness towards popular crusades. Once when reproached for backsliding by an opponent of the C. D. Acts, Florence remarked that her critic 'does not want to hear facts; she wants to be enthusiastic'.[165]

Militant feminism presented Edwardian professional women with a painful dilemma: personal success in their careers was at least as important to women's long-term emancipation as the winning of the vote, and militancy provided critics with a most convenient weapon to beat even the non-militant suffragists. 'The head mistress of the high school will probably be favourable', wrote Margaret Robertson in 1909, advising readers on how to establish a non-militant suffragist branch in a locality, 'but unwilling to appear prominently because of her position'.[166] So discrediting were militant suffrage connections that the suffragette Cicely Hale feared arrest lest her father, a suffragist London doctor, would suffer in his practice.[167] The young Marie Stopes, writing from Tokyo to her mother in 1908, was relieved to be safely distant from London, with all its suffragette excitements, 'for tho' I don't have so much sympathy with the rowdy ones, I should have probably got drawn into it, and it would have seriously damaged my career as a scientist'.[168] Then there was Dr Fairfield, the suffragist doctor,

[164] Elizabeth Garrett [Anderson], *An Inquiry into the Character of the Contagious Diseases Acts of 1866–9* (London, 1870), p. 16, cf. J. Manton (note 159), pp. 179–80, and see p. 317 for her attitude to anti-vaccinationism. See also M. Todd (note 46), p. 364.
[165] E. Cook (note 63), ii, p. 408.
[166] *Common Cause* (20 May 1909), p. 82.
[167] Tape-recorded interview with author, 6 Nov. 1974.
[168] Stopes Papers, f. 104: Marie Stopes to her mother, 29 Mar. 1908, British Library, additional MSS 58450.

advertising suffragette meetings by chalking on the pavement near her hospital in Nottingham. '*Dr Fairfield!*' exclaimed the consultant who saw her: 'What are you doing on your knees in the market place?' Fortunately he took the matter no further, but when Dr Fairfield moved to London she presented her problem to Mrs Pankhurst, adding that she was nonetheless ready for militant work. Over sixty years later, she recalled Mrs Pankhurst's understanding reply: 'my dear, you will be much the most useful person if you increase your status in the medical profession, so you've no reason to think about that again. We have *plenty* of volunteers'.[169]

The need for caution was by no means the only disability suffered by the woman doctor in comparison with her male colleagues. The need for an established tradition as a basis for achievement was as important here as in the writing of novels. 'The medical solitude is really awful at times', wrote Elizabeth Blackwell from New York to her sister in 1854: her loneliness eventually led her to adopt a small orphan girl. As a practising doctor in Edinburgh, Sophia Jex-Blake decades later felt disadvantaged by her exclusion from male colleagues' shop-talk on difficult cases.[170] We must therefore reject the third hypothesis, that substantial improvements in women's health between 1840 and 1940 can be ascribed to the woman doctors.

Our three hypotheses could have been dismissed from other directions, for the analysis has so far been founded only on sources internal to the feminist movement: by pointing to the lack of any coincidence in timing between feminist progress and improvements in women's health, for example. The decline in female mortality began well before the British feminist movement was established in the 1860s; nor does there seem to be any subsequent correlation between feminist success and such statistical indications as we possess for changes in women's health. It has even been argued, in the American context, that there is an inverse correlation between women's recruitment as doctors and the campaign for the vote[171] – though more plausible explanations for the twentieth-century deceleration in women's recruitment to the medical profession seem to be the changing attitudes to child-rearing and the professional

---

[169] Tape-recorded interview with author, 21 Dec. 1976.
[170] E. Blackwell (note 57), p. 200, cf. *ibid.*, pp. 195, 198; M. Todd (note 46), p. 459.
[171] M. R. Walsh (note 40), pp. 185–6, 214.

woman's changing domestic situation which have already been discussed.

Women were not enfranchised in Switzerland till 1971, yet the Swiss decline in infant mortality (deaths of infants under one year old per 1000 live births) has been just as fast as in Britain. Indeed, in only five years between 1900 and 1945 (in 1903, 1905, 1907, 1909 and 1920) was the Swiss mortality rate higher than in England and Wales: in many years it was much lower. Feminism as an influence on women's health interacts with many other factors; it may even, in some circumstances, cause women to subordinate the pursuit of health to other objectives – to risk lung cancer in seeking social poise through the cigarette, to risk dangerous careers in pursuing equal opportunity and, most obviously, to resist the compulsory treatment of women infected by venereal disease in championing an equal moral standard. Many feminists were angry in October 1916 when Mrs Pankhurst and others demanded compulsory notification and treatment of women suspected of carrying the disease. The rising female contribution to traffic accidents reflects the wider social role which women have been acquiring. In the 1870s, only 15 per cent of those killed on the roads and 7 per cent of those killed on the railways were female. By the 1930s these figures had risen to 22 per cent and 10 per cent respectively and by 1967 women were contributing 30 per cent of all road deaths.[172]

None of this excludes the possibility that feminists will have considerable impact on women's health in the future. Indeed, the medical profession is far more alert to women's needs now than in the past – not least to the needs of women doctors. It is already recruiting a rising proportion of women and needs to recruit more, not simply on the ground of improving women's opportunities for employment, but because women's abilities and sheer presence are greatly needed in the medical sphere. Woman doctors, simply by virtue of the fact that they are women, are more likely to comprehend the symptoms of woman patients. This is important, because women are likely to constitute a majority among them: they bear children, they live longer, and they are relatively eager to seek medical advice. The married woman doctor who is also a mother

[172] B. R. Mitchell, *European Historical Statistics 1750–1970* (London, 1975), p. 131; Nevinson Diary, 23 Oct. 1916, Bodleian Library, MS Eng. Misc. c 620/1; P. E. H. Hair, 'Deaths from Violence in Britain: A Tentative Secular Survey', *Population Studies*, xxv (1971), p. 9.

will be better equipped on some aspects of children's medicine, which provides a quarter of a general practitioner's work. There is even some evidence that women are (for whatever reason) better suited than men to the counselling role which is so centrally important in primary medical care.[173]

IV

The improvement in women's health has been central to their emancipation. It is a change which British feminism has assisted through encouraging more open discussion in the sexual sphere: through assisting an overall change in attitudes to women in society, to which doctors in the long term have to respond: and through broadening out opportunities for women in British life, either directly within feminist organizations, or indirectly through the legislative and other changes they promote. The relationship between psychological and physiological illness is too complex for its impact on this third dimension of health to be measured precisely. The fact that British feminists have not done more than this is hardly surprising: not only were they penetrating to the heart of the enemy camp by challenging male supremacy in the medical sphere: they were also subject to major handicaps in competing with men once they had entered the medical profession. Nor is it unusual in public life for there to be a partial or even total disjunction between the activities of reforming movements (male or female) and the advent of the changes most likely to promote their underlying objective: indeed, in certain areas – woman suffrage between 1912 and 1914, for example, or temperance throughout the nineteenth century – there has been an actual conflict between the two. Reforming leaders are no better than politicians at predicting the future, and it is hardly surprising in reforming causes – as in politics overall – that there is sometimes a disjunction between intention and outcome.

But to reveal the relative unimportance of feminist influences on the medical profession since the 1840s does no more than clear a small part of the ground before major explanatory structures can

[173] Office of Health Economics, *Compendium of Health Statistics* 2nd edn (London 1977), Section, 5, p. 4; A. M. Carr-Saunders, D. C. Jones and C. A. Moser *A Survey of Social Conditions in England and Wales* (Oxford, 1958), p. 235; *Journal of the Royal College of General Practitioners* (Apr. 1979), pp. 197–8.

be erected. As was emphasized earlier, the doctor's role in improving the health of the people is itself controversial for much of the period under discussion. There are many other areas in which the efforts of feminists, and of women in general, could have contributed towards the change. With a view to this wider inquiry, no more than suggestions as to three possible influences can be offered here. The first is, paradoxically, the prevalence in Britain and elsewhere of an attitude central to anti-feminism: the desire to keep up the birth-rate. It was feared that the entry of women into political life would undermine Britain's international standing by causing the birth-rate to fall. Acutely conscious of military threats from abroad, anti-feminists wanted citizenship linked to fighting capacity. 'You have at the present moment certain statistics which show that both the birth and marriage rate are decreasing', said that staunch anti-suffragist Sir Charles Hobhouse on 19 June 1917, in the House of Commons debate on the Franchise Bill: 'can you adopt at this time a policy which might mean an immense destruction of the population of the country which it is essential should not only be retained, but increased?'[174]

The prestige of motherhood was boosted further by the eugenists, a group whose eagerness to improve the quality of the population led them frequently to diverge from the feminists. Francis Galton's *Hereditary Genius* (1869) emphasized the great national gains to be made from getting the strong strains in the population to marry earlier and the weak strains to marry later; his late-Victorian disciples were alarmed that the birth-rate was falling fastest among the educated classes.[175] The spread of birth control throughout the working class seemed urgent to such people for non-feminist reasons and the twentieth-century expansion in the birth control movement owed much to them. A healthy population, it was argued, would also be more efficient for war and/or industrial production – a belated echo of many a memorandum drafted in the 1860s by Edwin Chadwick and Florence Nightingale. Here is one of the roots of the Edwardian preoccupation with infant welfare clinics, regulation of midwifery, registration of nurses and provision of school meals: healthy and abundant children could be produced only by healthy mothers. Of the seventy-five

---

[174] House of Commons Debates, 19 June 1917, col. 1654.
[175] F. Galton, *Hereditary Genius. An Inquiry into its Laws & Consequences* (London, 1869), pp. 352–6; R. McWilliams-Tullberg (note 47), p. 103.

officers or council members of the Eugenics Society at some time during the six years 1930–6, fourteen held some kind of official position in the National Birth Control Association (N.B.C.A., ancestor of the Family Planning Association), and some were very active in both. Lord Horder was president of the N.B.C.A. throughout the period, and vice-president of the Eugenics Society for five of the six years. Sir Humphrey Rolleston, president of the Eugenics Society in 1933–4, was also on the N.B.C.A.'s Birth Control Investigation Committee throughout the period. C.P. Blacker, General Secretary of the Eugenics Society, was also very active in the N.B.C.A., and Eva Hubback, who played a major role in launching the N.B.C.A., was on the Eugenics Society council for four of the six years.[176]

The birth control campaign did not aim merely at enabling mothers to produce more healthy children. It attacked problems of sterility – aiming to solve the particular problem of the individual parent, male or female, as well as to tackle social problems conceived on a national scale. As early as 1923, Marie Stopes' Holloway birth control clinic was encouraging conception as well as preventing it,[177] and by the mid-1930s the N.B.C.A. was giving an emphasis to 'planned parenthood' – an emphasis which was soon to produce a change of name and an alteration in formal 'objects'.[178]

The desire for healthy mothers and children was by no means confined to anti-feminists. Indeed, among the strongest of the suffragist arguments had always been the claim that women need the vote because the state – in promoting the health and welfare of the domestic population – has *already* involved itself in the areas of national life where women are best informed.[179] Eva Hubback was a prominent feminist and her work was supplemented by the interwar campaign of that distinguished feminist Eleanor Rathbone for improved nutrition and for the family allowances which were designed to assist it. An immense impact on the health of the population must have been made by the advent of the welfare state, whose origins owed much to pressure from women, many of them feminist women. Although the pioneering British feminists of the 1860s included many who resisted the spread of birth control and

[176] Information from annual reports of the Eugenics Society and of the N.B.C.A.
[177] M. Stopes, *Contraception (Birth Control). Its Theory, History and Practice* (London, 1923), p. 388.
[178] N.B.C.A. *6th Annual Report*, 1935–6 (London, n.d.), p. 4.
[179] See, e.g., Forsyth, House of Commons Debates, 26 Apr. 1876, col. 1662; Campbell Bannerman, *ibid.*, 8 Mar. 1907, cols. 1110–11.

of factory regulations specific to women, who believed that woman's place was in the home, and who favoured votes and careers only for widowed and unmarried women – early twentieth-century feminists were becoming increasingly preoccupied with the plight of the overburdened housewife and mother. There were always close affinities between the Labour Party and feminists of both militant and non-militant camps and the considerable overlap between feminism and socialism is epitomized in the careers of Emmeline Pethick-Lawrence, Ellen Wilkinson and Sylvia Pankhurst. Collaboration between feminists and anti-feminists in promoting welfare measures is one of the factors submerging feminism as a distinct political alignment after 1918.

Even more important was women's contribution to a second, and more generalized influence assisting improvements in women's health. This can only be described as the humanitarian and secularized preoccupation with improving the health of the population as a whole for its own sake. It is not so much that feminism produces the improvement here, as that both feminism and the improvement originate in the same cause: in the growth in this-worldly values which from the beginning of the period encouraged preoccupation with the health of males and females, young and old, rich and poor, free man and slave. Feminism was but one constituent in a crusade for social and moral reform which had many facets: indeed, many feminists entered public life as social reformers and began campaigning for the vote partly with the aim of extending their influence in that role.

The history of the British campaign for birth control usefully illustrates the broad humanitarian influences, feminist and non-feminist, which go to make up a change which is as central to improvements in women's health as any other; at this point, it deserves rather more extended discussion. The control of pregnancy was integral to women's emancipation – perhaps even more important to it than winning the vote, if only because birth control would make it easier for women to participate in politics. But the social and sexual emancipation entailed by birth control was even more important. When analysing her first 10,000 cases, Marie Stopes detected a positive correlation between the number of a woman's pregnancies and the number of her children who died.[180] Sexual fulfilment was impossible for women terrified of pregnancy:

[180] M. Stopes, *Preliminary Notes on Various Technical Aspects of the Control of Conception* (Mothers' Clinic for Constructive Birth Control, 1930), p. 9.

'I am so afraid of conception', one Manchester woman told her in 1921, 'that I cannot bear for my husband to even speak kindly to me or even put his hand on my shoulder for fear he wants his rights'.[181] In the essays on *Maternity* of 1915, sexual advances from the husband are seen almost as menacing threats and only the possession of what is called 'a good husband' makes life tolerable amid the bewildering complex of obligations which repeated pregnancies involve. As one of the authors pointed out, in the midst of childbearing, the mother 'is still the head and chancellor of the exchequer. If she were confined on Friday, she would still have to plan and lay out the Saturday money, and if it did not stretch far enough, she would be the one to go short or do the worrying'.[182]

One might have expected British feminists to take the lead in a campaign so central to women's health and welfare. Yet in the sexual and even in other spheres, as has already been shown, the British feminist who aimed at political results in the short term felt the need for caution. Even the feminists who spoke out – such as Christabel Pankhurst or Josephine Butler – were in many respects conservative on sexual matters and most feminists preferred to keep silent. For like the doctors, they were insecure in their status and could not afford to challenge too many contemporary attitudes at once. Just as doctors were using science to undermine powerful religious and social attitudes, so the feminists were subverting deeply-held political and family conventions. Eleanor Rathbone's *Disinherited Family* (1924) admits that tactical considerations had restrained her comments on birth control during the fight for improved education and the vote, 'but now that those irrevocable gifts have been given, we can afford to speak our minds'.[183] But the British feminists' conservatism in sexual matters was not merely tactical. 'Better not think about those subjects', was Mrs Sidgwick's response, when approached on Josephine Butler's crusade. Rare is the reformer who is progressive in every sphere, and by modern British and contemporary European and American feminist standards, British feminists were relatively conservative on topics such as birth control, which they began discussing publicly only somewhat tentatively in the 1920s.[184]

---

[181] Quoted in R. Hall (note 23), p. 171.
[182] M. Llewelyn Davies (note 21), p. 89.
[183] E. Rathbone, *The Disinherited Family. A Plea for the Endowment of the Family* (London, 1924), p. 246.
[184] E. Sidgwick (note 47), p. 189; see also A. McLaren (note 64), p. 111; Ray

British feminist reticence did not prevent unobtrusively feminist influences from inspiring the British pioneers of birth control – William Thompson, Richard Carlile, Robert Dale Owen and J. S. Mill – all of whom were inspired by women.[185] But the official feminist movement was alarmed even by Josephine Butler's movement (highly conservative on sexual matters, in several respects) let alone by the type of feminist whom Bishop Hensley Henson encountered in 1930. Why should unmarried women not have lovers, she asked him, 'and by the help of contraceptives, have no children? Who would be injured by their doing so? And, if no one was injured, why was it wrong?'[186] It was not in these terms that British feminists in the 1920s quietly launched their public discussion of contraception. The sexual emancipation they envisaged was decidedly limited.

Apart from Marie Stopes, who was for a short time a militant, it was the former non-militants, organized in the National Union of Societies for Equal Citizenship (N.U.S.E.C., heir to the National Union of Women's Suffrage Societies) who were most prominent in this discussion. N.U.S.E.C.'s organ, *The Woman's Leader*, insisted during 1921 that a platform must be provided for discussing a topic on which 'the interchange of serious thought ... is too often avoided or repressed'.[187] In its number of 6 May, Marie Stopes argued that political freedom 'is less to each individual than her personal and bodily freedom: and without control over her own motherhood no married woman can have bodily freedom'.[188] Vigorous discussion followed in the correspondence columns, and several feminists – Margaret Ashton, Lady Constance Lytton, Mrs Despard, Maude Royden – were among the patrons of Marie Stopes's first clinic in Holloway.[189] An undercurrent of controversy on birth control continued in *The Woman's Leader* throughout 1923–4 and in 1925 N.U.S.E.C.'s annual council approved a resolution urging the Ministry of Health to provide information at child welfare centres. Married women's access to birth control information was included among N.U.S.E.C.'s objectives in 1928

Strachey, *Millicent Garrett Fawcett* (London, 1931), pp. 88–9.
[185] A. McLaren (note 64), pp. 94–5, 98, 101.
[186] H. Hensley Henson, *Retrospect of an Unimportant Life*, 3 vols. (London, 1943), ii, p. 270.
[187] *Woman's Leader* (15 Apr. 1921), p. 166.
[188] *Ibid.* (6 May 1921), p. 211.
[189] See M. Stopes (note 177), p. 325.

and in the following year Mary Stocks was pressing for this policy within the National Council of Women.[190] In 1930, N.U.S.E.C. was among the societies which convened the conference on publicity for birth control techniques: Eva Hubback, one of N.U.S.E.C.'s most prominent members, added one more to the many feminist achievements of the non-militants: she took a key role in getting doctors and laymen to back the National Birth Control Association which emerged from the conference.[191] The Association attracted subscriptions and support from feminists as prominent as Eleanor Rathbone and Lady Astor and achieved the difficult feat of welding together a national network of birth control clinics.

Yet even at this stage, feminists were by no means united behind birth control. In 1920 a prominent suffragist woman doctor like Mary Scharlieb could describe even the discussion of contraceptive methods as 'lowering to the moral sense and to the innate reserve and purity of decently brought-up young people'.[192] Helen Fraser refused to speak on the subject, and in 1922 Emmeline Pethick-Lawrence declined Marie Stopes's invitation to speak, now that the movement had been launched.[193] In 1924 the Women's Freedom League (third in importance among the Edwardian suffragist organizations) went out of its way to stress its lack of commitment on the issue. In the House of Lords debate of 1926 on the provision of birth control information, Mary Scharlieb could be cited by Viscount Fitzalan of Derwent as opposing the idea – together with the Fabian suffragist and Catholic Dr Letitia Fairfield and the prominent gynaecologist Dr Louise McIlroy.[194] Even Marie Stopes's ideas on sexual matters – for example on sexual deviance, masturbation and sexual intercourse outside marriage – now seem narrow-minded.[195] If there is a dominant theme on sexual matters within the British feminist movement, it is the pursuit of an equal

[190] *Woman's Leader* (20 Mar. 1925), p. 61; N.U.S.E.C. *Annual Report, 1929* (London, n.d.), p. 14.
[191] Author's tape-recorded interview with Dr Helena Wright, 27 Feb. 1977.
[192] Quoted in R. Hall (note 23), p. 184.
[193] For Helen Fraser, author's tape-recorded interview with Mrs Helen Moyes [*née* Fraser], 19 Aug. 1975; for Emmeline Pethick-Lawrence see Marie Stopes Papers: Emmeline Pethick-Lawrence to Marie Stopes, 4 Oct. 1922, British Library, Additional MSS 58555.
[194] *The Vote* (21 Nov. 1924), p. 372; House of Lords Debates, 28 Apr. 1926, col. 1034.
[195] R. Hall (note 23), p. 307.

moral standard which involves elevating male standards rather than lowering female. Campaigns for social purity, attacks on state-regulated prostitution, belief in the morally elevating impact of woman suffrage on politics – these are its hallmarks.[196] In Britain, as in America, birth control was too closely associated with prostitution – the ideal of motherhood was too generally assumed to go with marriage – for more radical sexual attitudes to prevail.[197]

Furthermore, the British birth control movement was by no means exclusively feminist in inspiration. The sequence of enthusiasms was often the other way round: birth controllers inspired by other motives were impressed in the course of their work with the need for justice to women and added feminism to their other causes. Furthermore the importance of the anti-feminist contribution to the N.B.C.A. has already been stressed. Eva Hubback was a feminist, but her interests were always broader: she was a Fabian, a Liberal Party backroom policy-maker and a eugenist, and she was soon to help found the Association for Education in Citizenship; she had also played a crucial role in launching the Townswomen's Guilds. Marie Stopes had been a suffragist and suffragette and her support for birth control reflected her belief that women should seek full enjoyment of sexual intercourse; but as with so many pioneers in this field, she was preoccupied with broader social and racial problems and aimed at giving working people the knowledge of contraception which the educated classes had hitherto withheld.[198] The two key figures in moulding the Family Planning Association – Margaret Pyke and Lady Denman – had never been prominent suffragists. Margaret Pyke's introduction to the work lay simply through her need for employment when she separated from her husband in the late 1920s and through her sympathy with birth control on general humanitarian grounds; she was never active in specifically feminist organizations.[199] Lady Denman was a Liberal Party suffragist before 1914 and subsequently a major figure in the Women's Institutes, but these bodies had originated outside the feminist movement and – like the

[196] See, e.g., Christabel Pankhurst in *Suffragette* (8 May 1914), p. 87, and the incident in Mrs Pankhurst's trial reported *ibid.* (11 Apr. 1913), p. 422.
[197] Cf. L. Gordon in M. S. Hartman and L. Banner (note 5), p. 65.
[198] K. Briant, *Marie Stopes. A Biography* (London, 1962), pp. 128–9, 134, 144.
[199] Author's tape-recorded interview with Dr David Pyke, 19 July 1977.

Townswomen's Guilds – were never narrowly feminist in mood.[200]

Birth controllers exclusively feminist in intention could never have courted the medical profession as effectively as did the N.B.C.A. in the 1930s. The 1911 census revealed that doctors had the smallest families of all occupational categories,[201] so that the ground had already been unobtrusively prepared for the profession's public shift in attitudes. But in the 1920s doctors' professionalism was still being affronted by the unscientific attitudes prevalent in this sphere; Marie Stopes's *Married Love* contained several unfounded physiological assertions and her sectarian insistence that her clinics should use only the small high-domed pessary in preference to the Dutch cap made her a laughing-stock among doctors,[202] who feared the prominence of lay people and medically unqualified nurses at her clinics.[203] It was the N.B.C.A.'s major achievement in the 1930s simultaneously to harness the energies of Marie Stopes, to amalgamate the existing birth control clinics, to win over key figures in the medical profession and to cultivate important links with government. Such achievements were not of course won at the expense of feminist objectives, but they could be attained only through strategies and motives which were broader in scope.

It was what Lord Buckmaster in the House of Lords debate of 1926 called 'an increased respect for the sanctity of life'[204] which lay behind the spread of birth control: increased respect for the lives of man, woman and child. In this debate, as elsewhere between the wars, the secularized pursuit of happiness and health through birth control had to be justified against opposition from religious leaders, particularly against Roman Catholics who felt that these objectives were being given too much prominence, or at least were unattainable by such means. The N.B.C.A.'s initial object was 'to advocate and to promote the provision of facilities for scientific contraception so that married people may space or limit their families and thus mitigate the evils of ill-health and poverty'.[205] This objective was eminently compatible with feminism, but trans-

---

[200] G. Huxley, *Lady Denman, G.B.E. 1884–1954* (London, 1961), pp. 35–8.
[201] A. McLaren, (note 64), p. 134.
[202] R. Hall (note 23), pp. 130–2; cf. A. McLaren (note 64), p. 118.
[203] R. Hall (note 23), pp. 189, 309; M. Stopes (note 180), p. 8.
[204] House of Lords Debates, 28 Apr. 1926, col. 998; cf. Earl de la Warr, *ibid.*, col. 1037.
[205] N.B.C.A. *1st Annual Report, 1930–1* (London, 1931).

cended it. According to the Association's first annual report, experience in the clinics had shown that 'the health of the working mother is one of the most neglected problems of our time';[206] but its appeal here was humanitarian, racial and hygienic – an appeal more broadly based than the feminist and eugenic support to which the Association owed so much. Its second annual report pointed out that actual economies in public health expenditure would result from the spread of birth control.[207] Although Dr Helena Wright, one of the earliest doctors involved in the Association, had been a suffragist, she recalls her involvement with it as humanist rather than feminist in inspiration, an activity requiring co-operation between the sexes and the education of doctors, most of whom were men.[208]

The N.B.C.A. consolidated its hold on the doctors in the 1930s by encouraging a scientific professionalism where appropriate – most notably in the certification of contraceptive products – and by confining the gradually shrinking role of the layman to fund raising, propaganda and relieving the administrative burden on the doctors at the clinics. Contraception was spreading anyway and many doctors shared the Association's desire that it should spread only under expert guidance with government aid. Much effort was devoted to training doctors in contraceptive practice and among its earliest 'functions' was 'to keep in touch with scientific research on contraception and to assist in the making known of suitable new methods'.[209] In July 1934 the N.B.C.A. set up a subcommittee of doctors to co-ordinate the experience of doctors in the clinics and of others who had been teaching birth control technique.

The Association's desire for government co-operation was present in one of the earliest of its 'functions': 'to encourage the recognition by public health authorities and by hospitals or other voluntary health organizations, of the need for making available medical advice on methods of birth control'.[210] In thus collaborating with and galvanizing government departments, this inter-war pressure group contrasted markedly with the late-Victorian radical crusades which attracted so many early feminists and antagonized

[206] *Ibid.*, p. 6.
[207] N.B.C.A. *2nd Annual Report, 1931–2*, p. 10.
[208] Tape-recorded interview with author, 27 Feb. 1977.
[209] N.B.C.A. *1st Annual Report 1930–1931*. See also Helena Wright, 'Fifty Years of Family Planning', *Family Planning* (Jan. 1972, Apr. 1972).
[210] N.B.C.A. *1st Annual Report, 1930–31*.

so many doctors. One of the N.B.C.A.'s first actions was to publish a pamphlet which clarified a Ministry of Health memorandum on local authority provision of birth control information.[211] By these methods, birth control gained influential support between the wars and doctors became fully involved in the clinics. After the second World War, this basis was to be extended through the courageous espousal of birth control by leading doctors who, with Iain Macleod's aid, helped produce the Family Planning Association's final breakthrough in the 1950s. A new and more fruitful relationship between feminism and the doctors had at last made its appearance.

The third and final dimension of the campaign to improve women's health should now be apparent and should perhaps after all have been discussed first: the internal dynamic of scientific inquiry, powered by a rationalist, empirical and humanitarian ethic. However controversial the impact of medical research on health during the nineteenth century, there is less dispute about its contribution to the dramatic decline in maternal mortality from the late 1930s, a time of relative quiescence in the British feminist movement. Antibiotics seem to have been largely responsible for the fall from 3.29 maternal deaths (in pregnancy and child-birth) per thousand live births in the United Kingdom in 1940–2 to 0.88 in 1950–2.[212] It would of course be wrong to assume that the sole channel by which feminists could have influenced British doctors was through the British feminist movement: scientific research operates internationally, and feminist pressures may – on investigation – prove to have been influential on the overseas doctors whose medical discoveries were later applied in Britain. But even then, feminist influences would merely supplement the internal dynamic of scientific research. During the nineteenth century in all countries, obstetrics and gynaecology emerged as specialisms simply as a reflection of the growth in scientific professionalism and the sophistication of technique. About 400 varieties of the speculum, for instance, were introduced between 1800 and 1900 and the curette and uterine sound were developed as valuable adjuncts.[213] These developments did not have any immediate or dramatic

[211] Margaret Pyke, 'Pimlico to Knightsbridge', *Family Planning* (Jan. 1956), p. 5.
[212] *1976 Annual Abstract of Statistics* (H.M.S.O. 1976), p. 48; see also J. Donnison (note 59), p. 196; J. M. M. Kerr *et al.* (note 2), p. 223.
[213] J. V. Ricci (note 4), p. 23; cf. P. Branca (note 2), pp. 63–5.

impact on women's health, but their longer-term significance was considerable.

The internal dynamic lying behind medical research on questions of crucial importance to women is well illustrated from the history of the N.B.C.A. Beginning with a concern purely to promote knowledge of contraception, the clinics moved on to providing treatment for minor gynaecological ailments, guidance on marital practice, training for doctors in contraceptive technique and certification of contraceptive products.[214] From there the N.B.C.A. moved forward to combating sterility and thence to diagnosing pregnancy; in 1944, the Family Planning Association (as it had now become) set up a seminological centre and in 1949 a pregnancy diagnosis centre.[215] By the 1950s it was beginning to concern itself with the psycho-sexual dimension and so on. There was an internal logic about the process, a continuing responsiveness to day-to-day problems, which expanded the activities of the Association beyond its founders' dreams. The impulse came – not from the small groups who pioneer changes in political attitudes – but from the much larger group of ordinary patients whose problems are thrown up in the course of routine treatment. As Dr Wright puts it, 'the patients taught us'.[216]

While the biographical, institutional and internal approach to the history of medicine can be overdone, it seems that there is a strong case here for giving detailed study to the personalities involved and to the detailed sequence of the scientific discoveries they made. But this will not be adequately achieved without analysing the full impact of patient upon doctor and the major impact of the surrounding society (including the women he encountered) on the problems the doctor set himself and on the solutions he devised. In the introduction to his textbook, Ricci points out that the impact of the industrial revolution on women 'was not without some influence on the development of minor therapy in gynaecology'.[217] It is strange that so important a connection should be made only in passing: this point – and others like it – surely deserve extensive elaboration.

[214] See Mrs Spring-Rice, in *Family Planning* (Jan. 1956), p. 9; N.B.C.A., *6th Annual Report, 1935–6*, p. 4.
[215] Margaret Pyke, *Family Planning* (Jan. 1956), pp. 6–7.
[216] Tape-recorded interview with author, 27 Feb. 1977.
[217] J. V. Ricci (note 4), p. 1.

# 2. Working-Class Mothers and Infant Mortality in England, 1895–1914

CAROL DYHOUSE

Writing in 1882, the economist Stanley Jevons had complained that in spite of the steady appearance of articles in learned periodicals on the subject of infant death rates in large towns in Britain, he feared that infant mortality in general remained 'far too wide and vague an idea to rivet the attention of the public.'[1] If there was justice in this observation in the 1880s, the situation changed rapidly over the next ten years, and between 1900 and World War I it is reasonable to assert that prevailing rates of infant mortality in England became defined by contemporaries as one of the major social problems of the time.

It is not difficult to understand why this came to be so. Infant mortality had remained high throughout the nineteenth century (averaging about 149 deaths per 1000 live births); but this rate had attracted little attention while general death rates also remained high. However, between the 1860s and 1900 the general death rate (or deaths per 1000 in the total population) had fallen by about 15 per cent. Further, as the Registrar General emphasized in 1907, while the death rate for children aged from one to five years had fallen by 33 per cent over the preceding forty years, that for infants under one year had remained as high for the decade of the 1890s as it had been for the 1860s.[2] Meanwhile, of course, the birth rate had entered upon a period of steady decline; from 35.5 per thousand in 1871–75 to 29.3 per thousand in 1896–1900.[3] In other words, by 1900 fewer babies were being born, a high proportion of whom continued to perish in the first twelve months of life. Anxieties over the implications of a declining population undoubtedly gave a strong impetus to the early infant welfare movement in Britain.[4]

This paper was first published in *Journal of Social History*, xii (1978), pp. 248–67.
[1] W. Stanley Jevons, 'Married Women in Factories,' *Contemporary Review* (Jan., 1882), p. 38.
[2] *Supplement to 65th Annual Report of the Registrar General of Births, Marriages and Deaths in England and Wales 1891–1900* (part 1, 1907, col. 2618), cv.
[3] G. F. McCleary, *The Maternity and Child Welfare Movement* (London, 1935), p. 5.
[4] G. F. McCleary, *Infantile Mortality and Infants' Milk Depots* (London, 1905), p. 13. See also (*inter alia*) Sir J. Gorst, *The Children of the Nation* (London, 1906), p. 16; R. A. Bray, *The Town Child* (London, 1911), pp. 88–9; H. Llewelyn Heath, *The Infant, The Parent and The State* (London, 1907), pp. 45–9.

The first ten years of this century generated a spate of investigations and publications on the subject of infant mortality by various medical, sanitary and statistical experts. A first National Conference on Infant Mortality was held in 1906, followed by a second two years later. Activity was motivated by the growing conviction that a large proportion of the current wastage of infant life was in fact preventable. This conviction stemmed not least from an observation of the wide regional and topographical variations in infant mortality rates within Britain: a much higher proportion of babies perished in the towns than in the countryside, and rates were particularly high in the overcrowded urban-industrial and mining districts of the Midlands and North. It was an interest in the environmental dimensions of infant mortality that led Dr (later Sir) George Newman to entitle his famous monograph, published in 1906, 'Infant Mortality: A *Social* Problem.'[5]

Enthusiasm for schemes for the protection of infant life was also stimulated directly by the success of pioneering experiments abroad, particularly in France and Belgium. In 1899, St Helens town council, acting on the advice of the local Medical Officer of Health, Dr Drew Harris, had appointed a committee to visit Fécamp, where Dr Léon Dufour had established a *Goutte de Lait* to provide mothers who had difficulty with breast-feeding with a supply of sterilized milk for their babies. St Helens established its own 'milk depot' in 1899, many other towns following suit in the early 1900s.[6] A number of other schemes that had originated on the continent were also tried out in Britain at this time. Voluntary associations, such as the Birmingham Infants' Health Society, experimented with the provision of free dinners for nursing mothers, inspired by Henri Coullet's restaurants in Paris.[7] Most of the early infant welfare institutions and 'Mothers and Babies' Welcomes' established in England at this time provided individual advice on infant feeding more or less along the lines of the *Consultations de Nourissons* pioneered by Budin in France. The first English 'School for Mothers', established in St Pancras in 1907, owed its origin in part to the efforts of Alys Russell, who, visiting Belgium with a group of the Women's Co-operative Guild in 1906, had found herself greatly

[5] G. Newman, *Infant Mortality: A Social Problem* (London, 1906).
[6] G. F. McCleary, *Infantile Mortality and Infants' Milk Depots* (note 4), p. 71.
[7] *Birmingham Infants' Health Society, Report for 1908* (Birmingham Reference Library), p. 8.

impressed by the network of services for the education of mothers and protection of infant life organized by Dr Miele in Ghent.[8]

Some organizations and local authorities in England evolved their own highly original schemes to combat high rates of infant mortality. In Huddersfield, for instance, Benjamin Broadbent celebrated his mayoralty by distributing promissory notes to newly-delivered women, offering them a one pound reward if their babies should live to see their first birthday.[9] The reverse side of these promissory notes was printed with instructions and advice on infant hygiene and feeding. Huddersfield acquired a national reputation for infant welfare work early in this century, as a result of the energetic efforts of Dr S. G. Moore, local Medical Officer of Health, and of Alderman Broadbent. In 1906, the Corporation was the first in the country to require that notification of all births in the town be given within 48 hours to the local Medical Officer. The health department of the Corporation worked closely with a local voluntary organization (The Huddersfield and District Public Health Union) to establish a comprehensive system of home visiting for mothers in the area between 1905 and 1908.[10]

Altogether the *range* of institutions that developed for the promotion of infant welfare in England at this time was quite impressive. There were baby shows (popular in Yorkshire and the North of England) offering prizes for breast-fed babies.[11] There were Nursing Mothers' restaurants, milk depots, Schools for Mothers, Mothers' and Babies' Welcomes and At Homes. The sudden proliferation of activity in towns all over the country meant that nomenclature remained fluid – it was essentially a period of experimentation and hence it is difficult to draw hard and fast distinctions between the work of the various kinds of institutions that appeared at this stage. Most infant welfare centres offered infant consultations, which involved keeping a check on the weight of babies brought for attention and offering advice on feeding. The

[8] Alys Russell, 'The Ghent School for Mothers', *The Nineteenth Century* (Dec. 1906); E. M. Bunting, D. E. L. Bunting, A. E. Barnes and B. Gardiner, *A School for Mothers* (London, 1908).
[9] Sir G. Newman, *The Building of a Nation's Health* (London, 1939), pp. 318–19.
[10] B. Broadbent, *Education for Motherhood and Instruction for Mothers* (Paper read before Second National Conference on Infant Mortality, 23–25 March, 1908), see *Report of Proceedings* (Westminster, 1908), pp. 54–69.
[11] Dr H. Kerr, 'Modern Educative Methods for the Prevention of Infantile Mortality', *Public Health* (Jan., 1910), p. 131.

majority of centres also developed schemes for visiting mothers in their own homes. Some institutions – particularly the Schools for Mothers – offered organized classes in hygiene and infant care. The distribution of dried milk became a very important part of the business of many centres after 1907, commonly superseding the work of the milk depots, which had been established a few years earlier. A survey of infant welfare centres published in 1913 catalogues an endless variety of ancillary services.[12] Many foundations had started up provident clothing clubs and maternity savings schemes. Others had developed a thriving business in selling cradles made out of banana boxes, or lending out perambulators, enamelled saucepans and 'patent playgrounds'. A few centres tried to attract fathers to attend meetings – a departure looked upon somewhat askance by the author of the 1913 survey, I. G. Gibbon, who commented: 'The better type of father will probably keep away. He regards the whole thing as the wife's business'.[13]

The rapid mushrooming of infant welfare centres was the result of both voluntary and municipal effort. The first School for Mothers, as has already been mentioned, was founded in St Pancras in 1907. A report compiled by the National League for Physical Education and Improvement three years later noted the existence of eighty similar institutions; most of these were being administered by voluntary societies, but often with the close co-operation of local medical officers of health and health visitors.[14] Before 1914, infant welfare work was severly hampered, in many areas, by lack of funds. The Board of Education was able to make grants to Schools for Mothers and similar institutions, but only in respect of organized class teaching. This was the kind of activity that many institutions had quickly discovered to be one of the least satisfactory aspects of their work – most of the women who attended the centres preferred the opportunities for personal attention and relative informality of individual consultations. After 1914, the government began to make funds available for infant welfare work through the Local Government Board on a much wider basis.[15] By 1918, when the Maternity and Child Welfare Act came

[12] I. G. Gibbon, *Infant Welfare Centres: The Work of Infant Consultations, Schools for Mothers, and Similar Institutions* (London, 1913); see also his earlier *Report on Existing Schools for Mothers and Similar Institutions* (London, 1910).
[13] *Gibbon Infant Welfare Centres* (note 12), p. 27.
[14] Gibbon, *Report on Schools for Mothers* (note 12), Appendix, pp. 26–32.
[15] McCleary, *Maternity and Child Welfare Movement* (note 3), p. 12.

into operation, there were about 1278 maternity and child welfare centres in existence, 578 of which depended on voluntary
effort.[16]

Infant mortality declined spectacularly in Britain during the
early decades of the present century, the rate falling from about 128
per 1000 births between 1901 and 1910 to 53 per 1000 on the eve of
World War II. Historians have yet to discover precisely why this
happened. The decline certainly coincided with the rise of the infant
welfare movement, but this need not have been a simple relation of
cause and effect, and, in any case, we cannot rest content with
explanations on this level of generality.

The whole question of infant mortality in late nineteenth-century
and early twentieth-century England awaits detailed research by
historians of medicine and demography skilled in techniques of
quantification, and the subject is undoubtedly highly complex.
There are of course the usual problems which beset those who
would embark upon investigations of this kind – alterations in
official requirements for the registration of demographic data; a
growing sophistication in the diagnosis of various kinds of disease
and categorization of causes of death, and so forth, all rendering
generalization and secular comparison more difficult. But if there
are problems associated with the historical analysis of the *physiological* causes of infant deaths, the investigator finds himself or
herself on even less secure ground when moving on to try to make
sense of the various social and environmental factors at work. The
growing recognition of the significance of these factors in the early
years of this century did not by any means imply a consensus over
their precise nature, or over the relative importance of the various
factors involved.

There were two areas in which there was a broad measure of
agreement amongst most authorities. The correlation of high infant
mortality rates with high-density urban living was incontrovertible.
More particularly, most contemporary investigations discovered an
extremely close relationship between certain inadequate forms of
sewage disposal – the conservancy or privy-midden system – and
high rates of infant deaths.[17] Secondly, most authorities found
themselves in harmony when pointing out the increased risks of

[16] *Ibid.*, pp. 17–18.
[17] See especially Dr A. Newsholme, 'Second Report on Infant and Child Mortality' *42nd
Annual Report of Local Government Board 1912–13*, Supplement in Continuation of
Report of the Medical Officer of the Board (1913), xxxii, p. 88 and *passim.*

artificial feeding over breast-feeding, or at least, the dangers associated with certain forms of artificial feeding early in the century
before safe, pasteurized supplies of liquid milk or dried milk
became widely available (I shall return to this subject shortly). But
beyond these two areas of general agreement amongst medical
authorities and others concerned with infant welfare, there was vast
scope for controversy.

In this paper I want to look at two of the most contentious
theories put forward by contemporaries involved in discussing the
causes of infant mortality during the period, both of which helped
to mould the policy and outlook of early infant welfare work. The
first of these highlighted the employment of married women as an
important cause of infant deaths. The second theory, which gained
widespread currency after 1900, laid the blame for high infant
mortality rates on working-class mothers, generally depicted as
ignorant and incompetent in matters of infant care. Assessment of
the nature and validity of these arguments opens the way for
consideration of the causes of changes in the physical facts of
infancy and the extent to which they related to mothering.

The conviction that the employment of mothers outside the
home entailed a high rate of infant mortality had been widespread
during the nineteenth century. Married women who worked regularly in factories, it was argued, would be unable to breast-feed
their babies and were rarely able to make proper provision for their
care and supervision during the daytime.[18] Obviously, generalizations of this kind are likely to reveal as much about the values of
those making them as about the common practices of the time.
Middle-class Victorians generally believed that women should stay
at home and this necessarily led them to define women's employment outside the home as a social problem: the assumption that a
working mother entailed a neglected child was sacrosanct. The
most thorough investigation of this nineteenth-century assumption
that married women's work entailed the sacrifice of infant lives that
has yet appeared in print is still that of Margaret Hewitt, whose
*Wives and Mothers in Victorian Industry*, originally published in
1958, has now become something of a classic. In reviewing the mass

[18] M. Hewitt. *Wives and Mothers in Victorian Industry* (London, 1958), see especially
chapters 8–10.

of evidence adduced by nineteenth-century observers in support of their hypothesis, Hewitt remained consistently aware of the bias of their social values: this alerted her to the more extravagant claims and highly-coloured indictments of 'the factory mother' which were frequently made. Even so, she appears to have been convinced by the arguments and figures produced at the turn of the century by two authorities, Drs George Reid and George Newman, both of whom adhered strongly to the viewpoint that there was indeed a clear causal connection between infant mortality and the occupation of mothers outside the home. Hewitt concludes by accepting this viewpoint.[19]

George Reid, Medical Officer of Health for Staffordshire, delivered a paper embodying the results of his inquiry into infant mortality in that county at the Public Medicine section of the annual meeting of the British Medical Association in 1892.[20] In this paper he described how his curiosity had been aroused by dissimilarities existing between infant mortality rates to the north and to the south of Staffordshire over the 1881–89 period. These discrepancies, he believed, could only be explained by recourse to the fact of the differing extent of women's employment in the two areas. Openings for women's work were plentiful in the pottery towns to the north of the county, the area distinguished by the higher infant mortality rates; scarce in the coal-mining and iron-working districts to the south. In order to test his hypothesis. Reid had collected data for three classes of towns in Staffordshire 'with distinctly artisan populations.' The first class of towns he described as having 'many women engaged in work'. This group showed an average infant mortality rate of 195 over the 1881–90 period. The second group of towns, described as having 'fewer women engaged in work', showed an average rate of 166 over the same period. The third group, where, according to Reid, 'practically no women worked' averaged an infant mortality rate of only 152. The classification of towns itself seems to have been based upon the somewhat impressionistic testimony of local medical officers, supplemented here and there by the experience of local employers. Reid main-

[19] *Ibid.*, pp. 99–122.
[20] 'Report of Proceedings of Public Medicine Section of Annual Meeting of British Medical Association', in *The British Medical Journal* (July, 1892), pp. 275–8; see also Dr G. Reid's contribution to Chapter V, 'Infant Mortality and Factory Labour', in T. Oliver (ed.), *Dangerous Trades* (London, 1902).

tained that in all respects other than the extent of female employment, conditions in the three groups of towns were strictly comparable.

In the course of discussion following the delivery of Reid's paper, those present at the Public Medicine section of the meeting carried a resolution to call the attention of the Parliamentary Bills Committee of the B.M.A. to his work 'with a view to taking action for obtaining parliamentary inquiry into the influence of the employment of women in factories on the mortality of infants'. Reid's paper certainly impressed many of his colleagues and contemporaries, and his findings were to be quoted time and again in the literature that emerged on the subject of infant mortality over the next twenty years. In 1894, the Royal Statistical Society awarded its Howard Medal prize to Dr H. Jones in recognition of a long analytical essay entitled *The Perils and Protection of Infant Life*.[21] Dr Jones cited Reid's work as crucial, arguing that figures he himself had collected further afforded 'strong confirmatory evidence' of the association between the employment of women and a high rate of infant deaths. He concluded:

The children of women engaged in industrial occupations suffer from the effects of maternal neglect. They are handicapped from the moment of birth in their struggle for existence, and have to contend not only against the inevitable perils of infancy but also against perils due to their neglect by their mothers and to the ignorance of those to whose care they are entrusted.[22]

Categorical assertions of this kind did not escape unchallenged. During the Royal Statistical Society's formal dicussion of Dr Jones' paper, one of the participants, Mr Noel Humphreys, said that he believed that the question had been prejudged without sufficient evidence.[23] He pointed out that in Durham and South Wales, areas where very few women took jobs outside the home, infant mortality rates were markedly higher even than in the textile-manufacturing districts, such as the West Riding of Yorkshire, where large numbers of women worked. His own inquiries led him to suspect that overcrowding and other generally insanitary conditions were the crucial variables. Mrs Fawcett, also present at the discussion,

[21] Dr H. Jones. 'The Perils and Protection of Infant Life,' *Journal of the Royal Statistical Society*, lvii (Mar. 1894), pp. 1–98.
[22] *Ibid.*, p. 56.
[23] *Ibid.*, pp. 99–105.

agreed. She pointed out that although in some instances children might suffer from the absence of their mothers from the home, in others they might positively benefit from the extra nourishment and better conditions their mother's wages could purchase.

Four years later, a more detailed attack upon Dr Jones' argument was mounted in a paper read before the Royal Statistical Society by Clara E. Collet.[24] Clara Collet had recently (1893–94) served as assistant commissioner to the Royal Commission on Labour, which had investigated conditions of women's work, with, amongst its terms of reference, a specific injunction to inquire into: 'the effects of women's industrial employment on their health, mortality and the home'. The figures that Dr Jones had used to demonstrate what he alleged to be an important association between women's employment and infantile mortality, Collet argued, were both imprecise and impressionistic. A closer examination of data from the 1891 census on the extent of female employment and infant mortality returns for twenty-seven large towns, from 1889 to 1893, showed some slight correspondence between infant mortality and the percentage of the female population above the age of ten (whether married or single) who were returned as occupied. But this observation was too slender to support the weight of any alleged relationship of cause and effect. There appeared to be a much stronger connection, on the other hand, between infant mortality and the proportion of the female population returned as indoor domestic servants in 1891. It was clear that considerations of social class – the presence of sizeable middle-class residential areas in certain cities – were obscuring the issue. In order to test Jones' hypothesis more accurately, Collet proceeded to calculate the proportion of married or widowed working women in the population of certain homogeneous working-class districts, and to compare these percentages against the appropriate infant mortality data. No regular pattern emerged.

Collet took care to dissociate herself, in her paper, from any feminist advocacy of the compatibility between employment and motherhood. She herself believed the employment of married women with young children to be inadvisable. At the same time, she feared that: 'there is nothing so likely to weaken the power and to

---

[24] Clara E. Collet, 'The Collection and Utilization of Official Statistics Bearing on the Extent and Effects of the Industrial Employment of Women,' *Journal of the Royal Statistical Society* (June 1898), pp. 219–61.

relax the efforts of the medical officers of health as the easy-going policy of a sanitary committee which believes itself entitled to attribute high death-rates to the moral habits of the community, quite apart from such factors as overcrowding and bad sanitary conditions'.[25]

The Inter-Departmental Committee on Physical Deterioration, reporting in 1904, paid considerable attention to the problem of infant mortality, arguing that 'the facts seem to point to a strong presumption' that the loss of infant lives was greater where women went out to work.[26] The Committee admitted the need for more precise investigation here, whilst recording their unshakeable conviction that the employment of mothers was in any case an evil to be discouraged as strongly as possible.[27]

Partly in response to both this report, and to resolutions passed at the First National Conference on Infant Mortality in 1906, which included a call upon the Government to extend the period of legal prohibition on the industrial employment of women after childbirth from one to three months, the Home Office determined to investigate the question further.[28] In May 1907, a circular went out at the direction of the Home Secretary, Herbert Gladstone, addressed to the Medical Officers of Health 'of a number of representative industrial centres', soliciting their opinion on whether further legal restrictions were desirable.[29] In November 1907, these Medical Officers were invited to a conference at the Home Office during which it was agreed to mount over the following year, a more systematic enquiry into the question of whether maternal employment had any significant effect on infant mortality. Medical Officers were asked to carry out their own surveys on this subject, and also to give particular thought to the problem of whether new restrictions on married women's work might lead to a further fall in the birth rate or through increasing poverty in homes previously dependent on maternal income, actually *diminish* the chances of infant survival.[30]

Apparently the evidence collected in response to this scheme of

[25] *Ibid.*, p. 239.
[26] *Report of Inter-Departmental Committee on Physical Deterioration* (1904), xxxii, para. 241.
[27] *Ibid.*, para. 260.
[28] Home Office Correspondence (P.R.O./HO 45 10 335/138532).
[29] P.R.O./HO 158/13 circular dated 10 May 1907, no. 126388/9.
[30] *Ibid.*, 17 Dec. 1907, no. 152746.

inquiry was never collated properly: certainly not in any published form.[31] However, some reports of local investigations survive, one of which had been carried out under the aegis of Dr John Robertson, Medical Officer of Health in Birmingham.[32] This survey had been carried out in St Stephen's and St George's wards, two of the poorest and most overcrowded areas in the city, both of which were characterized by a high proportion of old, back-to-back houses, and in both of which about half the married women inhabitants were estimated to go out to work. All babies born during 1908 in these wards were visited regularly and their progress was carefully monitored. The results showed clearly that the mortality among infants whose mothers were in employment was actually *lower* (190 per 1000 births) than that amongst those whose mothers were not industrially employed (207 per 1000 births).

Commenting upon these findings, Dr Robertson described the importance of the mother's earnings in many working-class households. Those working women who were prepared to take on the extra responsibility of a job outside the home, he suggested, in addition to their domestic chores, were often the most energetic and capable section of the community. Far from *neglecting* the needs of their families, they sought work in order to buy extra nourishment for their children.

Not surprisingly, Robertson's report, published in 1910, achieved a good deal of publicity. In April 1910, the journal *Public Health* featured an editorial commenting:

The importance of the industrial employment of married women as a factor in the causation of infant mortality is a subject upon which the current opinion has been gradually changing in recent years. Formerly it was almost universally held to be an etiological factor of preponderating importance, but the application of more precise methods of investigation has cast grave doubts on this view, and has called for a restatement of the whole question.[33]

[31] See reference in *Report of Women's Employment Committee* of Ministry of Reconstruction (1919), xiv, p. 52.
[32] City of Birmingham Health Department, *Report on Industrial Employment of Married Women and Infantile Mortality* (Birmingham, 1910), Birmingham Reference Library 22451.
[33] 'The Industrial Employment of Married Women and Infantile Mortality', *Public Health*, xxiii (Apr. 1910), p. 229.

One way in which the historian can attempt to test the validity of the hypothesis that the larger the proportion of married working women in the population, the higher the associated infant mortality rate, is by using conventional linear regression analysis. Some calculations of this kind are described in an appendix to this paper: the results do not suggest a positive relationship between the two variables.

Almost all those who had pointed to women's work as a major cause of infant deaths over the last half-century or more had argued their case on the grounds that the rate of survival among babies who were spoon or bottle-fed was far lower than among those fed at the breast. Between the 1890s and the outbreak of World War I, however, the dangers associated with artificial feeding were substantially reduced in this country. Since this undoubtedly reduced the risks involved in mothers leaving their infants for substantial periods of the day, the subject merits some attention at this point.

The turn of the century saw the publication of a whole spate of manuals on infant feeding by French, American, and English authorities such as Budin, Rotch, Chapin, Vincent, and Pritchard.[34] Almost unanimously, these writers deprecated the use of the patent foods that had proliferated on the market since the 1860s. According to one rather lurid account:

> Under their persuasive influence the infant sometimes grows visibly and ponderably fatter, and to the parents' inexpressible delight may present the appearance of an infant Hercules. Who cannot recognize at sight a patent food baby veiling under his outward serenity the germs of a latent and inevitable trouble? Large and square-headed, fatuously complacent, pot-bellied, spade-handed and dumpy-footed, for all the world presenting the appearance of animated jelly.[35]

The majority of the patent foodstuffs sold for infants in late Victorian and Edwardian England were unsuitable or even dang-

[34] Inter alia: P. Budin, Le Nourrison (Paris, translated into English 1907) and Manuel Practique d'Allaitement (Paris, 1907); T. M. Rotch, Pediatrics: the Hygiene and Medical Treatment of Children (Philadelphia, 1896); H. D. Chapin, The Theory and Practice of Infant Feeding (London, 1903); R. Vincent, The Nutrition of the Infant (London, 1904); E. Pritchard, The Physiological Feeding of Infants (London, 1904).

[35] Pritchard, op. cit., p. 13.

erous for younger babies, because they generally contained a
high proportion of farinaceous material and were deficient in fat
and protein.[36]

Manuals on infant feeding from this period usually devoted some
space to discussing recent advances in modifying cow's milk to
approximate to the composition of human milk, a process generally
involving dilution, with the addition of cream, sugar and lime water
(the latter to reduce acidity). Rotch's 'percentage method' marked
the culmination of this approach. By about 1900, however, most
authorities were pointing out that minute changes in the composition of the mixture fed to babies were of little importance
beside cleanliness, and that the essence of the matter involved the
guarantee of a pure milk supply.[37]

M. W. Beaver has recently argued in *Population Studies* that the
sharp, impressive decline in infant mortality in England this century had its origin in the growing availability of pathogen-free milk,
whether in liquid, condensed, or dried form, rather than in any
general rise in living standards or improvements in midwifery or
health visiting services.[38] One must be cautious here, however: the
majority of working-class mothers (Dr Arthur Newsholme,
Medical Officer to the Local Government Board, estimated about
80 per cent)[39] had probably always breast fed their babies where
they could easily do so, not least because this method of feeding
was relatively cost-free. The evolution of safe forms of artificial
feeding was undoubtedly of crucial importance in cases where
it was difficult or impossible for mothers to breast feed, but it
is difficult to rest content with any monocausal explanation
that would attribute demographic change on such a scale to this
factor.

Condensed milk became widely available in the United Kingdom
in the 1890s: between 1895 and 1901 importations of tinned
condensed milk doubled from about 545,394 to 919,319 cwt; it was

[36] F. J. H. Coutts, *On the Use of Proprietary Foods for Infant Feeding*. Reports to
Local Government Board on Public Health and Medical Subjects. NS, no.
80, H.M.S.O. 1914.
[37] Chapin (note 34), pp. 3–5.
[38] M. W. Beaver, 'Population, Infant Mortality and Milk', *Population Studies*, xxvii
(1973).
[39] *30th Annual Report of Local Government Board*, 1909–10, Supplement to Report
of Board's Medical Officer, Containing A Report on Infant and Child Mortality
(1910), xxxix, pp. 70–4.

also manufactured in England.[40] Unsweetened, full-cream condensed milk appears to have been a reasonable substitute for fresh
cow's milk when used for feeding infants, although there was a
problem in that the substance was liable to contamination quickly, once the tin had been opened; many authorities holding that
the risks of epidemic diarrhoea were increased where its use was
widespread, especially in the hot summer months.[41] However,
separated, sweetened, and machine-skimmed varieties of condensed
milk were not considered suitable for infant feeding; they contained
too much carbohydrate and insufficient fat. It has been thought
that the Sale of Food and Drugs Act, 1899 (which prohibited the
sale or importation of 'condensed, separated, or skimmed milk,
except in tins or other receptacles which bear a label wherein the
words 'machine-skimmed milk' or 'skimmed milk' are printed in
large and legible type') would help to diminish the practice of
feeding babies on these forms of condensed milk. A report on the
subject, written for the Local Government Board in 1911, pointed
out that this had not been the case.[42] In fact Dr F. J. H. Coutts, the
author of this report, believed that the use of these inferior forms of
condensed milk for infant feeding in working-class homes was
increasing. This was not least a reflection of poverty – skimmed
milks were much cheaper than full cream varieties. But misleading
labelling was also to blame. Coutts pointed out that even where the
words 'machine-skimmed' were actually printed in bold type on
tins, some women took this to indicate an especially pure quality of
product, i.e., 'untouched by human hand', or even 'the thick rich
milk from the top'.[43]

The problem of ensuring a supply of uncontaminated liquid milk
suitable for infant feeding preoccupied those active in the earliest
years of the infant welfare movement. Articles regularly appeared in
the public health and medical journals disclosing the putrid character of samples taken in towns all over the country. Reference has
already been made to the municipal milk depots, modelled on the
French *gouttes de lait*, which were founded in the early 1900s in
Britain; these had generally distributed sterilized, modified milk in
specially designed bottles sufficient for one feed. From about 1907,

[40] F. J. H. Coutts, *Report to Local Government Board on an Inquiry as to Condensed Milks; with Special Reference to their Use as Infants' Foods* (London, H.M.S.O., 1911), pp. 3–7.
[41] *Ibid.*, p. 35.
[42] *Ibid.*, pp. 31 ff.
[43] *Ibid.*, p. 34.

however, many of these institutions had given up their original practice of supplying pasteurized or sterilized liquid milk in favour of the dried milk powders that were becoming widely available on the market.[44]

Although 'desiccated milk' had evidently been used in the making of some proprietary infant foods in the late nineteenth century, it did not come into any considerable use on its own until after the development of the Just Hatmaker process of manufacture, patented between 1903 and 1906.[45] Its use by infant welfare institutions thereafter spread rapidly. George Newman, as Medical Officer of Health for Finsbury, recommended it highly in his Annual Report of 1907. Centres in Sheffield and Leicester began distribution on a large scale – by 1911 the Sheffield Dried Milk Depot claimed to have fed nearly 3000 babies on cost-price Glaxo. In Manchester, it was reported that dried milk had significantly diminished the threat of the outbreaks of summer diarrhoea that had formerly proved so destructive of infant life.[46] Detailed reports to the Local Government Board in 1918 were wholly enthusiastic about the properties of dried milk as an infant foodstuff.[47] Altogether, this apparently meant something of a revolution in the practice of safe artificial feeding.

Most of the early infant welfare ventures had begun operations secure in the assumption that one of the most effective methods of combating infant mortality lay in encouraging mothers to breastfeed. The assumption was not to pass unchallenged. In Birmingham, for instance, from 1907 onwards the newly formed Infants' Health Society began a campaign in St Bartholomew's ward to promote breast-feeding. By 1911, the Society's annual reports show it reluctantly forced to recognize that the artificially-fed babies of working mothers whose wage bought a slightly better standard of living for their families showed a better rate of survival than did the breast-fed babies of mothers in similar social circumstances who stayed at home.[48]

[44] McCleary, *Maternity and Child Welfare Movement* (note 4), pp. 42–3.
[45] F. J. H. Coutts, *Report upon an Inquiry as to Dried Milks, with Special Reference to their Use in Infant Feeding.* (Reports to Local Government Board on Public Health and Medical Subjects, N s no. 116, H.M.S.O., 1918, pp. 58 ff.
[46] *Ibid.*, pp. 61–2, 66–7.
[47] *Ibid., passim,* see also G. Winfield, *Some Investigations Bearing on the Nutritive Value of Dried Milk,* Report on an Inquiry Undertaken on Behalf of the Medical Research Committee (H.M.S.O., 1918).
[48] Birmingham Infants' Health Society, *Annual Reports for 1907–8, 9* and *Annual Reports for 1911,* pp. 14–18 (Birmingham Reference Library).

The second, and equally controversial, explanation of infant mortality that came to dominate discussion before World War I focused on the quality of maternal care. Patricia Branca has documented some of the changing attitudes to reproduction and child care that developed among middle-class families in late nineteenth-century Britain.[49] Middle-class parents were having fewer children, a tendency that was paralleled by a declining sense of fatalism, a growing reluctance to accept a high probability of death in early infancy as part of the natural order of things. Manuals and magazine articles offering advice on child-rearing to middle-class mothers proliferated during the last quarter of the century. The evolution of prescriptive attitudes towards child care among doctors and other professional groups went hand in hand with a growing conviction among many of these authorities, early in the present century, that high infant mortality rates were rooted in 'faulty maternal hygiene,' or the widespread ignorance of working-class mothers in matters of child care, whether they were employed or not.

The report of the Physical Deterioration Committee in 1904, its pages littered with references to a new generation of women ignorant of domestic management and disinclined towards their duties in the home, helped prepare the ground for the ready reception of the interpretation.[50] Any random perusal of a journal such as *Public Health* in the 1900s will demonstrate the growing popularity of the view that women were themselves largely to blame for the loss of their babies. Dr Alex Robb, Medical Officer of Health in Paisley, suggested in 1908 that about one-third of the infant death rate was preventable and could only be attributed to the ignorance of mothers.[51] Dr Harold Kerr, Assistant Medical Officer in Newcastle-upon-Tyne, argued:

> The terribly heavy death-rate among young children in our towns is of course due to a certain extent to the relative unhealthiness of their surroundings, but that is by no means the chief cause. The factor that is of primary importance is maternal mismanagement. I use this word advisedly, because all mothers, with very few exceptions, love their babies and desire to do the

[49] P. Branca, *Silent Sisterhood, Middle Class Women in the Victorian Home* (London, 1975).
[50] *Report of Physical Deterioration Committee* (note 26), pp. 55–6 and *passim*.
[51] Dr A. Robb. 'Infantile Mortality in Paisley', *Public Health* (June, 1908), p. 162.

best for them: but every visitor in the homes of the working class knows only too well the hopeless ignorance of the majority of the mothers in regard to everything connected with the rearing of healthy offspring.[52]

The chief proponent of the 'maternal ignorance' theory was Sir George Newman. Throughout his professional life, Newman maintained the opinion that sanitation, substandard housing, and poverty were of secondary importance to anyone wishing to get at the root cause of infant mortality, that 'the most injurious influences affecting the physical condition of young children arise from the habits, customs and practices of the people themselves rather than from external surroundings or conditions'.[53] His appointment as Chief Medical Officer to the Board of Education gave Newman ample opportunity to publicize this viewpoint; and his Annual Reports, from 1910, continually reiterated his conviction that the infant death rate in Britain was 'more largely due to maternal ignorance, negligence and mismanagement than to any other single cause'.[54]

Newman contended that infant mortality should be fought through Schools for Mothers, the establishment of day nurseries and crèches (but only where these could be shown not to encourage women to find work outside their homes), and through the modification of the curriculum in public elementary schools to include the teaching of mothercraft and infant hygiene to girls.[55] This last suggestion was one frequently voiced through the 1895–1914 period; it being popularly believed that girls' education had 'gone too far' under the influence of feminists bent on securing wider opportunities and emulating the successes of boys' schools.[56] Many authorities on infant care, like Truby King (visiting England from New Zealand in 1913–14)

[52] Dr H. Kerr, 'Modern Educative Methods for the Prevention of Infantile Mortality', *Public Health* (Jan, 1910), p. 129.
[53] Board of Education Circular 940, *On Education and Infant Welfare*, containing Reprint from Report of Chief Medical Officer of the Board, 1914 (H.M.S.O., 1916), p. 2, para. 50.
[54] *Annual Report of Chief Medical Officer of the Board of Education, 1913* (1914–16), Reports of Commissioners, xviii, p. 19, para. 26.
[55] Board of Education Circular 940, *On Education and Infant Welfare* (1916), pp. 6–34
[56] C. Dyhouse, 'Good Wives and Little Mothers: Social Anxieties and the Schoolgirl's Curriculum, 1890–1920'. *Oxford Review of Education*, ii, no. 1 (1977).

maintained that too much interest in intellectual achievement spoilt women for motherhood.[57]

In 1910, Dr Christopher Addison introduced a bill into the House of Commons that would have required all public elementary schools to give instruction in infant care to girls over twelve years of age.[58] The bill was unsuccessful: Addison blamed the Board of Education for its downfall.[59] But, as I have shown elsewhere, the Board became very interested in the whole question of the extent to which the curriculum in girls' schools included domestic training and a preparation for motherhood during this period.[60] Morant had already asked the Medical Department to draw up a memorandum on the teaching of infant care in elementary schools, and Janet Campbell's fairly detailed suggestions on the subject were circulated to local authorities in 1910.[61]

Newman's insistence upon maternal ignorance as the major cause of infant death in early twentieth-century Britain was coming increasingly under attack by the time of World War I. One of the most obvious limitations of the thesis was its failure to explain the marked and persistent variations in the *distribution* of infant mortality rates. Dr William Brend, for instance, writing for the Medical Research Committee in 1916, objected:

> We cannot assume that the Connaught peasantry – many of whom can neither read nor write – are so much better instructed in the care of infants that in spite of poverty and hard conditions infant mortality among them is half that among the mothers of Kensington, and one third that of Bradford, where so much has been done to instruct mothers by means of health visitors and schools for mothers.... If instead of areas social classes be examined, it will be found that the wives of woodsmen and foresters must be credited with as great a knowledge of the conditions governing infant welfare as that possessed by the

---

[57] See Truby King's comments in discussion following Dr Caroline Hedger's paper on 'The Relation of the Education of the Girl to Infant Mortality'. *Report of the Proceedings of the First English-Speaking Conference on Infant Mortality, London August 1913* (London, 1913), pp. 287–94.

[58] Parliamentary Bills, 1910, no. 262, p. 627: *Elementary Schools Instruction in Hygiene* (19 July 1910).

[59] C. Addison, *Politics from Within, 1911–18.* (London, 1924), i, pp. 18–19.

[60] C. Dyhouse, 'Good Wives and Little Mothers' (note 56).

[61] Board of Education Circular 758, *Memorandum on the Teaching of Infant Care and Management in Public Elementary Schools* (H.M.S.O., 1910).

professional groups, and it must be believed that the wives of agricultural labourers and shepherds excel in this respect all other classes of manual workers.[62]

Many doctors argued that comparisons between infant mortality figures in towns distinguished by energetic schemes of welfare education and health visiting, like Bradford or Huddersfield, and those from other towns without such provision revealed remarkably similar trends and fluctuations.[63] Newman's work was criticized by contemporaries in the first place for underestimating the significance of environmental factors – poverty, inadequate housing and sanitation, atmospheric pollution conducive to respiratory disease (an important cause of infant deaths) – and secondly, for paying too little attention to epidemiological factors, such as the periodicity of epidemics of zymotic diseases.[64] With something of the benefit of hindsight, we could add a further criticism: Newman (and here in common with most of his contemporaries) paid surprisingly little attention to the category of 'developmental and wasting diseases' that consistently accounted for a large proportion of infant deaths.[65] The full realization of the important connection between this category of deaths (particularly the problem of death through premature birth) and the nutrition and physical condition of the mother herself came after World War I. The Women's Co-operative Guild helped draw attention to the medical profession's neglect of the problems of maternal health, pregnancy and child-

[62] Dr W. A. Brend, 'The Relative Importance of Pre-natal and Post-natal Conditions as Causes of Infant Mortality', National Health Insurance Medical Research Committee, *The Mortalities of Birth, Infancy and Childhood* (London, H.M.S.O., 1918), p. 11.

[63] Dr D. S. Davies, 'Infant Mortality Statistics', *Public Health* (March, 1908), p. 40; Dr L. Findlay, 'The Causes of Infantile Mortality', National Health Insurance Medical Research Committee, *The Mortalities of Birth, Infancy and Childhood* (London. H.M.S.O., 1918), p. 37.

[64] Brend (note 62), pp. 16–17; Findlay (note 63), p. 39.

[65] A point developed independently by Professor Anthony Wohl in an unpublished paper entitled 'Working Wives or Healthy Homes?' read before the Annual Conference of the Society for the Social History of Medicine at New Hall, Cambridge, July 1977. A Registrar General's Report published in 1907 groups the causes of infantile deaths into five major categories. Between 1891 and 1900 the tabulations show that 'Wasting Diseases' carried off the largest number of babies under one year (44.44 per 1000 births). This category referred rather loosely to 'premature birth, congenital defects and injury at birth, want of breast milk and starvation, atrophy, debility and marasmus', see *Supplement to 65th Annual Report of the Registrar General* (London, 1907), p. 111, table III.

birth with their publication of a remarkable book entitled Maternity: Letters from Working Women, in 1915.[66]

Explanations of high infant mortality rates in terms of married women's work or the ignorance of mothers proved remarkably tenacious in early twentieth-century Britain. Ultimately, faith in these explanations was knitted into the fabric of contemporary assumptions about social class and the nature of family life. In spite of the efforts of middle-class feminists to widen employment opportunities for women towards the close of the nineteenth century, popular opposition to married women's work grew even more widespread in England.

One reason for this was that the middle-class ideal of family organization – wife securely ensconced in the home by a husband working for a family wage – became diffused more widely down the social ladder as living standards rose amongst some sections of the skilled working class.[67] At the same time, working-class opposition to women's employment was fuelled by the anxieties of male trade unionists who resented female workers as a source of cheap competition in the labour market, effectively undercutting union wage-rates. The near-hysterical outburst against married women's work that characterized John Burns' inaugural addresses (as president of the Local Government Board) before the first two National Conferences on Infant Mortality in 1906 and in 1908 illustrate this complex of anxieties. Burns insisted upon married women's work as the demon responsible not only for infantile mortality, rickety and anaemic children, but also for broken homes, unhappy and emasculated fathers, 'idle and loafing husbands', and lowered standards of wages – indeed for almost every imaginable kind of dire social ill. 'We have got to restrict married women's labour' he concluded fervently, 'as often and as soon as we can.'[68]

Even when faced with the near-impossibility of marshalling any convincing evidence in support of the theory that the employment

[66] Women's Co-operative Guild, Maternity: Letters from Working Women, with a preface by the Rt. Hon. Herbert Samuel (London, 1915).

[67] P. N. Stearns, 'Working-class Women In Britain, 1890–1914', in M. Vicinus (ed.), Suffer and Be Still: Women In the Victorian Age (Bloomington and London, 1972).

[68] Report of Proceedings of National Conference on Infantile Mortality ... with address by the Rt Hon. John Burns, M.P. (London, 1906) and Report of Proceedings of Second National Conference on Infantile Mortality (Westminster, 1908).

of mothers meant a significant loss of infant life, many authorities refused to abandon their conviction that this *must* be the case. The attitude of Arthur Newsholme, who, as Medical Officer to the Local Government Board, was responsible for three major detailed reports on infant mortality between 1909 and 1914 is instructive.[69] In the first of these reports, published in 1909–10, Newsholme admitted that the statistical evidence available did not enable him to make any precise statement about the scale of the influences exerted by women's work on infant mortality rates. Nevertheless, he insisted: 'Such employment must, however, tend on balance to increase infant mortality and to lower the health of older children in the same family. Even when the mother's earnings are necessary for the bread-winning of the family such earnings are secured by some sacrifice of the interests of the next generation'.[70] In the last analysis, the opposition of a man like Arthur Newsholme to women's employment in industry was grounded in a vision of social order hallmarked by a specific sexual division of labour – the woman's sphere was domestic; a mother should stay at home. This becomes abundantly clear to anyone perusing his *Report on Infant Mortality in Lancashire*. For instance, he argues that: 'In a wider sense *all* industrial occupation of women, whether married or unmarried, may be regarded as to some extent inimical to home-making and child care. This is so even in the case of girls and their industrial employment should be associated with systematic training in domestic economy'.[71]

It will hardly surprise the reader to learn that Newsholme was dismissive of the significance of Dr Robertson's study of 1909–10 in Birmingham (discussed earlier);[72] nor, of course, that the results of this later research were greeted with delight by feminists.[73] Members of the Fabian Women's Group and of the Women's Industrial Council were keen to defend the right of women to

[69] *39th Annual Report of Local Government Board* (London, 1909–10); supplement to *Report of Board's Medical Officer*, containing a 'Report on Infant and Child Mortality' (London, 1910), p. xxxiv; *42nd Annual Report of L.G.B.*, supplement containing a 'Second Report on Infant and Child Mortality' (London, 1913), p. xxxii; and *43rd Annual Report of L.G.B.*, containing a 'Third Report on Infant Mortality, dealing with Infant Mortality in Lancashire' (London, 1914), p. xxxix.
[70] Newsholme, *Report on Infant and Child Mortality* (1910) (note 69), p. 75.
[71] Newsholme, *Third Report on Infant Mortality* (note 69), p. 19.
[72] Newsholme, *Report on Infant and Child Mortality* (note 69), p. 57.
[73] Fabian Society Women's Group, *Summary of Eight Papers and Discussion Upon the Disabilities of Mothers as Workers* (1910), p. 22.

combine work with motherhood when they wished to do so,[74] but they were all too painfully aware of the strength of social disapproval that they faced.

Feminists such as B. L. Hutchins and Clementina Black continually emphasized the fact that the majority of working-class mothers seeking employment outside their homes had little choice; they needed to work in order to find the money to feed their families properly. An enlightened social policy, argued B. L. Hutchins, 'should aim at better conditions and shorter hours, at maternity insurance and the establishment of well-ordered crèches, but not at the prohibition of married women's work'.[75]

The strength of the social assumption that women should stay at home militated against any widespread provision of crèches or other arrangements for day-time care that would have come to the aid of the working mother during the period and coloured the policy of much early infant welfare work. In Huddersfield, for instance, Benjamin Broadbent justified his enthusiasm for home visiting by arguing that, unlike other schemes for educating mothers, the scheme positively discouraged women from leaving their houses in the daytime.[76]

Similarly, the belief that the ignorance of working-class women was a major cause of high infant mortality rates moulded the character of the early infant welfare movement in Britain. The first government grants for infant welfare were made, as pointed out earlier, through the Board of Education to the Schools for Mothers. Most infant welfare institutions saw their role as predominantly educational; they set out to instruct working-class women, whether in organized classes or in their own homes, in techniques of home management and child care. This emphasis on instruction, and the conviction among some welfare workers that their main task was one of inculcating or elevating standards of parental responsibility among working women, was frequently accompanied by an extreme wariness about the provision of any material aid in the form of dinners for expectant mothers, subsidized dried milk, or what-

[74] *Ibid.,* and Clementina Black (ed.), *Married Women's Work: Being the Report of an Enquiry Undertaken by the Women's Industrial Council* (London, 1915), pp. 1–14.

[75] Fabian Society Women's Group, *The Disabilities of Mothers as Workers* (note 73), pp. 22–3.

[76] County Borough of Huddersfield, *Infantile Mortality: The Working of the Huddersfield Scheme* (October, 1907), pamphlet in Huddersfield Public Library.

ever. I. G. Gibbon, writing in 1910, confessed himself particularly anxious lest too much charitable assistance should erode the sense of family responsibility, and spoke approvingly of one School for Mothers where necessitous women were provided with dinners worth twopence per head in exchange for 'the equivalent value in needlework'.[77] Several institutions, however, seem to have been brought up sharply against the problem faced by the Birmingham Infants' Health Society in 1907–08 – that pressure on mothers to breast-feed babies could have little effect where these women were too poor and ill-nourished to do so.[78] Indeed, Mary King, recollecting Truby King's experience of visiting London in 1913–14, commented thirty years later that: 'The stupendous problem of appalling poverty so dominated the infant welfare situation at this time that help to mothers was restricted mainly to philanthropic patronage and doles. So much help was needed for the poor that the paramount need of practical education in domestic hygiene and mothercraft had been almost lost sight of'.[79]

Historians need to find out more about the character of early infant welfare work in Britain; about attendance at centres; about the relationships between doctors, health visitors and their 'clients'; about the kind of instruction and knowledge disseminated during the period. One might perhaps have expected the Schools for Mothers and early welfare centres to have attracted wives of the skilled and better-off sections of the working class. Some contemporary reports by Medical Officers of Health in London and Yorkshire confirm that in their experience this was indeed the case.[80] Many centres resorted to a range of inducements such as free tea, cakes and buns, prizes for regular attendance, and so forth, to try to attract a wider clientele (Gibbon even mentions one centre that attempted to lure the more timid mothers along, with the advertisement that 'Ladies and the clergy sing sometimes'.[81]) Even so, it seems not improbable that many working-class mothers, discouraged by the atmosphere of middle-class philanthropy

[77] Gibbon, *Report on Schools for Mothers* (note 12), p. 10.
[78] Birmingham Infant's Health Society. *Annual Report for 1907–8* (Birmingham, 1908), p. 9.
[79] M. King. *Truby King – The Man* (London, 1948), p. 214.
[80] See, *inter alia*, reports of Dr Thomas (Medical Officer of Health in Finsbury) and Dr Moore (Medical Officer in Huddersfield) quoted in Carnegie United Kingdom Trust, *Report on the Physical Welfare of Mothers and Children* (London, 1917), pp. 275, 295.
[81] Gibbon, *Infant Welfare Centres* (note 12), pp. 30–1.

Mission and Board School that clung around many early welfare institutions, would have kept well away.

However sound the advice on child care offered to working-class mothers by medical officers of health and health visitors may have been, it was sometimes offered in a condescending, patronizing way. The medical profession's growing interest in infant care and hygiene almost inevitably implied a devaluation of the knowledge and experience working-class women had inherited on the subject.[82] This is clearly reflected in the numerous anecdotes about the ignorance of mothers and the stereotyped versions of 'old wives' tales' enshrined in the pages of public health and medical journals of the time. Dr Harold Kerr, for instance, writing in *Public Health* in 1910 referred to grandmothers as 'infanticidal experts', lamenting that: 'We have all learned in the course of our duties that the esteem in which a woman's erudition is held is often in direct ratio to the number of babies she has lost, and the higher this is, the greater the assurance and effrontery with which she delivers her dicta'.[83] Or again: 'In Newcastle ... one does not meet with so many of the grosser outrages upon the infantile digestive organs as one sometimes hears of elsewhere, such as feeding a three months' child with pickled onions or soothing him when fractious with a whelk soaked in gin'.[84]

The tone and condescension in remarks of this kind were far from untypical: one is tempted to sympathize with the working mothers of Rochdale who were complained about by a local clergyman in discussion at the second Conference on Infant Mortality in 1908. This well-meaning gentleman reported in injured tones that: 'When he had endeavoured to tell the members of his mothers' meeting how to bring up their babies, those Lancashire women had told him to go and play at marbles.'[85]

It becomes abundantly clear that before we can attempt any realistic assessment of the impact of the infant welfare movement in Edwardian England, we need to know more about traditional methods of infant care in working-class families. A large proportion of the accounts of working-class family life in the Victorian period

[82] On this theme see A. Oakley, 'Wisewoman and Medicine Man. Changes in the Management of Childbirth,' in A. Oakley and J. Mitchell (eds.). *The Rights and Wrongs of Women* (London, 1976).

[83] Kerr (note 52), p. 129.

[84] *Ibid.*, p. 131.

[85] *Report of Proceedings of National Conference on Infantile Mortality* (Westminster, 1908), p. 78.

bequeathed to us by middle-class observers are accusatory rather than descriptive: they tell us more about the viewpoint and values of the observer than about those being observed. One suspects that more than a few of the stereotyped accounts of 'ignorant old women' 'doping' their small charges with opiates while their mothers worked in the factory fall into this category. The historian has no real reason to assume that the majority of those women who undertook the day care of the children of working mothers were wholly unqualified for their task. Most of them had probably accumulated a good deal of experience with babies of their own in the past. A large proportion of them may have been relatives, if not the grandmothers of the infants involved.[86] And it is by no means unlikely that the spirit of neighbourly support and mutual aid prompted as many women into undertaking the care of young children as did need for the small sums of material remuneration involved.

Accounts of working-class family arrangements left by early twentieth-century observers present the historian with the same kind of difficulty. But here there is the additional resource of memory to fall back upon: if we are to discover anything of value about popular child-rearing practices during the period, it is clear that we need to exploit the techniques of the oral historian to the full. The anecdotal material and apocryphal stories gleaned from the pages of medical journals tell us a good deal about social distances, but next to nothing about working-class motherhood.

APPENDIX[87]

In his *Supplement to the 39th Annual Report of the Local Government Board, 1909–10, Containing a Report on Infant and Child Mortality*, Arthur Newsholme quoted infant mortality rates for thirty separate counties (representing the highest, medium and lowest counties of England and Wales for infant mortality in 1908); together with figures indicating the number of married and widowed women employed in these counties (from the 1901 census).

It has already been pointed out in the preceding pages that Newsholme himself was keen to demonstrate that infantile mortality rose in areas

---

[86] M. Anderson's recent work on family structure and co-residence in industrial Lancashire is suggestive here. See his *Family Structure in Nineteenth Century Lancashire* (Cambridge, 1971), esp, chapter 6.
[87] I would like to express my thanks to Dr G. N. von Tunzelmann for his help with the statistical material in the *Appendix*. Any errors in calculation are mine.

where a high proportion of women worked; hence it is reasonable to assume that he would have cited potentially favourable material for his case.

We can test the relationship by conventional linear regression analysis as follows:

$$IMR = 168.5 - 1.108 \text{ WFP} \ldots R^2 = 0.333$$
$$(3.487)$$

where:   IMR  = Infant mortality rate, per 1000 births
WFP  = Number of married and widowed women engaged
in occupations per 1000 females aged 10 years or older.

The regression shows that on the basis of these data for 1908 the correlation betweeen infant mortality rates and female workforce participation rates was on average *negative* rather than positive. As the t-value shows (quoted in parentheses beneath the coefficient) there is less than a 0.005 chance that the relationship between the two variables could be nonexistent, or indeed positive. Each rise of 1 per cent in the proportion of working women was associated with a fall of 1.1 per cent in the infant mortality rate across counties, on average. The $R^2$ estimated shows that the linear equation explains only about one-third of the total variance in the infant mortality rate, although this is enough to be significant at standard levels of confidence.

There are, clearly, problems involved in using data for areas as large and as mixed in character as counties. Similar tests were therefore carried out using infant mortality figures published in the annual report of the Registrar-General for 1905 for individual towns. The report listed thirty-four of the 217 chief towns in England and Wales with populations over 20,000 characterized by *high* rates of infant mortality (above 160 per 1000 births), and thirty-two towns with *low* rates (below 100 per 1000 births). The figures for the proportion of married and widowed women in employment were taken, as before, from the 1901 census.

Regressions were calculated (1) using the data for towns with the high rates of infant deaths and (2) taking the data for both groups of towns together.

The results were as follows:

(1) $IMR = 181 + 0.163 \text{ WFP}$
$(0.540)$          $R^2 = 0.009$
(2) $IMR = 114 + 1.620 \text{ WFP}$
$(1.837)$          $R^2 = 0.051$

In other words, the first equation showed no significant correlation between the variables. When all towns were taken together, there was a weak positive correlation (not significant at the 0.95 level). The group of towns characterized by low rates of infant mortality were mainly spas, middle-class residential areas, and seaside resorts, such as Tunbridge Wells, Wimbledon, and Worthing. It seems extremely likely that this correlation is accounted for by the class and income skew in the data.

# 3. Theories of the Cell State in Imperial Germany

## PAUL WEINDLING

The cell as a social concept now normally refers to a unit of political organization.[1] But the concept of an organism as a cell state, or *Zellenstaat*, has a neglected history associated with the rise of cell biology in nineteenth-century Germany. Professors of anatomy propagated the theory that an organism was a 'social arrangement of parts' both in their teaching and as a means of scientific explanation in their research.[2] Moreover on the basis of their privileged social position many professors drew on biological theories to formulate opinions on national issues like the feminist movement, naval expansion or war strategy. German scientific achievements in cell biology may be considered as a form of nationalism, if it is accepted that social ideals were intrinsic to the scientific formulation of concepts of life.

That the theory of the cell as the elementary organism permeated other aspects of culture raises questions about the prestigious authority of science in Imperial Germany. Relations between scientific theory, institutional aspects of teaching and research, and broader social questions pose complex historical problems. German universities were to a considerable extent state financed and controlled. But academics also vociferously defended their privileges, arguing that German scientific achievements were the result of national traditions of academic freedom. The resulting conflict of interests raises the question examined here with regard to anatomy

---

[1] For the cell as a sociological concept, see W. Bernsdorff, *Wörterbuch der Soziologie* (Stuttgart, 1969), pp. 1309–11; H. Sacher (ed.), *Staatslexikon* (Freiburg i.B., 1932), v, pp. 1559–62; M. Kossitsch, 'Zellen und Cliquen', *Kölner Zeitschrift für Soziologie*, v (1952–3), pp. 233–53.
[2] R. Virchow, *Cellular Pathology as based upon Physiological and Pathological Histology*, translated from 2nd German edn. (Berlin, 1859) by F. Chance (Philadelphia, 1863), reprinted New York, 1971, with introduction by L. J. Rather, p. 40; P. Diepgen, *Geschichte der Medizin. Die historische Entwicklung der Heilkunde und des ärztlichen Lebens*, 2nd edn., 2vols. (West-) Berlin, 1965), ii. pt. 1, pp. 114–15; ii, pt. 2, pp. 42–3; G. Mann, 'Medizinisch-biologische Ideen und Modelle in der Gesellschaftslehre des 19. Jahrhunderts', *Medizinhistorisches Journal*, iv (1969), pp. 1–23.

from the 1880s to 1918 at Berlin: to what extent was the theory of the cell state a response to the state's institutional control of the universities?

Although it is often said the activities of university professors in party politics declined with the establishment of the Empire in 1870, many maintained a highly diverse range of interests and social commitments. This study is focused on two major figures in German medical science, the professors of anatomy at Berlin, Oscar Hertwig (1849–1922) and Wilhelm Waldeyer (1837–1921). A biographical approach is appropriate as an integrated account of their biological research, institutional activities and social opinions is revealing of the underlying institutional structure and cultural assumptions prevalent in Imperial Germany.

The scientific use of social concepts by Hertwig and Waldeyer also provides a corrective to schematic accounts of the history of biology as the progressive application of mechanisms reducing biological processes to mechanistic or physico-chemical terms. Darwinian natural selection has been over-emphasized in this context, because it was not dependent (directly, at least) on any particular physiological viewpoint. Hertwig stressed that as biology dealt with the organization of life, it was more akin to the social sciences than the physico-chemical sciences.[3] Investigation of biological debates in Imperial Germany shows that Darwinism itself was transformed by existing preoccupations with cell theory and embryology. Many distinguished cell biologists and researchers into heredity were opposed to Darwinism. They argued in terms of environmental and regulative factors. These were readily formulated as social analogies, and were also directly relevant to social questions.

This study therefore endeavours to present the broader social and institutional ramifications of the theory of the cell state. The first section examines the tension between the needs of industrializing society for adequate medical care as perceived by the state, and the expansion of medical education and biological research in Imperial Germany. In Berlin there was a conflict of interests

[3] O. Hertwig, *Der Staat als Organismus, Gedanken zur Entwicklung der Menschheit* (Jena, 1922), p. 1; *idem*, 'Der Mensch ein Zellenstaat und die Gesetze des Zellenlebens. Vortrag, im Verein für Volkshygiene', *Blätter für Volksgesundheitspflege*, iv (1904), pp. 1–5, 17–22.

between the state anxious to increase division of academic labour, and the medical faculty determined to restrict the number of chairs. This background forms the context for consideration of the application of social concepts in the scientific research of Hertwig and Waldeyer. They were initially allied to opposed factions of anatomists, who had taken up contrasting positions over Darwinism and cell theory. Their biological views extended into explicit theorizing about the social organism, which was also subject to diverse interpretations. Finally career structure and the social sectors from which the Berlin medical faculty were recruited are investigated, in order to evaluate how representative Hertwig and Waldeyer were, and the extent to which full professors in the faculty may be considered a homogeneous group expressing its social interests by means of a distinctive organicist ideology.

## MEDICAL SCIENCE AND THE STATE

Historical approaches to the medical and biological sciences and their institutions in Imperial Germany diverge widely. These are at the one extreme preoccupied with the march of scientific progress, and at the other with the more lurid aspects of biological racism and Aryan physical culture. Consequently ideological and institutional implications of the theory of the cell state have been overlooked. Historians of the medical sciences have conventionally attributed institutional growth and the proliferation of medical specialities to the accumulation of discoveries.[4] But this assumes that the state, responsible for the endowment of new chairs and institutes, was at the beck and call of scientists. The alternative approach of treating all biological references to society as 'Social Darwinism' has been based on unwarranted overgeneralizations. Schematic accounts of Social Darwinism as a proto-fascist ideology concentrate on natural selection, forgetting that this was only one biological concept from which laws of social development were derived. The relationship between organicist ideology and the social structure of Imperial Germany has frequently been reduced to doctrines of the survival of the fittest as expressing

[4] J. L. Pagel, *Die Entwickelung der Medizin in Berlin von den Ältesten Zeiten bis auf die Gegenwart* (Wiesbaden, 1897), p. 15; H.-H. Eulner, *Die Entwicklung der medizinischen Spezialfächer an den Universitäten des deutschen Sprachgebietes* (Stuttgart, 1970).

aristocratic and militarist interests, rather than seeing organicist theories as also a product of the growth of the middle class.[5]

It may be noted in passing that there was only minimal continuity between those generations of professors appointed to full chairs in the Berlin medical faculty before 1918 and the faculty of the Third Reich (see Table 2). This discontinuity is further emphasized by the emigration of over 42 per cent of German university teachers in medicine after 1932.[6] In Imperial Germany only a small proportion of those gaining teaching posts in medicine came from families which were designated as lower middle class. But it was recognized that increasing numbers were coming from the commercial sectors of the middle class. In 1890, 75 per cent of those gaining teaching posts had fathers with university degrees; by 1910 this had decreased to 60 per cent.[7]

Possession of a university degree was traditionally the criterion for belonging to the *Bildungsbürgertum*, the educated intelligentsia. It was said that whoever in Germany had no academic education lacked a social distinction for which neither riches nor noble birth could compensate.[8] In order to assess the validity of this highly idealized view, the social status of university professors is crucially important. For this elite claimed leadership of public opinion. There has been a substantial amount of research on the social views of professors, tracing shifts in their opinions from the Navy League in the 1890s to the conduct of the 1914–18 war and the establishment of the new republic. But the political opinions of

[5] The term 'Social Darwinism' was used by Steinmetz, the sociologist, as early as 1901. For the complex history of the term 'evolution' see M. Briegel, *Evolution. Geschichte eines Fremdwortes in Deutschen* (Freiburg i. B., 1963). Representative studies of Social Darwinism are H. W. Koch, *Der Sozialdarwinismus. Seine Genese und sein Einfluss auf das imperialistische Denken* (München, 1973) and P. von zur Mühlen, *Rassenideologen. Geschichte und Hintergründe* ((West-) Berlin, Bonn-Bad Godesberg, 1974). For bibliography see G. C. Field, 'Nordic Racism', *Journal of the History of Ideas*, xxxviii (1977), pp. 523–40. For a critical perspective in relation to social structure see G. Eley, 'The Wilhelmine Right: How it Changed', in R. J. Evans (ed.), *Society and Politics in Wilhelmine Germany* (London, 1978), pp. 113–16. Studies of Darwinism in France have been more sophisticated than for Germany, see Y. Conry, *L'introduction du Darwinisme en France au XIXe siècle* (Paris, 1974); L. L. Clark, *Social Darwinism and French Intellectuals* (Univ. Microfilms, Ann Arbor, 1968).
[6] C. von Ferber, 'Die Entwicklung des Lehrkörpers der deutschen Universitäten und Hochschulen 1864–1964' in H. Plessner (ed.), *Untersuchungen zur Lage der deutschen Hochschullehrer*, 3 vols. (Göttingen, 1956), iii, pp. 145–6.
[7] *Ibid*, pp. 185–6.
[8] F. Paulsen, *Die deutsche Universitäten und das Universitätsstudium* (Berlin, 1902), p. 150.

natural scientists, university professors of medicine and physicians have been relatively neglected.[9] In many respects medical professors were no different in their opinions than those of their colleagues in the humanities. There were, however, additional issues raised by the provision of laboratories and clinics, which affected relations between professors and the state. University professors of medicine also considered themselves as spokesmen for the medical profession and agitated or were called on by the state to improve standards of public health. Thus while at least among professors party politics declined, there were new spheres of institutional and professional power which became subject to conflicts and rivalries.

The increasing resources of the Prussian state after the industrial take-off in the 1870s provided funds to establish laboratories and institutes, so facilitating the systematic investigation of the cellular mechanisms of heredity and disease. This situation was complicated by the administrative structure of both health care and the universities remaining in the grasp of individual states, rather than wholly subject to a centralized imperial administration. It was to an extent possible for a particular state to regulate conditions so that certain universities could be pre-eminent. But rivalries between states and academic factions made such plans difficult to realize. In the 1870s the cellular pathologist and liberal politician Rudolf Virchow complained in the state assembly that Berlin was losing its prestige to rival universities like Leipzig in Saxony.[10] The Prussian state subsequently fostered Berlin's reputation by improving its research facilities. But state policies were also determined by priorities of fostering medical specialities for their practical therapeutic value, an issue over which the faculty, and in particular Virchow, would clash with the state.

It is important to appreciate the extent to which university professors were subject to competing demands. They required the esteem of their colleagues at a particular university, and also of representatives of their discipline at other universities. Not only were they appointed and paid by the state, a substantial part of their

[9] For politics and university professors of medicine, see E. Seidler, 'Der politische Standort des Arztes im Zweiten Kaiserreich', in G. Mann and R. Winau (eds), *Medizin, Naturwissenschaft, Technik und das Zweite Kaiserreich* (Göttingen, 1977), pp. 87–118; G. Jeschal, *Politik und Wissenschaft deutscher Ärzte im Ersten Weltkrieg* (Pattensen, 1977).
[10] N. Andernach, *Der Einfluss der Parteien auf das Hochschulwesen in Preussen, 1848–1918* (Göttingen, 1972), pp. 58–9.

income also came from student fees for attending their lectures. In addition, successful authors of textbooks and popular expositions of their subject could earn further amounts: for example, the popularizer of Darwinism, Ernst Haeckel in 1882 nearly trebled his salary from the 6000 marks professorial stipend paid by the state to as much as 20,000 marks from publications.[11] Thus university professors felt both a duty and a financial incentive to be more than just efficient researchers. Discoveries in cell biology were presented in terms of relevance to medical students, the medical profession, and the general public. Professors' socially influential position provided them with an incentive to develop theories such as the cell state. Indeed it was said by the anatomist Martin Heidenhain, that most teachers of anatomy used the theory of the cell state in their lectures.[12]

It is of particular interest to assess the implications of the diverse aims and allegiances of the Berlin professors since their faculty constituted both a national and an international model of medical education. Humboldt's concern at the foundation of the university in 1809 was that scientific teaching and research be linked to clinical instruction. There were many admiring foreign observers of conditions at Berlin, like Abraham Flexner, whose views on medical education in German universities were to be decisive for developments in the U.S.A. Flexner commented in 1912 that whereas at the beginning of the nineteenth century the German universities furnished only a fraction of those practising medicine and surgery, by 1909 there were 30,558 physicians for a population of 63 million giving a ratio of 1:2000. Between 1885 and 1909 the number of physicians increased almost 100 per cent, a rate three times as fast as the population growth in the same period.[13]

The status of physicians was consequently perceived as particularly dependent on the scientific standards of the universities. Professors saw themselves as leading representatives of an increasingly influential medical profession. For example, Hertwig and Waldeyer were active in providing courses enabling physicians to

[11] C. Hünemörder and I. Scheele, 'Das Berufsbild des Biologen im Zweiten Deutschen Kaiserreich – Anspruch und Wirklichkeit', in Mann and Winau (see note 9), p. 137.
[12] M. Heidenhain, Plasma und Zelle, 2 vols. (Jena, 1907–11), i, pp. 26–9.
[13] A. Flexner, Medical Education in Europe (New York, 1912), pp. 7–9, 17–20.

keep abreast of the latest scientific research. The consequent sense of the profession's dependence on the state, reinforced by Bismarck's social insurance legislation, was expressed in the observation that every physician was like an irreplaceable cell in the organism of the state; like a migratory *Wanderzelle* the physician was responsible to intervene, wherever there was irritation or infection from foreign bodies.[14]

By the 1890s Humboldt's mechanism of institutional growth based on independent scientific activity was failing to function efficiently. The number of full professorial chairs (*Ordinarien*) no longer kept in step with the expansion of numbers of associate professors (*Extraordinarien*) and lecturers (*Privatdozenten*). Thus in 1897 there were ninety-six *Ordinarien* and a total of 334 university teachers in Berlin; in 1907 there were ninety-two full professors, but overall 478 teachers.[15] The resulting tensions were particularly acute in the Prussian medical faculties as the numbers of medical students declined in proportion to total student numbers. Thus whereas medicine had in 1895 occupied 28.1 per cent of Prussian students, by 1906 this had fallen to 11.6 per cent.[16]

Despite this stagnation, the state continued to press for an increased number of chairs. This was, however, resisted by the established *Ordinarien*, who sought to preserve their elite position. In Berlin of 1870 there were thirteen *Ordinarien*, twelve *Extraordinarien* and twenty-nine *Privatdozenten* for 229 medical students. By 1910 there were thirty-one *Ordinarien* and an additional thirteen honorary professors with personal chairs, forty-two *Extraordinarien* and 129 *Privatdozenten* for 1568 students.[17] As a proportion of the total number of teachers in the medical faculty, the numbers of *Ordinarien* fell from 19 per cent in 1870 to 15 per cent in 1909.[18] The differentials in incomes, however, greatly increased. In 1870 the average earnings of a full professor of medicine were 4221 marks and an associate's were 950 marks. By 1910 this had further widened: the average earnings of a full

[14] L. Seidler, 'Der politische Standort des Arztes im Zweiten Kaiserreich', in G. Mann and R. Winau (note 9), p. 88.
[15] M. Lenz, *Geschichte der Königlichen Friedrich-Wilhelms-Universität zu Berlin*, 4 vols. (Halle, 1910–1918), iii, p. 491.
[16] K. H. Jarausch, 'The Social Transformation of the University: the Case of Prussia 1865–1914', *Journal of Social History*, xii (1979), p. 614.
[17] M. Lenz (note 15), iii, p. 491.
[18] *Ibid.*, iii, p. 402.

professor had risen to 6789 marks; but an associate's were only 1247 marks, and nearly half of these posts in Berlin carried no salary at all. Associate professors and lecturers were considered a species of academic proletariat.[19]

There came to prevail among the professors the sense that industrialization was inimical to the traditions of academic freedom. Scholarship conducted on a mass scale of a large business concern was graphically described by Theodor Mommsen as *der Grossbetrieb der Wissenschaft*.[20] This development meant the state extended its power in university life. Increased funds were available for the state to endow specialized institutes and clinics. Indeed Max Weber was to observe that the large institutes of medicine and natural science were state capitalist enterprises.[21] As assistants' posts needed state approval this undermined the value placed on the independence of the *Privatdozent*.[22] As faculty appointments, the latter reflected the ideal of individual scholarship, and in many cases the prerequisite of private financial means. Despite the prevailing cultural pessimism to which Weber gave expression, whether full professors actually became increasingly subservient to the state is a moot point. For clinics and institutes provided a new sphere for the wielding of autocratic power by their directors. Many professors also became increasingly vociferous in the defence of their socially privileged status and in their financial demands.

In medicine, tensions due to differing conditions of employment were particularly acute. On the clinical side there tended to be less dependence on the state than in other faculties. In clinical specialities, the *Privatdozent* or *Extraordinarius* could have a hospital post or private practice, which could bring earnings in excess of 20,000 marks, especially if a practitioner had gained the title of 'Professor'. But in non-clinical subjects like anatomy and physiology, a *Privatdozent* would be assistant at an institute, con-

[19] *Ibid.*, iii, p. 532; F. Eulenburg, *Der 'akademische Nachwuchs': eine Untersuchung über die Lage und die Aufgaben der Extraordinarien und Privatdozenten* (Leipzig, 1908), pp. 129, 130.
[20] L. Stern (ed.), *Die Berliner Akademie der Wissenschaften in der Zeit des Imperialismus, 1, Von den neunziger Jahren bis zur Grossen Sozialistischen Oktoberrevolution* (Berlin, 1975), pp. 12–13.
[21] M. Weber, 'Science as a Vocation', in H. H. Gerth and C.W. Mills (eds.), *From Max Weber: Essays in Sociology* (London and Boston, 1974), p. 131.
[22] A. Busch, 'The Vicissitudes of the *Privatdozent*: Breakdown and Adaptation in the Recruitment of the German University Teacher', *Minerva*, i (1962–3), pp. 319–41.

sequently losing independence.[23] As will be shown, there was considerable resentment by full professors on the faculty of certain clinical specialities.

Not only was the elite position of the *Ordinarius* challenged by the state's promoting of new specialisms, but the state fostered institutions such as the *Technische Hochschulen* for applied science excluded from the universities. The state also founded institutes for scientific research which were independent of the universities and academies of sciences. Similarly in medicine the imperial administration sponsored measures against typhus, tuberculosis, infant mortality and syphilis. In Prussia, Koch's *Institut für Infectionskrankheiten* in 1891 opened a new era of such independent research establishments. There followed the *Krebsforschungsinstitut* and Wassermann's institute for experimental therapy, and public health laboratories were established.[24] When an institute for neurobiology was opposed by the Berlin faculty, it was supported by Althoff, the Prussian ministerial director responsible for university affairs, and financed by the industrialist Gustav Krupp von Bohlen und Halbach. Even when professors took an initiative to demand the establishing of specialized research institutes, as did Hertwig and Waldeyer in 1907, the resulting conglomeration of research institutes, the *Kaiser-Wilhelm-Gesellschaft*, was administratively outside the University or Prussian Academy of Sciences.[25] A further novel feature was that its finance was provided by industrialists. Hertwig and Waldeyer were only able to act as representatives of the University and Academy on governing committees.[26]

Examination of the records of appointments to the Berlin medical faculty reveal that there was considerable resistance to state intervention. It must be emphasized that only full professors were faculty members. Although the state made appointments, the faculty had the right to make recommendations. There was, consequently, opposition to many of the new full chairs established in the Berlin

---

[23] F. Eulenburg (note 19), pp. 52, 116–17, 144.
[24] F. Pfetsch, *Zur Entwicklung der Wissenschaftspolitik im Deutschland des 19 und beginnenden 20. Jahrhunderts* ((West-) Berlin, 1973), pp. 91–2.
[25] G. Wendel, *Die Kaiser-Wilhelm-Gesellschaft 1911–1914. Zur Anatomie einer Imperialistischen Forschungsgesellschaft* (Berlin, 1975); L. Burchardt, *Wissenschaftspolitik im Wilhelminischen Deutschland. Vorgeschichte, Gründung und Aufbau der Kaiser-Wilhelm-Gesellschaft zur Förderung der Wissenschaften* (Göttingen, 1975).
[26] R. B. Goldschmidt, *Portraits from Memory. Recollections of a Zoologist* (Seattle, Wash. 1956), pp. 78–80.

medical faculty under Althoff, the mastermind of the Prussian university system from 1882 to 1907.[27] Echoing the Berlin faculty's fears, the medical historian Julius Pagel condemned increasing numbers of medical specializations, as increasing intellectual poverty.[28]

Thus the current view that accumulating medical discoveries resulted in the proliferation of medical specialities is untenable. For the institutionalization of medical specialities reveals conflicts over the state's policy towards the expansion of teaching and research grounded on the intellectual and social aspirations of university professors. Not only have the implications of the institutional basis of cytology in anatomy been overlooked, but schematic accounts of specializations neglect consequences for anatomy as an already established discipline. For although from anatomy there developed the specialisms of physiology and pathological anatomy, anatomy remained a live area for scientific research.[29] Cytology, histology and comparative anatomy provide examples of innovative applications of new scientific methods in anatomy. These furthered the importance of anatomy as the instrumental basis of medicine and surgery, as well as raising fundamental scientific and philosophical questions.

From this perspective the customary identification of a correspondence between the processes of the foundation of new institutes and increasing specialization is unsatisfactory. It is customary to see the appointments of Virchow as pathological anatomist in 1856 and of Du Bois-Reymond in 1858 as representing the first stages in progressive specialization from anatomy.[30] But another distinguished Berlin *Ordinarius*, Ehrenberg, had for many years been lecturing on physiology, and objected to the appointment of Du Bois-Reymond. Similarly Virchow gained his chair at the expense of a histologist and pathologist Robert Remak, who was renowned for his achievements in neurocytology[31] (see

[27] For Althoff and medicine, see A. Sachse, *Friedrich Althoff und sein Werk* (Berlin, 1928), pp. 118–19, 146–7. For a general study of Althoff, see B. vom Brocke, 'Hochschul- und Wissenschaftspolitik in Preussen und im Deutschen Kaiserreich 1882–1907: das "System Althoff," in P. Baumgart, M. Schlenke and H. G. Zier (eds.), *Staat und Bildung in Preussen und im Deutschen Kaiserreich* (Stuttgart, in press).

[28] J. L. Pagel, 'Die Berliner medizinische Fakultät in ihrem ersten Jahrhundert', *Deutsche medizinische Wochenschrift*, xxxvi (1910), p. 1844.

[29] W. Waldeyer, *Geschichte des anatomischen Unterrichts an der Berliner Universität* (Berlin, 1899); idem, 'Anatomie' in W. Lexis (ed.), *Die deutschen Universitäten, für die Universitätsaustellung in Chicago*, 2 vols. (Berlin, 1893), ii, pp. 187–233.

[30] H.-H. Eulner (note 4), p. 513; M. Lenz (note 15), ii, pt. 2, p. 312.

[31] B. Kisch, 'Forgotten Leaders in Modern Medicine', *Transactions of the American Philosophical Society*, xliv (1954), pp. 279–82.

Table 1 for titles of appointments). Professors continued to promulgate elaborate synthetic philosophies, and were not blinkered in the pursuit of their specializations. They sought, as Ringer observes in his study of the German mandarin type, philosophical truths affecting 'the totality of man's nature'.[32] Thus neurologists, pathological anatomists, histologists and physiologists all contributed to the theory of the cell state.

The medical faculty defended their privileged position by using a tactical argument over scientific standards to resist state proposals to increase the numbers of full chairs. Bound by both academic and professional ties, the number of full chairs in the medical faculty was far smaller than in the philosophical faculty (only the universities of Göttingen, Strassburg and Dorpat had faculties for the natural sciences and mathematics separate from philosophy). Waldeyer described the medical faculty as a particularly closed and integrated body, for which new chairs posed especial problems.[33] New specialities like otology, laryngology and dermatology were condemned as not fully legitimate sciences.[34] It was argued that these specialities did not deal with the body as a whole, and were consequently only partial sciences. In 1905 the faculty scathingly dismissed a whole range of specialities such as orthopaedics, dentistry, urology and tuberculosis. The faculty accused the Prussian ministry of engineering the fall of theoretical science as such specialities were for mere 'technicians'.[35] This hostility corresponded to the opposition of philosophical faculties to applied sciences.

The expansion in the number of chairs was of two types, either replicating established disciplines or as the culminating mark of recognition for a new speciality. The faculty considered the duplication of chairs and clinics to be an acceptable means for coping with increased student numbers. The faculty's adherence to existing intellectual divisions meant that Hertwig was appointed to a duplicate chair of anatomy rather than, as the state had proposed,

[32] F. K. Ringer, *The Decline of the German Mandarins. The German Academic Community 1890–1933* (Cambridge, Mass., 1969), pp. 106–9.
[33] Universitätsarchiv der Humboldt-Universität zu Berlin Aktenbestand des Anatomisch- und des Anatomischen Biologischen Instituts, Bd. 3, Bl. 3.
[34] 'Neue Professuren', *Vossische Zeitung* (6 August 1910). For dermatology see: M. Stürzbecher and G. Wagner, *Die Vorgeschichte der Berufung von Edmund Lesser an die Charité* (Kiel, 1962); Zentrales Staatsarchiv, Dienstelle Merseburg, (ZSTA Merseburg), Ministerium der geistlichen, Unterrichts- und Medizinalangelegenheiten, Rep. 76 Va Sekt. 2 Tit. IV Nr 46 Bd 17 Bl. 2–3.
[35] ZSTA Merseburg, Rep. 76 Va Sekt. 2 Tit. IV Nr 46 Bd 17 Bl.5.

Table 1. *The Berlin medical faculty in 1870*

| Name | Dates | Year of appointment as *Ordinarius* | Age on appointment | Title of chair | Religion | Father's occupation |
|---|---|---|---|---|---|---|
| Schultz-Schultzenstein, Carl Heinrich | 1798–1871 | 1833 | 35 | Physiology and botany | Evang. | Master-builder |
| Juengken, Johann Christian | 1793–1875 | 1834 (emeritus, 1868) | 41 | Surgery and ophthalmology | Evang. | Court physician at Magdeburg |
| Ehrenberg, Christian Gottfried | 1795–1876 | 1839 | 44 | History of medicine and physiology | Evang. | Municipal magistrate |
| Mitscherlich, Carl Gustav | 1805–71 | 1844 | 38 | Materia medica (*Arzneimittel-lehre*) | Evang. | Pastor |
| Romberg, Moritz Heinrich | 1795–1873 | 1845 (emeritus, 1865) | 49 | Special pathology and therapy (clinician and neuropatho-logist) | Evang. (bapt. Jew) | Merchant |
| Langenbeck, (von) Bernhard Rudolph Konrad | 1810–87 | 1848 | 38* | Surgery | Evang. | Church minister (uncle, prof. of medicine) |
| Virchow, Rudolf Carl | 1821–1902 | 1856 | 34 | Pathology and anatomy | Evang. | Merchant/municipal official/farmer |

| Name | Dates | Appointed | Age | Field | Religion | Father's occupation |
|---|---|---|---|---|---|---|
| Martin, Eduard Arnold | 1809–75 | 1858 | 47 | Obstetrics and gynaecology | Evang. | Jurist |
| Du Bois-Reymond, Emil Heinrich | 1818–96 | 1858 | 40 | Physiology | Reform | Watchmaker and representative of Prussian Neufchâtel (*Geh. Regierungsrat*) |
| Reichert, Karl Bogislaus | 1811–83 | 1858 (emeritus, 1883) | 46* | Anatomy and physiology | | Father: mayor. Stepfather: *Gymnasium* teacher |
| Frerichs, (von) Friedrich Theodor | 1819–85 | 1859 | 40* | Pathology and therapy | Evang. | Estate owner |
| Hirsch, August | 1817–94 | 1863 | 45 | Hygiene (pathology, medical history and literature) | Evang. (bapt. Jew) | Merchant |
| Graefe, (von) Wilhelm Ernst Albrecht | 1828–70 | 1866 | 38 | Ophthalmology | Evang. | Univ. prof. (medicine, Berlin) |
| Bardeleben, (von) Heinrich Adolf | 1819–95 | 1868 | 49 | Surgery | Evang. | Jurist and liberal politician |

*The age on appointment may be inaccurate by one year.

Table 2. *Ordinarien of the medical faculty, Berlin, appointed 1870–1918*

| Name | Dates | Year of appointment | Age | Title of chair | Religion | Father's occupation/status |
|---|---|---|---|---|---|---|
| Traube, Ludwig | 1818–76 | 1872 | 58* | Medicine (pathology and therapy) | Jewish | Wine merchant |
| Liebreich, Oscar | 1839–1908 | 1872 | 33 | Pharmacology | Evang. (bapt. Jew) | |
| Schweigger, Carl | 1830–1905 | 1873 (emeritus, 1900) | 42 | Ophthalmology | Evang. | University prof. (physics) |
| Westphal, Carl | 1833–90 | 1874 | 41 | Psychiatry | | Physician (*Geh. Sanitätsrath*) |
| Leyden, Ernst (von) | 1832–1910 | 1876–85; 1885 (emeritus, 1907) | 44 | Medicine II Medicine I | Evang. | Government official |
| Schroeder, Carl | 1838–87 | 1876 | 37 | Obstetrics | Evang. | School teacher |
| Gusserow, Adolf | 1836–1906 | 1878 (emeritus, 1904) | 41 | Obstetrics II | | Physician (*Geh. Sanitätsrath*) |
| Bergmann, Ernst (von) | 1836–1907 | 1882 (emeritus, 1907) | 45 | Surgery | Evang. | Pastor |
| Waldeyer, (-Hartz, von), Wilhelm | 1836–1921 | 1883 (emeritus, 1917) | 46 | Anatomy II | Catholic | Estate manager |
| Koch, Robert | 1843–1910 | 1885–91 | 41 | Hygiene | Evang. | Mining official |
| Gehrhardt, Carl | 1833–1902 | 1885 | 52 | Medicine I | Evang. | *Gymnasium* teacher |
| Olshausen, Robert (von) | 1835–1915 | 1887 | 51 | Gynaecology and obstetrics I | Evang. | Univ. prof. (orientalist) |
| Hertwig, Oscar | 1847–1922 | 1888 (emeritus, 1921) | 41 | Anatomy I | Evang. | Cigar manufacturer |
| Jolly, Friedrich | 1844–1904 | 1890 | 45 | Psychiatry | Reform | Univ. prof. (physics) |
| Rubner, Max | 1854–1932 | 1891–1909; 1909 (emeritus, 1922) | 37* 55* | Hygiene Physiology | | Locksmith |
| Heubner, Otto | 1843–1926 | 1894 (emeritus, 1913) | 52* | Paediatrics | Evang. | Lawyer (1848 revolutionary) |

| Name | Dates | Appointment (emeritus) | Age* | Chair/Subject | Religion | Father's occupation |
|---|---|---|---|---|---|---|
| Koenig, Franz | 1832–1910 | 1895 (emeritus, 1904) | 63* | Surgery II | Evang. | Court physician |
| Engelmann, Theodor | 1843–1909 | 1897 (emeritus, 1909) | 54* | Physiology | Evang. | Publisher |
| Michel, Julius (von) | 1843–1911 | 1900 | 57* | Ophthalmology | | Lawyer |
| Kraus, Friedrich | 1858–1936 | 1902 (emeritus, 1927) | 44 | Medicine II (physiology and pathology) | Catholic | Teacher |
| Orth, Johannes | 1847–1923 | 1902 (emeritus, 1917) | 55* | Pathological anatomy | | Physician |
| Hildebrand, Otto | 1858–1927 | 1904 | 46* | Surgery II | Evang. | Univ. prof. (economics) |
| Ziehen, Theodor | 1862–1950 | 1904–12 | 42* | Psychiatry | Evang. | Journalist/teacher |
| Bumm, Ernst | 1858–1925 | 1904–10; 1910 | 52* | Obstetrics I and II | Catholic | Teacher in deaf and dumb institution |
| Bier, August | 1867–1949 | 1907 (emeritus, 1932) | 46* | Surgery I | Evang. | Surveyor |
| His, Wilhelm | 1863–1934 | 1907 (emeritus, 1932) | 44* | Medicine I | Reform | Univ. prof. (anatomy) |
| Passow, Adolf | 1859–1926 | 1907 | 48* | Otology, ENT I | Evang. | Surveyor |
| Heffter, Arthur | 1859–1925 | 1908 (emeritus, 1925) | 48* | Pharmacology | Evang. | Wine merchant |
| Fluegge, Karl | 1847–1923 | 1909 (emeritus, 1921) | 62* | Hygiene | Evang. | Physician |
| Franz, Karl | 1870–1926 | 1910 | 40* | Obstetrics II | Catholic | Warden of a hospital |
| Lesser, Edmund | 1852–1918 | 1911 | 59* | Dermatology | Jewish | |
| Krueckmann, Emil | 1865–1944 | 1912 (emeritus, 1934) | 46* | Ophthalmology | | Physician |
| Bonhoeffer, Karl | 1863–1948 | 1912 (emeritus, 1938) | 49* | Psychiatry | Evang. | Lawyer |
| Czerny, Adalbert | 1863–1941 | 1913 (emeritus, 1932) | 50* | Paediatrics | Alt-katholisch | Apothecary |
| Lubarsch, Otto | 1860–1933 | 1917 (emeritus, 1929) | 57* | Pathology | Evang. (bapt. Jew) | Banker |
| Fick, Rudolf | 1866–1940 | 1917 | 51* | Anatomy II | Evang. | Univ. prof. (physiology) |

*The age on appointment may be inaccurate by one year.

for comparative anatomy and embryology.[36] The second type of new chair was sponsored by the state to provide more effective medical care. The state's influence was decisive for hygiene: opposition to this particular chair was led by Virchow, who objected to the appointment of Robert Koch in 1882.[37] Althoff also sponsored (and Virchow opposed) the introduction of paediatrics. A full chair was established for this in 1885 because of official concern with maintaining an adequate rate of population growth at a time when the state was particularly concerned to improve post-natal care and strengthen the family unit by social insurance provisions. While the state won its battles to introduce full chairs for dermatology, and for ear, nose and throat diseases as clinical specialities, this was not without opposition from the faculty. It has been suggested that Berlin was especially innovative as a university.[38] It must however be pointed out that this was more the result of state pressure on the university due to its location in the expanding imperial capital, rather than because of any open-mindedness on the part of the faculty.

It is in the context of such conflicts that organicist theories were used to justify restrictive attitudes. Hertwig considered that the corollary of division of academic labour was the integration of specialized sciences on a higher plane of intellectual synthesis. Cell theory provided the faculty with a common theoretical basis for experimental investigations. Hertwig and Waldeyer emphasized that cytology increasingly united the sciences of anatomy, physiology, zoology and botany. In 1904 Waldeyer supported the establishment of a chair for the study of unicellular animals (*Protistenkunde*) as relevant to practical medicine, social hygiene and general cytology.[39] Organicist views, exemplified by the theory of the cell state, can be seen as generated by the professorial community rather than by any theoretical demands imposed by the state.

[36] ZSTA Merseburg, Rep. 76 Va Sekt 2 Tit. IV Nr 46 Bd 10 Bl. 86–89.
[37] N. Andernach, *Der Einfluss der Parteien auf das Hochschulwesen in Preussen. 1848–1918* (Göttingen, 1972), pp. 146–9.
[38] F. B. Pfetsch and A. Zloczower, *Innovation und Widerstände in der Wissenschaft* (Düsseldorf, 1973), pp. 18–19.
[39] O. Hertwig, *Die Entwicklung der Biologie im 19. Jahrhundert. Vortrag auf der Versammlung deutscher Naturforscher zu Aachen am 17. September 1900* (Jena, 1900); W. Waldeyer, *Die neueren Ansichten über das Bau und Wesen der Zelle* (Leipzig, 1895); idem, '*Festrede*', *Sitzungsberichte der Preussischen Akademie der Wissenschaften*, (1896), p. 736; ZSTA Merseburg, Rep. 76 Va Sekt. 2 Tit. IV Nr 46 Bd 16 Bl. 325.

Althoff's correspondence shows that officially the state's primary concern was to secure capable teachers and researchers. But inquiries as to candidates' beliefs, for example whether a Roman Catholic was ultramontane, confirm Max Weber's observation: 'In Germany the freedom of learning exists only within the limits of officially accepted political and religious views'.[40] These limits were extended by Althoff along with his policy of fostering useful new academic specialisms. Waldeyer as nominally Catholic had not been eligible for habilitation at Königsberg.

The extent to which there was greater tolerance under Althoff may be seen in Waldeyer's personal belief as a free-thinker, and in Hertwig's humanist interpretation of the Christian ethic of brotherly love as essential for social cohesion. Hertwig had a number of Jewish assistants, although other professors could be unwilling to have Jews as assistants or block their careers by refusing to allow them to become *Privatdozenten*. The substantial number of Jewish honorary professors suggests that there were indeed cases of discrimination. It was felt that certain Jews had failed to achieve the *Ordinarius* which they merited; among these were the physiologist Munk, the ophthalmologist Hirschberg and the clinician Senator. Althoff also had difficulty in finding a suitable place for Ehrlich, for whom an institute was ultimately established at Frankfurt.[41]

Althoff's capacity to innovate could be hampered by the existing academic structure. Although he wished to institute chairs for anthropology in Prussian universities he was unsuccessful in this. He considered anthropology was of use to the state in military matters, in halting the decline in population and in combating the harmful effects of cities and industries on the lives of the working populace.[42] The case of anthropology suggests that there were interests both in the state and the universities opposed to its introduction into the university with a fully-fledged institute.[43]

[40] M. Weber, 'Die ,sogenannte "Lehrfreiheit" an den deutschen Universitäten', *Frankfurter Zeitung und Handelsblatt*, 53.262 (20 September, 1908), quoted in F. K. Ringer, *The Decline of the German Mandarins. The German Academic Community 1890–1933* (Cambridge, Mass., 1969), p. 143.
[41] For the failure of Munk to become *Ordinarius* despite the faculty's support, see ZSTA Merseburg, Rep. 76 Va Sekt. 2 Tit. IV Nr 46 Bd 14 Bl. 13, 16, 22, 181. 'Juden in der Wissenschaft', *Unterhaltungsblatt der deutschen Tageszeitung* (22 March 1897).
[42] ZSTA Merseburg, Rep. 76 Va Sekt. 2 Tit. IV Nr 46 Bd 18 Bl. 22.
[43] For the difficulties of an anthropologist see: Heller (Graf), 'Gustav Fritsch zum Gedächtnis', *Anatomischer Anzeiger*, lxiv (1927), pp. 257–69.

For a clinical innovation like dermatology, Althoff had to win the support of both the finance ministry and the educational administration.[44] The state was not an all-powerful monolithic body, and had also to contend with the established authority of professors. A skilled administrator like Althoff could manipulate academic factions to some extent; but in many respects professors were still able to use their monopolistic rights of authority in the faculty, or their personal academic status to influence the state administration.

## CELL THEORY AND POLITICS

Preliminary investigation of relations between professors of medicine and the state suggests that there was a discrepancy between the actual conflict-ridden course of relations and the idealistic expectations of the state prevalent among professors. It was their ideals of the state which became incorporated into biological theory. This suggests that the concept of the cell state must be assessed in relation to broader cultural preoccupations of the middle class. Darwinism was frequently criticized in Germany as the doctrine of an alien *laissez-faire* liberalism, its Malthusian competitive individualism threatening social disintegration. The theory of the cell state expressed the sense of social responsibility of the German professor to the nation, idealized as a *Kulturstaat*. Oscar Hertwig attributed the initial success of natural selection to the physical suffering in the early days of industrialization being justified as an inevitable consequence of social evolution. Hertwig considered that just as co-operative definitions of the social organism had come to prevail, so too had liberal individualism as an economic principle been replaced by trusts, syndicates and state supervision, in order to alleviate the harmful effects of competition.[45]

This transition in social thought was reflected in theories of the cell state. Among the pioneers of cell theory in the 1840s were liberal patriots like Schwann, Henle and Virchow, the latter subsequently being a founder of the liberal Progressive Party.

---

[44] M. Stürzbecher and G. Wagner, *Die Vorgeschichte der Berufung von Edmund Lesser an die Charité* (Kiel, 1962), p. 54.
[45] O. Hertwig, *Das Werden der Organismen. Zur Widerlegung von Darwins Zufallstheorie durch das Gesetz in der Entwicklung*, 3rd edn. (Jena, 1922), pp. 628–9.

Virchow's views on cell formation are historically well known, and were of particular importance and influence. In 1855 he took the step of interpreting an organism as a 'social arrangement of parts'. In the tracing of the genesis of such concepts of cellular organization, the historian encounters a complex interaction of microscopical observations, scientific theories and the intrusion of political and religious concerns. Yet the use of analogies should be interpreted with caution. An example of misrepresentation in the case of Virchow is a too simplistic equation of chemical reductionism with liberal democratic radicalism.[46] For, while attempts to establish methodological principles were influenced by sociological factors, Virchow's adherence to the theory of free cell formation as analogous to crystallization had by 1855 given way to a theory of cellular continuity as a continuous historical process; the resulting formation of organs and tissue was comparable to social organization.

The implications of free cell formation and then continuous cell division as tenets of materialism were complex. Certain mechanistic theories of cell formation still relied on distinctive living forces inherent in matter.[47] A recent study of scientific materialism by Gregory suggests that such materialism was the cover for metaphysically-based positions. A variety of conclusions for the political and social realm were derived from scientific principles. Karl Vogt denounced the Christian state in terms of 'social physiology', Ludwig Moleschott used nutritional theory to predict socialism, Heinrich Czolbe scientifically justified monarchism.[48] Similarly the cell state as assimilated into liberal ideology could be subject to diverse interpretations. It was an integral component of the theory of free associations and interest groups. This was known as *Genossenschaftslehre* – as the term was preferred to the foreign sounding *Assoziation*. Liberal politicians like Karl Twesten or Hermann Schulze-Delitzsch, a co-founder of the Progressive Party

---

[46] E. Mendelsohn, 'Revolution and Reduction: the Sociology of Methodological and Philosophical Concerns in Nineteenth Century Biology', in Y. Elkana (ed.), *The Interaction between Science and Philosophy* (Atlantic Highlands, N.J., 1974), pp. 407–26.

[47] For cell theory used in opposition to materialism and Darwinism, see M. J. Schleiden, *Ueber den Materialismus der neueren deutschen Naturwissenschaft, sein Wesen und seine Geschichte* (Leipzig, 1863).

[48] F. Gregory, *Scientific Materialism in Nineteenth Century Germany* (Dordrecht, 1977), pp. 165, 169, 188.

with Virchow, interpreted society as a living organism, personifying the unity of individual efforts.[49]

Virchow illustrates how the cell state as a liberal ideology could be accompanied by increasing defence of professional and institutional interests. He formulated his views on the cell state at a time when he was particularly anxious to rehabilitate himself with the Prussian authorities; he had been an active campaigner for political, medical and social reform in 1848. Virchow did not merely rely on his own intellectual attainments when he wished to obtain the chair of pathology in the Berlin medical faculty, but resorted to plagiarism of the theories of Remak, his academic rival. Remak had emphasized that all animals consisted of nucleated cells, and had observed that every nucleus in the development of the embryo came from the first nucleus of the fertilized cell by continuous division. In 1855 Virchow adopted Remak's theories, without acknowledging the latter's priority. That Remak was a Jew and that Virchow relied on influential connections to the Prussian military establishment, assisted Virchow to gain the chair of pathological anatomy at Berlin in 1856.[50] Virchow was also helped by the army's influence on appointments made at the *Charité*, Berlin's state hospital.

Further insight into the way Virchow related science and politics is provided by his opposition to state interference in academic affairs. In the Prussian assembly Virchow demanded freedom of critical research. He objected to all theories which were speculative. This meant he opposed the legitimacy of theology as a university discipline.[51] He also attacked the materialistic Darwinism of Haeckel, who suggested in 1876 that evolutionary theory should be taught in schools. Virchow considered that in the new Empire there was only room for established scientific facts.[52]

Virchow's concept of the cell state as an aggregate of cellular individuals became increasingly contested, as was the associated

[49] H. Schulze-Delitzsch, *Soziale Rechte und Pflichten* (Berlin, 1866), pp. 244–59.

[50] B. Kisch, 'Forgotten Leaders in Modern Medicine', *Transactions of the American Philosophical Society*, xliv (1954), pp. 279–82. M. Lenz (note 15), ii. pt. 2, pp. 172–82.

[51] N. Andernach, *Der Einfluss der Parteien auf das Hochschulwesen in Preussen. 1848–1918* (Göttingen, 1972), pp. 55–6.

[52] R. Virchow, *Die Freiheit der Wissenschaft im modernen Staat* (Berlin, 1877); E. Haeckel, *Freie Wissenschaft und freie Lehre. Eine Entgegnung auf Rudolf Virchow's Münchener Rede über 'Die Freiheit der Wissenschaft im modernen Staat'* (Stuttgart, 1878).

concept of the cell as the lowest unit of organic life. When Virchow in 1859 defined an organism as 'a society of living cells, a tiny well ordered state', he also emphasized that life was subject to unique laws of organization. He therefore observed that one could only describe the state as an organism insofar as it consisted of living citizens; conversely an organism was a state, society or family in that it consisted of living members of common origin. Just as a political state arose through the co-operative work of its citizens, so the organism arose through the co-operation of cells. But Virchow insisted that social processes were not reducible to the physical laws of atoms.[53]

Virchow's relatively egalitarian theory of the cell state contrasted with Haeckel's more hierarchical views. Haeckel compared cells to law-abiding citizens in an orderly *Kulturstaat* which grew by division of labour. In plants, cells only formed republics but in animals there was a cell monarchy. The organs formed from tissues were like state departments and institutions: rule by central government was comparable to the power of the brain as nerve centre.[54]

This conflict of interpretations of the cell state between Virchow and his former pupil Haeckel, affected the early scientific careers of Hertwig and Waldeyer. Hertwig, as Haeckel's disciple at Jena, had concentrated on invertebrate biology in order to gain insight into the primal forms and mechanisms of life. He had also made considerable use of mechanisms of natural selection, for instance to explain the development of dentine teeth from placoid fish scales or of germinal layers in the embryo. When he moved to Berlin and began to criticize Darwinism, Haeckel commented that Virchow would be delighted. Haeckel ascribed this change of allegiances to the bad Berlin air, the Berlin faculty having a reputation of considerable hostility to Darwinism.[55]

Waldeyer's scientific outlook was especially influenced by another early associate of Virchow, the anatomist and pathologist Jacob Henle.[56] As a liberal patriot, Henle had been unable to

[53] R. Virchow, 'Atome und Individuen', in *Vier Reden über Leben und Kranksein* (Berlin, 1862), p. 55; E. Richter, *Rudolf Virchow als Politiker* (Berlin, 1901).
[54] E. P. A. Haeckel, *Zellseelen und Seelenzellen. Vortrag gehalten am 22. März 1878 in der 'Concordia' zu Wien*, 2nd edn. (Leipzig, 1923), pp. 20–1.
[55] V. Franz (ed.), 'Der Meister und die Meisterschüler, Haeckel und die Hertwigs in ihrem Briefwechsel', in *Ernst Haeckel, sein Leben, Denken und Wirken* (Jena and Leipzig, 1943), i, pp. 50, 53–4.
[56] H. Hoepke (ed.), 'Wilhelm Waldeyer. Briefe an Jacob Henle 1863–1885. Erster Teil (1863–1872)', *Ruperto Carola*, lv (1975), p. 47.

reconcile himself to Prussia's repressive domestic politics in the 1850s. He consequently had refused the chair of anatomy in Berlin in 1858.[57] Henle came to despise Haeckel's Darwinism, as did the anatomist Wilhelm His, another associate of Waldeyer. Rejection of Darwinian speculation did not mean that biology and society were necessarily separate spheres. His, who was noted for application of mechanical principles to embryology, considered that the same mechanical causal forces operated in society.[58]

### HERTWIG, WALDEYER AND CONFLICTS IN ANATOMY

Anatomy as practised by Hertwig and Waldeyer was not only description or topography but also provided a causal analysis of morphology. Histology, embryology and comparative anatomy were therefore particularly favoured as explaining organic form in terms of cellular constituents. Hertwig emphasized the value of social theories of organization as an integral part of evaluating and formulating biological theories.[59] Waldeyer made considerable use of anthropology as in his investigations of the pelvis and placenta. Besides histological investigations of diverse areas of the body such as nerve fibres, auditory organs, the conjunctiva of the eyeball, the larynx and the embryology of the reproductive organs, Waldeyer was to achieve renown for his grasp of theoretical issues, as exemplified by his introduction of the terms 'neurone' and 'chromosome'.[60] Hertwig's scientific reputation was founded on his theory of fertilization as the fusion of two cell nuclei. This discovery provided the basis for his experimental investigations of inheritance and of the early stages of embryological development.[61]

[57] G. Rosen, 'Social Aspects of Jacob Henle's Medical Thought', *Bulletin of the History of Medicine*, v (1937), pp. 509–37; F. Merkel, *Jacob Henle, Ein Deutsches Gelehrten Leben* (Braunschweig, 1871), p. 314.
[58] W. Waldeyer, *Wilhelm His†. Sein Leben und Wirken* (Leipzig, 1904), pp. 7, 13, 23–4.
[59] O. Hertwig, *Die Lehre vom Organismus und ihre Beziehung zur Sozialwissenschaft. Universitätsrede* (Jena, 1899).
[60] Further biographical information may be found in: K. E. Rothschuh, 'Wilhelm von Waldeyer-Hartz', *Westfälische Lebensbilder*, vi (Münster, 1957), pp. 166–75; J. Sobotta, 'Zum Andenken an Wilhelm von Waldeyer-Hartz', *Anatomischer Anzeiger*, lvi (1922), pp. 1–43; R. Bochalli, *Die Berliner medizinische Schule vor 50 Jahren* (Melsangen, 1950), pp. 6–10.
[61] O. Hertwig, 'Dokumente zur Geschichte der Zeugungslehre. Eine historische Studie als Abschluss eigener Forschung', *Archiv für mikroskopische Anatomie*, xc (1918), pt. 2, pp. 30–6.

Hertwig applied the theory of progressive division of labour to explain the laws of cellular growth and differentiation with the formation of organs and tissues. The corollary of this was provided by Herbert Spencer's theory of organic integration: that the more an organism was differentiated, the higher was the level of correlation and co-adaptation.[62] Waldeyer adopted a similar explanatory structure. He described how in cell colonies increasing division of labour occurred, as in animal and human societies. The functional value of each resulting organ was comparable to diverse professional groupings.[63]

It was only after they had been in Berlin for some years that Hertwig and Waldeyer came to emphasize the regulative powers of the totality of the organism. Previously they were allied with opposed factions of anatomists. Waldeyer had primarily stressed the importance of explaining anatomical form in terms of physiological processes. This was directly applicable to human anatomy and, arguably, to clinical medicine. Hertwig's emphasis on comparative morphology and the importance of invertebrates to understanding the early stages of embryological development laid Darwinists open to the charge that their research lacked relevance to clinical medicine. Waldeyer opposed the candidature of Hertwig for the chair of anatomy at Jena in 1880 because of Hertwig's lack of experience of human anatomy.[64] Waldeyer complained to Henle that the Jena faculty should not have allowed itself to be so tyrannized by Haeckel, and that if more of such appointments were made, this would undermine the relevance of anatomy to clinical medicine.[65]

These competing academic factions were anxious to cultivate good relations with state administrations responsible for making appointments. Just as Haeckel was able to secure the appointment of Hertwig as *Privatdozent* and *Ordinarius* at Jena, so Henle consistently supported Waldeyer. Not only was Henle's recommendation often decisive at Göttingen where he occupied the chair

[62] O. Hertwig (note 45), pp. 139–78.
[63] W. Waldeyer, 'Befruchtung und Vererbung, Vortrag auf der Braunschweiger Naturforscher-Versammlung', *Verhandlungen der Naturforscher-Versammlung zur Braunschweig*, 3 vols. (Leipzig, 1898), i, p. 79.
[64] G. Uschmann, *Zur Geschichte der Zoologie und der zoologischen Anstalten in Jena 1779–1919* (Jena, 1959), p. 98.
[65] H. Hoepke (ed.), 'Wilhelm Waldeyer. Briefe an Jakob Henle 1863–1885. Zweiter Teil (1872–1880)', *Ruperto Carola*, lvi (1975), p. 176.

of anatomy, his opinions were sought by Althoff for appointments throughout Prussia.[66]

Jena provides an interesting example of how a small university, which was the responsibility of four minor duchies, could achieve the reputation of a citadel of Darwinism in the 1860s. This was due to the liberal policies of the state curator, Moritz Seebeck, who saw his office as the representative of professorial interests to the state. Haeckel counted Seebeck as one of his closest friends. Haeckel's extensive use of Goethe's term *Morphologie* had overtones of being a compliment to the tradition of patronage of national culture by the Dukes of Saxe-Weimar-Eisenach.[67]

Hertwig's father was the prosperous owner of a cigar factory and was thus able to subsidize the early stages of the academic careers of his sons.[68] Waldeyer did not have independent means and had to begin his academic career in the newer 'fringe' disciplines of physiology and pathological anatomy. He was initially assistant in the physiology department at Königsberg and then pathological anatomist at Breslau. At both universities he crossed swords with representatives of the old school of descriptive anatomists. On Henle's recommendation he was appointed professor of anatomy in 1871 at Strassburg, where another liberal administrator von Roggenbach was determined to erect this new imperial university into a bastion of German culture. Innovative research was to be combined with the sense of mission to germanify Alsace. Althoff himself also came from the ranks of the professors at Strassburg.[69]

Since Hertwig and Waldeyer both held duplicate chairs of anatomy at Berlin, it is possible to assess the degree to which the state required uniformity with regard to theoretical issues like Darwinism or to broader issues of politics and religion. Although when appointed Hertwig and Waldeyer held conflicting views on the cellular mechanisms of inheritance, the state hoped each in his

---

[66] F. Merkel, *Jacob Henle* (note 57), p. 314; W. von Waldeyer-Hartz, *Lebenserinnerungen* (Bonn, 1920), p. 68.

[67] M. Steinmetz (ed.), *Geschichte der Universität Jena*, 2 vols. (Jena, 1958–61), i, pp. 387, 449, 465; G. Uschmann, *Ernst Haeckel – Forscher, Künstler, Mensch* (Jena, 1954), pp. 52, 58, 62–3, 78.

[68] R. Weissenberg, *Oscar Hertwig 1849–1922. Leben und Werk eines deutschen Biologen* (Leipzig, 1959).

[69] J. Sobotta, 'Zum Andenken an Wilhelm von Waldeyer-Hartz', *Anatomischer Anzeiger*, lvi (1923), pp. 7–8; J. E. Craig, *A Mission for German Learning: the University of Strassburg and Alsatian Society 1870–1918*, (Stanford University, Dissertation, 1973).

way would bring to Berlin prestige as a teacher and researcher. Althoff made the personal acquaintance of both anatomists, who were conventionally patriotic and (like Althoff) undogmatic in their religious beliefs. That Hertwig and Waldeyer scientifically disagreed suggests that during Althoff's era the Prussian state accepted diverse theoretical approaches as long as these were rigorously grounded on systematic observation and experiment. Similarly Althoff furthered the career of Wilhelm Roux, whose mechanistic and Darwinist conclusions from embryological experiments clashed with Hertwig's emphasis on regulative organization.[70]

In the case of anatomy at Berlin, the state's efforts to establish a prestigious new chair (as the present incumbent Reichert was increasingly senile) was the occasion for a power struggle between competing academic interests. The tangled sequence of negotiations shows the effect of outside opinion on the state's decision-making processes. The appointment of Waldeyer in 1883 was due to the influence of former Strassburg colleagues in Berlin. On the faculty these were Leyden and Gusserow, and in the state Althoff's preference for the more energetic Waldeyer rather than the more eminent Kölliker was decisive.[71]

Waldeyer diplomatically agreed to the separation of human and comparative anatomy, so that Reichert could continue to be responsible for the latter until his death in December 1883. Althoff's task of filling the second chair proved to be a difficult job of reconciliation of the conflicting demands made by anatomists in other universities, of Waldeyer and the medical faculty concerned to maintain their independence, of numbers of medical students rising from 653 in the summer semester of 1882 to 1142 by 1886, and finally of the need to give the new professor adequate responsibilities and facilities so as to attract a talent of the highest order.

In 1884 Althoff received lengthy memoranda on the condition of anatomy at Berlin from Henle (the so-called Nestor of German anatomy), from Henle's son-in-law Merkel (professor of anatomy at Königsberg) and from Budge (professor of anatomy and physi-

[70] C.-E. Kretschmann, *Friedrich Althoffs Nachlass als Quelle für die Geschichte der Medizinischen Fakultät in Halle von 1882–1902*, (Halle-Wittenberg, Medizinische Dissertation, 1959), pp. 29–61.
[71] J. Sobotta, 'Zum Andenken an Wilhelm von Waldeyer-Hartz', *Anatomischer Anzeiger*, lvi (1923), p. 15.

ology at Greifswald. While emphasizing the importance of the physiological rather than the comparative approach to anatomy, they insisted on maintaining the unity of anatomy as the fundamental medical science. Although they recognized the need for a second chair, they argued against treating embryology and comparative anatomy as independent specialities or separating general and microscopic anatomy. Althoff's reaction was that since it was inadequate to separate only comparative anatomy, both embryology and histology should be added to the responsibilities of the new chair. Waldeyer, however, declined to give up histology at Althoff's request, although he relinquished embryology.[72]

Then began a struggle with the medical faculty. The faculty failed to comply with the ministry's request to propose three candidates for the new chair and informed the minister that the philosophical faculty would be more suitable for comparative anatomy. The situation was indeed complicated by there being expert microscopists in the philosophical faculty: these were F. E. Schulze, the professor of zoology and Schwendener, the plant anatomist. The medical faculty contested that as long as comparative anatomy had dealt with vertebrates closely related to man, the subject had been of value to medicine. But since the advent of evolutionary theory there had been increasing preoccupation with invertebrates, which had no medical relevance. Although Hertwig and Althoff were already discussing plans for a new institute in July 1887, the faculty was not informed. In January 1888 the faculty protested that the minister had caused it pain by departing from the established procedure of receiving suggestions for candidates. But the faculty had initially refused to propose candidates, it had delayed the appointment for four years, and it attempted to exclude an additional member by arguing that a science had advanced beyond the bounds of relevance: these tactics reveal the faculty as defiant, obstructive and vigorously independent.[73]

Waldeyer also disappointed Althoff by supporting the medical

[72] ZSTA Merseburg, Rep. 92, Althoff A I Nr 108 Bl. 22–31 (Merkel), Bl. 3–21 and 33–5 (Henle), Bl. 36–157 (Budge, 'Denkschrift über Fürsorge und Förderung der anatomischen Wissenschaft'); ZSTA Merseburg, Rep. 76 Va Sekt. 2 Tit. IV Nr 46 Bd 10, Bl. 16–22, dean (Du Bois-Reymond) and professors to the minister, 27 November 1886; ZSTA Merseburg, Rep. 76 Va Sekt. 2 Tit. X Nr 10 Bd. 9 Bl. 67, Waldeyer to Althoff, 22 November 1886.
[73] ZSTA Merseburg, Rep. 76 Va Sekt. 2 Tit. IV Nr 46 Bd 10 Bl. 179, dean to minister, 9 March 1887; ZSTA Merseburg, Rep. 92 Althoff. B Nr 68 Bd 2, Bl 82–3, Richard Hertwig to Althoff, 15 January 1885.

faculty and campaigning against Hertwig. Although Althoff had already contemplated the appointment of Hertwig in 1885, Waldeyer initially hoped that Gegenbaur, who had recently censured Haeckel's Darwinism, or van Beneden, a noted critic of Hertwig, could be won for the Berlin chair. Waldeyer, fearing a rival at close quarters, insisted on two completely independent anatomical institutes.[74] These tortuous negotiations show how Darwinism and its implications for embryology had significant repercussions for the institutionalization and division of scientific labour.

Hertwig was one of many professors appointed by Althoff, despite the opposition of a faculty. As Ringer comments: 'Of 1355 men appointed to German faculties of theology, law, and medicine between 1817 and 1900, no less than 322 were placed against or without faculties' recommendations'.[75] In Hertwig's case, the state compromised in that the title of his chair should remain that of general anatomy.[76] Brow-beating of the faculties by the state authorities could ultimately benefit academic disciplines. This increased academic competitiveness and furthered theoretical controversy. Althoff's decision-making frequently took account of a consensus of professorial opinions from other universities, enabling him to raise standards in a discipline.

Althoff's emphasis on an experimental approach also meant that Hertwig received one of eleven palatial new institutes for medical sciences at Berlin.[77] Such institutes were often the outcome of the state's concern either with academic standards or with broader considerations of state policy. The public museums of the institutes for hygiene and marine studies reflected the latter priorities. Reorganization of the university's anatomical collection in the 1880s resulted in the transfer of most specimens to a new public museum for natural history.

In Hertwig's case, the ministry supported the development of his institute into a specialized establishment for embryology and

[74] H. Hoepke (ed.), 'Wilhelm Waldeyer, Briefe an Jakob Henle 1863–1885, Dritter Teil (1881–1885)', *Ruperto Carola*, lvii (1976), p. 48; ZSTA Merseburg, Rep. 76 Va Sekt. 2 Tit. IV Nr 46 Bd 10 Bl. 23–4, Althoff to minister, 9 March 1887; ZSTA Merseburg, Rep. 92 Althoff B Nr 68 Bl. 3–4, O. Hertwig to Althoff, 4 August and 24 October, 1887.
[75] F. K. Ringer (note 32), p. 37.
[76] ZSTA Merseburg, Rep. 76 Va Sekt. 2 Tit. X Nr 131 Bd 1 Bl. 5, also *ibid.* Bd. 2 Bl. 212–4.
[77] O. Hertwig, 'Das anatomisch-biologische Institut', in M. Lenz, *Geschichte der Königlichen Friedrich-Wilhelms-Universität zu Berlin*, 4 vols. (Halle, 1910–18), iii, pp. 141–54.

microscopical anatomy (i.e., histology).[78] But Hertwig came to be
at loggerheads with the state complaining that the inadequate
budget for his institute restricted his activities. Both Hertwig and
Waldeyer repeatedly petitioned regarding their lack of assistants
and equipment. Waldeyer's grant was fixed at an estimate which
did not take account of mounting numbers of students. Hertwig
complained that he had to leave rooms unheated and had to
borrow equipment when histology acquired increased importance
in state medical examinations. Although, while Althoff was in office,
the state's budget for universities more than doubled, new institutes
and higher scientific standards as well as the overall rise in student
numbers meant additional burdens were imposed on the medical
faculty. Professors continued to feel that their facilities were
inadequate. Consequently there was antipathy to securing places
for research students. Despite Waldeyer's boast of having taught
over 20,000 students, he only allowed one of his doctoral students
to be habilitated at Berlin.[79]

Consideration of anatomy confirms that, as suggested more
generally with regard for the medical faculty, academics were not
subservient to the state. Not only were they able to manipulate
decision-making processes, but over many important questions
there were unresolved differences. There was no uniformity among
academics over key theoretical issues like Darwinism. Theories of
embryological development and inheritance were much contested
by diverse academic factions. These debates had, as has been
shown, important implications for academic appointments. It is,
however, necessary to investigate further scientific issues especially
those relating to cell theory, in order to assess the extent to which
social ideals and expectations influenced the formulation of scientific theories.

THE BIOLOGY OF THE CELL STATE

The growth of cell biology in nineteenth-century Germany must be
considered in relation to a broad range of factors. Among these
were, in addition to systematic observation and experiment, in-

---

[78] ZSTA Merseburg, Rep. 76 Va Sekt. 2 Tit. X Nr 131 Bd 2 Bl. 212–5, 227–34.
[79] J. Sobotta, 'Zum Andenken an Wilhelm von Waldeyer-Hartz', *Anatomischer Anzeiger*, lvi (1923), pp. 18–19. ZSTA Merseburg, Rep. 76 Va Sekt. 2 Tit. X Nr 131 Bd 1, Bl. 53, 112, 143, 175, 223 and *ibid*. Bd 2 Bl. 112, 130, 132. For examples of refusals for requests for funds F. K. Ringer (note 32), p. 51; W. von Waldeyer-Hartz (note 66), pp. 201–9.

tellectual stimuli such as the drive to locate the fundamental forms and processes of life; institutional factors as the expansion of university research facilities; social priorities as the hope that bacteriology would provide a panacea to the spread of disease; and technical factors such as the availability of aniline dyes for use in histological staining and the rise of the precision optical industry encouraged both by the state and certain enterprising university professors like Abbe who directed the Zeiss optical works at Jena. There was, consequently, increasing concern not only with the components of the cell like the chromosomes, but also with the interaction of cells as key elements in the structure and functioning of the body.

Subsequent commentators have tended to oversimplify scientific developments seeing a smooth transition from Darwinism as formulated in cellular terms by Weismann to the rediscovery of the Mendelian ratios. But not only had Darwinism been opposed by many innovative cell biologists and embryologists, like von Baer, Kölliker or Nägeli, many Mendelians were also hostile to Darwinism. Cytological investigations undertaken in Imperial Germany cannot be interpreted merely as a preliminary to Mendelian genetics. Many cell biologists like Waldeyer were indifferent or non-committal to Mendelism, while Hertwig was more interested in demonstrating environmental affects on embryological growth.[80]

Concern with organic regulation and environmental factors meant that social theories were perceived as particularly relevant. E. B. Wilson, the distinguished American cell biologist commented that the cell state 'offered a simple and natural point of attack for the problems of cytology and revolutionized the problems of organic individuality'.[81] The importance of social concepts was reflected in such cytological terms as 'cell territories', 'colonies', 'cultures', 'migration', and 'division of labour'. Contemporary debates raged over the legitimacy of the concept of the cell state, for instance between the anatomist Martin Heidenhain and the pathologist Ludwig Aschoff.[82] The following section examines the

---

[80] For Hertwig's qualified approval of Mendelism, see O. Hertwig (note 45), pp. 348–53.

[81] E. B. Wilson, *The Cell in Development and Heredity*, 3rd edn. (New York, 1925), p. 102.

[82] M. Heidenhain, *Plasma und Zelle*, 2 vols. (Jena, 1907–11), i, pp. 12–87; L. E. Aschoff, *Hundert Jahre Zellforschung* (Berlin, 1938), pp. 191–9.

importance of institutional and social concerns in the research of Hertwig and Waldeyer at Berlin.

The cytological investigations undertaken by Hertwig and Waldeyer resulted in different interpretations of inheritance. Not only was inheritance basically a legal term – as Hertwig pointed out, but differing interpretations also illustrate the institutional implications of theoretical controversies, as well as divergent attitudes to social issues such as women's demands for social equality.

Academic rivalries were apparent in differing theories of fertilization. Waldeyer submitted a review of these theories to the *Kultusministerium* in 1887 with the comment that it should be taken as an expression of his opinion of the candidates for the second chair of anatomy in Berlin. This review strongly criticized Hertwig's theory of a 'fusion' of male and female elements, in favour of the 'replacement' theory of the Belgian embryologist, Eduard van Beneden.[83] The latter theory of fertilization meant the replacement of ejected male nuclear elements in the egg by those from the sperm, which had earlier expelled female material as polar bodies. Hertwig disagreed with van Beneden's view of the egg and sperm as half nuclei produced from the hermaphroditic nuclei of the parent cell.

In what was a highly technical debate involving the first use of Zeiss apochromatic lenses, complex double staining and preparative techniques in order to follow the processes of formation of the sexual cells and the behaviour of their nuclear components during fertilization, this institutional background has been overlooked. In the discussion over the implications for heredity as to how the cell nucleus divided, were disagreements which had implications stretching beyond purely scientific issues. In 1888 Waldeyer supplanted Hertwig's term of *Kernsegmente* (for the nuclear threads visible during cell division) with the new name of 'chromosomes'. This was partly derived from van Beneden's term *amas chromatiques*.[84] Waldeyer also initiated research on the parasitic roundworm *Ascaris* by a researcher at his institute in support of van Beneden's theories.[85] When Hertwig gained his chair, the first

[83] ZSTA Merseburg, Rep. 92 Althoff B Nr 192 Bd 1 Bl. 82, Waldeyer to Althoff, 11 November 1887; W. Waldeyer, *Ueber die Karyokinese und ihre Bedeutung für die Vererbung. Vortrag gehalten im Verein für innere Medizin in Berlin* (Berlin, 1887).
[84] W. Waldeyer, 'Karyokinesis and its Relation to the Process of Fertilization', *Quarterly Journal of Microscopical Science*, xxx (1889), pp. 159–214.
[85] N. Kultschitzky, 'Die Befruchtungsvorgänge bei *Ascaris megalocephala*', *Archiv für mikroskopische Anatomie*, xxxi (1888), pp. 567–92.

project he undertook was to vindicate his own interpretation. He undertook a refutation of van Beneden's theories in a classic paper on gamete formation and maturation division in *Ascaris*. He aggressively entitled this 'A Basis for Cellular Controversies' as he was determined to extend cellular laws to the mechanisms of heredity.[86]

Although Hertwig was to establish cordial relations with Waldeyer, substantial differences remained between them about inheritance and social questions. Waldeyer supported a cellular interpretation of Weismann's neo-Darwinian theory of a hereditary germplasm: that the germinal substance was a monopoly of distinctive germinal cells.[87] The implications of this were determinist and selectionist, and could be used to legitimate social divisions on the basis of biological inequalities. In contrast, Hertwig emphasized, by invoking social comparisons of equal civic rights, that all cells were potentially reproductive cells, despite functional differentiation due to physiological division of labour.[88]

These different interpretations of heredity resulted in conflicting opinions on nature of male and female in general and in particular on the biology of sexual dimorphism. Waldeyer pointed to differences in the development of male and female reproductive cells: whereas the egg cell had a greater quantity of protoplasm, the spermocyte had more nuclein.[89] Despite the contrasting forms of the sperm and egg cells, Hertwig insisted that they contained equivalent amounts of the hereditary substance: egg and sperm preserved the same mass of chromatin and an equal number of chromosomes. The difference between male and female forms was due to the necessity of contriving that two fundamentally equal cell nuclei fuse, in order to initiate a new cycle of cell division. It was due to this that the sperm was particularly motile. Sexual differentiation was for Hertwig the effect rather than the cause of fertilization, as there was an equal contribution of male and female to heredity.

[86] O. Hertwig, 'Vergleich der Ei- und Samenbildung bei Nematoden. Eine Grundlage für celluläre Streitfragen', *Archiv für mikroskopische Anatomie*, xxxvi (1890), pp. 1–138.
[87] W. Waldeyer, 'Die Geschlechtszellen', in O. Hertwig (ed.), *Handbuch der vergleichende und experimentelle Entwicklungsgeschichte der Wirbeltiere*, 3 vols. (Jena, 1906), i, pp. 404–5 (first appeared in 1903).
[88] O. Hertwig, *The Cell. Outlines of General Anatomy and Physiology*, (translated M. Campbell, ed. H. J. Campbell) (London, 1895), pp. 291, 313, 345–6.
[89] W. Waldeyer (note 87), pp. 411–15.

The scientific differences between Hertwig and Waldeyer on heredity were reflected in their divergent opinions on the admission of women as students. The Berlin medical faculty was particularly opposed to women studying medicine, having argued that exposure to human bodies would harm the female character. The faculty voted unanimously against women students in 1892 and when in 1896 the state permitted women to sit in on lectures, eight professors refused to admit them.[90] Waldeyer was an outspoken opponent, whereas Hertwig when rector of the university in 1905 supported the views of a more enlightened minority in favour of the admission of women.[91] Waldeyer used anthropological evidence that the size of women's brains was smaller; therefore they had fewer nerve cells and thus less capacity for learning. He considered men and women were fundamentally unequal, women being more suited to family life.[92]

Theories of heredity also influenced opinions on university extension classes. These had been opposed by a majority of professors on the university's senate as beyond the official function of the university.[93] But an active minority of professors organized an association to provide such classes. Waldeyer supported these, considering that as heredity was predetermined, there could be intellectual genius in all classes of society.[94] Hertwig recognized that while people were born with unequal physical and mental potentials, historical and geographical conditions also affected intelligence. Public lectures were thus a means for certain pro-

[90] Universitätsarchiv der Humboldt-Universität zu Berlin Medizinische Fakultät Nr. 101, Frauenstudium, Bl. 2; A. Blumenthal, 'Diskussionen um das medizinische Frauenstudium in Berlin', (West-) Berlin Phil. Diss. 1965); A. Kirchhoff, *Die akademische Frau. Gutachten hervorragender Universitätsprofessoren, Frauenlehrer, und Schriftsteller über die Befähigung der Frau zum wissenschaftlichen Universitätsstudium und Berufe* (Berlin, 1897); D. Tutzke, *Alfred Grotjahn* (Leipzig, 1979), p. 27.
[91] O. Hertwig, *Das Bildungsbedürfnis und seine Befriedigung durch deutsche Universitäten. Rede zur Gedächtnisfeier des Stifters der Berliner Universität König Friedrich Wilhelm III in der Aula derselben am 3. August 1905* (Jena, 1905), pp. 9–12.
[92] W. Waldeyer, *Ueber die somatischen Unterschieden der beiden Geschlechter* (Leipzig, 1895), pp. 27–8; idem, 'Das Studium der Medizin und die Frauen', *Verhandlungen der Gesellschaft deutscher Naturforscher und Aerzte*, (Köln, 1888), pp. 31–44; idem, *Lebenserinnerungen* (Bonn, 1920), pp. 196–200. See also Table 4 below.
[93] H. Siemering, *Arbeiterbildungswesen in Wien und Berlin* (Karlsruhe, 1911), pp. 70–2.
[94] W. Waldeyer, 'Festrede', *Sitzungsberichte der Preussischen Akademie der Wissenschaften* (1905), pp. 114–15.

fessors to fulfill their sense of responsibility to the rest of the social organism.[95]

Controversies over inheritance demonstrate that embryology and reproductive physiology were considered critical areas for the legitimatizing of social systems. Hertwig made a substantial contribution to the debate between Herbert Spencer and August Weismann regarding polymorphism in state forming insects. Weismann had attributed functional differentiation of each caste to selection from different sets of determinants in the germplasm. Spencer rejected this, and formulated the cause in environmental terms of nutrition during the larval period. During this controversy of 1893–4, Hertwig wrote a critique of Weismann's principle of the all-sufficiency of natural selection.[96] Hertwig related his embryological investigations to the researches of Grassi and Emery on the regulation of numbers of workers and soldiers, and the development of different parts of insects to the quantity of nutrition. These findings were compared to experiments in embryology, where the fertilizing sperms or eggs had been immersed in saline solutions, with the result that malformations occurred in the resultant embryo. Hertwig demonstrated that in the embryos subjected to abnormal environmental conditions, different cell material was used in the formation of organs. He concluded that the use of cell material depended not on inherited localized determinants, but on the actual process of development in relation to external circumstances.[97]

Experiments on the effects of chemical stimuli on embryonic development, led Hertwig to warn against unhealthy habits and environmental conditions. He inveighed against alcoholism which he regarded as having dire consequences during the early stages of pregnancy.[98] He suggested that certain human malformations like spina bifida and anencephalic conditions could be due to adverse environmental conditions.[99] He subsequently gave experimental proof that radium could bring about hereditary defects. This

[95] O. Hertwig (note 91), pp. 12–25.
[96] D. Duncan, *The Life and Letters of Herbert Spencer* (London, 1911), pp. 343–9.
[97] O. Hertwig, *Zeit- und Streitfragen der Biologie. Heft 1: Präformation oder Epigenese? Grundzüge einer Entwicklungstheorie der Organismen* (Jena, 1894), pp. 124–6.
[98] *Ibid.*, pp. 133–4.
[99] O. Hertwig, 'Die Entwicklung des Froscheies unter dem Einfluss schwächerer und stärkerer Kochsalzlösungen', *Archiv für mikroskopische Anatomie*, xlv (1895), pp. 324–6.

discovery contributed to his views concerning the genetic hazards resulting from unhealthy working conditions, as shown in the case of lead workers' children.[100] Such evidence refuted Social Darwinist opposition to reforms improving the social environment. Hertwig also used the analogy of the cell as worker in the body against Darwinist theories of germinal selection. He argued that an organism like society functioned with the co-operation of groups.[101] Such comparisons were made by many other colleagues of Hertwig. For example, the pathologist Lubarsch believed that disease was due to a refusal of the cellular proletariat to participate in the *Gesammtarbeit* of the body.[102]

Similar competitive rivalries as in controversies over research resulted from disputes over the demarcation of responsibilities for the teaching of students, or resentment of new clinical specialities as depriving those in established positions of 'material' (i.e., patients).[103] Hertwig as a teacher of histology was in competition with both Waldeyer and Gustav Fritsch. Until 1905 Fritsch headed a department for histology in the physiological institute. Hertwig's irritation with Fritsch as a rival was expressed in a complaint to the minister in 1905 that no teaching should be allowed in histology other than by those from the anatomical institutes.[104] Fritsch's university lectures on Darwinism and race would also have been uncongenial to Hertwig.

Waldeyer, like Hertwig, was concerned with how the diverse parts of an organism were integrated. His hierarchical view of the constitution of an organism can be illustrated by the conceptual innovation marked by the introduction of the term 'neurone' in 1891 to describe the cellular unit of the nervous system.[105] In contrast, Virchow had supported the rights of the 'third estate' of

[100] O. Hertwig, 'Die Radiumkrankheit tierischer Keimzellen. Ein Beitrag zur experimentellen Zeugungs- und Vererbungslehre', *Archiv für mikroskopische Anatomie*, lxxvii (1911), Part 2, pp. 1–95, 97–164; idem, 'Keimesschädigung durch chemische Eingriffe', *Sitzber. Kgl. Preuss. Akad.* (1913), pp. 579–82.

[101] O. Hertwig, *Zur Abwehr des ethischen, des sozialen, des politischen Darwinismus* (Jena, 1918), pp. 68–97.

[102] O. Lubarsch, *Ein bewegtes Gelehrtenleben. Erinnerungen und Erlebnisse, Kämpfe und Gedanken* (Berlin, 1931), p. 591.

[103] For these matters at Heidelberg, see R. Riese, *Die Hochschule auf dem Wege zum wissenschaftlichen Grossbetrieb* (Stuttgart, 1977), pp. 112–34.

[104] ZSTA Merseburg, Rep. 76 Va Sekt. 2 Tit. IV Nr 46 Bd 18 Bl. 58, also *ibid.* Bd 21 Bl. 124.

[105] W. Waldeyer, 'Ueber einige neuere Forschungen im Gebiete der Anatomie des Centralnervensystems', *Deutsche medizinische Wochenschrift*, xvii (1891), pp. 1213–19, 1244–6, 1267–9, 1287–9, 1331–2, 1350–6.

cellular elements when he criticized neural pathology as over-emphasizing the 'aristocratic' nature of the nervous system.[106] Waldeyer correlated a variety of new embryological discoveries to conclude that the nervous system was itself cellular in nature rather than a net-like structure of fibres. The cell was the fundamental psychological unit, the 'Denkorgan'. Each neurone consisted of a ganglion cell, protoplasmic processes or dendrites and the axis-cylinder process. The term 'neurone' thus defined what was a higher type of organic unit functioning as the basic component of the integrative and controlling system of the body. These neurones were distinctive units since histologically they were not in contact but only adjacent and contiguous.

The Bonn physiologist Max Verworn explicitly interpreted Waldeyer's neurone theory in terms of the theory of the cell state: that the centralized supervision of the nervous system over the organism enabled far-reaching differentiation and the development of new powers. Verworn recommended that sociologists should study constitutions of different types of cell states: current ideas about social reform would then have to be reappraised. Hertwig attributed hierarchical superiority to the ganglion, which he compared to Nietzsche's *Uebermensch*.[107]

Waldeyer's favouring of an aristocracy of the intellect was also apparent in his investigations of cranial anatomy. He described dissections of the brains, the craniometrical measurements and the facial features of national figures like Schiller or Frederick the Great in order to isolate unique characteristics.[108] Waldeyer's anatomical institute had a particularly extensive collection of racial skulls, and he also conducted comparative investigations of the skulls and brains of primates. As an influential member of the Berlin and German Anthropological Societies, Waldeyer's views

[106] G. Rath, 'Der Kampf zwischen Zellularpathologie und Neuralpathologie im neunzehnten Jahrhundert', *Deutsche medizinische Wochenschrift*, lxxxii (1957), pp. 740–3.
[107] M. Verworn, *General Physiology. An Outline of the Science of Life*, translated F. S. Lee, (London, 1899), pp. 580–5; idem, *Biologische Richtlinien der staatlichen Organisation. Naturwissenschaftliche Anregungen für die politische Neurorientierung Deutschlands* (Bonn, 1917), p. 9.
[108] W. Waldeyer, 'Der Schädel Schillers. Bericht über die Mitteilung A. v. Frorieps auf der Anatomen-Versammlung in München 22. April 1912', *Deutsche medizinische Wochenschrift*, xxxviii (1912), pp. 1199–2000. idem, *Die Bildnisse Friedrichs des Grossen und seine äussere Erscheinung. Rede gehalten in der Festsitzung der Königlich Preussischen Akademie der Wissenschaften am 25 Januar 1900* (Berlin, 1900), pp. 19–33.

had considerable authority. He particularly wished to see a change of emphasis from craniometrical measurements, an area which Virchow had pioneered, to cerebral anatomy, which he considered merited a special institute. Indeed he supported research into the biological and psychological bases of social morality.[109] Waldeyer's use of science to legitimate thinly veiled prejudices was shown by his opinion of the limited cerebral capacity of women. But his anthropology was nonetheless scientifically far more sophisticated than popular *völkisch* racism and vulgar Social Darwinism. He concluded that a brain of a habitual murderer, dissected to verify Lombroso's criminological theories, was anatomically normal.[110] Waldeyer dismissed Gobineau's studies of racial inequality as worthless. When the Social Darwinist Ludwig Woltmann requested financial support from the Academy of Sciences, Waldeyer said that while he was in favour of a combination of ethnology and anthropology applied in historical research, Woltmann's racist conclusions regarding the determination of physical qualities were not valid.[111] In a popular lecture during the war, Waldeyer gave anthropological descriptions of the enemy races opposing Germany.[112] This criticized Anglo-Saxon aggression, but Waldeyer's acknowledgement that Germany's opponents had equivalent physical and mental racial qualities shows that he maintained a degree of scientific objectivity. Many commentators have overexaggerated the extent of naive racist chauvinism prevailing in German anthropology. Virchow's influential craniometrical surveys of school children disproved Aryan racial stereotypes. Virchow had particularly set the tone for non-Darwinian theories of variation, by arguing that all evolutionary changes were pathological.[113] German states were very cautious in

[109] W. Waldeyer, 'Ueber anthropologische Untersuchung des Gehirns und über Gehirnsammlungen', *Correspondenzblatt der deutschen anthropologischen Gesellschaft*, xviii (1887), p. 159.
[110] W. Waldeyer 'Das Gehirn des Mörders Bobbe', *Correspondenzblatt der deutschen anthropologischen Gesellschaft*, xxxiii (1901), pp. 140–1.
[111] L. Stern (ed.), *Die Berliner Akademie der Wissenschaften in der Zeit des Imperialismus.* 2 vols. (Berlin, 1975), i. pp. 90–1.
[112] W. Waldeyer, 'Die im Weltkriege stehenden Völker in anthropologischer Betrachtung', *Deutsche Reden in schwerer Zeit*, xxxii (Berlin, 1915).
[113] F. B. Churchill, 'Rudolf Virchow and the Pathologist's Criteria for the Inheritance of Acquired Characters', *Journal of the History of Medicine and Allied Sciences*, xxxi (1976), pp. 117–48; R. Virchow, 'Eröffnungsrede', *Correspondenzblatt der deutschen anthropologischen Gesellschaft*, xxv (1894), pp. 80–7; C. Posner, 'Rudolf Virchow und das Vererbungsproblem', *Archiv für Frauenkunde und Konstitutionsforschung*, viii (1922), pp. 14–23.

their support of anthropology, the only chairs established by 1910 being at Berlin and Munich.[114]

## THE STATE AS AN ORGANISM

Insight into the motivations behind the use of social concepts in anatomy is provided by Hertwig's and Waldeyer's views on the state as an organism. As university professors they felt it was their responsibility to be leaders of public opinion. But unlike Virchow, neither Hertwig, Waldeyer nor indeed most of the Berlin medical professors were active in party politics. Academic outsiders were politically more active like the dermatologist Oskar Lassar, who was chairman of the National Liberal Party in Berlin. Interestingly it was the faculty members rather than Althoff, who failed to recommend Lassar for the chair of dermatology.[115] Even a committed member of the nationalist Pan-German League like the pathologist Lubarsch considered party politics as secondary to social and nationalist aims. Lubarsch illustrates the complexity involved in any categorization of political affiliations: for elections to the *Reichstag* he voted National Liberal or Conservative, but he never apparently voted Conservative for the Prussian *Landtag*.[116] The professorial pronouncements of Hertwig and Waldeyer were similarly critical of the divisiveness of party politics. Science reinforced their calls for national unity, especially with regard to establishing Germany as a world power.

Waldeyer used his authority as a Secretary of the Academy of Sciences to call for internal political unity.[117] During the colonial crisis of 1909, he expressed his opinion on the relationship between science and patriotism:

Should the Academy not limit itself to the field of science?

---

[114] The first *Ordinarius* for anthropology in Berlin was Fritz von Luschan appointed in 1909 (P. doz. 1889, Ao. 1899). Besides G. Fritsch appointed in 1872 and F. Boas in 1886, there were two other *Privatdozenten*, Hans Friedenthal and Paul Bartels with affiliations to anatomy and physiology respectively. S. Westphal-Hellbusch, 'Hundert Jahre Ethnologie in Berlin, unter besonderer Berücksichtigung ihrer Entwicklung an der Universität', in H. Pohle and G. Mahr (eds.), *Hundert Jahre Berliner Gesellschaft für Anthropologie, Ethnologie und Urgeschichte 1869–1969*, 2 vols. ((West-) Berlin, 1969–70), i. pp. 157–83.

[115] M. Stürzbecher and G. Wagner, *Die Vorgeschichte der Berufung von Edmund Lesser an die Charité* (Kiel, 1962), p. 32.

[116] O. Lubarsch, *Ein bewegtes Gelehrtenleben* (Berlin, 1931), p. 535.

[117] L. Stern (ed.), *Die Berliner Akademie der Wissenschaften in der Zeit des Imperialismus*. 2 vols. (Berlin, 1975), i, pp. 80–5, 99–101, 126, 174–7, 190, 228.

Certainly. But we are also members of the fatherland, which the Academy serves like all other institutions. Everything in the state is like an organism, living and inter-related; so that the state can remain healthy the Academy should not separate science and politics. In 1918 Waldeyer expressed opposition to party politics, by making comparisons to a view of an organism as resolving conflicting forces. Waldeyer's ceremonial speeches also demanded expansion of the Academy's resources, this being a national necessity since culture was the life blood of the nation, and vital also internationally for retention of Germany's pre-eminence in international scientific circles. Hertwig was also of the opinion that Germany had to make up for its lack of colonies by cultural achievement.[118]

Hertwig and Waldeyer had both publicly supported naval expansion at the turn of the century. This was an issue on which the middle class felt strongly in favour; the navy was seen as providing an alternative to the army dominated by the landowning aristocracy. Six other Berlin professors of medicine participated in this campaign as well as such noted zoologists of other universities as Eimer, Haeckel, Richard Hertwig, Kölliker, Weismann and Ziegler. They supported an association which would promote objective and scientific arguments for the navy.[119] That this association was founded in 1899 in reaction to the officially sponsored Navy League, suggests that nationalist feeling among professors was in many respects autonomous of the state.[120]

Hertwig and Waldeyer pronounced that the 1914–18 war was only justified as a war of defence.[121] They both opposed Pan-Germanist Social Darwinism, which proclaimed the inevitability of the war as a racial struggle. A substantial number among the

[118] *Ibid.*, pp. 83–4; W. Waldeyer, 'Ansprache', *Sitzber. Kgl. Preuss, Akad.* (1909), pp. 106–7 (translated by Weindling); *ibid* (1918), pp. 9–10; *idem*, 'Festrede', *ibid.* (1896), pp. 734–6; (1905), pp. 117–21; O. Hertwig (note 91), pp. 28–30.

[119] A. Kirchhoff (ed.), *Deutsche Universitätslehrer über die Flottenvorlage. Gutachten hervorragender deutscher Universitätslehrer über die Bedeutung der Flottenvorlage. Gesammelt von der Berliner Wissenchaftlichen Korrespondenz* (Berlin, 1900), pp. 5–6. For an introduction to this key issue in the mobilization of public opinion see: J. Steinberg, 'The Kaiser's Navy and German Society', *Past and Present*, no. 28 (1974), pp. 102–10. See also Table 4 below.

[120] W. Marienfeld, *Wissenschaft und Schlachtflottenbau in Deutschland 1897–1906* ((West-) Berlin, Frankfurt a. M., 1957), pp. 46–8, 110–15.

[121] O. Hertwig, *Zur Abwehr des ethischen, des sozialen, des politischen Darwinismus* (Jena, 1918), pp. 116–19. W. von Waldeyer-Hartz (note 66), pp. 361, 380.

academic community justified the war as primarily defensive although this concealed an increasingly divergent range of opinions.[122] Waldeyer later explained that his experience of Strassburg had convinced him of the futility of foreign annexations.[123] He had however assumed a prominent role in the mobilization of public opinion in support of the German war effort. He signed the so-called 'Address to the Civilized World' of 1914 as did Rubner and Wassermann. This welcomed the war as a struggle which would result in the spiritual rebirth of the German nation. Waldeyer was also Secretary of the *Kulturbund*, which sought to win the support of foreign intellectuals for Germany.[124]

Hertwig in contrast was deeply disturbed by the 1914 declaration, having been privately critical of the bellicose foreign policy of the Kaiser due to such incidents as the Agadir crisis of 1911 (when Germany had challenged French control of Morocco).[125] During the war he published substantial attacks on Social Darwinism and the scientific errors of eugenics. For he felt that the errors of Darwinism had repercussions far beyond the limits of biology as an academic discipline.[126] He hoped that just as cells co-operated in an organism, so states should co-operate in the European federation of *Mitteleuropa*, proposed by the social liberal Friedrich Naumann.[127] In contrast Oscar Hertwig's brother, Richard, professor of zoology at Munich, was active in the expansionist Pan-German League, having remained faithful to Haeckel's Darwinism.[128]

With the collapse of imperial institutions after the war, Oscar Hertwig's final book fully elaborated his view of the state as an organism. This opposed scientific assertions of the necessity of class struggle as well as of racial struggle. Hertwig did not, however,

---

[122] For reactions of university professors to the war, see K. Schwabe, *Wissenschaft und Kriegsmoral. Die deutschen Hochschullehrer und die politischen Grundfragen des Ersten Weltkriegs* (Göttingen, 1919); professors of natural science and medicine, however, are omitted.

[123] W. von Waldeyer-Hartz (note 66), p. 360.

[124] G. Jeschal, *Politik und Wissenschaft deutscher Aerzte im Ersten Weltkrieg* (Pattensen, 1977), p. 26.

[125] Personal communication from Prof. Dr Paula Hertwig.

[126] O. Hertwig (note 45), pp. vii–ix; *idem, Zur Abwehr ... des Darwinismus* (note 101).

[127] *Ibid.*, pp. 110–15.

[128] K. von Frisch, *Richard von Hertwig* (München, 1938), p. 20; Senkenbergische Bibliothek, Frankfurt a M., Fürbringer Nachlass, R. Hertwig to Fürbringer, 12 February 1918; personal communication from Richard Hertwig's daughter, Marianne Hertwig.

abandon organicist arguments but distinguished between the false premises of Darwinism and socially valid laws of cellular functions and growth. This organic analogy was the basis for an analysis of the social pathology of the German nation.[129] He considered that just as every cell was of use to the body as a whole, so every worker had a responsibility to society. In the animal organism work was a co-operative *Gemeinschaftsarbeit*; similarly in human society there was both a duty and a right to work. Hertwig therefore criticized the Taylor system of rigorous division of labour as inhumane.

Occupational hygiene proved the necessity of increased leisure; machine operating ought therefore to free the individual for higher spiritual interests.[130] He proposed that the state should organize a national festival at Whitsun for all working people to symbolize unity between employers and employees; Christmas should become a secularized festival of the readiness of the individual to sacrifice self-interest to the community.[131] Hertwig's visionary proposals show how it was possible for academics to see festivals, which were a distinctive feature of the corporate nature of German political life, as a means of disseminating ideals of national culture and order. These illustrate how scientific innovations were combined with humanist university traditions, Christian ethics and nationalist politics as a means of preserving the supremacy of the intelligentsia in a newly democratic and industrialized society.

Although the social opinions of Hertwig and Waldeyer had idiosyncratic elements, they merit consideration as academic exponents of a broader movement of organicist social thought. Their concern with the impact of mechanization and the survival of corporate national spirit was shared by such noted figures as Spengler and Rathenau. It must, however, be noted that while Hertwig's critique of Social Darwinism ran to a second edition in 1921, the total number of copies printed was only 4000 and there were 2000 copies of his book on the state as an organism.[132] These circulation figures were miniscule when compared with Spengler's great popular success, or with academics like Haeckel or the philosopher Eucken whose popular writings inspired the foun-

[129] O. Hertwig, *Der Staat als Organismus* (note 3), pp. 173–98.
[130] *Ibid.*, pp. 207, 211, 213.
[131] *Ibid.*, pp. 248–56.
[132] Publication figures were kindly made available by the Volkseigene Verlage für Medizin und Biologie, Berlin GDR.

dation of public associations.[133] The faith of Hertwig in popular exposition of scientific theories was to a great extent naive, although the influential academic position held by Hertwig meant that his opinions made a more substantial impact on leading intellectuals than sheer publication figures might suggest.

The birth of the new republic was the occasion for the proliferation of organicist philosophies. Theories using natural selection, although by no means uncommon, were only one type among the many variants of organicist ideas. Darwinism was much criticized. The environmental biologist von Uexküll, for example, also elaborated a theory of the cell state. He said that social rather than mechanical analogies were more appropriate to biology; for every living body differed from a machine in that an organism consisted of living cells which were both self-supporting and combined in unity.[134]

Hitherto, accounts of organicist social thought have tended to concentrate on certain of the more extreme Social Darwinists and racists. Thus academic outsiders like the eugenicists Schallmayer, Ploetz and Tille have received attention, but not other types of organicism.[135] It has for example been customary to identify Social Darwinism with Spencer's social thought (so protecting the reputation of Darwin and subsequent Darwinists as unbiassed scientists). This approach to Social Darwinism is simplistic. Hertwig shows how it was possible to formulate a theory of the social organism in Spencerian terms in order to establish the errors of Darwinism. The dangers of any historical analysis attempting to separate objective science from subjective politics may be seen when Fritz Lenz, one of the leading eugenicists and racial theorists, said that his work on the biological roots of social inequalities had to be differentiated from the subsequent implementation of such views under the Nazis. Therefore, at an historical congress in 1959, to commemorate the centenary of Darwin's publication of *The Origin of Species*, he objected to Hedwig Conrad Martius'

---

[133] D. Gasman, *The Scientific Origins of National Socialism. Social Darwinism in Ernst Haeckel and the German Monist League* (London and New York, 1971); H. Lübbe, *Politische Philosophie in Deutschland. Studien zu ihrer Geschichte* (München, 1974), pp. 176–85.

[134] J. von Uexküll, 'Der Organismus als Staat und der Staat als Organismus', *Der Leuchter*, i (1919), pp. 79–110.

[135] For example, H. G. Zmarzlik, 'Der Sozialdarwinismus in Deutschland', in G. Altner (ed.), *Kreatur Mensch* (München, 1969), pp. 147–56.

pioneering history of eugenics, which had implicated Lenz. The latter unrepentantly replied that his scientific studies had merely established that the western *Kulturvölker* risked racial degeneration, although he now doubted whether eugenic measures could be adequate to prevent this.[136]

The explanation of the development of scientific racism like that of Lenz was not merely the logical consequence of the theory of natural selection. Racism cannot be explained by the intellectual genealogy of eugenicist theories, without reference to the changing institutional and social context. Laboratory research was subject to both conscious and unconscious social influences. The institutional roots and means of propagation of Social Darwinism require more systematic investigation than they have hitherto been accorded. Just as eugenics may be considered institutionalized Social Darwinism, so other environmental philosophies gave rise to diverse associations for improving national health and efficiency. These associations attempted with greater or lesser success to win state approval, although the pressure on municipalities and the state to institute eugenic measures only began to be effective in the 1920s.

Among academics, opinions were subject to considerable variation, especially when certain independent-minded *Privatdozenten* are taken into account. It was thus possible for Social Darwinism to be used in support of genuine pacifism: like militarism, pacifism had been elevated into a science. Friedrich Nicolai, a cardiologist at Berlin, defiantly justified his pacifism in biological terms. Although he considered there was a universal 'struggle for life', he uncompromisingly condemned the war as a struggle against life. War therefore prevented the development of humanity. Unlike Hertwig, who was careful not to offend the state authorities with his criticisms of Social Darwinist militarism, Nicolaí was prevented from lecturing at the university on the biology of war, and was ultimately forced into exile.[137]

Hertwig and Waldeyer were among those academic *Vernunftre-*

---

[136] F. Lenz, 'Die soziologische Bedeutung der Selektion', in G. Heberer and F. Schwanitz (eds.), *Hundert Jahre Evolutionsforschung. Das wissenschaftliche Vermächtnis Charles Darwin* (Stuttgart, 1960), pp. 185–95. For Lenz's support of Hitler's racial hygiene, see B. Schreiber, *The Men behind Hitler* (London, 1975), pp. 143–58; H. Conrad-Martius, *Utopien der Menschenzüchtung. Der Sozialdarwinismus und seine Folgen* (München, 1955).

[137] F. Nicolai, *Die Biologie des Krieges* (Zürich, 1917); W. Basler, 'Zur politischen

*publikaner* who accepted the necessity of fundamental constitutional change, although at heart they had been staunchly imperialist.[138] Waldeyer echoed Hertwig's Spencerian theory of the state as an organism, since he believed that only by dismembering Prussia and Bavaria and establishing a truly federal Germany based on the *Gau* could a truly strong nation develop.[139]

Although Spencer had been opposed to the state, in Germany Spencerian organicism was used to legitimize the state. The federal constitution of the Weimar Republic, which was drawn up by the Berlin *Privatdozent* Hugo Preuss, revealed the influence of organicist theories on natural law. Preuss had compared the state to an integrated cellular body consisting of differentiated single cells and composite territorial cells, in order to establish that the state was formed not by law as an artificially rational system, but by the common life of men.[140] Preuss subscribed to the theories of natural law of Otto von Gierke, the distinguished *Ordinarius* in the faculty of law in Berlin. Gierke had held Hertwig's opinions on the close relationship between the biological sciences and the *Staatswissenschaften* in high esteem.[141]

There had been opposition to biological analogies in the social sciences throughout the Empire. For example the political theorist Jellinek was a noted opponent of Gierke's theories of natural law.[142] After the collapse of the Empire, criticism of organicist

Rolle der Berliner Universität im ersten imperialistischen Weltkrieg 1914 bis 1918', *Wissenschaftliche Zeitschrift der Humboldt-Universität Berlin, Mathematisch-Naturwissenschaftliche Reihe*, x (1961), pp. 197–9; R. Chickering, *Imperial Germany and a World without War. The Peace Movement and German Society, 1892–1914* (Princeton, 1975), pp. 94–108.

[138] For reactions of professors to the political upheavals after the collapse of the Empire, see K. Töpner, *Gelehrte Politiker und politisierende Gelehrte. Die Revolution von 1918 im Urteil deutscher Hochschullehrer* (Göttingen, Zürich, Frankfurt a. M., 1970). For a more systematic analysis see H. Döring, *Der Weimarer Kreis. Studien zum politischen Bewusstsein verfassungstreuer Hochschullehrer in der Weimarer Republik* (Meisenheim am Glan, 1975).

[139] W. von Waldeyer-Hartz (note 66), pp. 390–1.

[140] H. Preuss, *Gemeinde, Staat, Reich als Gebietskörperschaften. Versuch einer deutschen Staatskonstruktion auf Grundlage der Genossenschaftstheorie* (Berlin, 1889), pp. 214 (for the state as cell tissue), 230–4 (for theory of social organism).

[141] O. Gierke, *Das Wesen der menschlichen Verbände* (Berlin, 1902), pp. 13–14.

[142] G. Jellinek, *Das Recht des modernen Staates. Allgemeine Staatslehre* (Berlin, 1900), pp. 132–8. F. W. Coker, *Organismic Theories of the State. Nineteenth-century Interpretations of the State as Organism or as Person* (New York and London, 1910); E. T. Towne, *Die Auffassung der Gesellschaft als Organismus, ihre Entwicklung und Modifikation* (Halle, 1903).

theories came to a head with the institutionalization of sociology as a university discipline. It was on the basis of sociology having distinctive rational criteria that Tönnies criticized Hertwig's theory of the state as outmoded. Certain sociologists like Franz Oppenheimer (who had initially studied medicine at Berlin), Paul Barth and Gustav Salomon continued to give serious consideration to organicist social theory.[143] Moreover even sociologists like Tönnies anxious to establish the discipline on independent rational criteria, could exert influence on innovations in medical theory; Tönnies influenced the development of Grotjahn's social hygiene for which a chair was established at Berlin in 1920.[144]

Grotjahn described how as professor of the new discipline of social hygiene in 1920, he felt that fundamental differences separated him from the old guard of professors in the faculty like Hertwig, Rubner and Waldeyer.[145] The republican administration proposed a variety of new chairs for specialisms previously condemned as scientifically peripheral. Pharmaceutical chemistry, laryngology, dental surgery (which received no less than four *Ordinarien*) and certain outpatient clinics now were given the ultimate accolade of recognition, full professorships. New chairs were also proposed for approaches to medicine which had previously been considered totally unscientific. There was a series of pitched battles fought between the ministry and the medical faculty over the academic status of specialisms like nature therapy (*Naturheilkunde*), insurance medicine, psycho-analysis and a special chair for problems of prostitution.[146] Political groups and public associations were particularly instrumental in pressurizing the ministry to support these. The state also proposed to promote all *Extraordinarien* to the full status of *Ordinarien*, and to integrate into the 'organism' of the

[143] P. A. Sorokin, *Contemporary Sociological Theories* (New York, 1926), p. 201; F. Tönnies, review in: *Niemeyers Zeitschrift für internationales Recht*, xxx (1922), pp. 303–4.
[144] A. Grotjahn, *Erlebtes und Erstrebtes. Erinnerungen eines sozialistischen Arztes* (Berlin, 1932), pp. 56–7, 110.
[145] *Ibid.*, p. 210.
[146] For nature therapy see ZSTA Merseburg, Rep. 76 Va Sekt. 2 Tit. IV Nr 46 Bd 21 Bl. 335–6, 408; *ibid.*, Bd 22 Bl. 121, 133–188, 203; *Der Tag*, no. 123, 9 June 1920, for nature therapy as an achievement of revolution. For prostitution, see ZSTA Merseburg, Rep. 76 Va Sekt 2 Tit. IV Nr 46 Bd 22 Bl. 7, 33–4. For insurance medicine see ZSTA Merseburg, Rep. 76 Va Sekt. 2 Tit. IV Nr 46 Bd 23 Bl. 42. For psycho-analysis, see ZSTA Merseburg, Rep. 76 Va Sekt. 2 Tit IV Nr 46 Bd 22 Bl. 550.

university previously disenfranchised groups of teachers and students.[147]

The faculty claimed to stand not only for the traditions of academic freedom but for the defence of the medical profession. Berlin professors had the reputation of hostility to the new republican administration. In a particularly heated exchange, the medical faculty remarked that for a long time ministers had used quacks (*Kurpfuscher*) for their personal medical needs, but now the ministry wished to dismantle science and integrate quackery into officially recognized medical practice.[148]

The medical faculty managed to resist the major part of these proposals, due to a combination of its own tactics of prevarication, the state's lack of finance and the changing political situation. This confrontation underlines the extent to which the imperial administration had sustained academic privileges. The response of university professors to the republican innovations was to reemphasize corporate traditions, reinforced by the latest scientific theories. Even the more liberal minority like Hertwig, who had supported certain reforms like the admission of women and university extension classes, wished to keep the university's independence intact as based on its traditional privileges.

ORGANICIST IDEOLOGY AND SOCIAL MOBILITY

These events raise the question as to whether it is possible to interpret certain organicist social theories as legitimizing the socially privileged position of university academics. It has, however, been shown there were diverse interest groups among professors; there were also differences between two professors in a single discipline as Hertwig and Waldeyer. In order to consider the extent to which university professors may be seen as a distinctive group, it is necessary to undertake a more systematic analysis of the relation between ideology and social status. It is with this aim that the following preliminary survey of the formation of the professorial elite of the Berlin medical faculty has been undertaken.

The status of intellectuals in Imperial Germany has been the subject of considerable disagreement among historians. Using

[147] E. Wende, *C. H. Becker. Mensch und Politiker. Ein biographischer Beitrag zur Kulturgeschichte der Weimarer Republik* (Stuttgart, 1959), pp. 124–5, 130–1.
[148] ZSTA Merseburg, Rep. 76 Va Sekt. 2 Tit. IV Nr 46 Bd 21 Bl. 327.

criteria based on contemporary opinions, many subsequent commentators have considered the intelligentsia as a distinctive social class.[149] Their criterion is that of a university degree, reinforced with evidence as to the difficulty of even the lower middle class to gain access to university education.

There have, however, been studies which have isolated the professorial elite as a distinctive ruling class. Among the most persuasive of such accounts has been Ringer's account of academics' perceptions of the changing social structure. Ringer identifies professors as a 'mandarin aristocracy', equivalent in status to the upper levels of the bureaucracy; 'The non-entrepreneurial upper middle class, the mandarin aristocracy of cultivation had become the functional ruling class of the nation. University professors, the mandarin intellectuals, spoke for this distinctive elite and represented its values'.[150] According to this interpretation, university professors may be seen as the chief ideologists of the imperial state.

But the extent to which professors and bureaucrats ever formed a 'functional ruling class' is, in practice, difficult to determine. The validity of this concept can be questioned here on the basis of this case study of the aims and motivations of Hertwig's and Waldeyer's organicist ideology. For although they both were staunch patriots, their ideals reflected more the concerns of broader groups among the middle class. While Du Bois-Reymond's view of Berlin university as the intellectual bodyguards of the Prussian monarchs accurately conveys the sense of social engagement of professors, they were far from subservient.

An alternative interpretation denying that German 'scientists' had any political pretensions, as suggested by Ben-David, fails adequately to account for social influences on the production of scientific theories or the ideological uses of science. Ben-David has analysed bureaucratically organized scientists pursuing their careers in a 'socially insulated system of higher education'.[151] This overlooks the situation that both ideologically, with such theories as division of labour, and in terms of career structure there was increasing penetration by representatives of the newly enriched commercial sectors of society.

[149] See for example, K. Vondung (ed.), *Das wilhelminische Bildungsbürgertum* (Göttingen, 1976), pp. 12, 24, 31.
[150] F. K. Ringer (note 32), pp. 6–7.
[151] J. Ben-David, *The Scientist's Role in Society, A Comparative Study* (Englewood Cliffs, 1971), pp. 109–10.

The sectors of society from which students and university teachers were recruited need to be ascertained in order to assess ideological convictions of the professorial elite. Their fears that universities would become factories for mass learning and technical education may be seen as grounded in increasing penetration by the commercial middle classes into the hallowed sanctity of the universities. Despite their deficiencies, statistics suggesting this for medicine are revealing of contemporary prejudices. Regarding the social origins of medical students at Berlin, the numbers who were from the intelligentsia, as traditionally defined, decreased from 48 per cent in 1850 to 25 per cent in 1880 and remained around 30 per cent until 1910.[152] The proportion of students from commercial sectors of the middle class like industrialists, merchants or property owners correspondingly increased from 34 per cent in 1850 to 48 per cent in 1880, and remained around this figure until 1910. The percentage of students from middle or lower grades of officials, primary schoolteacher, artisan or agricultural worker backgrounds also increased from 18 per cent in 1880 (in 1810 it had been as high as 42 per cent) to 27 per cent in 1910. The numbers of medical students at Berlin rose overall from 233 in the winter semester 1849–50 to 585 in 1879–80 and to 1568 in 1909–10. The resentment among *Ordinarien* to a lowering of standards may thus be linked to an increasing number of students from a broadening social spectrum.[153]

The same trend of increasing numbers from the commercial sectors of the middle class may be detected among *Privatdozenten* and *Extraordinarien*. Eulenburg in an examination of this rise, showed that by 1906 for the social origins of 623 of the 725 medical *Privatdozenten* and *Extraordinarien* in Germany and Austria, 217 had backgrounds in commerce, 133 were sons of physicians, 97 of university professors, 58 of manufacturers, 42 of estate owners, 28 of clergy, 19 of lawyers, 19 of *Gymnasium* teachers and 10 were sons of apothecaries.[154] Although occupation as an indicator of a family's social standing requires a degree of caution (there might be commercial investments made by a physician), the results of this survey were widely discussed. A more recent analysis of occu-

[152] This category includes higher officials, clergy, lawyers, university and *Gymnasium* teachers, physicians, apothecaries, architects, engineers, authors and artists.
[153] M. Lenz (note 15), iii, pp. 494–8, 522.
[154] F. Eulenburg, *Der 'akademische Nachwuchs': Eine Untersuchung über die Lage und die Aufgaben der Extraordinarien und Privatdozenten* (Leipzig, 1908), p. 18.

pations undertaken by Ferber suggests that whereas between 1860 and 1889, of the 1273 university teachers 63.2 per cent were recruited from 'traditional' *Akademikerberufe*, 28.1 per cent came from independent commercial occupations and 8.7 per cent from those in dependent employment. But between 1890 and 1919 for a total of 3012 university teachers only 49.4 per cent came from the *Akademikerberufe*, yet 39.9 per cent had independent positions in the commercial sector and 10.7 per cent had fathers in dependent employment. For 1860–89, 140 came from physicians' families, as did 217 between 1890 and 1919.[155] That the German academic community is comparatively well-documented, so providing material for a systematic study of university education as a means of social mobility, makes it all the more important to appreciate distinctive variation from these overall trends as will be shown in the case of the Berlin medical faculty.[156]

The occupational groups from which the *Ordinarien* in the Berlin medical faculty were recruited contrasted to this general trend for *Privatdozenten* and *Extraordinarien*. According to Eulenburg, for 331 *Privatdozenten* and *Extraordinarien* in Berlin approximately 39 per cent (126 in all) came from the intelligentsia, 38 per cent (123) from commercial backgrounds, 10 per cent (33) from the lower middle class and dependent occupations.[157] In the Berlin medical faculty of 1870, eight *Ordinarien* came from the traditional intelligentsia. From the commercial sector of the bourgeoisie came four professors, and two had prosperous artisan backgrounds. A preliminary survey of the backgrounds of subsequently appointed *Ordinarien* suggests that not only did the traditional intelligentsia retain its pre-eminence but that there was an increasing proportion who were sons of physicians or university professors. For of the thirty-four *Ordinarien* (out of a total of thirty-six), whose fathers' occupations I have identified, twenty-six were recruited from the intelligentsia (nine came from medical families and six had fathers who were university professors); only four came from the entre-

[155] C. von Ferber, 'Die Entwicklung des Lehrkörpers der deutschen Universitäten und Hochschulen 1864–1954', in H. Plessner (ed.), *Untersuchungen zur Lage der deutschen Hochschullehrer* (Göttingen, 1959), iii, pp. 177–8, 185–6.

[156] For the comparable case of Bonn, see K. H. Jarausch, 'The Social Transformation of the University: the Case of Prussia 1865–1914', *Journal of Social History*, xii (1979), pp. 609–36.

[157] F. Eulenburg, *Der 'akademische Nachwuchs': Eine Untersuchung über die Lage und die Aufgaben der Extraordinarien und Privatdozenten* (Leipzig, 1908), p. 18.

preneurial and propertied sectors of the bourgeoisie and four appointments were made of those whose parents were either artisans as Rubner, whose father was a locksmith, or surveyors (see Tables 1, 2, and 3).[158]

Lubarsch's denial that family connections were important for an academic career is unconvincing. By 1918, as Lubarsch himself admitted, five out of eighteen *Ordinarien* were either sons of, or related to, university professors; and Lubarsch did not mention those others who were also sons of *Akademiker*. Social rather than regional differences became increasingly decisive for the composition of the medical faculty. The numbers of native Prussians occupying seventeen posts in Berlin in 1866 amounted to eleven.[159] Lubarsch commented that for eighteen *Ordinarien* at Berlin in 1918, only three were Prussians.[160]

The training of military physicians and surgeons was also a concern of the Berlin medical faculty. Experience in the army medical corps was an important factor in subsequent careers at Berlin as in the cases of von Bergmann, Virchow, Koch and von Leyden. Military cadets from the *Kaiser-Wilhelms-Akademie* formed a substantial proportion of students attending lectures. For example of the 1319 auditors at Hertwig's lectures between 1890 and 1893, 513 were military cadets.[161] The composition of the *Ordentliche Honorar-Professoren* was partly determined by the emphasis placed by the army on medical science, and partly by the state's fostering of specialisms relevant to public health. Their social origins show that the balance between those with parental backgrounds in commerce or the intelligentsia was more even. These honorary professors had status equivalent only to *Extraordinarien*. With no official duties they represented an attempt to strengthen ties between the university and the medical profession (see Table 3).

That the Berlin medical faculty was distinctive was also borne out by the increasingly late age at which a chair was secured. The

[158] Sources for Berlin include J. Asen, *Gesamtverzeichnis des Lehrkörpers der Universität Berlin*, i, 1810–1945 (Leipzig, 1955); *Chronik der königlichen Friedrich-Wilhelms-Universität zu Berlin*. In Tables 1, 2 and 3, in certain cases, marked with an asterisk, the age on appointment may be inaccurate by one year.
[159] T. Billroth, *The Medical Sciences in the German Universities* (New York, 1924), p. 176.
[160] O. Lubarsch, *Ein bewegtes Gelehrtenleben* (Berlin, 1931), p. 327.
[161] *Chronik der königlichen Friedrich-Wilhelms-Universität zu Berlin* (1890–2), iii, p. 101; iv, p. 86 and v, p. 100. W. von Waldeyer-Hartz *Lebenserinnerungen* (Bonn, 1920), p. 209.

average age of the Berlin faculty in 1870 had been on appointment 41.7 years. For the twelve members called to the faculty between 1860 and 1884 their average age was 43.3 years. For Germany as a whole in the same period, Ferber states this to be 36.1 years. The twenty-two *Ordinarien* appointed at Berlin between 1885 and 1909 were on average fifty years of age. Between 1910 and 1918 the eight new full professors had an average age of 50.6 years, in contrast to this period 1910–19 in Germany the average age was 44.3.[162] The main reason for this discrepancy was that many appointed at Berlin had occupied full chairs at other universities. In the second half of the nineteenth century, the faculty was decreasingly recruited internally from those who had spent their whole career at Berlin. Higher incomes, the recruiting of distinguished outsiders and new institutes meant that Berlin steadily increased in prestige. Coupled with the fact that after Virchow's death in 1902, professors were not particularly active in liberal politics, the rising average age of the faculty contributed to its ethos of conservatism.

Evaluated in the context of these trends, Hertwig and Waldeyer were, relatively speaking, outsiders. But although their social rise was greater than most, particularly for Waldeyer, being among the very few professors admitted into the hereditary aristocracy, there were nonetheless certain predisposing factors in their family backgrounds (after 1870 only six professors in the medical faculty, of which three were *Ordinarien*, were ennobled). In Hertwig's case, his father had been a student of Liebig but had neither the financial means nor a suitable assistantship for an academic career. Hertwig's uncle was also a cigar manufacturer, whose son became a professor of engineering at the *Technische Hochschule*, Aachen. Since both Hertwig's son Günther and daughter Paula became university professors after having worked in their father's laboratory, Hertwig may be seen as exemplifying the growing tendency for university professors' children to have successful academic careers. Waldeyer's semi-Catholic Westphalian background made him somewhat more of an outsider, despite his mother coming from a school teacher's family who had aristocratic ancestry. Waldeyer's son chose one of the most prestigious occupations open to the middle class – that of the navy in which he became admiral.

---

[162] C. von Ferber, 'Die Entwicklung des Lehrkörpers der deutschen Universitäten und Hochschulen 1864–1954', in H. Plessner (ed.), *Untersuchungen zur Lage der deutschen Hochschullehrer* (Göttingen, 1956), iii, pp. 129–30.

This analysis of career structure sheds additional light on organicist ideology as a means of legitimatizing the faculty's privileged status. It does not, however, seem justified to see the faculty as fundamentally distinct from other sectors of the professional middle class. Differences between the social outlook of Hertwig and Waldeyer have already been stressed. The faculty always contained competing groups. Naunyn, the experimental pathologist and clinician, described how as an assistant he was obliged to support Frerichs, noted for his pathological investigations, in a feud against the pathological anatomist Virchow. Allied with Frerichs were Reichert and Jüngken. For a combination of scientific, political and professional reasons they were opposed to an alliance of Virchow, Traube, Du Bois-Reymond, Gräfe and Langenbeck.[163] Later, representatives of new specialisms would also be seen as outsiders. The unity of the faculty as a single interest group therefore should not be overemphasized.

Waldeyer was increasingly drawn into official circles. He has been presented as an outspoken representative of German imperialism in the important study of the Prussian Academy of Sciences edited by Stern. Waldeyer combined his role as presenting the natural sciences in the service of imperialism, with demands that the state contribute yet more money to science, so enhancing the status of academics in established positions and opening new career opportunities. He was also active in a great variety of professional organizations, anthropological and medical societies. In addition he was a member of prestigious intellectual associations in Berlin like the *Mittwochs-Gesellschaft*, in which there were not only academics but also artists, writers and generals. Thus Waldeyer associated with a wide variety of groups and not merely with academics.[164]

Hertwig, although far more introverted than Waldeyer, showed in his general writings broader identification with the ideals of popular authors like Lagarde, Nietzsche and Langbehn in their extolling of the national spirit. Hertwig also assimilated into his theories the writings of social critics like Bellamy, Kropotkin and Popper-Lynkeus. Similar broader concerns may be detected among Hertwig's colleagues in the faculty. There was considerable interest in the physical condition of the population and its rate of increase.

[163] B. Naunyn, *Die Berliner Schule vor 50 Jahren* (Leipzig, 1908), pp. 223–4.
[164] W. von Waldeyer-Hartz (note 66), pp. 272–8.

Table 3. *Ordentliche Honorar-Professoren in the medical faculty, Berlin, 1880–1918*

| Name | Dates | Year of appointment | Age | Institutional affiliation/rank | Special-ization | Reli-gion | Father's occu-pation/status |
|---|---|---|---|---|---|---|---|
| Lauer, von Gustav | 1808–99 | 1880 | 73* | *General-Stabsarzt der Armee. Chef des Sanitätscorps. Prof. d. med. chirurg. Akad. f. Militär.* | Semeiotics, surgery, forensic med. and therapy | Evang. | Pastor |
| Rose, Edmund | 1836–1914 | 1881 | 44 | *Leitung des Krankenhaus Bethaniens* | Ophthalmology | | Univ. prof. (min-eralogy, Berlin) |
| Koch, Robert | 1843–1910 | 1891 | 48* | *Dir. d. Institut f. Infections-krankheiten* | Bacteriology | Evang. | Mining official |
| Skrzeczka, Karl Friedrich | 1833–1902 | 1891 | 58 | *Polizeipräsidium Mitgl. des Kais. Gesundheitsamts.* | Forensic medicine | Evang. | Teacher |
| Coler, von Alwin | 1831–1901 | 1892 | 61 | *Generalstabsarzt der Armee. Chef des Sanitätscorps. Dir d. militärärztl. Bildungsanstalten.* | Military hygiene | Evang. | Tax collector and post master |
| Fraenkel, Bernhard | 1836–1911 | 1897 | 62* | *Dir. Klinik u. Poliklinik f. Hals u. Nasenkrankheiten* | Otology, laryngology and rhinology | Reform (bapt. Jewish father) | Military physician |
| Munk, Hermann | 1839–1912 | 1899 | 60* | *Dir. Tierärztliche Hochschule* | Physiology | Jewish | |
| Lucae, August | 1835–1911 | 1899 | 64* | *Dir. Staatliche Ohrenpolikl.* | Otology | | Apothecary |
| Senator, Hermann | 1834–1911 | 1899 | 65* | *Dir. Polikl. Inst. f. innere Med.* | Internal medicine | Jewish | |
| Fritsch, Gustav | 1838–1927 | 1899 | 62* | *Abt. Vorst. Inst. f. Physiol.* | Anatomy and anthropology | | Architect (*kgl. Baurat*) |
| Hirschberg, Julius | 1843–1925 | 1900 | 57* | Private clinic | Ophthalmology | Jewish | Merchant |

| Name | Dates | Appointed | Age* | Position | Field | Religion | Father's occupation |
|---|---|---|---|---|---|---|---|
| Leuthold, von Rudolf | 1832–1905 | 1901 | 69* | *Generalstabsarzt der Armee. Chef des Sanitätskorps u. d. Medizinalabteilung d. Kriegsministeriums* | Military medicine | | |
| Schjerning, Otto von | 1853–1921 | 1906 | 53* | *Generalstabsarzt der Armee* | Military medicine | Evang. | |
| Goldscheider, Alfred | 1858–1935 | 1907 (Ordinarius 1919) | 49* | *Dir. Medizinische Polikl.* | Internal medicine | Evang. | Physician |
| Sonnenburg, Eduard | 1848–1915 | 1908 | 59 | *Leiter Chirurg. Abt. d. Krankenhaus Moabit* | Surgery | Evang. | Gymnasium teacher |
| Ewald, Karl Anton | 1845–1915 | 1908 | 62 | *Dir. Innere Abt. Berliner Augusta-Hospital* | Internal medicine, hygiene, dietetics | Evang. (bapt., Jewish father) | |
| Salkowski, Ernst | 1844–1923 | 1909–10 | 65 | *Vorst. chem. Abt. Pathol. Inst.* | Medical chemistry | Evang. | Pastor? |
| Gaffky, Georg | 1850–1918 | 1912 | 60* | *Dir. Inst. f. Infections-Krankheiten* | Infectious diseases | Evang. | Shipping agent |
| Wassermann, August von | 1866–1925 | 1911 | 45* | *Dir. Inst. f. Experimental-therapie* | Internal medicine and bacteriology | Jewish | Banker (Bavarian nobility, 1910) |
| Krause, Fedor | 1857–1937 | 1915 | 57* | *Dir. Augusta-Hospital* | Surgery (neurology) | Evang. | Kreisgerichtssekr. |
| Hansemann, David von | 1858–1920 | 1914 | 55* | *Prosektor Rudolf-Virchow-Krankenhaus* | General pathology and pathological anatomy | Jewish | Factory owner |
| Virchow, Hans | 1852–1940 (emeritus 1922) | 1917 | 65* | *Prosektor Anat. Inst.* | Anatomy | | Univ. prof. (pathological anatomy) |

*The age on appointment may be inaccurate by one year.

Berlin professors were active in promoting dietary and environmental therapies, such as heat, water and physio-therapy.[165] They also took a leading role in public associations for gymnastics. swimming pools, holiday colonies for children and measures to secure better living conditions. These environmental schemes were based on medical and biological theories; indeed many could justly be termed Social Lamarckism. These broader interests suggest that the social activities and organicist ideology of the medical faculty can only be understood with reference to more general issues agitating Imperial Germany.

There was, as Lukács has demonstrated, a rising tide of irrational and idealistic *Lebensphilosophie* disseminated both within and outside the universities.[166] Among these, as has been suggested here, were many theories incorporating the latest biological research. These theories were publicized by both academic and more popular journals, by diverse types of authors, and were also encouraged by the patronage of industrialists such as Alfred Krupp. Social Darwinism became an integral part of the ideology of nationalist pressure groups as the Pan-German League or the *Bund der Landwirte*.[167] Evans has described the German women's movement as a case of liberal associations succumbing to increasingly conservative Social Darwinism.[168] Kuczynski has analysed a number of extreme nationalist and racist public associations as propaganda organizations of monopoly capitalism. In the Pan-German, Colonial and Navy Leagues he has detected a common nucleus of publicists like the Berlin professor of history Dietrich Schäfer, the Leipzig professor of chemistry Eugen Hasse and the eugenicist Alexander Tille who was subsidized by industrialists' associations.[169]

It is hoped that the presentation of the theory of the cell state

---

[165] F. Munk, *Das medizinische Berlin um die Jahrhundertwende* (München, (West-) Berlin, 1956), pp. 40–1.

[166] G. Lukács, *Die Zerstörung der Vernunft*, vol. 2, *Irrationalismus und Imperialismus* (Darmstadt and Neuwied, 1974), pp. 88–100, 136, 207. Lukács saw an increasing dichotomy between the mythical concepts of *Lebensphilosophie* and biological science.

[167] H.-J. Puhle, *Agrarische Interessenpolitik und preussischer Konservatismus im wilhelminischen Reich (1893–1914)* (Bonn-Bad Godesberg, 1975), pp. 90–3.

[168] R. J. Evans, *The Feminist Movement in Germany 1894–1933* (London, Beverly Hills, 1976), pp. 158–70.

[169] J. Kuczynski, *Studien zur Geschichte des deutschen Imperialismus*, vol. 2, *Propagandaorganisationen des Monopolkapitals* (Berlin, 1948), p. 311.

may add an additional dimension to the solid foundations for a study of organicist ideology laid by the above studies. In particular non-Darwinian or anti-Darwinian formulations of the social organism have been emphasized here. Organicist theories of society require assessment in the context of occupational practices, institutional affiliations and broader political and social opinions. Study of the views of Hertwig and Waldeyer in the context of the Berlin medical faculty reveals how apparently disparate spheres of activity – scientific teaching and research, career structure, and social views – were interrelated. These connections were explicitly made in the pronouncements on the social issues of these two professors of anatomy.

Consideration of the opinions held by professors, as exemplified by the theory of the cell state, suggests that these contrasted to the institutional demands of the state for efficient training of increased numbers of medical practitioners and scientists. The state's conception of teaching and research was at variance with the elaborate synthetic philosophies, which were fabricated from scientific observations deriving from such areas as cell biology and a mixture of humanist and nationalist idealism. The origins of the theory of the cell state must be sought in middle class nationalist sentiments. The motivations for subsequent elaborations of this theory may be investigated in terms of the middle class response to industrialization and imperialism. While the state and the academic community were apparently united in believing that the sciences should be given priority as a national enterprise, their views differed as to how this was to be achieved. Even among scientists there was considerable divergence of opinions, as shown by debates over the social implications of Darwinism. Regarding their impact on the state, while academics' opinions on technical, medical or educational issues were taken seriously, there is a lack of evidence that opinions offered by professors on general questions such as the conduct of the war had much effect on those in power.[170] The theory of the cell state as a social theory can be interpreted as reflecting the liberal accommodation with imperialism.

While political activism declined, science was a cultural form which could be exploited to neutralize political contrasts and enhance the status and the institutional powers of medical pro-

[170] J. B. Joll, review of K. Schwabe, *Wissenschaft und Kriegsmoral, EHR*, lxxxv (1970), pp. 202–3.

fessors. The pre-eminence of economic analogies as the division of labour meant the theory of the cell state marked changing responses to industrialization and the establishment of the *Reich*, as shown by the emergence of co-operative theories of the social organism.

On the basis of this case study of practitioners of anatomy, certain assumptions about the development of modern university science may also be questioned. Generalizations of increasing specialization of sciences with a growing recognition of natural science as distinct from both the social sciences and humanistic disciplines cannot be confirmed. Moreover increasing numbers of students did not result in a corresponding opening of the senior positions in the academic hierarchy.

If higher education and the medical profession are to be counted among what has been termed the tertiary sector of services in a modern industrialized society, these paradoxically expanded at a very early stage during Germany's industrial 'take off' from the 1870s. Those investigating the emergence of a 'modern research university' would be hard pressed to separate 'traditional' features from 'modern' and 'progressive' features in this case. Instead, it has been suggested that scientific research, the values attached to academic freedom, the activities of the medical faculty and the policies of the state must be understood in the context of developing middle-class social groupings forming the complex structure of Imperial Germany. Rational explanation of fundamental processes of life, did not in this case result in narrow specialists and (to use Weber's terms) a disenchanted world view and medical science only as 'a practical technology'; but the scientific investigations of Hertwig and Waldeyer were used to disseminate social philosophies.[171]

While there was an apparently progressive accumulation of discoveries in cytology and embryology, integral to these were organicist ideas which have been viewed as retrogressive as a form of social thought. These ideas were shaped by the institutional and social structure of Imperial Germany, which was reflected in the theories of the state as an organism held by Hertwig and Waldeyer. The Berlin faculty's defence of academic freedom thus concealed tensions between the state bureaucracy and university professors.

[171] M. Weber, 'Science as a Vocation', in H. H. Gerth and C. W. Mills (eds.), *From Max Weber: Essays in Sociology* (London and Boston, 1972), pp. 142, 144, 149.

Scientific achievements attributed to academic freedom reflected middle-class idealization of the Imperial German state.

Table 4. *Views of Berlin professors.*

|  | Views on women studying medicine | Supporters of expansion of navy, 1900 |
|---|---|---|
| Bergmann | Opposed | X |
| Fick |  | X (at Göttingen) |
| Fritsch | Opposed | X |
| Gusserow | In favour if better educated |  |
| Hertwig | In favour | X |
| Heubner |  | X |
| Jolly |  | X |
| Lesser | Opposed |  |
| Leyden | Undecided |  |
| Munk, H. | In favour |  |
| Olshausen | Opposed |  |
| Orth | Opposed (at Göttingen) |  |
| Rubner | Undecided | X |
| Schweigger | Opposed |  |
| Senator | Undecided |  |
| Virchow | Opposed |  |
| Waldeyer | Opposed | X |
| Wassermann | Opposed |  |

## ACKNOWLEDGEMENTS

Earlier drafts of this paper were given to the history of science seminar, University of Leeds, and to the Society for the Social History of Medicine. I would particularly like to thank Ludmilla Jordanova and Karl Figlio for comments. The paper has benefited from the recollections of Dr H. Blaschko, F.R.S. and Prof. Dr Walter Pagel, both former students of Oscar Hertwig, as well as from conversations with his daughter Prof. Dr Paula Hertwig.

I also wish to pay tribute to the late Dozent Dr Hans-Heinz Lötzke, Oberarzt am anatomischen Institut, Bereich Medizin (Charité), Humboldt-Universität, Berlin, as a historian of anatomy.

# 4. Innate Character in Animals and Man: A Perspective on the Origins of Ethology

JOHN R. DURANT

> I should like to have the complete biography of every animal.
>
> C. G. Leroy[1]

In the aftermath of a scientific controversy which has bordered at times on the outrageous, it is appropriate that historians should turn their attention to 'The Roots of Sociobiology'. Of course, this is no easy task. For one thing, it is too early to be sure of the precise nature of the subject with which we are dealing. The biologist Richard Dawkins highlighted this problem recently, when he asked almost despairingly: 'What on earth is sociobiology?' According to the philosopher David Hull, this question cannot be answered in terms of a set of simple defining characteristics, or even by exclusive reference to the substantive content of the subject. Sociobiology, Hull argues, has no 'essence'; in the last analysis it is what its practitioners make it.[2] This approach introduces another element of uncertainty, since at the present time it is far from clear exactly who are the sociobiologists. When Edward Wilson published his massive volume *Sociobiology. The New Synthesis* in 1975, some biologists were surprised that so much fuss should be made over a subject which they had been teaching in undergraduate courses for several years, and others wondered whether they were not witnessing a 'political game' involving the naming and renaming of fields.[3] Finally, the problems facing the historian are compounded by the fact that the sociobiology debate is highly polarized, and the literature abounds with tendentious and superficial

---

[1] C. G. Leroy, *The Intelligence and Perfectibility of Animals from a Philosophic Point of View. With a few Letters on Man* (London, 1870), p. 11.
[2] R. Dawkins, 'Defining Sociobiology', *Nature*, cclxxx (2 Aug. 1979), pp. 427–8; R. Hull, 'The Sociology of Sociobiology', *New Scientist*, lxxix (21 Sept. 1978), pp. 862–5.
[3] G. P. Baerends *et al.*, 'Multiple Review of Wilson's Sociobiology', *Animal Behaviour*, xxiv (1976), pp. 698–718.

historical judgements. At close range it is often difficult either to ignore these judgements altogether, or to bring them into the sharp focus which is necessary for the purpose of critical assessment.[4]

All this serves as a warning against any simple-minded exploration of the roots of sociobiology. However, it need not dissuade us altogether from the task. Certain general features of sociobiology and the sociobiology debate seem to be clear and undisputed. For example, it is widely agreed that sociobiology is concerned with the biological analysis of 'social behaviour', and that this analysis draws upon both theoretical population genetics on the one hand, and animal behaviour studies on the other. Moreover, no one appears to dispute the fact that sociobiology is most controversial when it is applied to human societies. On this basis, the history of sociobiology may be approached through some of the older disciplines upon which it draws, and insights into the current controversy may be sought through the investigation of earlier debates concerning the relationship between biology and the social sciences. The contributions of Mackenzie, Searle and Norton in this volume all bear on the latter question. This paper consists of a preliminary exploration of one of the major disciplines out of which sociobiology has grown: ethology.[5]

The science of ethology deserves greater attention from historians, philosophers and sociologists of science than it has hitherto received.[6] Still a comparatively young subject, it has a well-

---

[4] I have discussed these problems at greater length in a forthcoming essay review, 'Exploring the Roots of Sociobiology', to be published in *British Journal for the History of Science*, xiii (Mar. 1980).

[5] The precise nature of the relationship between ethology and sociobiology remains to be investigated. But that ethology is an important antecedent of sociobiology is beyond dispute. See E. O. Wilson, *Sociobiology: The New Synthesis* (Cambridge, Mass. and London, 1975), pp. 5–6; T. H. Clutton Brock and P. H. Harvey (eds.), *Readings in Sociobiology* (Reading and San Francisco, 1978), preface.

[6] There is no adequate general work on the history of ethology, but see P. H. Klopfer and J. P. Hailman, *An Introduction to Animal Behaviour: Ethology's First Century* (London, 1967) and W. H. Thorpe, *The Origins and Rise of Ethology* (London, 1979). The following are useful articles on particular aspects of the subject, P. H. Gray, 'Douglas Alexander Spalding: The First Experimental Behaviourist', *Journal of General Psychology*, lxvii (1962), pp. 299–307; P. H. Gray, 'The Descriptive Study of Imprinting in Birds from 1873–1953', *Journal of General Psychology*, lxviii (1963), pp. 333–7; P. H. Gray, 'The Early Animal Behaviorists: Prolegomenon to Ethology', *Isis*, lix (1968), pp. 372–83; J. Jaynes, 'The Historical

established reputation as one of the most distinctive and influential branches of modern biology. Broadly speaking, the history of ethology may be divided into three phases. In the first 'formative' phase (the period up to about 1930), the term 'ethology' became associated fairly widely with the study of animal behaviour, and a number of pioneering studies were undertaken. The second 'classical' phase occupies the twenty years up to 1950. During this period coherent traditions of ethological research were established in northern Europe, particularly under the influence of Konrad Z. Lorenz and Nikolaas Tinbergen, and these rapidly elaborated a substantial body of theory and practice. By 1950 the subject had developed to the point where two of Tinbergen's former students were able to publish an 'introduction' to the ethology of one family of fish which ran to almost 250 pages; and a year later, Tinbergen himself published *The Study of Instinct*, a book summarizing the major achievements of classical ethology, and described by none other than Edward Wilson as 'possibly the single most influential synthesis of animal behaviour published in this century'.[7] After 1950, ethology entered a third or 'mature' phase. Now a well-established discipline, it began to emerge from the comparative isolation of the pre-war period and to attract a much wider audience. In 1949 Tinbergen moved from Leiden to Oxford, and almost simultaneously, W. H. Thorpe set up a field station near Cambridge for the study of bird behaviour. Over the next few years, English ethology expanded very rapidly.[8] At the same time, there was increasing contact between Europe and America, and ethology began to benefit from interaction with other traditions of be-

Origins of "Ethology" and "Comparative Psychology"', *Animal Behaviour*, xvii (1969), pp. 601–6; T. J. Kalikow, 'History of Konrad Lorenz's Ethological Theory, 1927–1939', *Studies in History and Philosophy of Science*, vi (1975), pp. 333–41; T. J. Kalikow, 'Konrad Lorenz's Ethological Theory, 1939–1943: "Explanations" of Human Thinking, Feeling and Behaviour', *Philosophy of the Social Sciences*, vi (1976), pp. 15–34; R. J. Richards, 'The Innate and the Learned: The Evolution of Konrad Lorenz's Theory of Instinct', *Philosophy of the Social Sciences*, iv (1974), pp. 111–33.
[7] G. P. Baerends and J. M. Baerends Van Roon, 'An Introduction to the Study of the Ethology of Cichlid Fishes', *Behaviour*, supplement 1 (1950), pp. 1–243; N. Tinbergen, *The Study of Instinct* (Oxford, 1951); T. Eisner and E. O. Wilson (eds.), *Animal Behaviour: Readings from 'Scientific American'* (San Francisco, 1955–75), p. 2.
[8] W. H. Thorpe (note 6), gives some valuable personal reminiscences of this period (pp. 108–25).

havioural research.[9] The unexpected and controversial climax of this last phase came in 1973, when Lorenz and Tinbergen, together with Karl von Frisch, were awarded the Nobel Prize for Physiology and Medicine.[10]

What is ethology? A more or less random survey of literature from the mature phase reveals a fairly close and possibly predictable consensus on this question. For Lorenz, ethology is 'the biology of behaviour', or alternatively, 'the *comparative* study of behaviour'. For Tinbergen, it is 'the biological study of behaviour'. Thorpe defines his subject as 'the comparative study of the natural behaviour of animal species', while the ethologist and historian P. H. Gray describes it as 'the study of the behaviour of animals in their natural environments'. Finally, for the authors of a text-book subtitled 'Ethology's first century', ethology is 'the study of animal behaviour from a biological viewpoint'.[11] These general statements are clear enough, at least as far as they go. However, their clarity belies what is a very complex and significant history. For the term 'ethology' has been given a number of distinct meanings, and it is only relatively recently that biologists have appropriated it for their

[9] The debates of the 1950s deserve a special study of their own. Classical ethology came under attack from a number of American biologists and comparative psychologists, see, for example, D. S. Lehrman, 'A Critique of Konrad Lorenz's Theory of Instinctive Behaviour', *Quarterly Review of Biology*, xxviii (1953), pp. 337–63; T. C. Schneirla, 'Interrelationships of the "Innate" and the "Acquired" in Instinctive Behaviour', in P. P. Grassé (ed.), *L'Instinct dans le Comportement des Animaux et de l'Homme* (Paris, 1956), pp. 387–452. Lorenz eventually replied to these and other criticisms in his *Evolution and Modification of Behaviour* (Chicago and London, 1965).

[10] Details of the prize-giving ceremony, together with brief autobiographical sketches of the three men and their Nobel lectures, are given in *Les Prix Nobel en 1973* (Nobel Foundation, Stockholm, 1974), pp. 11–46, 158–218. The announcement of the award was unexpected, since it broke with the tradition that the prize be given for basic physiological or medical research. Controversy centred on the question of Lorenz's political views. Some of his papers from the war-period were described as being pro-Nazi, and Simon Wiesenthal, Head of the Jewish Documentation Centre in Vienna, wrote asking Lorenz to decline the prize. The awards and the subsequent controversy were reported in *The New York Times*, 12 October 1973 and 15 December 1973. The most critical article of the period was probably W. Cloud, 'Winners and Sinners', *The Sciences*, xiii, no. 10 (1973), pp. 16–21.

[11] K. Lorenz, in Charles Darwin, *The Expression of the Emotions in Man and Animals* (Chicago, 1965), preface, p. xi; K. Lorenz, *Studies in Animal and Human Behaviour*, 2 vols. (London, 1970–1), i, p. xvi (hereafter, these volumes will be referred to as *Studies*, i and ii); N. Tinbergen, 'Ethology', in R. Harré (ed.), *Scientific Thought 1900–1960* (Oxford, 1969), p. 238; Thorpe (note 6), p. viii; P. H. Gray, 'The Early Animal Behaviorists: Prolegomenon to Ethology' (note 6), p. 373; P. H. Klopfer and J. P. Hailman (note 6), p. ix.

own use. There is a great deal to be learnt from the way in which this process took place.

The *Oxford English Dictionary* (1973) gives three definitions of ethology: (1) the portrayal of character by mimicry, (2) the science of ethics, also, a treatise on morals, (3) the science of character. The first two definitions are the oldest, and they appear to have become entirely obsolete. The last is rather more recent, and is taken from the work of John Stuart Mill. In the second volume of his *Logic*, Mill proposed the establishment of two distinct sciences of the human mind: psychology, which was to investigate the general or universal laws of human nature; and a subordinate subject, having to do with the way in which these laws, operating in particular circumstances, gave rise to individual human characters. Mill wrote: 'A science is thus formed, to which I would propose to give the name Ethology, or the Science of Character; from the Greek *ethos*, a word more nearly corresponding to the term "character" as I here use it, than any other word in the same language'.[12]

Mill's definition was perfectly reasonable, given the etymology of the term he had chosen, but for all that, his new science met with little success. Only for a few years at around the turn of the century did Millean ethology find favour in America, and in Europe it appears to have been almost totally ignored. Instead, the term was taken up by biologists. Julian Jaynes notes that in 1859 Isidore Geoffroy Saint Hilaire 'rather casually recreated ethology' as the branch of biology devoted to the study of animals in their natural habitats. Jaynes interprets this move as part of the conflict in early nineteenth-century France between the claims of laboratory analysis on the one hand, and those of naturalistic observation on the other; and he argues that this conflict underlay the separate origins in the latter part of the century of laboratory-based comparative psychology and naturalistic ethology.[13] However, while comparative psychology became rapidly and securely established after 1870, ethology remained in a state of considerable confusion. The reasons for this are not hard to find. Not only did the term itself now have at least two distinct meanings, but one of them (Geoffroy's 'biological' ethology) overlapped extensively with 'Oecologie', Ernst Haeckel's new discipline, whose exact nature was itself a matter of

---

[12] J. S. Mill, *A System of Logic Ratiocinative and Inductive* (1st edn. 1843, repr. of 8th edn., 1872), 2 vols. (Toronto, 1973–4), ii, p. 869.
[13] J. Jaynes (note 6), pp. 601–6.

debate. Thus, Haeckel's early definition of ecology as 'the science of the economy, of the habits, of the external relations of organisms to each other', was virtually indistinguishable from Alfred Giard's slightly later use of the term ethology to cover 'the study of the customs of animals and their mutual relationships'.[14]

This confusion proved fatal for ethology in England and America. In 1902, the *Zoological Record* of the Zoological Society of London began using the term in its elaborate classifications of the zoological literature. Ethology appeared as a subdivision of a section devoted to 'Textbooks, General Works, Evolution, Essays'. By 1907, it had its own section, but this was devoted to works on 'Behaviour, habits, plankton, psychology, symbiosis, parasitism', and the scope of ethology was anything but clear. Doubt persisted in the *Record* until as late as 1940, when ethology was finally dropped altogether, its place being taken by a section on 'Ecology and Habits'.[15] Similarly, in America the well-known zoologist William Morton Wheeler began a campaign for ethology in 1902. In an article revealingly entitled 'Natural history, Oecology or Ethology?', Wheeler argued that zoologists were in urgent need of a new term which would cover their interest in the relationship between the habits of animals and their habitats. He wrote: 'The only term hitherto suggested which will adequately convey the study of animals, with a view to elucidating their true character as expressed in their physical and psychical behaviour towards their living and inorganic environment, is *ethology*'.[16] Over the next few years, Wheeler used the term ethology in the titles of a number of his scientific papers.[17] But it seems that he was alone in seeing a need for the new term, and eventually he dropped it altogether. His argument had been that ecology was to botany what ethology should be to zoology. When it became clear that ecology had established a secure position in both sciences, he reluctantly con-

[14] For Haeckel, see R. C. Stauffer, 'Haeckel, Darwin and Ecology', *Quarterly Review of Biology*, xxxii (1957), pp. 138–44. The work of Alfred Giard is discussed by Jaynes (note 6), pp. 603–4.
[15] See *The Zoological Record*, xxxix (1902) – lxxvii (1940).
[16] W. M. Wheeler, '"Natural History", "Oecology" or "Ethology"?', *Science*, xv (1902), p. 974.
[17] See, for example, 'Ethology and the Mutation Theory', *Science*, xxi (1905), pp. 535–40; 'An Ethological Study of Certain Maladjustments in the Relations of Ants to Plants', *Bulletin of the American Museum of Natural History*, xxii (1906), pp. 403–18; and 'Comparative Ethology of the European and North American Ants,' *Journal für Psychologie und Neurologie*, xiii (1908), pp. 404–35.

ceded defeat. In his retiring address as President of the American Association for the Advancement of Science in 1923, Wheeler commented:

I admire Haeckel, but I dislike his term 'ecology' and have repeatedly pointed out that it belongs in the synonymy with a number of other terms, ranging in order of priority as follows: 'natural history' (eighteenth and nineteenth centuries), 'ethology' (Isidore Geoffroy Saint Hilaire, 1859), 'ecology' as 'Relationsphysiologie' (Haeckel, 1866), 'Biologie' in the restricted German sense (later nineteenth century to the present), 'bionomics' (E. Ray Lankester, 1889), 'behaviour', 'comportement', 'Gebaren' (past three decades). In this country the inept Haeckelian term, largely as a result of the afore-mentioned silo and saleratus botanists and their zoological camp-followers, has won the day and my adrenals are now too weak to offer further resistance.[18]

After so many false starts, it was finally in Germany and Holland that ethology became permanently established. In a series of articles published during the 1890s, the zoologist Friedrich Dahl urged the need for greater importance to be attached to what he termed 'comparative ethology', by which he meant the comparative study of the life habits of related groups of animals.[19] For a time his argument was no more successful than Wheeler's, but eventually it gained the support of the Assistant Director of the Berlin Zoological Gardens, Oskar Heinroth. Heinroth is arguably the single most important figure in the early history of ethology. In the course of ornithological studies which culminated in the publication of a definitive four-volume work on *Die Vögel Mitteleuropas* (1924–33), he laid the methodological and theoretical foundations of classical ethology. In a key paper entitled 'Contributions to the Biology, and particularly to the Ethology and Psychology of the Anatidae', Heinroth wrote:

I have always been interested, not in what we commonly refer to as biology ... but rather in the more subtle life habits, manners and customs [of animals], that is, in the sort of thing students refer to as rituals. I soon found that ethological literature of this type was more or less non-existent, and so I entered a largely

[18] W. M. Wheeler, 'The Dry-Rot of our Academic Biology', *Science*, lvii (1923), p. 66.
[19] See for example, F. Dahl, 'Die Ziele der Vergleichenden "Ethologie"', *Verhandlungen des V Zoologischen-Kongresses zu Berlin*, v (1902), pp. 296–300.

unworked field of study, where the first essential was to plough a straight furrow.[20]

For Heinroth, ethology was as close to psychology as it was to ecology. More strictly, it was an independent field of inquiry which deserved a place of its own amongst the sciences of life. During the 1920s and 1930s, it was Heinroth's vision of what ethology could be which inspired not only Konrad Lorenz but also an important group of Dutch workers which included G. F. Makkink, A. F. Portielje, J. Verwey, and, of course, Niko Tinbergen. In the writings of these men, the term ethology became firmly linked with the biological study of animal behaviour.

However, it is worth noting in passing that even now there was some ambiguity in the use of terms. Indeed, the most important mouthpiece for the new science of ethology throughout the classical period was a journal called Die Zeitschrift für Tierpsychologie.

Enough has now been said to indicate that the establishment of the term ethology within biology was a long and complex process. Over a period of around seventy-five years the term was taken up in a variety of contexts which overlapped at one extreme with ecology and at the other with psychology. Clearly it would be a mistake to assume either that the term had a single meaning in biology during this period, or that all who were of like mind on the subject of animal behaviour called themselves ethologists. Nevertheless, the growing use of the term, particularly after 1900, reflected a significant movement of thought amongst naturalists and zoologists which it is the purpose of this paper to identify. In summary, it may be said that the early ethologists shared a distinctive view of animal behaviour and of the way in which it should be studied. This view held that animals possess specific, innate 'characters' which can be understood, often by direct ana-logy with human character, on the basis of prolonged and sym-pathetic observation.

The remainder of the paper attempts to put flesh on to the dry bones of this summary by means of an examination of the aims and

---

[20] O. Heinroth, 'Beiträge zur Biologie, namentlich Ethologie und Psychologie der Anatiden', Verhandlungen des V Internationalen Ornithologen-Kongresses (Berlin, 1911), p. 589 (hereafter, this paper will be referred to as 'Beiträge'). In her biography, Heinroth's second wife records that her husband was influenced by Dahl in matters of nomenclature and it therefore seems likely that it was from him that he adopted the term ethology. See K. Heinroth, Oskar Heinroth. Vater der Verhaltensforschung, 1871–1945 (Stuttgart, 1971), p. 64. I am extremely grateful to Dr R. W. Burkhardt for making available to me his copy of this book.

methods of different groups of workers in America and Europe. It will be argued that, in its most important manifestation, the idea of innate character in animals (and man) was central to the work begun by Heinroth and continued, in particular, by Lorenz. This idea gave to classical ethology some of its most distinctive features; it underlay many of its greatest successes, as well as giving rise to a number of fundamental problems, some of which are still unresolved at the present time. Paradoxically, the centrality of the notion of innate character to the project of early ethology brought it within sight of Mill's original plan for a science of the formation of human character. But to see how this happened, it is necessary to return to some of the early calls for a reformulation of the science of animal behaviour.

When William Morton Wheeler championed the cause of ethology in the first decade of this century, he did so in the context of a general plea for 'a renascence of zoology'. Wheeler was concerned to combat the increasing domination of zoology by a laboratory-based preoccupation with morphological and physiological research. A life-long naturalist and myrmecologist who never quite adjusted to the new experimental biology of his day, he opposed what he saw as a widespread obsession with the physical characteristics of (mostly dead) specimens. Wheeler was never a man to mince his words, and he lashed out at the prevailing ethos of his profession: museums had become 'mausoleums of animal and plant structures'; creatures were widely regarded as being of interest only when they had been 'fixed in some fluid recommended in a German laboratory'; and in fact biology as a whole was in danger of being swept off course by 'ephemeral laboratory fads'. What was needed was nothing less than a return to fundamentals. Wheeler wrote:

> History shows that throughout the centuries, from Aristotle and Pliny to the present day, natural history constitutes the perennial root-stock or stolon of biological science and that it retains this character because it satisfies some of our most fundamental and vital interests in organisms as living individuals more or less like ourselves.[21]

But if natural history was the stolon of biology, then ethology was its most vigorous bud, for it was concerned with just those areas of

[21] See W. M. Wheeler (note 16), pp. 974, 976; *idem*, 'Ethology and the Mutation Theory' (note 17), pp. 537–8; *idem* (note 18), p. 67.

research which were most in need of support: studies of 'the accustomed seat, haunt, habitat or dwelling of men and animals'; of 'habits, manners, etc.'; and of the 'character', 'dispositions', 'nature', or 'psychology' of animals. Wheeler argued that an organism's ethos or character was as distinctive as its physical form. Thus, if taxonomy and phylogeny were not to remain 'deplorably defective and one-sided', it was essential that 'comprehensive, comparative study of behaviour' be given top priority.[22]

Wheeler's characterization of ethology clearly reflected his own work with the social insects, and particularly the ants, where close attention to both physical environment (e.g., the nest) and behaviour was often essential for accurate identification and classification.[23] In addition, however, his views reflected the general orientation of a small but extremely influential group of zoologists of which he had been a member during the early stages of his career. Wheeler was born and brought up in Milwaukee, and it was here during the 1880s that his scientific interests were shaped under the influence of such people as Carl Akeley, George W. Peckham and Charles Otis Whitman. Akeley is now regarded as the founder of modern taxidermy, and he revolutionized the art of museum display by introducing the 'diorama', an exhibit in which animals and plants are presented naturalistically, in typical groups and settings. For a time, Wheeler and Akeley worked together at the Natural Science Establishment of H. A. Ward in Rochester, New York, and they became extremely friendly. The significance of Akeley's work may be judged from Wheeler's tribute to his friend, written many years later:

> [Akeley] was thoroughly convinced that an animal is meaningless, except to a hard-shelled zoologist, unless it is presented in such a manner as to convey something of its real character, or *ethos*, which is manifested by its specific motor behaviour in a specific natural environment. The development of the taxidermic 'group' follows naturally from such a conviction.[24]

[22] See W. M. Wheeler (note 16), p. 975; *idem*, 'Ethology and the Mutation Theory' (note 17), p. 539.

[23] See W. M. Wheeler, 'Comparative Ethology of the European and North American Ants' (note 17), pp. 404–35; *idem*, *The Social Insects, Their Origin and Evolution* (London, 1928).

[24] W. M. Wheeler, 'Carl Akeley's Early Work and Environment', *Natural History*, xxvii (1927), p. 141. This article is a valuable source of personal reminiscences concerning Wheeler's early life. Further biographical details, including a lengthy discussion of Wheeler's time in Milwaukee, are contained in M. A. Evans and H. E. Evans, *William Morton Wheeler, Biologist* (Cambridge, Mass., 1970).

If Wheeler was impressed by Akeley's work, he was even more influenced by that of George Peckham. In 1885, Wheeler returned from Rochester to Milwaukee to take up a position in the Milwaukee High School, of which Peckham was then principal. Peckham had been a biology teacher, and he and his wife were keen students of the behaviour of spiders and insects. They were also enthusiastic Darwinists. Of Peckham, Wheeler wrote: 'Every year he most conscientiously read, as a devout priest might read his breviary, Darwin's *Origin* and *Animals and Plants under Domestication*'.[25] This devotion found more lasting expression in a series of classic papers on the 'courtship' behaviour of spiders. On the basis of detailed and often painfully laborious observations of a great number of different species, the Peckhams fully corroborated Darwin's widely criticized theory of sexual selection. Wheeler helped with the illustrations for these papers, and he went on to assist the Peckhams in field-work which resulted in equally important publications on the behaviour and evolution of wasps.[26]

Of all those who influenced Wheeler during the 1880s, undoubtedly the most important was C. O. Whitman. Whitman was a leading figure in late nineteenth century American zoology: he is generally credited with the responsibility for having introduced European ideas and methods into America; he founded the *Journal of Morphology* in 1887; and a year later he became the first Director of the Marine Biological Laboratory at Woods Hole, a post which he held for twenty years.[27] During the late 1880s, Whitman was for a time Director of the Allis Lake Laboratory in Milwaukee, and it was here that he became part of the circle of friends which included Wheeler, Akeley and the Peckhams. Although not widely known during his life-time for his interest in behaviour, Whitman left his mark on ethology through a series of lectures delivered at Woods Hole in 1897 and 1898, through a work on the behaviour of pigeons which was published posthumously in 1919, and, perhaps above all, through his influence on

[25] W. M. Wheeler (note 24), p. 137.
[26] See G. W. and E. G. Peckham, 'Observations on Sexual Selection in Spiders of the Family Attidae', *Occasional Papers of the Natural History Society of Wisconsin*, i (Milwaukee, 1889), pp. 1–60. This was the first of six papers by the Peckhams on the Attidae which were published by the Natural History Society of Wisconsin between 1889 and 1896. See also their *Wasps, Social and Solitary* (Cambridge, Mass., 1905).
[27] The best biographical source on Whitman is F. R. Lillie, 'Charles Otis Whitman', *Journal of Morphology, Whitman Memorial Volume*, xxii (1911), pp. xv–lxxvii, but see also, E. S. Morse, 'Charles Otis Whitman', *Biographical Memoirs of the National Academy of Sciences*, vii (1913), pp. 269–88.

his students, among whom Wheeler and Wallace Craig were outstanding.[28]

It was on the basis of detailed studies of animals as diverse as the leech *Clepsine*, the salamander *Necturus*, and the pigeons, that Whitman advanced his distinctive views on behaviour. In the Woods Hole lectures, he defended what he took to be the 'Darwinian' theory of instinct against the 'Lamarckian' notion of the inheritance of acquired habit. Instincts were not isolated, disconnected phenomena which had developed in unrelated groups of organisms through simple experience. Rather, they were fundamental biological entities, subject to the laws of variation and natural selection. Drawing not only on the work of Darwin himself, but also on that of the Peckhams, Whitman argued that instincts were 'evolved, not improvised'; their genealogy was 'as complex and far-reaching as the history of their organic bases'. It followed directly from this that, as he put it, 'Instinct and structure are to be studied from the common standpoint of phyletic descent'.[29] Whitman went on to put this principle into practice in his monumental study of pigeons, where behavioural and morphological evidence was integrated in an attempt to reconstruct the evolutionary interrelationships among nearly forty wild species, as well as a number of domesticated varieties. Wallace Craig found inspiration in this work for a theory of animal instinct which eventually crossed the Atlantic and had an important influence on European ethology.[30]

[28] In recent years, ethologists have come to revere Whitman as the true founder, with Heinroth, of their discipline. See, for example, P. H. Klopfer and J. P. Hailman (note 6), pp. 46, 52; K. Lorenz, *Studies*, i (note 11), p. 370.

[29] C. O. Whitman, 'Animal Behavior', *Biological Lectures of the Marine Biological Laboratory* (Woods Hole, Mass., 1898), pp. 300, 328.

[30] See C. O. Whitman, 'The Behaviour of Pigeons' in O. Riddle (ed.), *C. O. Whitman: Posthumous Works*, 3 vols. (Washington, 1919), iii. In one of his earliest papers on pigeons, W. Craig noted that the long term aim of his research was to study the characteristic sounds and bodily movements of one species and to compare them with 'all the species in Professor Whitman's large collection of living birds', see 'The Expressions of Emotion in the Pigeons: 1. The Blond Ring-Dove (*Turtur risorius*)', *Journal of Comparative Neurological Psychology*, xix (1909), p. 30. Craig went on to publish a series of studies which culminated in his important theoretical paper, 'Appetites and Aversions as Constituents of Instincts', *Biological Bulletin*, xxxiv (1918), pp. 91–107. Although this paper had a great influence on Lorenz, Craig soon lost contact with developments in ethology. Thorpe (note 6), pp. 48–9, describes how, after giving a lecture at Harvard in 1951, he was amazed to learn that Craig was in the audience. He had assumed him to be dead and few others present even knew who he was!

In both his research and his teaching, Whitman followed the basic precept that nothing could be understood about behaviour without the most prolonged and intimate acquaintance with animals. As a boy, he is said to have been fascinated by pigeons, keeping them and watching them endlessly, 'intensely interested in their feeding, their young, and everything they did'. Later in life, when the study of these birds had become almost an obsession, Whitman transferred his pigeons from Chicago to Woods Hole and back again each summer. Indeed, the problems involved in this annual pilgrimage appear to have influenced his decision to resign as Director of the Woods Hole Laboratory in 1908. By this time, his home had become one enormous pigeon-cote, and his student and biographer, F. R. Lillie, records that: 'He thus actually lived with his birds constantly, and very rarely was absent from them even for a single day. He made observations and kept notes on all aspects of the life and behaviour of each species, as well as of such hybrids as he was able to produce'.[31]

Whitman wrote only one popular article on the subject of animal behaviour, and it is significant that it took the form of a sustained critique of the current state of research. Directing his attack particularly at the laboratory-based psychologists – at those who, as he put it, 'hoped to reach the heights of comparative psychology through a few hours of parlour diversion with caged animals' – he insisted that 'The one qualification absolutely indispensable to reliable diagnosis of an animal's conduct is an intimate acquaintance with the creature's normal life, its habits and instincts.'[32] This was the high standard Whitman set for his students. He is said to have encouraged them not to allow anything their animals did to escape attention; and they are reported to have greeted each other, not with 'What is your special field?' but rather with, 'What is your beast?'[33] At this point, it is worth remembering that chief among Whitman's students was Wheeler himself. Not only did Wheeler work under Whitman at the Allis Lake Laboratory, but subsequently he followed him first to Clark University in Worcester, Mass., and then to Chicago.[34] Thus, the similarity of outlook between the two men was no coincidence. In his campaign for a 'renascence of zoology' based upon the treatment of animals as 'living individuals more or less like ourselves', Wheeler was following very

---

[31] F. R. Lillie (note 27), pp. xvi, lxxi.
[32] C. O. Whitman, 'Myths in Animal Psychology', *The Monist*, ix (1899), p. 530.
[33] M. A. Evans and H. E. Evans (note 24), p. 9.
[34] See 'William Morton Wheeler', *Dictionary of American Biography*, xxii, suppl. II (1958), pp. 707–8.

largely in his mentor's footsteps. His use of the term ethology to cover 'the study of animals, with a view to elucidating their true character as expressed in their physical and psychical behaviour towards their living and inorganic environment', simply gave the most appropriate name to a project on which Whitman had been engaged for many years.

At the same time that Wheeler was making his case for ethology in America, similar arguments were being put by Oskar Heinroth in Germany. In many ways, Heinroth was the Whitman of northern Europe. A trained zoologist with a life-long and passionate interest in the lives of birds, he too used naturalistic observation and experiments with hand-rearing to explore the nature and development of animal behaviour. As Whitman's comparative study of the pigeons broke new ground in America, so Heinroth's comparative study of the ducks, geese and swans paved the way for later developments in Europe. Linking the two men together as the joint founders of ethology, Konrad Lorenz has asserted (rather modestly) that 'My scientific merit lies in discovering Whitman and Heinroth'.[35]

Heinroth's obsession with birds dominated his life. At school he hated formal academic study, and his one real interest earned him the nickname 'Duck Henry' (*Entenheinrich*). Later, during long and frustrating years of medical training and military service, he took every available opportunity to return to his first love. Finally, in 1896, he entered the Friedrich-Wilhelms-Universität in Berlin to read zoology, and now he was able to spend much more time studying the birds in the neighbouring Berlin Zoological Gardens. Before his training was even complete, Heinroth was acting as unpaid assistant to the Director of the Gardens; and he continued in this role for several years until money could be found to make his position official. In her biography, Heinroth's second wife, Katharina, notes that her husband made considerable sacrifices, both of money and of the prospects for an academic career, in order to remain in the one place where he could pursue his ornithological studies without interruption.[36]

From the outset, Heinroth brought a distinctive approach to his

[35] R. I. Evans, *Konrad Lorenz. The Man and His Ideas* (New York and London, 1975), p. 7.
[36] K. Heinroth (note 20), p. 89. All biographical information concerning Heinroth has been taken from this volume.

work with birds. In his important paper on the *Anatidae* (ducks, geese and swans), he began by contrasting his own interests with those of his contemporaries. He had always been preoccupied, he wrote, not with the general biology of birds, but rather with their more subtle life habits, manners and customs ('*die feineren Lebensgewohnheiten, die Sitten und Gebräuche*') – that is, with their ethology. Heinroth criticized his colleagues for having neglected this dimension of bird life: he pointed out that ornithological handbooks almost always failed to distinguish the quite different call-notes of male and female ducks; and he ridiculed one unfortunate author who had confused two distinct species of swan:

> When I came across the picture of the Whooper Swan in the New Neumann, I could hardly believe my eyes, for there was a bird holding its wings in the manner of the Mute Swan! The fact is that the two species hold their wings quite differently, and one might almost say that their distinct life-habits are embodied in their distinct postures ... Without exaggerating, in ethological terms this is as if, in representing an enraged dog, one were to use an irritated cat as a model!

Having illustrated the inadequacies of earlier studies, Heinroth explained what was meant by the term ethology:

> Before I go on to present my modest and unfortunately incomplete ethological observations, we should first be quite clear about ethology itself. As you know, the term 'ethos' refers to customs and manners in a human sense. Strictly speaking, this word is not really applicable to animals, since in our case language, customs and manners are taught and learnt, whereas a duck brings its language and rituals – which I shall describe in due course as its communication system [*Verkehrsformen*] – with it into the world, and exercises both without ever having heard or seen another member of its own species. Thus we speak in this instance of instinctive or inborn customs and manners, and we use the term ethos in a way which is quite different from its original meaning.[37]

Heinroth's preliminary discussion clarifies the nature of his interests. He was concerned to investigate in animals the sort of behaviour which in man is often described as gestural, symbolic or

[37] O. Heinroth, 'Beiträge' (note 20), pp. 589–90.

expressive. Heinroth saw his birds as possessing, by analogy with man, innate characters or personalities. The task of the ethologist was to analyse these characters with a view to gaining a better understanding of the part which they played in the birds' lives. In addition, by comparing groups of closely related species, the ethologist could use his understanding of innate character to reconstruct evolutionary genealogies.

In the bulk of his paper, Heinroth went on to show how this project could be tackled by means of a comprehensive survey of the *Anatidae*. On the basis of a life-time's personal experience with these birds, he reconstructed the nature or character of each species. Using photographs to supplement his detailed and evocative descriptions, he tried to give a complete account of the activities of the birds, and to interpret their different meanings. He described the 'incitement' behaviour (*Hetzen*) of female ducks, the 'display postures' (*Imponierstellungen*) of the males, and the 'triumph ceremonies' (*Triumphgeschreien*) which were performed by swans and geese; he discussed how apparently trivial actions might serve as 'greeting signals' (*Begrüssungszeichen*) or 'intention movements' (*Intentionsbewegungen*); and he recounted the way in which the innate responses of hand-reared birds were often re-directed to man.[38] Like Whitman before him, Heinroth used hybridization experiments to back up his comparative studies, and he did not hesitate to use his understanding of the birds' natures to revise accounts of their taxonomy. For example, in the section on swans, he wrote: 'The Black Swan has been made the sole representative of a special genus *Chenopsis*: biologically, and particularly ethologically, this is quite wrong, since its character [*Wesen*] bears a close resemblance to that of the Mute Swan, whereas with the Whooper Swan it has absolutely no affinity'.[39]

Heinroth's attractive and sympathetic accounts of bird life were

---

[38] It is often difficult to translate Heinroth's descriptive terminology into English. Where possible, I have followed the conventions adopted by A. Heymer, *Ethological Dictionary: German, English, French* (New York and London, 1977). Like many other contemporary ethologists, Heymer mistakenly attributes to Lorenz a number of Heinroth's concepts and terms (see, for example, '*Hetzen*', p. 86 and '*Triumphgeschrei*', p. 180). Lorenz took up Heinroth's work on the re-direction of innate responses in his study of 'imprinting' ('*Prägung*'); see 'Companions as Factors in the Bird's Environment', *Studies*, i (note 11) pp. 101–258.

[39] O. Heinroth, 'Beiträge' (note 20), pp. 602–3. Heinroth paid a great deal of attention to the results of hybridization experiments and he included photographs illustrating the outcome of particular crosses (see his Table 4).

based on the interpretation of behaviour as a complex of external signs which expressed internal psychological or emotional pre-dispositions. This interpretation was reflected in the very terms which he chose to describe behaviour – 'intention movement', 'triumph ceremony', etc. – and it depended upon his willingness to identify with the animals that he watched. This identification rested in turn, of course, upon the fundamental analogy between animal and human character. In the *Anatidae* paper, Heinroth argued that animals could be understood just like people, by observing their 'involuntary facial expressions and unintentional emotional out-bursts'.[40] Elsewhere, he described animal language as being 'like our laughing and crying'.[41] In the introduction to their major work, *Die Vögel Mitteleuropas*, Heinroth and his wife wrote that their aim had been to study the subtle details of bird behaviour 'in order to gain some idea of how things look from the point of view of the bird'. Once again, this aim was achieved by means of evocative descriptions which moved freely between observed exter-nal signs and attributed internal feelings. Here, for example, is an account of the relationship between a hand-reared corncrake called Liliput and Magdalena Heinroth:

> The love relationship of Liliput with my wife was formed in the following way. Especially if she held out her hand, he took on a proud bearing, extending his wings and cleaning his stomach and sides with his beak: cleaning movements in the bird world are in fact often an expression of excitement, and particularly of amorousness, or perhaps they correspond to an expression of embarrassment, as when a man puts the finishing touches to his moustache or necktie and a woman fusses over her clothes? Man and animals certainly possess extraordinarily similar feelings which are often expressed in the same way ... In jest, we usually express our point of view thus: animals are emotional people of extremely poor intelligence.[42]

It would be difficult to over-estimate Heinroth's role in the foundations of ethology. At the level of methodology, his vision of the need for complete inventories of the characteristic behaviours of

---

[40] O. Heinroth, 'Beiträge' (note 20), p. 621.
[41] O. and K. Heinroth, *The Birds* (London, 1959), p. 119.
[42] Quoted by K. Heinroth (see note 20), pp. 108, 130–1, from O. Heinroth *Die Vögel Mitteleuropas in allen Lebens-und Entwicklungsstufen photographisch aufgenommen und in ihrem Seelenleben bei der Aufzucht vom Ei ab beobachtet*, 4 vols. (Berlin, 1924–33).

animals, compiled on the basis of exhaustive naturalistic observation, became a major preoccupation amongst later workers.[43]
Similarly, at the level of theory, Heinroth's analysis of the emotional life of birds and of the expressive nature of their behaviour
entered into the mainstream of classical ethology, particularly
through the work of Lorenz. The question of the relationship
between Heinroth and Lorenz deserves greater attention than can
be given to it here, but in summary it may be said that Heinroth
was the single most important influence on Lorenz during the
1920s and 1930s. In the decade after 1926, when Lorenz's fiancée
typed up his notes on the behaviour of a hand-reared jackdaw and
sent them to Heinroth without Lorenz's knowledge, the two men
developed their ideas in such close collaboration that it is often
impossible to distinguish their separate contributions. For example,
Lorenz has written of one of his most important early papers that it
was 'an attempt, on my side, to bring some sort of preliminary
order into a host of observational facts partly collected by myself
and partly inherited from Oskar Heinroth'. It is a measure of his
respect for the older man's work, as well as of his characteristically
vague method of presentation, that Lorenz did not even bother to
tell his readers which material was his own, and which
Heinroth's.[44]

Lorenz looked to Heinroth for the framework of his entire early
research programme. In a series of publications during the 1930s
which are widely regarded as having established the boundaries of
classical ethology, he took up one after another of the major
themes in Heinroth's work. Using exactly the same techniques of
naturalistic observation, hand-rearing, and hybridization, Lorenz
extended his mentor's views concerning the role of instinct in the
life of birds; he developed a more sophisticated analysis of the

[43] This was particularly true of the early Dutch ethologists. See, for example, A. F. J.
Portielje, 'Zur Ethologie bezw. Psychologie der Silbermöwe (Larus argentatus
argentatus Pont.)', Ardea, xvii (1928), pp. 112–49; J. Verwey, 'Die Paarungsbiologie
des Fischreihers', Zoologische Jahrbücher, Abteilung für allgemeine Zoologie,
xlviii (1930), pp. 1–120; G. F. Makkink, 'An Attempt at an Ethogram of the
European Avocet (Recurvirostra avosetta), with Ethological and Psychological
Remarks'. Ardea, xxv (1936), pp. 1–60. Makkink's term 'ethogram' has come to be
widely used to signify 'an exact catalogue of all behaviour patterns occurring in an
animal species', Heymer, Ethological Dictionary (note 38), p. 64.
[44] K. Lorenz, Studies, i (note 11), p. xviii. On the whole, Lorenz has been quite
candid about the extent of his debts to Heinroth (see note 35), but this has not
prevented the existence of widespread misconceptions concerning the authorship of
ideas (see note 38).

communicative and 'releasing' functions of so-called 'ritualized' behaviour; and he refined the comparative ethology of the *Anatidae.*[45] This was the most productive period in Lorenz's scientific career, and throughout it he was in regular correspondence with Heinroth, discussing everything from successes and failures with the rearing of birds to the prospects for a unified science of animal and human behaviour. In 1931, Lorenz wrote admiringly to his teacher: 'Are you ... aware, Herr Doktor, that you are really the founder of a science, namely animal psychology as a branch of biology?' Five years later, the two men were discussing how best to introduce their views into the newly-formed *Gesellschaft für Tierpsychologie.* In the end, their efforts were so successful that Lorenz was appointed joint editor of the Society's Journal, and with this move ethology found important official recognition.[46]

Perhaps the most significant similarities between the work of Heinroth and that of Lorenz existed not at the level of theory, but rather at that of method. Using the same observational techniques as Heinroth, Lorenz depended equally heavily for ethological insight upon a close personal relationship with his animals. Over and again, his writings return to the theme of the basic need to know an animal thoroughly, to have an intuitive 'feel' for its character, before attempting any ethological analysis. In the introduction to a collection of his early papers, Lorenz described the 'deep disappointment and disillusionment' which he had felt on encountering the work of earlier animal psychologists such as Spencer, Lloyd Morgan, and McDougall: 'They were no experts!', he exclaimed, 'They simply did not know enough about animals!' In contrast, he portrayed ethologists – the 'starers-at-animals' – as experts of a very unusual kind. Their work depended upon thorough familiarity

[45] The most important of Lorenz's papers from this period are: 'Beiträge zur Ethologie sozialer Corviden', *Journal für Ethologie,* lxxix (1931), pp. 67–127; 'Der Kumpan in der Umwelt des Vogels', *Journal für Ornithologie,* lxxxiii (1935), pp. 137–214, 289–413; 'Uber den Begriff der Instinkthandlung', *Folia Biotheoretica,* ii (1937), pp. 18–50; (with N. Tinbergen) 'Taxis und Instinkthandlung in der Eirollbewegung der Graugans', *Zeitschrift für Tierpsychologie,* ii (1938), pp. 1–29; 'Vergleichende Verhaltensforschung', *Zoologische Anzeiger Supplement,* xii (1939), pp. 69–102; and 'Vergleichende Bewegungsstudien an Anatinen', *Journal für Ornithologie,* lxxxix (1941), pp. 194–294.
[46] Much of the correspondence between Heinroth and Lorenz is reprinted in K. Heinroth (note 20), pp. 151–62. The quotation is from p. 155. Lorenz was invited to share editorial control of the *Zeitschrift für Tierpsychologie* with Otto Koehler, an early convert to his ideas about instinct, and a keen supporter of ethology.

with a group of related animals, and such familiarity was not easily achieved. He went on: 'In fact, it seems necessary to become emotionally involved to the point of "falling in love" with such a group in the way many bird-lovers and aviculturists and other kinds of "amateurs" do'.[47]

It is the role of this emotional involvement in Lorenz's work that makes the familiar image of him being followed by his 'family' of goslings, or swimming with them in the lake at his home in Altenberg, so much more than a romantic diversion from the serious business of ethology. Lorenz chose for detailed study only those birds with which it was possible to strike up a genuine friendship; and his interpretation of their behaviour was based on an ability to understand, and often to speak, their 'language'.[48] The reason for this personal involvement is not hard to find. Like Heinroth before him, Lorenz sought insights into the behaviour of his birds by trying to see things from their point of view.[49] His close rapport with individual birds enabled him to establish with comparative ease the symbolic significance of their gestures, postures, and so forth. Once again, a process of identification was involved, and animal behaviour was interpreted by analogy with human experience. In the early paper which made extensive use of Heinroth's observations, Lorenz concluded with some reflections on the nature of instinct:

> After years of close contact with animals, one is forcibly struck with the impression that instinctive behaviour patterns are correlated with subjective phenomena which correspond to feelings and passions. No genuine animal observer can overlook the

[47] K. Lorenz, *Studies* (note 11), i, p. xvi.

[48] This, of course, was the theme of Lorenz's popular book, *King Solomon's Ring* (London, 1952). The English title is less revealing than that of the original German, *Er redete mit dem Vieh, den Vögeln und den Fischen* (He talked with the beasts, the birds and the fish) (Vienna, 1949). The fact that this was a popular rather than a professional work in no way reduces its significance. The same style, and even on occasion the same anecdotes, appear in Lorenz's early scientific papers.

[49] In this context, Lorenz was influenced not only by Heinroth but also by the physiologist Jakob von Uexküll. Uexküll coined the term *Umwelt* to designate the subjective or phenomenal world of an individual, and he devised many ingenious techniques for exploring and explaining how things look from an animal's point of view. See J. von Uexküll, *Umwelt und Innenleben der Tiere* (Berlin, 1909) and *idem*, 'A Stroll Through the Worlds of Animals and Men. A Picture Book of Invisible Worlds', in C. H. Schiller (ed.), *Instinctive Behavior* (London, 1957), pp. 5–80. Lorenz's paper 'Der Kumpan in der Umwelt des Vogels' (1935) was dedicated to Uexküll on the occasion of his seventieth birthday.

homologies which exist between man and animals and which virtually impel one to draw conclusions about the subjective processes within animals.

Having established the crucial link between man and animals, Lorenz went on to endorse his teacher's oft-repeated motto: 'Animals are emotional people of extremely poor intelligence'.[50]

At this point, it would be possible to follow the progress of classical ethology in some detail, starting perhaps with the meeting between Lorenz and Tinbergen in 1936, and moving on to the increasingly sophisticated studies which they, their colleagues, and their students undertook in the turbulent years up to 1950.[51] However, besides being well beyond the scope of a single paper, this exercise would not add materially to the main theme of the present discussion, namely the question of the underlying attitudes and interests which fostered the rise of ethology. This theme may be pursued more profitably by extending the survey of early contributions to ethology in America and Europe to include contemporary developments in England. In particular, it is worth pausing over a group of English ornithologists whose work was ethological in style, though not in name.

In 1930, the Dutch ethologist Jan Verwey opened an influential account of the behaviour of the heron by noting that, though the number of ornithologists was extraordinarily large, the number of those who concerned themselves with 'the most intimate Biology of birds', and whose work thus acquired a more profound significance, was still very small. To illustrate the sort of work he had in mind, Verwey cited the 'distinguished studies' of Heinroth and a number of his Dutch colleagues. In addition, he mentioned two Englishmen: Edmund Selous and Julian Huxley.[52] In fact, Selous and Huxley were early representatives of a long line of English ornithologists in this century who have been interested in the study of bird behaviour.[53] Their work may be characterized in a number

---

[50] K. Lorenz, *Studies* (note 11), i, p. 251.

[51] Once again, it must be emphasized that this story remains to be told in anything like adequate detail. However, relevant information may be found in A. Nisbett, *Konrad Lorenz* (London, 1976), chapters 5 and 8; G. Baerends, C. Beer & A. Manning (eds.), *Function and Evolution in Behaviour. Essays in Honour of Professor Niko Tinbergen* (Oxford, 1975), pp. xi–xxii; and Thorpe (note 6), chapters 5 and 7.

[52] J. Verwey (note 43), p. 2.

[53] This line includes E. A. Armstrong, H. Eliot Howard, J. S. Huxley, F. B. Kirkman, D. L. Lack, W. P. Pycraft, E. Selous and W. H. Thorpe, all of whom made important contributions to the rise of ethology.

of different ways. At one level, they were simply amateur or at best semi-professional bird-watchers who were interested in the close observation of animals in their natural environments. At another, they were evolutionists who attempted to test some of Charles Darwin's ideas, and particularly his theory of sexual selection, through the study of the reproductive habits of birds. Finally, however, they may be seen as two of the earliest students of that 'most intimate Biology' which was ethology.

Edmund Selous was a shy and solitary man who appears to have pursued his passion for ornithology untiringly, but alone.[54] A prolific author of books and articles on different aspects of natural history, he embodied to perfection Lorenz's image of the ethologist as a 'starer-at-animals'. To judge from his published work, it would seem that Selous spent the greater part of his adult waking life crouched in hides taking notes on what he called the 'domestic habits' of birds. Many of his publications were simply observational diaries – direct transcripts of these notes, as they had been taken in the field. Selous recorded blow-by-blow accounts of what his birds did, together with his immediate thoughts on the meaning of what they had done, and thereafter he preferred not to alter a single word. Of course, this was not always possible. For one thing, the birds were often so active that, as he put it, 'One has ... to scribble very fast in order to keep up ... and so must leave a few things to be added';[55] and for another, publishers were frequently reluctant to accept the long and ungainly manuscripts which were the result. In one of his later works, which was itself compiled directly from diaries, Selous confessed that his consistent refusal to edit or compress his notes had often stood in the way of publication. He wrote:

> But I will hope better things ... At any rate, so long as I can publish at all I will not recount scantily what – in so far as it has seemed to me evidential – I have observed more fully. I value my notes as they are, not as turned into something else, as the strength of my evidence, not as the weakening of it. I will not de-pioneer myself.[56]

[54] Biographical information concerning Selous is extremely hard to find. There is a large collection of manuscript material in the Edward Grey Institute in Oxford. I have looked at this material only very briefly, and it may be that it contains some of the clues which are so conspicuously absent from Selous's published work.

[55] E. Selous, 'An Observational Diary of the Habits – mostly Domestic – of the Great Crested Grebe (*Podiceps cristatus*)', *The Zoologist*, v (1901), p. 173.

[56] E. Selous, *Evolution of Habit in Birds* (London, 1933), p. xvi.

Selous's chosen method of publication reflected his obsession with capturing as directly as possible the finest nuances of bird life. A severe critic of the experimental methods of the laboratory psychologists, as well as of the widespread disinterest in behaviour amongst his fellow-ornithologists, Selous aimed to establish the study of the everyday habits of birds upon a secure foundation of detailed observation. In this task, he saw himself as no more than a passive vehicle through which the birds could, as it were, speak for themselves. In another volume of observational diaries, he described himself as 'but the birds' amanuensis', adding: 'only I wish that they themselves had been sometimes a little more explicit, which would have rendered unnecessary a comment, here and there, for which I must take responsibility'.[57] Here, Selous was acknowledging that it was not always possible to live up to the ideal of the completely passive observer. However, in reality he was far more actively engaged than he knew. Not only was he a committed Darwinist, but many of his studies were undertaken specifically in order to test the Darwinian theory of sexual selection. Moreover, in his concern to interpret the significance of what he saw, Selous brought to his investigations exactly the same willingness to identify with his birds which characterized the work of the German ethologists. From the great wealth of his writings, perhaps a single example will serve to illustrate the effect of this identification. In the course of one description of an almost trivial incident in the 'courtship' of a pair of birds, Selous broke into his own narrative as follows:

> It is in watching such *imponderables*, such by-products or unessentials, as one may call them ... that the automaton theory as applied to animals ... entirely breaks down. One sees now not a mere species acting on certain definite lines necessary to its salvation, but two tenderly affectionate little *persons*, behaving, because they both feel like that, in very much the same way as a pair of young human lovers.[58]

It was because this sort of interpretation ran through all of his work with birds that Selous was able to state as a general conclusion:

> It follows ... as the result of my observations, that the 'brute beast' is a more intelligent, more emotional, more affectionate

---

[57] E. Selous, *Realities of Bird Life. Being Extracts from the Diaries of a Life-loving Naturalist* (London, 1927), p. 11.
[58] *Ibid.*, p. 64.

and generally fuller-feeling being than he has yet been acknowledged to be, having been too much killed and (even where protected) too little observed to allow of this justice being done him. For the most part, such observation as he has received has not been of a sympathetic (which means understanding) kind.[59]

Selous's general view of bird character had important implications for his theoretical work. For example, in the spring of 1906 he spent some time in Holland observing the breeding habits of the ruff and a number of other species with a view to testing Darwin's theory that many female birds actively select their mates on the basis of subjective preference. This theory attributed both aesthetic sensibilities and the power of choice to birds, and it was widely criticized in the late nineteenth century on the grounds of gross anthropomorphism.[60] However, in the observational diary which resulted from his trip, Selous strongly supported Darwin's view. His notes reveal that he was impressed, above all, by the drama of the birds' lives – by the evocative nature of their antics, and by the charged atmosphere of their 'courtship rites'. Selous did not hesitate to attribute conscious feelings to the birds, and he relied upon an intuitive grasp of their character as a basis for assessment. Of one pair of ducks, he wrote that 'their married relations are ... very much like our own at their best'; and when it came to the ruffs, his conclusion was clear: 'The selection on the part of the Reeves is most evident. They take the initiative throughout, and are the true masters of the situation. Quiet and unobtrusive as they are, compared to the Ruffs, their whole manner betrays conscious power'.[61]

Partly as a result of his isolation, Selous always felt that he was being ignored by his contemporaries. In fact, his influence was considerable, both in England and on the continent. In particular,

[59] Ibid., p. 341.
[60] Among others, Alfred Russel Wallace could not accept the theory of sexual selection by female choice. See Wallace, 'The Descent of Man', The Academy, ii (1871), pp. 177–83; J. Marchant (ed.), Alfred Russel Wallace: Letters and Reminiscences, 2 vols. (London, 1916), i, pp. 157, 203, 212, 227, 298. The anthropomorphic structure of the theory, and its place in Darwin's work, are discussed in more detail in my doctoral thesis: J. Durant, 'The Meaning of Evolution: Post-Darwinian Debates on the Significance for Man of the Theory of Evolution, 1858–1908' (Univ. of Cambridge PhD thesis, 1977), pp. 157–65.
[61] E. Selous, 'Observations Tending to Throw Light on the Question of Sexual Selection in Birds, including a day-to-day Diary on the Breeding Habits of the Ruff (Machetes pugnax)', The Zoologist, x (1906), pp. 201–19, 285–94, 419–28; ibid, xi (1907), pp. 60–5, 161–82, 367–80. The quotations are from ibid., x, p. 202 and xi, p. 375.

his work was cited extensively by Julian Huxley, who undertook very similar studies of his own. In his autobiography, Huxley recollected that, as a young zoology lecturer at Oxford, he had combined his duties with 'something that I knew intuitively would be of much greater importance for my future career – scientific bird-watching'.[62] Huxley's interest had first been aroused by one of Selous's books, which he read at about the time that he left school; and it grew to the point where, a year after he went up to Balliol in 1906, he was able to deliver a paper on 'Habits of Birds'.[63] Over the next two or three decades, Huxley combined a successful career as a biologist with what always remained a more or less amateur involvement in 'scientific bird-watching'. In the end, however, his early intuition was borne out, for his studies of birds were to have an influence which far exceeded the rather marginal place that they occupied in his work.

Throughout his life, Huxley was fascinated by bird 'courtship'. His first chance to study this phenomenon came in 1911, when he organized a reading party in North Wales during the spring vacation. While there, he was able to observe the 'courtship' of a number of redshanks, and later he wrote of having discovered 'a whole new world of watching ... rich in sights fascinating in themselves, and full also of meanings ... to be puzzled out and unravelled'.[64] Huxley's most important work on 'courtship' was the product of another spring holiday two years later at Tring in Hertfordshire, during which he studied the behaviour of the great crested grebe. Watching his birds over a period of a fortnight, Huxley was struck, as Selous had been before him, by the drama of their lives. He came to see the elaborate movements involved in the birds' lengthy 'courtship' as the gestures and postures of two performers caught up in some sort of evolutionary play. In order to reconstruct the plot of the play, Huxley gave an evocative account of the roles which the birds performed. He described the 'courtship'

[62] J. S. Huxley, *Memories I* (Harmondsworth, 1972), p. 79.
[63] J. S. Huxley, 'Habits of Birds', Huxley MSS, Miscellaneous Item A, Edward Grey Institute of Field Ornithology, Oxford. The paper is dated 1907 and was read to the Decalogue Club, Balliol College, Oxford. It shows the clear influence of Selous's work, and deals for the most part with sexual selection in birds and the evolution of habit and instinct. Huxley acknowledged his debt to Selous in his Introduction to Selous's *Realities of Bird Life* (note 57) pp. xi–xvi.
[64] J. S. Huxley, *Bird-Watching and Bird Behaviour* (London, 1930), p. 63, cf. Huxley, *Memories I*, p. 79.

as being rather like a 'curious set ritual'. From time to time, this 'ritual' was interrupted by apparently irrelevant actions which were performed almost absent-mindedly, 'as one may sometimes see a man wind up his watch in the day-time, just because he has been changing his waistcoat'. Huxley suggested that movements which were once of direct use to the birds had been transformed into gestures of purely symbolic value, and that from here it was but a short step – 'one that has taken place often enough in various human affairs' – to the development of 'mere rituals'.[65] When it came to the question of the meaning of these 'rituals', Huxley relied upon a sympathetic understanding of the birds' characters. He concluded that a great deal of the 'courtship' was enjoyed by the grebes for its own sake. Rather than being simply a prelude to mating, many of the 'rituals' were 'self-exhausting'; they permitted 'an interplay of consciousness or emotion' between the birds, and thus served to form and strengthen the all-important bonds of 'marriage'.[66]

Huxley's interpretation of the 'courtship habits' of the grebe was enormously influential. His concept of 'ritualization' was taken up by many continental ethologists, and indeed, it is still widely used today.[67] However, what is of more immediate concern here is the nature and style of Huxley's analysis. Like so many of those whose work has now been discussed, he possessed a distinctive view of

[65] J. S. Huxley, 'The Courtship-habits of the Great Crested Grebe (*Podiceps cristatus*); with an Addition to the Theory of Sexual Selection', *Proceedings of the Zoological Society*, xxxv (1914), pp. 496–7, 506–7. This paper has become something of a classic and an abridged version of it has been published, together with a foreword by Desmond Morris, in the form of a book, see J. S. Huxley, *The Courtship Habits of the Great Crested Grebe* (London, 1968).

[66] This was one of a number of points on which Huxley took issue with Darwin's version of the theory of sexual selection. Over the years, Huxley returned to this theme in a number of his papers, and it is clear that Darwin's theory formed the framework within which much of his work on bird behaviour was conducted. See J. S. Huxley, 'Darwin's Theory of Sexual Selection and the Data Subsumed by it, in the Light of Recent Research', *American Naturalist*, lxxii (1938), pp. 416–33.

[67] Although Huxley is usually credited with the 'discovery' of 'ritualization', it should be noted that this idea was implicit in the work of Heinroth (see note 20). Lorenz, of course, was familiar with the work of both men, and he made extensive use of the term in his early papers, see *Studies* (note 11), i, pp. 82, 95–6 and ii, pp. 21, 61, 101, 103, 106. It is some measure of the amount of interest that this concept has attracted in recent years that in 1965 Huxley was asked by the Royal Society to organize a conference on the Ritualization of Behaviour in Animals and Man. The proceedings of this conference appeared in *Philosophical Transactions of the Royal Society, London*, B. ccli (1966), pp. 247–524.

bird life and of the way in which it should be studied. He saw birds as individual personalities whose conduct was dominated by complex emotions; and he insisted that the path to a true understanding of them lay in a close acquaintance with their ordinary lives. Huxley wrote:

> Every kind of bird has its own particular quality or character, so to speak, which derives partly from its size and colouring and voice, partly from its temperament and habits, partly from its surroundings ... to go out on a country walk and see and hear different kinds of wild birds is thus to the bird-watcher rather like running across a number of familiar neighbours, local characters, or old acquaintances. The walk becomes a series of personal encounters.[68]

For Huxley, the necessary starting-point of any investigation was an intimate acquaintance with a bird's character. On this basis, he sought direct insight into the bird's mental and emotional life 'by comparing ... [its] actions with our own in circumstances as similar as possible'.[69] The logical outcome of this approach was the now-familiar account of the 'symbols' and 'ceremonies', the 'dances' and 'rituals' which together constituted the 'courtship' of the great crested grebe.

Not long after the publication of his work on grebes, Huxley wrote an article on 'Bird-Watching and Biological Science'. He lamented the gulf which existed between amateur naturalists and professional biologists, and recommended 'scientific bird-watching' as an effective bridge between the two. The straightforward observation of the private lives of birds was capable of yielding profound conclusions in the realms of evolutionary theory and comparative psychology. Huxley wrote: '... all my observations have gone to root deeply in me the conviction that birds have a mind of the same general nature as ours, though of course more rudimentary', and he concluded with these words:

[68] Huxley (note 64), pp. 4–5.
[69] Huxley, 'The Courtship Habits of the Great Crested Grebe (*Podiceps cristatus*); with an Addition to the Theory of Sexual Selection' (note 65), p. 510. Huxley's 'Ils n'ont que de l'âme: an Essay on Bird-Mind', in *Essays of a Biologist* (London, 1923), pp. 105–28, was an explicit defence of his view of birds as emotional creatures 'untrammelled by much reason', against the behaviourist argument that discussion should be confined to 'the objective description of directly observable behaviour'. Huxley's position was captured perfectly in the full quotation from which the title of the article was taken: '*Ils n'ont pas de cerveau – ils n'ont que de l'âme*' ('They have no brains – they have only soul').

bird-watching is the foundation of a real science, the science of the behaviour of birds in their natural environment. Bird-watching, too, is in itself a sport, as all who have tried it well know; but those who attempt to understand the motives of the birds, the connection of their doings and the origin of their various habits, will find themselves not only experiencing the sportsman's thrill, but also the intellectual interest of the detective piecing together the broken chains of evidence, *and the human feelings of a spectator at the play* [my emphasis].[70]

Whether in matters of science or of history, it is always dangerous to generalize from a restricted number of examples. However, the range of studies which has been described represents a substantial cross-section of early contributions to ethology, and it is appropriate at this stage to step back and assess its wider significance. In the first instance, a number of themes stand out as being of obvious importance. For example, it is clear that the conventional view of ethology as a discipline founded upon naturalistic observation is fully justified.[71] Virtually all of those whose work has been discussed were either amateur naturalists, or else zoologists whose general orientation was towards natural history. Moreover, most of them were sharply critical of the experimental methods of the laboratory-based comparative psychologists. When Edmund Selous wrote that 'to watch an experiment made by nature is in nine cases out of ten much better than to make one oneself', he spoke not only for the whole of English 'scientific bird-watching', but also for many of his American and continental counterparts.[72] Similarly, there was undoubtedly a fairly broad community of theoretical interest amongst the early ethologists. This is most easily demonstrated by the fact that most of them saw

[70] J. S. Huxley, 'Bird-Watching and Biological Science', *Auk*, xxxiii (1916), pp. 143–4, 269.

[71] See J. Jaynes (note 6), pp. 601–6; and W. H. Thorpe (note 6), pp. vii–xi.

[72] E. Selous (note 55), p. 166. Although the commitment to naturalistic observation was general, it should be noted that it did not always take the same form. Thus, where the English ornithologists practised field observation, Heinroth and Lorenz kept and bred their birds in captivity. However, in both cases the emphasis was on observation rather than experiment, the natural environment rather than the laboratory. Even Tinbergen, who was what Lorenz described as 'a genius at devising ... unobtrusive experiments', wrote 'It cannot be stressed too much in this age of respect for – one might almost say adoration of – the experiment, that critical, precise and systematic observation is a valuable and indispensable scientific procedure, which we cannot afford to neglect ...', in *The Animal in its World. Explorations of an Ethologist, 1932–1972*, 2 vols. (London, 1972–3), ii, p. 100.

themselves as working within a 'Darwinian' tradition. Quite apart from the fact that they all employed a comparative and evolutionary approach to animal behaviour, Whitman defended what he took to be the Darwinian theory of instinct, most of the English ornithologists were preoccupied with the theory of sexual selection, and Craig and a number of others took up Darwin's work on the expression of emotions.[73] So far as their attitude to Darwin himself is concerned, perhaps Selous may be allowed, once again, to speak for the rest: 'Darwin, as it seems to me, has never been properly assimilated ... Instead of reading new works upon evolution it would be better – more profitable – to read him over and over again'.[74]

Although these methodological and theoretical issues are important, they are not the main objects of interest in this paper. Rather, the focus of concern here is the less tangible but certainly no less significant question of the prevailing style or 'ethos' of early ethology. As late as 1955, a Dutch zoologist wrote that 'ethology is not so much a separate science as a state of mind, a scientific reform movement'.[75] In a sense, this claim is borne out by the examples which have been discussed. Many of those who contributed to the rise of ethology shared a distinctive approach to the study of animals. Their work involved detailed and sympathetic observation of undisturbed individuals, the aim being to gain insight into their 'character', 'conduct' and general way of life. It was argued that only this sort of insight could provide a true understanding of the nature and meaning of animal habits. Heinroth caught something of the spirit of this approach when he spoke of his effort 'to gain some idea of how things look from the point of view of the bird', and Craig was also close to the mark when he described his debt to Whitman, who had 'always given helpful answers to my questions as to what a bird is thinking about when it does a certain act'.[76] However, both these statements are a little misleading, since they seem to entail a crude anthropomorphism which was quite foreign to their work. The point about the

[73] See for example, W. Craig, 'A Note on Darwin's Work on the Expression of the Emotions in Man and Animals', *Journal of Abnormal and Social Psychology*, xvi (1922), pp. 356–66.
[74] Selous (note 57) p. 227.
[75] A. Kortlandt, 'Aspects and Prospects of the Concept of Instinct', *Archives Neerlandaises Zoologique*, xi (1955), p. 215.
[76] See K. Heinroth (note 20), p. 108; W. Craig (note 30), p. 31.

early ethologists was not that they wished to project human
capacities into animals on a wholesale basis, but rather that they
believed that it was possible to understand animals in just the same
way that we understand our fellow-men. In the most literal sense
imaginable, they were fulfilling the eighteenth-century vision of the
French naturalist C. G. Leroy, who had wished to have 'the
complete biography of every animal'.[77]

The point of concentrating on the 'state of mind' of the early
ethologists is that it exerted a profound influence on almost every
aspect of their work. In the early stages of his correspondence with
Heinroth, Lorenz wrote of his enthusiasm for *Die Vögel
Mitteleuropas*: 'I can almost say it by heart, and that not through
frequent reading, but because your portrait of the birds' behaviour
left almost as vivid an impression on me, as if I had kept them
myself'. Several years later, Lorenz returned to this theme, writing:
'I find it so immensely impressive and convincing (particularly for
unbelievers), when you explain what an animal does, and more
especially, what it doesn't do!'[78] Lorenz was not simply flattering
his mentor. Rather, he was highlighting one of the most characteristic features of the work of the animal biographers. At a time when
many comparative psychologists were struggling to make their
work more 'objective' and more experimental,[79] the 'starers-at-
animals' held fast to a method which was based upon personal
insight. The fruits of this insight were often conveyed by means of
evocative prose which placed the reader within the animal's world,
there to be persuaded that he, too, understood the significance of
what was going on. When Heinroth spoke of Liliput's 'proud
bearing' in the presence of his wife, he not only described the bird's
movements but also evoked a sense of its whole character.
Description and interpretation were interwoven in a single, insight-
ful story.

The preoccupation with animal character inevitably introduced a
subjective element into the ethologists' work. Animals were seen as

[77] See note 1.
[78] Quoted in K. Heinroth (note 20), pp. 151–2, 161.
[79] In this context, it is worth noting the verdict of E. G. Boring: 'Experimental
animal psychology belongs to the first decade of the twentieth century', in *A History
of Experimental Psychology*, 2nd edn. (New York, 1950), p. 626. B. D. Mackenzie
provides a useful account of the development of comparative psychology in relation
to the development of behaviourism in his book, *Behaviourism and the Limits of
Scientific Method* (London, 1977), pp. 54–100.

actors in their own social worlds, and indeed the analogy with drama was extemely common. Wallace Craig described the 'cooing and gesturing' which commonly preceded fighting between pigeons as an elaborate 'pantomime', and Huxley summed up the attitude of many when he referred to 'the human feelings of a spectator at the play'.[80] Of course, this dramaturgical analogy opened up a whole range of interpretative possibilities. In particular, it directed attention to the question of the meaning or symbolic significance of behaviour. Typical in this respect was Selous, who noted that the 'wonderful drama ... of bird-life' often appeared almost absurd in its obvious formality. Over and again, he compared the antics of birds with human ceremony, and this led him to consider whether they might not serve some useful but purely symbolic purpose. In fact, it was Selous who first applied this idea to the 'courtship habits' of the grebe. Over a decade before Huxley undertook his more famous analysis, Selous wrote: 'In every essential except the clear consciousness that they were doing so ... these grebes, as it appears to me, went through a marriage ceremony'.[81]

With the notion that particular sounds and movements have symbolic significance, we come close to the heart of the enterprise of early ethology. In his comparative study of the Anatinae, Lorenz related a tale often told by Heinroth, about how long it had taken him to realize that the drinking which occurred when two ducks met on a pond was no chance phenomenon, but rather a *'pacific gesture'*.[82] This characterization of movement as gesture was a key element in the analogy between animal and human character. The *Oxford English Dictionary* (1973) defines gesture as 'Movement of the body or limbs as an expression of feeling', and of course it is the principal technique which is employed in the dramatic art of mime. Indeed, it is no exaggeration to say that Heinroth sought to understand his birds in just the same way that an audience understands a mimic. He saw sounds and movements as 'ritualized' acts of expression, giving insight into the feelings of the performer. It was in an early paper on the Carolina wood duck (*Lampronessa*) that Heinroth had analysed the meaning of what he termed 'display

[80] W. Craig, 'The Voices of Pigeons Regarded as a Means of Social Control', *American Journal of Sociology*, xiv (1908–9), p. 97; Huxley (note 70).
[81] E. Selous (note 55), pp. 349–50.
[82] K. Lorenz, 'Comparative Studies of the Motor Patterns of Anatinae', *Studies*, ii (note 11), p. 30.

drinking' (*Antrinken*). He wrote:

This performance is rather like the tail-wagging which goes on when two dogs meet, by means of which they indicate that they have no hostile intentions towards one another, and in the same way we can be sure that two ducks which converse in this way will get on with one another, at least for a time. If display drinking is repeated, it indicates greater affection: a pair will persist with the ritual, for example, if they meet again after a short separation. In *Lampronessa*, this drinking movement is performed very rapidly by the drake just before mating, and here it is an expression of tenderness.[83]

Discussions like this run through not just the work of Heinroth, but also that of Craig, Huxley, Lorenz and Selous. In each case, insights were obtained by treating birds as if they were characters in a silent play whose plot remained to be discovered.

The concept of gesture occupied a central position in the outlook of the early ethologists; it was the basic classificatory unit in comparative studies of innate movements or 'motor patterns', it was the starting-point for the analysis of the nature and functions of animal 'language', and it provided a theoretical link between observed motor patterns and inferred feelings or emotions.[84] On the last point, it should be noted that there was direct continuity between early preoccupations with emotional expression and later, less obviously anthropomorphic interest, in the question of motivation. For example, by interpreting movements as expressive signs, Heinroth explored the varied and changeable 'moods' (*Stimmungen*) which governed the lives of animals.[85] Similarly, Wallace Craig's interest in the subjective, psychological functions of emotion led him to develop a theory of the role of 'appetites' and 'aversions' in instinctive behaviour. He argued that these subjective aspects of instinct were manifested in specific 'bodily attitudes and gestures which are easily recognized signs or "expressions" of

[83] O. Heinroth, 'Beobachtungen bei einem Einbürgerungsversuch mit der Brautente (*Lampronessa sponsa* (L.))', *Journal für Ornithologie*, lviii (1910), pp. 120–1.
[84] In his Introduction to Lorenz's book, *King Solomon's Ring* (London, 1961), p. viii, W. H. Thorpe wrote that 'for the twentieth century pioneers of this new approach to the study of animal behaviour, the word ethology virtually meant the comparative anatomy of "gesture"'. Unfortunately, Thorpe has not (to my knowledge) followed up this insight in his later work on the history of ethology.
[85] See, for example (note 83), pp. 122, 124–5; *Die Vögel Mitteleuropas*, (Leipzig, 1967), ii, pp. 26, 47, 152.

appetite or aversion'.[86] Finally, it was under the combined influence of Heinroth and Craig that Lorenz developed ideas about
motivation which culminated in his controversial 'hydraulic drive'
model of instinct.[87] Throughout, the confidence with which these
men theorized about the inner lives of animals was a reflection of
their liberal use of the concept of gesture; and this, in its turn, was
part and parcel of their view that 'Animals are emotional people of
extremely poor intelligence'.

The early ethologists recorded in exhaustive detail the repertoire
of sounds, gestures and postures possessed by their animals, and,
believing with Huxley that *'emotions* and *attitudes* are just as much
*characters* as are *colours* or *structures'*,[88] they conducted comparative surveys with a view to the reconstruction of genealogical
relationships. It has been argued that much of this work was based
upon personal insight, and that much of this insight grew out of the
fundamental analogy between animal and human character. The
influence of this analogy (sometimes unspoken, but often explicit[89])
has been traced in the research style or ethos of early ethology, in

[86] Craig, 'Appetites and Aversions as Constituents of Instincts' (note 30), pp. 91–2,
95.
[87] Lorenz took up Heinroth's notion of 'mood' in his paper, 'Companions as Factors
in the Bird's Environment', *Studies,* i (note 11), pp. 163, 209, 219, 221, 239, and
especially 252. Also, it was at about this time that Lorenz discovered the work of
Craig and commenced a correspondence with him on the subject of instinct. Craig's
influence is very obvious in Lorenz's next important theoretical paper, 'The Establishment of the Instinct Concept', *Studies,* i (note 11), pp. 259–315. Here, Lorenz
began to develop a putatively physiological theory of instinct, while at the same time
retaining the subjectivist connotations of the earlier work of Heinroth and Craig.
These issues are discussed in greater detail by T. J. Kalikow in her 'History of
Konrad Lorenz's Ethological Theory, 1927–1939', pp. 331–41. Lorenz set out his
'hydraulic drive' model of instinct in his paper, 'The Comparative Method in
Studying Innate Behaviour Patterns', *Symposia of the Society for Experimental
Biology,* iv (1950), pp. 221–68. This paper was read at an important international
conference which was held in Cambridge in July 1949. Significantly, it contains a
lengthy discussion of Heinroth's notion of 'mood' and of Craig's theory of instinct,
see pp. 248–9, 261–5. Moreover, the list of ethological terms which was established
at the conference included 'Appetitive Behaviour', 'Drive', Instinct' and 'Mood' (as
quoted in Thorpe, *The Origins and Rise of Ethology* (note 6), pp. 99–100).
[88] Huxley, 'The Courtship-Habits of the Great Crested Grebe' (note 65), p. 528
(note).
[89] Several of those whose work has been discussed published explicit defences of
anthropomorphism. See for example Huxley, 'Ils n'ont que de l'âme: an Essay on
Bird-Mind' (note 69), pp. 105–128; W. M. Wheeler, 'On Instincts', in *Essays in
Philosophical Biology* (Cambridge, Mass., 1939), pp. 37–70. Wheeler wrote that 'it is
impossible to regard anthropomorphism as such a very terrible eighth mortal sin' (p.
47).

the conceptual vocabulary of the early ethologists, and in at least some of their theoretical interests. However, there is one final area in which the analogy between animals and man left its mark. Having brought an understanding of human character to bear on their work with birds, many of the early ethologists could not resist the temptation to apply the results back to man. Of course, this was a familiar feature of the ethology of the 1960s, but the basic position had been set out long before, and may be illustrated in the work of Heinroth and Lorenz.

In his paper on the Anatidae, Heinroth was at pains to point out the wider psychological and social implications of his work. For example, in his long discussion of the family life of geese, he remarked that, to the 'uninitiated', much of the birds' behaviour seemed 'extremely human and straightforwardly funny'. Stressing the fact that this social behaviour was 'charged with meaning', he went on:

> In all animals which are social and live in families, including man, similar habits are formed, even in the most disparate groups. For me, the behaviour of the geese is not a sign of man-like intelligence, but rather an indication of the fact that many of our relationships and forms of interaction ... are nothing more than social instincts ...[90]

Heinroth returned to this theme at the end of his paper, and he concluded with these words:

> In this treatise, I have paid particular attention to forms of communication, and it appears that the more sociable birds with which we have dealt are astonishingly human, particularly when the family, father, mother and children, form such a stable and closely-knit unit as is the case in the geese. The Sauropsidan order has developed all the emotions, feelings and customs which in man are associated with morality and intelligence. The study of the ethology of the higher animals – unfortunately still a largely unworked field – will greatly strengthen the conclusion that our behaviour towards family and strangers, our courtship, and so on, involve far more inborn and ancient influences than we commonly think.[91]

What emerges from these passages is Heinroth's willingness to exploit the analogy between animal and human character in both directions. Having used it to identify in birds a variety of essentially

[90] O. Heinroth, 'Beiträge' (note 20), pp. 618–9.
[91] Ibid., p. 702.

human emotions, feelings, and customs, he took it up again in order to reappraise the human condition. Of course, the effect of this move was to unite animals and man in a single theory of innate character.

It was left to Lorenz to follow up the implications of Heinroth's argument, and this he did with considerable zeal. In his autobiography, Lorenz's father remarked that he had not been at all keen on his son's choice of career, believing as he did that 'it was of no great importance to know whether herons were more or less stupid than they were thought to be'. He continued: 'Konrad contends that human psychology has much to learn from animal psychology and that there is no essential difference between these two branches of the science'.[92] Lorenz's interest in the relationship between animal and human psychology went back as far as the early stages of his correspondence with Heinroth. In 1931, having congratulated the older man on being the founder of 'the science of animal psychology as a branch of biology', he wrote:

> Who knows where today's human psychology will find itself, when once one knows of human behaviour what is due to instinct (*Triebhandlung*), and what to intelligence (*Verstandeshandlung*): who knows how human morality would appear, with its drives and inhibitions, if one could analyse it in the same way as the social drives and inhibitions of a jackdaw ...[93]

Over the years, Lorenz developed this vision into a comprehensive and extremely controversial theory of the innate components of human behaviour. Moreover, the path which he cleared was followed by many others, and human ethology soon became a major field of inquiry in its own right.[94] Throughout, this development was guided by the principle laid down by Heinroth in his correspondence with Lorenz: 'One should certainly learn to know and understand people through animals'.[95]

[92] Adolph Lorenz, *My Life and Work* (New York and London, 1936), p. 319.
[93] Quoted in K. Heinroth (note 20), p. 155.
[94] For the early development of Lorenz's ideas on the relationship between animal and human behaviour, see Kalikow (note 6), pp. 15–34. Lorenz's later views are set out, for example, in 'Part and Parcel in Animal and Human Societies', *Studies*, ii (note 11), pp. 115–95; K. Lorenz, *On Aggression* (London, 1966). Human ethology is now an enormous field, but the person who best represents the 'Lorenzian' tradition is perhaps Lorenz's student I. Eibl-Eibesfeldt. See, for example, I. Eibl-Eibesfeldt, *Ethology. The Biology of Behaviour* (New York and London, 1970), pp. 398–464, and *idem*, *Love and Hate. On the Natural History of Basic Behaviour Patterns* (London, 1971).
[95] Quoted in K. Heinroth (note 20), p. 156.

This final and important twist in the analogy between animal and human character brings us back to the introductory discussion concerning the meaning of the term ethology. It was stressed there that the term has been given a variety of definitions, the oldest of which appears to have been, 'the portrayal of character by mimicry'. In view of this, it would be easy to assume that the term was etymologically inappropriate within biology. Paradoxically, however, this turns out not to have been the case. The early ethologists were centrally concerned with the portrayal of character – even, it has been argued, with the portrayal of character by mimicry; and though they were primarily interested in animals, the nature of their work was such that it was readily applicable to the question of the formation of character in man. John Stuart Mill had looked forward to the establishment of a science which would be concerned with 'the formation of character'.[96] Although he undoubtedly had something rather different in mind, his description will stand as a summary of the aims of the early ethologists; for ethology came into existence when a relatively small group of naturalists and zoologists discovered that great progress could be made in understanding animals when they were treated as if, to all intents and purposes, they were really people.

[96] See note 12.

I should like to thank Dr R. C. Burkhardt for his helpful comments on an earlier draft of this paper. Part of the research on which the paper is based was undertaken with the help of a grant from the Wellcome Trust.

## 5. Genetics in the United States and Great Britain 1890–1930: A Review with Speculations

DANIEL J. KEVLES

In the last fifteen years, a rich body of historical scholarship has been published in the early history of genetics. Drawing upon the extensive manuscript collections becoming ever more available, this literature has focused on the emergence of the discipline from evolutionary biology and has given provocative attention to the celebrated dispute between the advocates of the then-competing paradigms of hereditary science – biometry and Mendelism.[1] Indispensable so far as it goes, the existing historiography neverthe-less omits approaches and subjects whose fruitfulness historians of science are, increasingly, coming to recognize. With some excep-tions, the literature of genetics covers its various topics in either the United States or England but not cross-nationally. Moreover, most of the scholarship does not go much beyond treatments of the principal actors or conceptual developments. Certainly it leaves unexplored the history of the overall corps of men and women, including the scientific commoners in research, who came to form the Anglo-American genetics community.[2] It is the aim of this

[1] The best reference for the newly available manuscript collections is *The Mendel Newsletter*, Library of the American Philosophical Society, Philadelphia, Pa., nos. 1–17, April 1968–June 1979.
[2] Entrée into recent literature on the history of scientific communities and com-moners may be gained through a variety of works, including: P. Forman, J. L. Heilbron and S. Weart, *Physics circa 1900: Personnel, Funding, and Productivity of the Academic Establishments*, vol. 5, 'Historical Studies in the Physical Sciences' (Princeton: Princeton University Press, 1975); K. Hufbauer, 'The Formation of the German Chemical Community' (University of California, Berkeley, Ph.D. dissertation, 1970); D. J. Kevles, *The Physicists; The History of a Scientific Community in Modern America* (New York: Knopf, 1978); idem, 'The Physics, Mathematics, and Chemistry Communities: A Comparative Analysis,' in Alexandra Oleson and J. Voss (eds.), *The Organization of Knowledge in Modern America, 1860–1920* (Baltimore: The Johns Hopkins University Press, 1979), pp. 139–72; G. Lemaine, R. MacLeod, M. Mulkay and P. Weingart (eds.), *Perspectives in the Study of Scientific Disciplines* (The Hague: Mouton, 1976); L. Pyenson, '"Who the Guys Were": Prosopography in The History of Science', *History of Science*, xv (1977), pp. 155–88. S. Shapin and A. Thackray, 'Prosopography as a Research Tool in the History of Science: the British Scientific

review, which brings to bear upon the literature both manuscript sources and a transatlantic perspective, to suggest that making up for these deficiencies would be worthwhile and, in certain respects, is necessary.

To summarize the recent scholarship, by the 1890s many younger biologists were growing restless with phylogenetic morphology and embryology, the traditional descriptive approaches to the much-debated problems of evolutionary theory. Eager to break away from these approaches, a number of these biologists – and some older ones such as Alfred R. Wallace – called for programs of quantitative or experimental research in evolution addressed in particular to the problems of heredity and variation. In England, Francis Galton inspired the most important quantitative research programme – W. F. R. Weldon's statistical analyses, developed in collaboration with Karl Pearson, of variations in large populations. Another important departure was the programme of hybridization experiments exemplified in the research of William Bateson. Pearson and Weldon helped establish the field of heredity studies known as biometry. The research of Bateson and others paved the way for the rediscovery in 1900 and then vigorous advocacy of the Mendelian paradigm.[3]

In England, the biometricians Weldon and Pearson hotly disputed the validity of Mendel's results, the merits of his conceptual

Community, 1700–1900', *History of Science*, xii (1974), pp. 1–28; Diana Crane, *Invisible Colleges: Diffusion of Scientific Knowledge in Scientific Communities* (Chicago: University of Chicago Press, 1972).

[3] On Galton, see K. Pearson, *Life, Letters, and Labours of Francis Galton*, 4 vols. (Cambridge: Cambridge University Press, 1914–1930); Ruth S. Cowan, *Sir Francis Galton and the Study of Heredity in the Nineteenth Century* (Ann Arbor: University Microfilms, 1969); D. W. Forrest, *Francis Galton: The Life of a Victorian Genius* (New York: Taplinger, 1974). Useful introductions to the early history of genetics are L. C. Dunn, *A Short History of Genetics* (New York: McGraw-Hill, 1965); A. H. Sturtevant, *A History of Genetics* (New York: Harper & Row, 1965); G. E. Allen, *Life Science in the Twentieth Century* (New York: John Wiley, 1975). On Bateson, see Beatrice Bateson, *William Bateson, F.R.S.; Naturalist, His Essays and Addresses, together with a Short Account of His Life* (Cambridge: Cambridge University Press, 1928); A. G. Cock, 'William Bateson, Mendelism, and Biometry', *Journal of the History of Biology*, vi, no. 1 (1973), pp. 1–36; L. Darden, 'William Bateson and the Promise of Mendelism', *Journal of the History of Biology*, x, no. 1, (1977), pp. 87–106; on Weldon and Pearson, see K. Pearson, 'Walter Frank Raphael Weldon', *Biometrika*, v (1906), pp. 1–52; Lyndsay A. Farrall, *The Origins and Growth of the English Eugenics Movement, 1865–1925* (Ann Arbor: University Microfilms, 1970); *idem*, 'W.F.R. Weldon, Biometry, and Population Biology' (unpublished manuscript copy with author); E. S. Pearson, *Karl Pearson: An Appreciation of Some Aspects of*

scheme, and even the integrity of his British advocates, especially Bateson. Bateson on his part found it 'impossible ... to believe that they [the biometricians] have made any honest attempt to face the facts' and doubted that they were 'acting in good faith as genuine seekers for truth'.[4] In the United States, while not biometricians, Edwin Grant Conklin and Thomas Hunt Morgan found a number of compelling reasons, notably the equality of sex ratios and echoes of preformationism, to doubt the Mendelian theory. In England the angry dispute between the biometricians and the Mendelians is said to have diminished considerably after Weldon's death in 1906, and in America Morgan was converted to Mendelism after 1909/10, when he began his celebrated research with *Drosophila*. Eventually, such scientists as William Castle showed how Mendelism allowed for small heritable variations liable to selection, and through the work of Ronald A. Fisher, Sewall Wright, and J. B. S. Haldane, the Mendelian and biometrical paradigms were formally demonstrated to be mutually complementary. The reconciliation was close to completion by 1930, when Fisher published *The Genetical Theory of Natural Selection*.[5]

In the celebrated dispute between the biometricians and Mendelians, various historical analyses have yielded certain key points of interpretation: in the most general treatment of the

*His Life and Work* (Cambridge: Cambridge University Press, 1938). On other aspects of the subject, see G. E. Allen, 'T. H. Morgan and the Emergence of a New American Biology', *Quarterly Review of Biology*, xliv (1969), pp. 168–88; J. S. Wilkie, 'Some Reasons for the Rediscovery and Appreciation of Mendel's Work in the First Years of the Present Century', *British Journal for the History of Science*, i (June 1962), pp. 5–17; W. E. Castle, 'The Beginnings of Mendelism in America', in L. C. Dunn (ed.) *Genetics in the Twentieth Century: Essays on the Progress of Genetics during its First 50 Years* (New York: MacMillan, 1951); A. H. Sturtevant, 'The Early Mendelians', *Proceedings of the American Philosophical Society*, cix (August 1965), pp. 199–204. See also the entries on Pearson, Bateson, Weldon and Galton in C. C. Gillispie (ed.), *Dictionary of Scientific Biography*, 16 vols. (New York, 1970–80).

[4] Bateson to C. C. Hurst, 24 March 1903, C. C. Hurst Papers, Cambridge University Library, Addn. 7955/3/12, Cambridge, England.

[5] For overall treatments of the biometrician–Mendelian controversy, see P. Froggatt and N. C. Nevin, 'The "Law of Ancestral Heredity" and the Mendelian-Ancestrian Controversy in England, 1889–1906', *Journal of Medical Genetics*, viii (1971), pp. 1–36; W. B. Provine, *The Origin of Theoretical Population Genetics* (Chicago: University of Chicago Press, 1971); Lyndsay A. Farrall, 'Controversy and Conflict in Science: A Case Study – The English Biometric School and Mendel's Laws', *Social Studies of Science*, v (1975), pp. 269–301. For Morgan, see G. E. Allen's series of articles 'Thomas Hunt Morgan and the Problem of Sex Determination, 1903–1910', *Proceedings of the American Philosophical Society*, cx (Feb. 1966), pp. 48–57;

subject, William Provine has argued that the issue turned on personal conflicts between the principals in the two camps. He has also concluded that this personal animosity delayed the reconciliation of Mendelism and biometry for a full fifteen years.[6] Without question public exchanges between the two sides were usually heated, and correspondence among the principals was replete with personal gibes. Bateson was not atypically intemperate in his *Mendel's Principles of Heredity: A Defence*. And Pearson, in pointing out errors, tended to use 'the ugliest means possible', the American geneticist Herbert S. Jennings observed, and to hit offenders 'over the head with a club'.[7]

Without question, too, the conflict among the principals put scientists who attempted to reconcile biometry and Mendelism at a disadvantage. The most formal expression of biometry was the 'law of ancestral heredity'. Fathered by Galton and modified by Pearson, this 'law' essentially apportioned various fractions of an organism's phenotypical expression to a distribution of ancestral influences. The suggestion, as early as 1902, of the British statistician G. Udny Yule that Galton's law and Mendelism actually complemented rather than contradicted each other was apparently ignored by Pearson.[8] A. D. Darbishire, a pupil of Weldon's at Oxford, after graduation commenced a course of research on inheritance in mice. As a result of this work, Darbishire, who began as an anti-Mendelian biometrician, gradually came to a qualified

'Thomas Hunt Morgan and the Problem of Natural Selection,' *Journal of the History of Biology*, i, no. 1 (1968), pp. 113–39; 'The Introduction of *Drosophila* into the Study of Heredity and Evolution, 1900–1910', *Isis*, lxvii (1975), pp. 322–33. What will surely become the standard biography of Morgan is Allen's *Thomas Hunt Morgan: The Man and His Science* (Princeton: Princeton University Press, 1978), which includes an extensive bibliographical essay. Other important studies include E. A. Carlson, 'The *Drosophila* Group: The Transition from the Mendelian Unit to the Individual Gene', *Journal of the History of Biology*, vii, no. 1 (1974), pp. 31–48; N. Roll-Hansen, 'Drosophila Genetics: A Reductionist Research Program', *Journal of the History of Biology*, xi, no, 1 (1978), pp. 159–210.
[6] W. Provine (note 5), pp. 63–64.
[7] H. S. Jennings to R. Pearl, 15 November 1909, R. Pearl Papers, American Philosophical Society Library, Jennings file. G. U. Yule, a friend of Pearson but an appreciator of Mendelism, said of Bateson's *Defence* that its preface was 'turgid and bombastic', its treatment of Weldon 'grossly and gratuitously offensive' and its style generally that of the 'religious revivalist.' G. U. Yule, 'Mendel's Laws and their Probable Relations to Intra-Racial Heredity', *New Phytologist*, i (1902), p. 194. See also L. Farrall (note 5), pp. 274–76; Froggatt and Nevin (note 5), see note 279.
[8] G. U. Yule, 'Mendel's Laws', *New Phytologist*, i (1902), pp. 193–207, 222–38. In this

acceptance of Mendelism. The qualifications displeased Bateson and his allies, the Mendelism annoyed Pearson. 'Darbishire', it has been observed, 'in trying to be objective and circumspect, pleased no one'.[9] Similarly, when Ronald A. Fisher submitted his ground-breaking paper reconciling biometry with Mendelism in 1918 to the Royal Society, Pearson, and Bateson's disciple Reginald C. Punnett, were called in as referees. Though neither recommended against publication in the *Proceedings*, neither was enthusiastically for it, and the paper was withdrawn.[10]

Yet Garland Allen has observed that Provine's stress on personality tacitly assumes that Bateson, Pearson and Weldon 'were not representative of a broader and more profound set of traditions. The further suggestion that the controversy largely ended because Weldon died, does considerable injustice to any understanding of how historical change comes about'.[11] Other students of the dispute have argued that profound scientific traditions did indeed lie behind the personal conflict. Philosophically, Bernard Norton has stressed, Pearson vigorously insisted upon avoiding the postulation of such unobservable entities as Mendelian factors. A positivist by conviction, Pearson preferred to describe, in a theory-free fashion, relations among phenotypic observables.[12] Adding

paper Yule hit upon a very restricted form of the later Hardy-Weinberg law. When in 1908 he learned of Hardy's general expression for the stability of a randomly breeding Mendelian population, he exclaimed 'Absolutely correct and solves the whole difficulty! I am kicking myself for never having seen it. The fact is that in my New Phytologist articles of 1902 I took the population as starting from a single D × R cross, which gives the 1:2:1 ratio as stable amongst the descendants, and *it never occurred to me that any other ratio could be stable*. It's extraordinary how stupid one can be. Pearson also follows in the same track in his Philosophical Transactions paper "On a generalized theory of alternative inheritance" and so *he* also gets the 1:2:1 ratio.' Quoted in R. C. Punnett to Bateson, 16 April 1908, William Bateson Papers, John Innes Horticultural Institute Archives, Box H. See K. Pearson, 'On a Generalized Theory of Alternative Inheritance with Special Reference to Mendel's Laws', *Philosophical Transactions*, cciiiA (1904), pp. 53–86.

[9] Froggatt and Nevin, 'The "Law of Ancestral Heredity"' (note 5), see note 309.

[10] B. Norton, 'A Note on the Background to, and Refereeing of R. A. Fisher's 1918 Paper ...', *Notes and Records of the Royal Society of London*, xxxi (July 1976), pp. 151–62.

[11] Allen, 'Genetics, Eugenics, and Society: Internalists and Externalists in Contemporary History of Science', *Social Studies of Science*, vi (1976), p. 111.

[12] Norton, 'Metaphysics and Population Genetics: Karl Pearson and the Back-

fuel to the controversy was the difference between the two sides over how biology was to be done – mathematically or traditionally.

While Pearson was a brilliant and Weldon an able mathematician, Bateson, who had suffered through mathematics while a Cambridge undergraduate, was mathematically inept. In 1902, though appreciating the value of Yule's idea on the basis of biological intuition, he was mathematically incapable of following it up. 'Yule's paper', he noted, 'is about the last word on the relation of M[endel] to G[alton], and in [the] future G's law will cease to be treated as a physiological statement at all and [will] merely become a statistical summary of the expectation as to the composition of a promiscuously breeding population. I tried to do the analysis he has carried through, but it was beyond me.'[13] Pearson was outspokenly intolerant of Bateson's inability – Pearson would have said refusal – to appreciate the techniques of correlation and regression. Still, many biologists agreed with the American biometrician and admirer of Pearson who remarked that for the most part Pearson had no first-hand knowledge of biological matters; he was 'apt to take a rather absurd position sometimes in regard to biologically obvious things'.[14]

Adding a social determination of scientific ideas to the analysis first advanced by William Coleman, Donald MacKenzie has argued that Bateson's socio-economic conservatism gave his intellectual temperament what Karl Mannheim would have called a 'conservative' cast; he was predisposed to analyse the particular case – the individual organism – in contradistinction to Pearson, a so-

ground to Fisher's Multi-factorial Theory of Inheritance', *Annals of Science*, xxxii (1975), pp. 537–53; *idem*, 'Biology and Philosophy: The Methodological Foundations of Biometry', *Journal of the History of Biology*, viii, no. 1 (1975), pp. 85–93. See also B. Norton, 'Karl Pearson and the Galtonian Tradition: Studies in the Rise of Quantitative Social Biology' (University College London, Ph.D. thesis, History of Science, 1978), pp. 78–81, 185.

[13] Bateson to Hurst, 8 February 1903, C. C. Hurst Papers (note 4), Addn. 7955/3/7.

[14] Pearl to Jennings, 8 October 1905, Pearl Papers (note 7), Jennings file. Pearl also remarked, 'I think the impression among biologists that biometry is proving rather a sterile field, comes from the unfortunate fact that (1) Pearson, who has grounded the subject mathematically, hasn't at all the biologist's point of view, and (2) that most of the biologists who have taken it up haven't gone to the trouble (or have been constitutionally unable) to work up thoroughly the mathematical side, so to know how to handle their data in an adequate way.' Pearl to Jennings, 4 February 1906, Pearl Papers (note 7), Jennings file.

cialist, who had a high propensity to see the world and nature in terms of collective populations. Bernard Norton has joined MacKenzie in arguing, similarly, that the commitment of Pearson and his allies to biometry was strongly reinforced, possibly even determined, by their embrace of eugenics; the line between eugenics and biometry, in their claim, ran through the eugenicist's eagerness to improve the quality of entire populations, no matter what the cost to individuals. In contrast, it was consistent for Bateson, the Mendelian, to be an anti-eugenicist; that position, like Mendelism, derived from a pro-individualist temperament.[15]

However suggestive, some post-Provine accounts of the dispute seem open to challenge. If Pearson knew no biology, his collaborator Weldon knew a great deal. In terms of intellectual temperament, Weldon was much closer to Bateson than to Pearson. Sharing Bateson's aesthetic sensibility, Weldon travelled often to Italy, loved classical and Renaissance art, frequently attended the opera. While Pearson tended to draw social meaning from literature, Weldon was attentive to individual character and circumstance. In social terms, while Pearson was indeed an ardent socialist and eugenicist, Weldon was neither. He was also decidedly alive to the role of environment in biological development. Weldon aside, both in Britain and America many eugenicists were Mendelians, and some biometricians were anti-eugenicists. One is hard put to find even a high correlation, let alone a necessary connection, between eugenic attitudes and position in the biometrician-Mendelian dispute.[16]

For the most part these interpretations have been applied to the British case and not to the American. Perhaps the reason is that Thomas Hunt Morgan, unlike Pearson, eventually embraced Mendelism. Nevertheless, it is curious that the opposition to

[15] W. Coleman, 'Bateson and Chromosomes: Conservative Thought in Science', *Centaurus*, xv (1970), pp. 228–314; D. A. MacKenzie and S. B. Barnes, 'Biometrician and Mendelian: A Controversy and Its Explanation', University of Edinburgh, Science Studies Unit Paper, September 1974; D. A. MacKenzie, 'Sociobiologists in Competition: The Biometrician-Mendelian Debate,' in *The Roots of Sociobiology* (London: The Past and Present Society, 1978); *idem*, 'The Development of Statistical Theory in Britain: A Historical and Sociological Perspective' (University of Edinburgh, Ph.D. thesis, 1977), pp. 13–30, 124–98, 246–308; B. Norton, 'The Biometric Defense of Darwinism,' *Journal of the History of Biology*, vi, no. 3 (1973), 283–316; *idem*, 'The Galtonian Tradition' (note 12), pp. 118–20, 138–9.
[16] Norton raises some of these objections in 'The Galtonian Tradition' (note 12), pp. 141–2, 181, 186, 188.

Mendelism of Weldon or Pearson seems to require special analysis, but that of Thomas Hunt Morgan does not. If Morgan's scepticism is perfectly explicable on scientific grounds, perhaps Weldon's at least is, too. In 1901, after subjecting Mendel's results to the chi-squared test, Weldon did not see that the results were 'so good as to be suspicious', but he did have doubts about the seeming difficulty of reproducing Mendel's results with further pea experiments. Weldon concluded that Mendel was 'either a black liar or a wonderful man'. 'If only', he remarked to Pearson, 'one could know whether the whole thing is not a damned lie!'[17] Weldon's extensive and newly available correspondence with Pearson suggests that a great deal more can be said about Weldon's scientific objections to Mendelism, and a cross-national perspective would seem to illuminate further the early history of genetics even as a story only of principal actors.

In all the historiography of early genetics the reception of Mendelism – the winning paradigm – obviously forms a principal topic. Some evidence suggests that in England, the opponents of Mendelism included a number of biologists who were not biometricians and that in the United States William Castle, as well as others, were sufficiently enthusiastic about Mendelism to celebrate Bateson during his visit in 1904. Yet one is left to wonder whether Bateson was atypical of British biologists in his embrace of Mendel's theory or whether Thomas Hunt Morgan was typical of his American colleagues in his early rejection of it. One is also left to wonder how both the enthusiasm and the opposition are to be accounted for. The difficulty lies in the lack of attention given to the less illustrious converts or antagonists of Mendelism, i.e., more generally, to the scientific commoners of genetic studies.

An assessment of scientific commoners seems no less pertinent to the dispute between the biometricians and the Mendelians. All the post-Provine treatments address primarily Weldon, Pearson and Bateson. But to account for the dispute mainly by scrutinizing the principal actors is to assume that a few key people set the scientific agenda and determined the intellectual commitments as well as research of the genetics community. To be sure, Lotka's Law tells

[17] Ibid., p. 175; Farrall (note 5), pp. 292, 295; W. F. R. Weldon to K. Pearson [November 1901], K. Pearson Papers, University College London, file 625.

us that a comparatively small fraction of the scientific community publishes a large proportion of the research, and one has no reason to doubt the validity of the law in the case of Anglo-American genetics.[18] But Weldon, Pearson, and Bateson were hardly the only publishers in genetics; research in biometry and Mendelism was done by a number of commoners. The story of these commoners, their significance in research, training programmes and the governance of the community, is a subject of interest in its own right. The commoners also form a useful arena of arbitration for the historiographic issues under consideration here. For to decide among the various explanations of the biometrical-Mendelian dispute, it would seem necessary to test their applicability among the community of geneticists at large. And to weigh the impact of the conflict on the course of genetics, it would seem imperative to know whether the angry sharpness of the debate extended through the entire British genetics community.

Apparently the dispute did not arise with similar acerbity in the United States. Between 1900 and 1915 about 25 per cent of the 230 articles published in the *American Naturalist* concerned biometry, including statistical studies of variation. Of course, much of this research was of less than compelling importance. Pearson remarked that in certain quarters biometry was becoming 'fashionable, and that to measure anything and throw a few figures together is considered biometrical research. In France, Italy, and America this type of biometry based on no adequate study of statistical mathematics is becoming unfortunately more and more common'.[19] Nevertheless, the United States certainly had able biometricians, including Raymond Pearl, who for a time was a collaborator of Pearson's, J. Arthur Harris, and, at least early in his career, Charles B. Davenport, the noted eugenicist and director of the Carnegie Station for Experimental Evolution at Cold Spring Harbor. And the American biometricians did face professional

---

[18] For a discussion of Lotka's Law and related subjects see D. J. de Solla Price, *Little Science, Big Science* (New York: Columbia University Press, 1963), especially chap. 2. See also, J. R. Cole and S. Cole, *Social Stratification in Science* (Chicago: University of Chicago Press, 1973). The validity of Lotka's Law for Anglo-American genetics is roughly borne out by a statistical study of genetics publishers now under way by the author.

[19] The figures are drawn from my own preliminary statistical analysis; Pearson to the President of the Carnegie Institution of Washington, 28 October 1905, Pearl Papers (note 7), Pearson file.

difficulties. In 1903 Pearl spoke of the 'prejudice in many quarters against biometrical work, and ... the small chance a young man without reputation stands to get the claims of biometry recognized'. Nevertheless, as Sewall Wright has recalled, while 'Mendelism was, indeed, ridiculed by most biologists, including those especially interested in evolution ... no such debate ensued as in England'. The Harvard geneticist W. E. Castle told a British colleague that he had 'no doubt about the ultimate victory of the Mendelians, but we must not so worship our pet theory as to become its slave. The deplorable results of such a course are seen in what you term the "Oxford opposition"', meaning, of course, Weldon.[20]

Why was there no dispute in America with the acerbity to match that in England? One is tempted to say: because, like the American Mendelians, the biometricians in the U.S. were not slaves of their paradigm either. At Cold Spring Harbor, Davenport aimed to foster 'co-operation among all biometrical workers and students of heredity', which included Mendelians while he remained a biometrician (and biometricians even after he embraced Mendelism). American biometricians like Pearl came out of a biological tradition and were engaged in experimental research. Pearl typically told Herbert Jennings, who was experimenting with *Paramecium*: 'How do you reconcile the sort of facts which you are getting in *P.* and I am getting in egg production, and the plant breeders are getting with their selection work with the "law of ancestral inheritance"?' Soon afterwards Pearl chided Pearson for refusing to accept the results of Wilhelm Johannsen's pure line experiments, which seemed to contradict Pearson's conviction that evolution must proceed by the selection of small variations. Pearl likened Pearson's denial of the existence of pure lines to someone's 'attempting to defend the thesis that black is white. If you could see, as I have repeatedly seen, acres of ground covered with pure line pedigreed cultures showing all the characteristics which Johannsen describes for such pure lines, I am sure that you could not make such a statement as you do'.[21]

[20] R. Pearl to C. B. Davenport, 5 October 1903, C. B. Davenport Papers, Pearl file (American Philosophical Society, Philadelphia, Pa., U.S.A.); S. Wright, 'Comparison of the Impact of Mendelism on Evolutionary Thought in England and America' (unpublished paper, copy in possession of Bernard Norton); W. E. Castle to C. C. Hurst, Jan. 18, 1904, Hurst Papers (note 4), Addn. 7955/4/47.

[21] Davenport to Pearl, 15 January 1904, Pearl Papers (note 7), Davenport file; Pearl to Jennings, 17 February 1909, Pearl Papers (note 7), Jennings file; Pearl to Pearson, 12 March 1910, Pearson Papers (note 17), Pearl file.

But Weldon, Pearson's ally in biometry, was an experimental biologist too, and a first-rate one at that. Clearly the grounding in biological tradition of the American biometricians does not fully explain the lack of an acerbic dispute in the United States. Certainly it fails to account for the vitriol generated by the debate in England. The interpretative stress on personal conflict does seem to get at the bitter and impassioned quality of the dispute between Bateson on the one side and Weldon and Pearson on the other, but it can scarcely account for the division into hostile camps – if such division existed – of other British students of heredity. In search of a more generally applicable explanation, it would seem worthwhile to view the Mendelian-biometrician battle against the background of the more common characteristics of British intellectual life. Here a cross-national perspective becomes particularly helpful. Bearing the United States in mind, one thinks immediately of the relatively close-knit nature of British science and scholarship. More specifically, one thinks also of its relatively limited institutional base.

A preliminary statistical analysis shows that, compared with the American, the institutional base of British genetics was decidedly limited. The American authors cited in the bibliography of Thomas Hunt Morgan, A. H. Sturtevant, H. J. Muller and C. B. Bridges, *Mechanism of Mendelian Heredity*, published in 1915, were employed at one time or another in twenty-six different institutions, nine of which had two or more authors. For the period 1916–30, the number of institutions represented by American authors in the journal *Genetics* totaled thirty-nine, with fifteen employing two or more such researchers and seven, four or more. These statistics may be matched against the number of institutions represented by British authors who published in the *Journal of Genetics* for the entire period 1910–30. The total number of institutions was twenty, about half the American figure; the number with two or more authors only five, about a third of the comparable American figure. More significant, almost all the authors in Britain were concentrated at only two institutions, Cambridge and John Innes, while in the United States genetics authors were spread widely through the research system, save for slight concentrations at Cold Spring Harbor, Harvard and Columbia.[22]

These institutional characteristics suggest the following hypothesis: that the biometrical-Mendelian dispute never reached a

---

[22] The figures are drawn from my own preliminary statistical analysis.

204 DANIEL J. KEVLES

level of vitriolic intensity in the United States because members of both camps operated in an environment of sufficient institutional opportunity to adopt a posture of intellectual tolerance towards advocates of the contrary paradigm. But in Britain the temperature of the dispute rose so high because the institutional situation encouraged members on both sides to see themselves in beleaguered positions. Both were seeking to establish a new field in an institutional environment so limited as to encourage the disputants to believe intellectual victory was required for satisfactory professional survival.

Lyndsay Farrall has noted that the principals in the dispute behaved as though they were in a state of siege, and so they did, even after Weldon's death. Bateson, often at odds with traditional biologists as well as with Pearson, denounced zoologists as 'nincompoops' – 'their ignorance and bigotry is beyond belief' – when a critically important paper on the inheritance of eye color by his collaborator C. C. Hurst was refused publication by the Royal Society. When in 1911 his colleagues Reginald C. Punnett and Rowland H. Biffen were denied election to the Society, Bateson pronounced the outcome 'disgraceful' and took it as a setback for 'all the Mendelian fraternity'.[23] To Pearson, on his part, attacks on biometry by Bateson marked the 'general tendency of the biologists here to discredit if possible the whole movement'. Pearson intended to do nothing which would 'give these folk an opening'. Pearson believed that his papers failed to receive a fair evaluation from the referees for the Royal Society, especially Bateson. In 1901, together with Weldon and a small group of fellow guarantors, he launched *Biometrika*. While ostensibly prepared to publish Mendelian materials, Pearson generally ran the journal with an iron intellectual hand. In 1903 he went so far as to discourage Davenport, a member of his editorial board, from publishing an article favorable to the (pro-Mendelian) mutation theory.[24]

In 1910, shortly after Davenport and Raymond Pearl, also a *Biometrika* editor, published comments favorable to Johannsen's pure line theory, Pearson summarily removed them from the

[23] Farrall, 'Controversy and Conflict' (note 5), p. 292, note 93; Bateson to Hurst, 30 June 1907, 18 June 1907, 27 June 1907, 3 March 1911, Hurst Papers (note 4), Addn. 7955/7/31; 28; 29, 7955/11/2.
[24] Pearson to Davenport, 27 January 1902, 23 May 1903, Davenport Papers (note 20), Pearson file.

editorial board by heavy-handedly abolishing the board altogether. 'It is a disadvantage to the Journal and the cause I have at heart', he explained to Pearl, 'to be told that the subeditors of the Journal are opposed to the principles for which it was founded'. Davenport he bluntly – and wrongly – accused of being 'no longer in sympathy with biometric methods and results'. Pearl, who regarded Pearson as a friend and mentor – he had spent a year learning biometry in Pearson's laboratory – was hurt and angry. He snapped to Pearson: You seem to want 'no one associated with you in the editorship of *Biometrika* who does not think exactly as you do on the questions of theoretical biology'. Herbert Jennings, Pearl's close friend, consolingly commented on Pearson's 'incredible' behavior: 'Whom the gods will destroy they first make mad'.[25]

Not mad, but, in the case of Pearson as well as Weldon and Bateson, perhaps professionally frustrated. Between 1894 and 1906 none was situated in professional comfort. Weldon, appointed Linacre Professor of Zoology and a fellow of Merton College at Oxford in 1899, at first found the university 'the place for a civilized man to live in, although men do talk about final causes after hall'. Soon, however, he discovered that the museum men were 'rank morphologists who prefer speculating about the pedigree of animals to any other more serious inquiry'. The museum funds were all tied up and he was unable to persuade the fellows of Merton to use the surplus college income – it amounted to £4000 per annum – for academic purposes rather than to invest it in new estates. 'We are therefore', Weldon lamented, 'removing from our possible means of helping knowledge a sum equal to the whole government grant for scientific research every year'. No less infuriating to Weldon was the unsympathetic attitude toward science which permeated the entire university. If a boy was found wanting in Greek, he was turned next to mathematics and, then, after learning 'the anatomy of the frog, and a shoddy hypothesis about the pedigree of animals', as a last resort given a science scholarship. Weldon had failed to get 'one man to care for any thing I say outside a textbook! Their tutors all tell them one is an amiable

[25] Pearson to Pearl, 27 January 1910, Pearl Papers (note 7), Pearson file; Pearl to Pearson, 15 February 1910, Pearson Papers (note 17), Pearl file; Jennings to Pearl, 5 March 1910, Pearl Papers (note 7), Jennings file. See also Pearson to Davenport, 27 January 1910, Davenport to Pearson, 5 February 1910, Davenport Papers (note 20), Pearson file.

crank, useless for the Schools [examinations] except when one says certain definite things'.[26]

At University College in Gower Street, Pearson was burdened by teaching – at least sixteen hours a week of lectures – and he also lacked financial support for research until grants from the Drapers' Company started in 1903; even then he had to battle with University College, which wanted to reduce his department's general budget support by an amount equal to half the Drapers' grant. When Raymond Pearl spent 1905 at Pearson's shop, he found conditions 'something of a disappointment', particularly in terms of inadequate laboratory space. 'The great biometric laboratory of University College is all comprised in one room with two windows [and] with six or seven other people, one of whom is Dr Alice Lee, whose most settled conviction is that the proper temperature of a room is *not over* 58°. I nearly freeze'. Pearson was always at loggerheads with the college, too, over the purpose of the institution; while he wanted to transform University College into a genuine institution of research, the administration insisted that it remain fundamentally a teaching college. Pearson lamented to Weldon: 'I wish we had both been born Germans; we should have established a new "discipline" by now and have had a healthy supply of workers'.[27]

Bateson, not so fortunate even as Weldon or Pearson, earned his livelihood as Steward of St John's College, Cambridge. To finance his research, he had to make do with small grants from the Evolution Committee and the British Association for the Advancement of Science. He also drew heavily on his own pocket and on collaborators in research, many of them women, all of whom earned their living by other means. Bateson's collaborator Punnett recalled, likely with considerable exaggeration, that early in the century the leading journals refused to publish the contributions of Mendelians; they had to depend on the reports of the Evolution Committee and the *Proceedings* of the Cambridge Philosophical Society until Bateson established the *Journal of Genetics* in 1910.[28]

[26] Weldon to Pearson, 12 April 1899; 19 May 1899, 21 May 1902, 11 July 1900, Pearson Papers (note 17), Weldon file.
[27] Weldon to Pearson, 31 July 1903, Pearson Papers (note 17), Weldon file; Froggatt and Nevin (note 5), p. 12; Pearl to Jennings, 8 October 1905, Pearl Papers (note 7), Jennings file; Pearson to Weldon, 9 October 1900, Pearson Papers (note 17), file 263.
[28] R. C. Punnett, 'Early Days of Genetics', *Heredity*, iv (April 1950), pp. 1–10.

At the turn of the century Pearson, dissatisfied with his post at University College London, applied four times unsuccessfully for different professorships at Oxford and Edinburgh. 'I fear ... you are the only part of the scientific public, which takes the least interest in my work', he told Galton plaintively. 'The mathematicians look askance at anyone who goes off the regular track, and the biologists think I have no business meddling with such things'. On his part, Weldon rued the day that he had left University College for Oxford, 'the greatest danger to England' that he knew. 'I hate it, and I hate myself because I have sold myself to it for money, instead of sticking to good old Gower Street, where there are live people who can be made keen'. Like Pearson, Bateson time and again offered himself for professorial posts at Cambridge. Rejected even after his election to the Royal Society and receipt of the Darwin Medal, he lamented to a friend: 'I have failed with my contemporaries; with posterity I hope to be more successful'.[29]

Of course Bateson was soon successful with his contemporaries. Appointed to the new, five-year chair of genetics at Cambridge in 1908, he achieved personal and professional security when he was made the director of the new John Innes Institute in 1910. The professional situation eased somewhat for Pearson after 1911, when a bequest established an endowed professorship for him and support for the Biometric and Galton Laboratories. To the degree that the dispute between the leading biometricians and Mendelians diminished in intensity after 1906, the reason was probably not simply that Weldon died. Quite possibly it was also because two of the chief contestants acquired more secure institutional status in the tightly knit world of British science for themselves, their paradigms, their research, and their training of students.

Cross-national attention to the commoners of genetics would likely help clarify another point of the existing historiography – that by 1915 the centre of Mendelian research was rapidly shifting from Britain to the United States. As early as 1907, British Mendelians were already avidly reading the *American Naturalist* and *Science*. And in 1921, when Bateson was elected a foreign

[29] Pearson to Yule, October 1901, Pearson Papers (note 17), Yule file; Pearson to Galton, 11 January 1898, Galton Papers, file 293C (I am indebted to Bernard Norton for this document); Weldon to Pearson, 21 October 1904, Pearson Papers (note 17), Weldon file; Bateson is quoted in Beatrice Bateson (note 3), p. 93.

associate of the National Academy of Sciences, he enthused to
Pearl: 'In our line American opinion is the best attainable, so I
really for once feel like somebody!'[30] The shift to American supremacy occurred, it has been suggested, because of Bateson's
disbelief in the central role in genetic transmission of chromosomes
and in the Morgan school's fecund research programme in chromosomal genetics. Not until 1922 did Bateson, fresh from a visit to the
United States, consider it 'practically essential that some try at the
cytology should be made ... It does tell an amazing lot as to the
significance of genetical problems'.[31] Bateson then hired a cytologist at John Innes. Still, whatever his attitudes toward cytology
and the chromosomal role in heredity, little can be said about the
effect of his beliefs without knowing a good deal more about his
influence after the very early years on the course of genetics
research in Britain. A number of British geneticists were on the staff
of the John Innes Institute, which Bateson directed from 1910 until
his death in 1926. One wonders what effect his antichromosomal
views had on the John Innes research programme and, going
beyond John Innes, what role they played in shaping genetic
research among scientific commoners in Britain through such
institutional mechanisms as journals, the Royal Society, the
Genetical Society, and the universities. More generally, one needs
to know the attitudes of British geneticists at large towards the
chromosomal theory of inheritance.

Any analysis of the relative vigour and quality of genetics
research in Britain and the United States must take into account
the institutional environment, or what Charles Rosenberg has
called the 'ecology' of the discipline. In Rosenberg's view, the swift
rise to prominence of the American school of genetics was made
possible by certain important institutional developments. One derived from the rapid enlargement after the 1890s of opportunities
for research and graduate training in American universities.
Between 1900 and 1915, doctorates awarded in America in botany
and zoology more than doubled. Between 1915 and 1930 the
prominent American geneticists William E. Castle and Edward M.
East, both at the Bussey Institution of Harvard University, each
trained twenty Ph.D.s. At Columbia between 1910 and 1930,

[30] Bateson to Pearl, n.d., Pearl Papers (note 7), Bateson file.
[31] G. E. Allen (note 3), p. 57; Bateson to Hurst, 12 February 1922, Hurst Papers,
(note 4), Addn. 7955/14/8.

Morgan produced a comparable number, including of course the graduates of the famed Fly Room, C. B. Bridges, A. H. Sturtevant and H. J. Muller. Such statistics are not yet available for Britain, but it is known that the total of advanced students in all fields at British grant-aided universities during 1913/14 was 172.[32] Another institutional advantage of importance to American genetics, Rosenberg has stressed, was the natural interest in the discipline of farmers and breeders who, though not always sympathetic to basic genetic research, nevertheless generally supported its prosecution at the newly established agricultural experimental stations attached to the land grant colleges and universities. Bateson caught the significance of the gathering institutional power of American biology when early in the century, stimulated by the establishment of Davenport's richly funded installation at Cold Spring Harbor, he remarked: 'We had read your vast programme of work with wonder and admiration. How any decent competition is to be kept up on our side I scarcely know!'[33]

Over the years the Cold Spring Harbor station actually produced less respectable genetics than it might have, but the agricultural experimental stations, especially after the passage of the Adams Act in 1906, provided an abundant source of fine genetics research. The Maine Experiment Station took advantage of the funds made available by the Adams Act to hire Raymond Pearl, for the purpose of mounting a thorough investigation of inheritance in poultry, particularly with regard to Mendelian phenomena. Pearl was delighted with the salary, facilities, budget, assistance and the degree, as he told Pearson, to which he would have a free hand. 'I am under no restrictions as to giving the work a practical turn. On the contrary I am expected to work exactly as if I were taking up the study of heredity for my own purely scientific ends'. Save for

[32] C. E. Rosenberg, 'The Social Environment of Scientific Innovation: Factors in the Development of Genetics in the United States,' in C. E. Rosenberg, *No Other Gods* (Johns Hopkins University Press, 1976), pp. 196–209; H. Cravens, 'The Role of Universities in the Rise of American Science, 1890–1930', manuscript version, pp. 31, 33, and note 50 (copy with author). See his shorter 'The Role of Universities in the Rise of Experimental Biology', *The Science Teacher*, xliv, January (1977); D. S. L. Cardwell, *The Organisation of Science in England* (revised edn., London: Heinemann, 1972), p. 215. On a special aspect of the institutional development of science in Britain, see G. L. Geison, *Michael Foster and the Cambridge School of Physiology: The Scientific Enterprise in Late Victorian Society* (Princeton: Princeton University Press, 1978).
[33] Bateson to Davenport, 25 April 1906, Davenport Papers (note 20), Bateson file.

occasional lapses, the administrators of the station followed through on the promise. In 1909 Pearl mused how he was protected at the station 'like a valuable piece of furniture'.[34]

Experimental station scientists who had to concern themselves, more than did Pearl, with practicality also contributed significantly to genetics. Particularly notable was the work of William J. Spillman, a plant scientist at Washington State College who in 1901, responding to the needs of local farmers, began to develop a variety of true winter wheat hardy enough for local conditions. Spillman knew nothing of Mendel, but he sensed that a useful route to follow might be hybridization. Smart and observant, Spillman recognized that the variations he observed in the $F_2$ generation were not fortuitous but the result of possible combinations of characters in the two hybrid parents. Calculating the percentages of plants displaying various characters, he found what he regarded as an astonishing regularity in these distributions over his different plants of wheat. Put on to Mendel's papers in 1902, Spillman realized that his results were entirely explicable on Mendelian theory. Upon reading Spillman's first wheat paper, published before he had yet heard of Mendel, C. C. Hurst exclaimed: 'As I read the copious facts given in the tables, the paper is biologically of the greatest importance and in the large numbers with which it deals is in my opinion the most valuable confirmation of Mendel published since his day, indeed in some respects it gives more facts than did he'.[35]

Yet if in the opportunities it gave to a Morgan, Pearl or Spillman, the United States had a numerical institutional advantage over Britain, it did not have any advantage in institutional setting or type. Research was gaining a stronger foothold in British universities after the turn of the century. Moreover, in the 1890s, anticipating Davenport, Francis Galton had joined leading English biologists to advocate the establishment of an experimental farm – it was to be located at Down, the Darwin family estate – to study variation and heredity. The effort had failed, but by the early twentieth century the agricultural utility of genetics research stations was under discussion in Britain. In 1904 the Cambridge

[34] Pearl to Pearson, 9 December 1906, Pearson Papers (note 17), Pearl file; Pearl to Jennings, 26 October 1909, Pearl Papers (note 7), Jennings file.
[35] W. J. Spillman to C. C. Hurst, 16 April 1903; 21 January 1904; Hurst to Wilkes, 21 January 1903, Hurst Papers (note 4), Addn. 7955/3/78–81 and 7955/3/54.

geneticist R. H. Biffen founded the *Journal of Agricultural Science*, declaring: 'The problem of heredity is going to be of such importance to agriculture that we propose to lay ourselves out for publishing it'.[36] The degree to which English breeders and horticulturalists were willing to lay themselves out is unclear. Older breeders of plants, horses and pigeons seem to have been skeptical; nevertheless, as a member of the City Columbarian Society, a London group of pigeon fanciers, told Hurst: 'It is the younger members who are gradually taking interest and disposed to breed on Mendelian lines'.[37] In 1909 Hurst himself transformed his family nurseries at Burbage in Leicestershire into the Burbage Experimental Station, which enjoyed considerable publicity when members of the British Association for the Advancement of Science, while meeting in nearby Birmingham in 1913, toured the facilities.[38] The British Army, alive to the uses of genetics, engaged Hurst and Cossar Ewart of Edinburgh in 1911 as scientific experts in a programme for breeding superior hunter-type horses for the military. By 1914 the British government was supplying funds to agricultural experiment stations at various universities.

In any event, the American institutional advantage did not make necessarily for higher quality science. Institutional opportunity can be undermined by perverse ideological commitments, e.g., Nazism or Lysenkoism, or by weakness in the scientific leadership of those in control. American physics operated in an institutional setting similar to that of genetics, yet American physics did not rank with British before World War I, when just two institutions, the Cavendish Laboratory and Manchester University, were enough to put Britain in the first rank. Before World War I the Carnegie Institution of Washington spawned two richly funded enterprises among others: the Station for Experimental Evolution under Charles B. Davenport and the Mt. Wilson Observatory under George Ellery Hale. The latter far outshone the former, not least because Hale's scientific taste and judgement were decidedly superior to Davenport's.

[36] R. H. Biffen to C. C. Hurst, 26 October 1904, Hurst Papers (note 4), Addn. 7955/5/58; Christabel S. Orwin and Edith Whetham, *History of British Agriculture, 1846–1914* (London: Longmans, 1964), pp. 373–86.
[37] C. R. G. Sanfort to Hurst, (n. d. [1908]). Hurst Papers (note 4), Addn. 7955/8/36.
[38] British Association for the Advancement of Science, 'Birmingham Meeting 1913, Visit to Burbage, 16 September 1913', pamphlet in Hurst Papers (note 4).

To account for the comparative quality of genetics in the United States and Great Britain, it would seem that the institutional situation must be considered in the total context of the discipline. Perhaps Mendelian genetics was somehow particularly well suited, in a way that physics was not, to the American scientific tradition or environment. Given the elitist nature of British academia, perhaps the loss in World War I of key younger geneticists was critically important to the fate of the discipline in England. Perhaps genetics in Britain was also affected by the fact that there, much more than in the United States, a large proportion of the people working in the discipline seem to have been breeders and horticulturalists, like C. C. Hurst, rather than professional scientists in universities. In 1924 the British Genetical Society had 108 members, forty-two of whom were private individuals and plant or animal breeders.[39] Also, perhaps the fate of genetics in the two countries was determined less by the relative number of institutional opportunities and more by the way those institutional opportunities were used for the training of students and the prosecution of research programmes.

The use was undoubtedly a partial function of the external forces that shaped them. In both the United States and Britain, economic expectations helped create the institutional environment for genetics research – at agricultural experimental stations and probably in university departments. Economic expectations aside, the pursuit of genetics was also, it seems, affected by social forces, notably the eugenics movement.

Expressing the aim of imposing through science a certain type of social control upon industrial society, the British and American eugenics movements included many geneticists before World War I and even some afterwards, when in the United States it turned increasingly conservative and racist. In both periods enthusiasts of eugenics seem to have supplied the institutional development of genetics research with certain benefits. At University College London Galton supported a Eugenics Record Office and a Research Fellowship in National Eugenics. Pearson, aching for funds, thought that 'the dear old fellow could have spent his money

[39] D. Lewis, 'The Genetical Society – The First Fifty Years', in J. Jinks (ed.), *Fifty Years of Genetics: Proceedings of a Symposium held at the 160th meeting of the Genetical Society on the 50th Anniversary of its Foundation* (Edinburgh: Oliver and Boyd, 1969), p. 1.

better', but his turn came soon, since it was Galton's will that established his endowed professorship of eugenics.[40] While Pearson's Drapers' Company grant was not given for eugenic purposes, it was used to aid statistical studies in heredity, and the Drapers' managers regarded the results favourably enough to continue the grant for some thirty years. Eugenic interests also played a role in the establishment of the chair of genetics at Cambridge University. Arthur Balfour, a longtime advocate of strengthening research in British universities and a member of the Eugenics Education Society, persuaded an anonymous donor – he was one William Watson – to endow the chair with £20,000.[41]

In the United States, eugenic convictions helped energize the research and scientific entrepreneurial activities of Charles B. Davenport at Cold Spring Harbor. There, in 1910 and with a substantial grant of funds from Mrs E. H. Harriman, Davenport founded a Eugenics Record Office, the American equivalent of the enterprise at University College. In 1921 the Office, further endowed by Mrs Harriman, became part of the Carnegie Institution's Department of Genetics, which between 1921 and 1930 spent almost $1.3 million for genetics and eugenics research.

Institutional considerations aside, eugenics seems to have helped recruit young scientists into genetics proper. In 1911 a group of faculty and undergraduates at Cambridge University, including R. C. Punnett, L. Doncaster, and R. A. Fisher, formed the Cambridge University Eugenics Society. In America, some colleges established special courses in eugenics, while many more taught biology, sociology and psychology with eugenically flavoured textbooks. Scarcely a major American university faculty failed to include one or more professors of biology who, espousing the desirability of eugenic goals, no doubt inspired some of their students into careers in genetics research.[42] Recruitment aside, eugenics or proto-eugenic convictions likely drew the attention of important scientists to

[40] Pearson to Yule, 30 October 1904, Pearson Papers (note 17), cabinet VI, drawer 5.
[41] L. A. Farrall (note 3), pp. 110–11, 126, 130–2; Viscount Esher to the Vice-Chancellor, 7 March 1912, Balfour Professorship of Genetics Guard Book, C. U. R. 39.47, Cambridge University Library; Esher to Balfour, 15 February 1912, Arthur Balfour Papers, British Library, Addn. 49719, item 214.
[42] K. Ludmerer, *Genetics and American Society* (Johns Hopkins University Press 1972), p. 82; G. R. Searle, *Eugenics and Politics in Britain, 1900–1914* (Leyden: Noordhoof International Publishing, 1976), pp. 13–14, 34–5.

problems in heredity. It certainly did so for Galton, Pearson and R. A. Fisher, whose work in the reconciliation of biometry and Mendelism was from his undergraduate days fuelled by his eugenic concerns.[43]

Despite the suggestiveness of the above examples, not a great deal can yet be said with confidence about the role – or lack of it – of eugenics or of economic expectations in the development of genetics research. Indeed, before much more can be said with confidence about the early history of genetics generally, it would seem that a set of important queries needs to be addressed:

Who were the early converts and opponents of Mendelism in the United States and Great Britain, and how is their position to be accounted for?

Who were the biometricians, and did they all oppose Mendelism?

To what degree did the angry biometrical-Mendelian dispute extend through the Anglo-American genetics community?

What role did Bateson's anti-chromosomal views play in the course of British genetics?

How did eugenics and agriculture actually affect in genetics the growth of its institutions, the recruitment of its practitioners, and the nature of the research they pursued?

To answer such queries – indeed, even to raise them – is to acknowledge with much of the recent historiography of genetics that the subject simply cannot be dealt with as the history of a body of knowledge produced largely by disembodied actors extracted from their personal, professional, or institutional contexts and engaged altogether in purely rational scientific debate. It is also to recognize that the rise of the Anglo-American genetics community forms a fertile field of historical investigation that can now be cultivated with the aid of extensive manuscript collections. The

---

[43] Important work stressing the role of social propensities in the history of genetics and biometry include: Ruth S. Cowan, 'Francis Galton's Statistical Ideas: the Influence of Eugenics', *Isis*, lxiii (1972), pp. 509–28; *idem*, 'Francis Galton's Contribution to Genetics', *Journal of the History of Biology*, v. no. 3 (1972), pp. 389–412; D. A. MacKenzie, 'Statistical Theory and Social Interests: A Case Study', *Social Studies of Science*, viii (February 1978), pp. 35–84; B. Norton, 'Karl Pearson and Statistics: The Social Origins of Scientific Innovation', *ibid.*, pp. 3–34; W. Coleman, 'Bateson and Chromosomes: Conservative Thought in Science', *Centaurus*, xv (1970), pp. 228–314. See also B. Norton, 'The Galtonian Tradition'; D. A. MacKenzie, 'Statistical Theory in Britain' (note 15); G. Allen (note 11).

subject invites the consideration, through cross-national comparison, not only of research but of practitioners and patrons, institutions and governance; as such, it promises profitable returns in the as yet dimly perceived arena where the history of ideas and the history of institutions come together.

# 6. Eugenics and Class

G. R. SEARLE

Even to discuss eugenics in class terms is an enterprise of which many British eugenists earlier in the century would have disapproved, since they clung tenaciously to the view that the ideology they were propounding was sanctioned by science. Eugenics, they claimed, rested upon 'laws of biology', which no more admitted of subjective interpretation than did the 'law of gravity'; those who denied these laws were guilty of the same sort of anti-scientific obscurantism which, a generation earlier, had led pious Christians into seeking to deny the validity of Darwinian biology. On the other hand, some eugenists did also devote much time and energy to debating the class implications of their creed and in the course of doing this they were to elaborate a highly idiosyncratic explanation of the British social system.

At the heart of eugenics was a fear about the likely consequences of differential class fertility. Eugenists interpreted the tendency of better-off groups to have smaller families than those beneath them in the social and economic scale to mean that the 'superior' stocks were dying out, while the 'unfit' continued to multiply; this demographic process, they argued, was producing progressive racial deterioration, alarming symptoms of which could already be seen. Eugenists were concerned, therefore, to stimulate the fertility of the better stocks ('positive eugenics') and to take whatever steps were feasible and politically acceptable to slow down the rate of reproduction at the bottom end of the social scale, steps which might include the placing of certain diseased and degenerate groups of people under custodial care so that they could be sexually segregated ('negative eugenics').[1]

These opinions were clearly predicated upon the view that social class expressed, to a certain extent, men's genetic endowment. Karl Pearson, for example, contended that 'class distinctions (were) not entirely illusory' and that 'certain families pursued definite occupations, because they (had) a more or less specialized aptitude for

[1] G. R. Searle, *Eugenics and Politics in Britain, 1900–1914* (Leyden, 1976).

217

them'.[2] From this standpoint, the working classes, and more particularly, the unskilled 'residuum' and the socially dependent, could be dismissively referred to as an 'army of the biologically unfit'. In generous mood, eugenists might admit the existence of the 'unlucky pauper', but the drift of their argument was to demonstrate that if, for example, a man was unemployed, this was because he was 'unemployable'. Intelligent, socially ambitious manual labourers, with valuable contributions to make to national life, would already have achieved upward mobility – either their innate energy would have enabled them to break down all social barriers to their advancement, or else they would have been picked out by the educational system and encouraged to receive a training for a middle-class career. This process of social sifting, said the eugenists, had left the working class inferior on average to their 'social betters', in respect of their health, physique and mental ability, while the lowest strata of manual workers contained a high percentage of men and women from 'tainted stock'.

It must not be supposed, however, that many eugenists were entirely happy with social arrangements as they stood. The existing distribution of wealth, political authority and social esteem did not, they admitted, altogether mirror the distribution of inherited mental ability among the population at large. For example, the principle of primogeniture by no means ensured that an able man who was ennobled would necessarily transmit his title and his acquired possessions to the descendant who had inherited most of his natural ability. For this reason, eugenists were inclined to denigrate the existing aristocracy as a 'sham aristocracy', devoid of biological significance. Even worse, they argued, the tendency in the late nineteenth and early twentieth centuries for English aristocrats to revive their financial fortunes by marrying rich heiresses from 'dubious' social backgrounds must have been harmful, firstly, because it threatened to degrade the stock, and, secondly, because it had the effect of converting the aristocracy into a plutocracy. Few eugenists felt much respect for the mere possession of wealth; indeed, the more radical elements among them argued that inherited, as distinct from acquired, wealth operated in a dysgenic way, by encouraging idleness and habits of selfish luxury, both of which were likely to weaken a healthy racial instinct.

[2] K. Pearson, *The Groundwork of Eugenics* (London, 1909), p. 32.

But neither did eugenists view with much favour the operations of big business. From both the socially conservative wing of the eugenics movement (e.g., the Whethams, Dean Inge) and from radical eugenists with socialist sympathies there came the charge that capitalism encouraged and profited by the multiplication of the unfit, because of its need for a large pool of surplus labour. Capitalism's orientation towards profit and short-term economic advantage might, in such ways as these, work against orderly racial progress.[3]

Who, then, were to act as the custodians of the racial health of the community and hold a watching brief for the interests of the unborn? Even a cursory glance through eugenical literature makes it clear that this central role was to be played by the professional middle classes. Two reasons are given for this. Firstly, eugenists claimed that the careers which professional men adopted assumed a high degree of mental ability and that this was kept up by the intensely competitive nature of professional life. But, secondly, the professional middle classes were said to be important since upon their skills and expertise rested all hopes of constructing a rational society informed by eugenical principles.

An examination of the occupations pursued by members of the British Eugenics Society confirms the impression, derived from a reading of the literature it produced, that eugenics was a creed which appealed almost exclusively to men and women from professional middle-class backgrounds. Lyndsay Farrall has taken the names of members of the Society's Council between 1908 and 1920, plus a random sample of sixty members and associate members in the years 1912–13, and has discovered that most middle-class professions are represented therein, with the two major groups being medical men and academics: twenty-six and eighteen, respectively, out of a total of sixty-three members about whom evidence was available.[4] Because of the high proportion of unknown members in Farrall's sample, Donald MacKenzie has carried out a more detailed investigation of his own, based upon the forty-one elected Council members for 1914. This investigation simply confirms Farrall's conclusions: doctors, scientists and academics comprise more than half of MacKenzie's group, the remainder

[3] G. R. Searle (note 1), chap. 5.
[4] Cited in D. MacKenzie, 'Eugenics in Britain', *Social Studies of Science*, vi (1976), pp. 523–4.

being divided between lawyers, writers, clergymen, headmasters and housewives.[5] A similar test applied to the Council of 1933 does not suggest that the social composition of the British Eugenics Movement was any different in the inter-war years to what it had been in the Edwardian period.[6] What all three investigations show, predictably, is an almost total absence of manual workers, trade union officials and the like; also, again not surprisingly in the light of eugenical propaganda, very few members from the business, commercial or financial worlds. All the evidence so far assembled seems to suggest that, in Britain at any rate, eugenics was, indeed, 'a movement *of* the professional middle classes, ideologically *for* the professional middle classes'.[7]

But what precisely was the relationship between eugenics as an ideology and the interests of those social groups which provided it with the bulk of its supporters? In a number of important and stimulating papers, Donald MacKenzie has presented eugenics not just as one of a variety of ideologies competing for the allegiance of the professional middle classes, but as the ideology which, together with its close ally, Fabianism, best represented the interests of professional men in general, but more particularly those in 'modern', scientific and technological occupations – its 'ideas were taken up when thought likely to be useful to their carrier groups, and later, when changed circumstances made them less appropriate, they were discarded'.[8] MacKenzie assigns particular importance in this process to the statistician and biometrician, Karl Pearson, the first Professor of Eugenics at London University; Pearson, he argues, acted as the ideologist, *par excellence*, of the professional middle classes, not because most professional men happened to agree with his scientific and political views, but because Pearson's thought expressed their interests in a 'pure' form, uncontaminated by the sort of political opportunism which 'distorted' the writings of the Fabians, and uncontaminated also by particular vocational commitments which could sometimes obscure

[5] D. MacKenzie, *ibid.*, pp. 524–7.
[6] Of fifty-two officers and members of the Society's council I have been able to trace the occupations of forty-two. Sixteen are doctors, seven scientists and two university teachers in non-scientific subjects.
[7] D. MacKenzie, review article, *British Journal for the History of Science*, xi (1978), p. 90.
[8] D. MacKenzie (note 4), p. 501.

the fundamental needs and outlook of this social stratum.[9] How much credence should be given to this interesting proposition?

Of course, as MacKenzie is the first to admit, the professional middle classes have never formed a homogeneous unit; there is an important distinction to be drawn, he writes, between, on the one hand, the church and the legal profession, which 'relied on traditional spheres of knowledge', and, on the other hand, 'many of the newer professions (and increasingly the older profession of medicine)', which sought to legitimate their social role 'in such fields as natural science and empirical social research'.[10] One would expect that the appeal of eugenics would be largely directed to the latter group, and an analysis of the social composition of the Eugenics Society apparently confirms this hypothesis.

Scientists, doctors and university lecturers have always dominated the British eugenics movement. It is no coincidence that nearly all the provincial branches of the Society set up before 1914 were located in towns which possessed a university college (for example, Oxford, Birmingham, Belfast and Liverpool), and that, typically, the initiative in setting up these organizations originated with one or two well-established academics, usually drawn from the faculties of medicine or biology.[11] This draws our attention to the very close relationship which existed from the very start between eugenics as a political movement and those emerging academic specialisms which formed the scientific basis of eugenics or were, in some other way, intimately connected with it. As MacKenzie and other historians of science have demonstrated, there was a dialectical interaction between eugenics as a set of political beliefs and eugenics as a set of scientific theories; several scientists, including Galton and Pearson, developed a concern for the scientific study of heredity as a *consequence* of a prior commitment to race-culture.[12]

In other cases professional self-interest probably drove into the Eugenics Society academics engaged on research into heredity and population problems, in particular, demographers, statisticians, psychologists and geneticists. It is surely significant that, with the important exception of William Bateson, nearly every distinguished

[9] D. MacKenzie, 'Karl Pearson and the Professional Middle Classes', *Annals of Science*, xxxvi (1979), p. 138.
[10] D. MacKenzie (note 4), p. 501.
[11] G. R. Searle (note 1), p. 60.
[12] E.g., D. MacKenzie (note 4), p. 502.

geneticist of the first generation joined the Eugenics Society. Even if, partly through pressure of work, partly through innate caution, they held back somewhat from general eugenical propaganda, they none the less submitted material for publication in the *Eugenics Review*, gave papers to eugenics conferences, and in this way put their professional prestige at the disposal of the cause. The same is true of psychologists strongly disposed to hereditarian explanations of mental ability, among them William MacDougall and Cyril Burt; indeed, the relationship between eugenics and the development of I.Q. testing is worth a more detailed examination than it can receive in this paper.

Even academics suspicious of the larger claims being made for eugenics must have been aware of the boost it could give to their professional work. For a start, eugenics provided their new intellectual specialisms with valuable general publicity. More particularly, the Eugenics Society was often able to support their research, both by providing facilities for publication and, increasingly in the inter-war period, by directly sponsoring and subsidizing specific research projects. Thus, the Society set up in 1936 a Population Investigation Committee 'to examine the trends of population in Great Britain and the Colonies and to investigate the causes of these trends, with special reference to the falling birthrate'. The Research Secretary of this Committee was the demographer, D. V. Glass, a lecturer at the London School of Economics, who was helped, in this way, to collect and process the material out of which was fashioned his book, *The Struggle for Population* (1936).[13] Or, to take another example, the Society was awarding from 1935 onwards a series of Darwin Research Studentships worth £250 and tenable for two years; the first award went to Dr R. B. Cattell, the Director of the School Psychological Clinic at Leicester,[14] whose psychometric investigations were later published in book form under the title, *The Fight For Our National Intelligence* (1937).

It is also reasonable to assume that eugenics attracted scientists in such emergent academic disciplines as demography, psychometry and genetics, because it promised them a future in which their professional expertise would guide and shape social policy. The

[13] Faith Schenk and A. S. Parkes, 'The Activities of the Eugenics Society', *Eugenics Review*, lx (1968), pp. 151–2.
[14] *Ibid.*, p. 150.

same consideration would apply to 'experts' outside the academic world whose specialized aptitudes would be of crucial importance in an eugenically organized State. As MacKenzie graphically puts it, 'the eugenic solution to social problems, employing as it would the statisticians' figures, the biologists' studies, the psychologists' tests, the social workers' case reports and ultimately the psychiatrists' custodial care or the surgeons' scalpel, was one which would give potentially full play to the skill of the developing scientific professions'.[15]

So far there seems to be considerable substance in MacKenzie's thesis. However, it is necessary to make the qualification that, even within the 'modern', scientifically educated section of the professional middle classes, eugenics ran into considerable opposition. Nor is this surprising when one considers that eugenists, in extolling the merits of certain academic disciplines and professional skills, were unavoidably drawn into denigrating others. Karl Pearson, in particular, drastically narrowed down the appeal of eugenics by his insistence that solid advances in the understanding of social and biological problems could only take place through the use of the statistical methods being devised by himself and his research assistants at the Eugenics Laboratory. Adopting the Royal Society's motto, *Nullius in verba*,[16] Pearson denied the scientific status of investigations that did not rest on a mathematical footing: a stance which led him to disparage the importance of Mendelian genetics and triggered off a bitter dispute between rival factions in the eugenics movement.[17] It also involved him in disputes with a number of expanding groups of professional men whose antagonism eugenics could ill afford to incur.

One such group of critics was formed by the Medical Officers of Health, who were already angry as a result of being constantly told by eugenists that their attempts to soften the environment meant a dangerous interference with the process of natural selection, which

[15] D. MacKenzie (note 7).
[16] K. Pearson, *Social Problems: Their Treatment, Past, Present and Future* (London, 1912), p. 17.
[17] For the scientific aspects of this controversy, see D. A. MacKenzie and S. B. Barnes, 'Biometrician versus Mendelian: A Controversy and Its Explanation' (University of Edinburgh, Science Studies Unit, September 1974); P. Froggatt and N. C. Nevin, 'The "Law of Ancestral Heredity" and the Mendelian-Ancestrian Controversy in England, 1899–1906', *Journal of Medical Genetics*, viii (1971), pp. 1–36.

was allowing a higher proportion of the unfit to survive. Sporadically, eugenists tried to win the profession over to their side. The Secretary of the Eugenics Society, Mrs Gotto, in a paper delivered to a Health Congress in Paris in 1913, expatiated on the importance of the health officer as a gatherer of the large quantity of data upon which eugenical research depended, and also saw a role for him in instructing school-teachers in elementary biology and sex hygiene, which information the teachers could then pass on to the children under their charge.[18] Pearson himself was on the same tack when he claimed that the M.O.H. was 'concerned with what makes for the racial efficiency of future generations' and therefore 'must *nolens volens* become a eugenist'.[19]

But the health officers, with their commitment to preventive medicine, to improved hygiene and to sanitary reform, were not likely to find eugenics attractive, and it is little wonder that this group should have gravitated towards the Webbs, who went to considerable lengths to woo them, particularly at the time of the debate over the Poor Law Reports.[20] By contrast, they saw the eugenists' preoccupation with heredity as a threat both to their *raison d'être* and to their career prospects. Thus, Arthur Newsholme, a former M.O.H. who held the position of Chief Medical Officer at the Local Government Board between 1907 and 1918, was still smarting at the ridicule which he had received at Pearson's hands, when he wrote his memoirs in the 1930s. 'Environment', Newsholme stoutly maintained, 'has a preponderant influence in determining the magnitude of infant and child mortality in a community; and the increasing efforts of hygienists to improve environment ... need not be embarrassed by suggestions that such efforts may exert an

[18] A. C. Gotto, 'The Relation of Eugenic Education to Public Health', *Journal of State Medicine*, xxi (1913), pp. 623–31.
[19] K. Pearson, *Darwinism, Medical Progress and Eugenics* (London, 1912), p. 3.
[20] Sidney Webb, a guest of honour at the Annual Dinner of the Society of Medical Officers of Health in October 1909, said in his speech: 'It was very largely to them that we had to look for the success of the scheme formulated in the Minority Report. He could not help thinking that the medical officers of health were doing already more than any other public officers to regenerate England – to make England even a more productive nation than it would otherwise be', *Public Health*, xxiii (1909), p. 66. A review of the Webbs' *The State and the Doctor* (1912), printed in *Public Health*, the journal of the Association of M.O.H.s, stated: 'Probably no one outside the ranks of the public health service has ever paid so much attention to the official writings of medical officers of health' than the Webbs have done, *Public Health*, xxiv (1910), p. 29.

inimical influence on the quality of mankind'. Eugenics, he complained, had dampened the enthusiasm and usefulness of not a few medical officers of health who had been unable to check the statistics employed by biometricians or to identify the flaws in them.[21] Newsholme's own chief interest in life was in combating tuberculosis by improvements in sanitary conditions and by removing infected patients for treatment in sanatoria, and he was incensed when Pearson argued that Nature had much better ways of her own for reducing the phthisical death-rate and that '£1,500,000 spent in encouraging healthy parentage would do more than the establishment of a sanatorium in every township'.[22] Another victim of Pearson's sarcasm, Dr Leslie Mackenzie, Chief Medical Officer at the Scottish Local Government Board, also hit back vigorously against eugenics and, like Newsholme, poured ridicule on the notion that biological 'fitness' coincided with either social position or financial success.[23] This collision between a predominantly hereditarian and a predominantly environmental social philosophy is a theme to which I shall later return.

But other medical men, too, felt the keenest antipathy towards eugenics. Major Darwin, the Society's president, expressed his perplexity at this state of affairs: 'Medical men must, no doubt, strive to keep the unfit alive; but are they not therefore doubly bound to join us in our efforts to diminish the multiplication of the unquestionably degenerate types?', he asked.[24] It is true that the Eugenics Society had a stroke of good fortune in 1912 when one of its Vice-Presidents, Sir James Barr, President of the B.M.A. for that year, chose to use his position to deliver an eugenical address at the Association's Annual Conference, but this does not mean, as one historian has recently claimed, that 'the eugenic creed received the imprimatur of the British Medical Association'.[25] It never did receive such an imprimatur, unless one so designates the decision of the B.M.A. to set up a 'Medical Sociology' Section in 1913, which eugenists quickly came to dominate. Significantly, several of the leading medical journals, including the *British Medical Journal*,

[21] A. Newsholme, *The Last Thirty Years in Public Health* (London, 1936), pp. 208–10.
[22] K. Pearson, *Tuberculosis, Heredity and Environment* (London, 1912), pp. 45–6.
[23] W. Leslie Mackenzie's review of the Whethams' *The Family and the Nation* (London, 1909), printed in *Sociological Review*, iii (1910), pp. 327–30.
[24] *Fifth Annual Report of the Eugenics Education Society* (London, 1912–13), pp. 8–9.
[25] A. McLaren, *Birth Control in Nineteenth-Century England* (London, 1978), p. 112.

showed consistent hostility to eugenics over a period of years.[26] In short, medical men may have been one of the largest groups within the Eugenics Society, but they comprised only a small minority of the profession as a whole.

Moreover, those who were active in the eugenics cause turn out, almost without exception, to belong to one of a number of specialized medical sub-groups. Some were medical authors and journalists, with a wide spread of interests (Havelock Ellis, Caleb Saleeby). Others were leading surgeons and consultants connected with the big teaching hospitals or holding university appointments. Most prominent of all were specialists in pathological conditions and diseases thought to be hereditary in their transmission, such as Dr F. W. Mott, pathologist to the London County Asylum, Dr A. F. Tredgold, author of the frequently re-published book, *Mental Defect*, and Dr Myles Bickerton, a senior ophthalmic surgeon, whose alarmist address on 'The Menace of Hereditary Blindness' was picked up by the popular press in 1934.[27]

This division between specialists and experts, on the one hand, and the mass of ordinary G.P.s, on the other, is especially noticeable in the 1930s, when the Eugenics Society, under the guidance of its general secretary, Dr C. P. Blacker, himself a doctor, deliberately tried to move the emphasis away from larger social and political issues to medical and psycho-medical problems likely to concern citizens of every ideological and party-political persuasion. At the centre of this strategy was a determined attempt by the Society, in alliance with other sympathetic associations, to persuade the Government to support a Bill that would legalize voluntary sterilization for certain specific groups. But although the Sterilization Campaign secured the backing of the Royal College of Surgeons and the Royal College of Physicians, the B.M.A. itself held aloof; and there is evidence that this was a major consideration when the Minister of Health was deciding what line the Government should take on the issue.[28]

Medical resistance to eugenics can best be examined under three heads. Firstly, as eugenists never ceased to complain, few doctors

[26] E.g., *British Medical Journal* (23 August 1913), pp. 508–10.
[27] *British Medical Journal* (20 January 1934), pp. 93–8.
[28] G. R. Searle, 'Eugenics and Politics in Britain in the 1930s', *Annals of Science*, xxxvi (1979), 159–69. I am also preparing an article on the sterilization issue in inter-war Britain.

possessed even a rudimentary understanding of statistics or genetics. When in 1913 the Eugenics Society attempted to get eugenics added to the medical curriculum, the leaders of the profession blandly rejected the idea with the argument that the curriculum was already too crowded.[29] As late as 1936 the distinguished physician, Lord Horder, the Society's Chairman, was still urging that somehow a place must be found for genetics in the training of medical students.[30] There seems some truth, therefore, in the charge that in this, as in other matters, the medical profession displayed an obstinate, and unreasonable, conservatism. But this conservatism may in part have stemmed from an understandable reluctance to become saddled with the frightening responsibility of deciding who was and who was not fit for parentage; the mere suggestion of 'marriage certificates', to be signed by a doctor, caused shudders of apprehension to run through the profession.[31] Also, the B.M.A. dared not offend its Catholic members, who had shown total hostility to eugenics from the very start – a hostility which increased after the Pope had singled out eugenics for censure in the Encyclical, *Casti Connubii*, issued in December 1930.

Finally, and perhaps most important of all, many doctors were clearly alienated by the tone adopted by what might be called the 'Better Dead' school of eugenists. Sir James Barr seemed on occasions to be blaming the degeneration of the race on to the medical profession, when he commended 'Nature's method of adapting the individual to the environment, which is the surest method of progress'.[32] But for a doctor to suggest that there was something reprehensible about the indiscriminate saving of life provoked outrage both within and outside the profession. Similar dismay greeted the remarks of another doctor sympathetic to eugenics, who proposed that surgeons should only save the lives of certain groups of sufferers on the understanding that no children should be born to them afterwards![33] Such language was a downright challenge to the doctors' cherished professional ethics, which enjoined them to save life and relieve suffering without regard to

[29] *Eugenics Education Society Minutes* (London, 24 April 1913).
[30] Lord Horder, 'Eugenics', *Eugenics Review*, xxvii (1936), p. 280
[31] G. R. Searle, (note 1), pp. 97, 99–100.
[32] J. Barr, *The Aim and Scope of Eugenics* (Edinburgh, 1911), p. 10.
[33] H. Campbell, 'Eugenics From the Physician's Standpoint', *British Medical Journal* (2 August 1913), p. 226.

consequences. Nor was anything to be gained by eugenists scolding doctors for not taking their racial responsibilities more seriously, as Dean Inge did when he addressed the International Congress of Medicine in 1913,[34] and as Major Darwin did in his Presidential Address, from which I have already quoted.

We come now to an equally formidable body of critics within the ranks of the 'modern', professional middle classes – namely, those involved in philanthropy, social work and social reform. It is true, of course, that the more tactful of the eugenists tried to scotch the notion that they had a fundamental quarrel to pick with any of these reforming groups; eugenics and social reform, they said, should be seen as complementary, not competing, creeds.[35] But eugenists as a group were not distinguished by their tact. More characteristic was Karl Pearson's blunt assertion: 'There is no real comparison between nature and nurture; it is essentially the man who makes his environment, and not the environment which makes the man'.[36] Social reformers were not likely to take kindly to Carr-Saunders' contention that 'the reason why slum dwellers are stunted or dull is because they come of a stunted and dull stock, which will produce similar offspring'.[37] The factory inspectorate had every reason to feel apprehensive about Pearson's remarks about the harmful racial consequences of the Factory Acts.[38] The schoolmaster and the educationalist would have been similarly displeased when Major Darwin mused out loud about whether education might not have had a dysgenic effect by 'throwing an additional strain on parents by lengthening the period during which they must remain without any help from the earnings of their children'.[39]

The cumulative impression left by all these pronouncements was that eugenists held the activities of social workers and social reformers in derision, and believed that, at best, attempts to raise the living conditions of the poor were superficial or irrelevant responses to a more deep-seated malady, and, at worst, that effort in this direction did positive racial harm. Of course, some charity workers and some officials in the public services might have been

[34] *The Times*, 11 August 1913.
[35] G. R. Searle (note 1), p. 47.
[36] O. Pearson, *Nature and Nurture: The Problem of the Future* (London, 1910), p. 27.
[37] A. M. Carr-Saunders, 'Some Recent Eugenic Work', *Economic Review*, xxi (1911), p. 23.
[38] K. Pearson, *The Problem of Practical Eugenics* (London, 1909), *passim*.
[39] *Fifth Annual Report of the Eugenics Education Society* (London, 1912–13), p. 7.

attracted by this aspect of eugenics. In his study of the American Eugenics Movement, Mark Haller has discovered many converts to 'hereditarianism' recruited from the ranks of social workers who were disillusioned by the seeming inability of the disadvantaged and the socially dependent to 'respond' to the treatment they were being offered;[40] some British eugenists seem to belong to this same category.[41]

But, clearly, most social reformers of all schools saw eugenics as an assault on all that they held dear. And this is highly relevant to our argument since a high proportion of these philanthropists and reformers came from the professional middle classes. Thus, Gareth Stedman Jones has shown that the most active and prominent members of the London branch of the Charity Organisation Society 'tended to be drawn from the Church of England, law, medicine, the army and navy, and the civil service';[42] the social composition of the leaders of the Settlements Movement was apparently similar. Also, the 'New Liberalism' revolved around the activities of professional men and intellectuals, notably journalists, writers, schoolteachers and university lecturers – all occupations undergoing rapid expansion in the early twentieth century.[43] Finally, the Fabian Society, as Eric Hobsbawm has demonstrated in a famous essay, can be identified from the social composition of its membership as a pressure group which represented the interests of 'the salaried, middle class', 'the trained, impartial and scientific administrators and expert advisers', who believed themselves to be neutrals in the battle between capital and labour.[44]

For the moment I will leave other philanthropic and radical groups and concentrate on the Fabian Society, if only because Fabianism plays an important part in MacKenzie's thesis. Following Hobsbawm's analysis, MacKenzie makes the claim that

[40] E.g., M. Haller, *Eugenics: Hereditarian Attitudes in American Thought* (New Brunswick, 1963), p. 77. Lancelot Hogben explained the appeal of eugenics in similar terms; it was, he suggested, a reaction against the erroneous view of an eighteenth-century humanitarianism that insisted that an improved environment and humanitarian care could restore idiots to a useful life; L. Hogben, *Science for the Citizen* (London 1959 edn., first published 1938), p. 1087.
[41] Searle (note 1), p. 114.
[42] G. Stedman Jones, *Outcast London* (Oxford, 1971), p. 268.
[43] See H. V. Emy, *Liberals, Radicals and Social Politics, 1892–1914* (Cambridge, 1973), especially pp. 53, 101.
[44] E. Hobsbawm, 'The Fabians Reconsidered', in *Labouring Men* (London, 1964), pp. 250–71.

Fabianism and eugenics were ideologies which expressed the same class interests, the interests of the rising class of salaried experts. More than that, the two ideologies, he argues, had a good deal in common with one another: 'On this view, Fabianism and eugenics were not political opposites but different (though overlapping) variants of the same adaptation. Eugenics was the kind of reform that the Fabians liked: scientistic, involving state action, legislation and (no doubt) an expansion of bureaucracy'.[45] Like Bernard Semmel before him, MacKenzie notes the participation of leading Fabians at the meeting held in 1904 to launch eugenics as a socio-political movement; and, again like Semmel, he quotes from Sidney Webb's notorious letters to the *Times* in 1906 on the declining birth-rate, as evidence that Webb can appropriately be dubbed a 'Fabian eugenist'.[46] Complementary to this is his insistence that Pearson, who continued throughout his life to call himself a socialist, was in fact the most consistent of Fabians,[47] even though he never joined the Fabian Society (just as the Fabians never joined the Eugenics Society). A picture is thus painted in which Fabianism and eugenics (or at least Pearson's version of eugenics) differ in the emphasis they place on environmental and hereditary factors, but are seen as being complementary and compatible creeds. Far from this being the case, I would argue that there is a clear differentiation between the two groups both at the intellectual level and in the type of professional man which each recruited.

It is, indeed, true that the Fabians sometimes employed a rhetoric with a strong eugenical colouration. For example, in a sympathetic review of W. H. Dawson's *The Vagrant Problem*, E. R. Pease claimed that tramps begot tramps and social wastrels, destined for the prison and the workhouse, and declared it 'deplorable folly to let this breeding of social pests go on year after year, while parliament spends its precious day in discussing precisely what theological dogmas are to be taught to small children and how many Dreadnoughts Germany will really possess in 1925'.[48]

---

[45] MacKenzie (note 4), p. 512, also, 'Pearson's pro-imperialism and enthusiasm for eugenics was shared by leading Fabian socialists such as Bernard Shaw, H. G. Wells and Sidney Webb. They, like Pearson, saw no incompatibility between eugenics and socialism; indeed, eugenics fitted very well with their elitist and scientistic views'; D. A. MacKenzie and S. B. Barnes (note 17), see fn. 61.
[46] B. Semmel, *Imperialism and Social Reform* (London, 1960), pp. 50–1.
[47] D. MacKenzie (note 9).
[48] *Fabian News*, January 1911, p. 18.

Moreover, both Webb and Shaw sometimes chose to describe themselves publicly as eugenists. Nor was this *merely* a matter of rhetoric. The leading Fabians, with their general commitment to the notion of a planned society, were clearly attracted by the possibility of *genetic* planning, and they were not by temperament squeamish about the sort of bureaucratic interference in family life which such planning would indubitably involve. It is also interesting to note that in 1909 and 1910 there existed a 'Biology' Group within the metropolitan Fabian Society and that this group, chaired by Hubert Bland, was apparently being steered by its secretary, Dr Lionel Taylor, in a eugenical direction; in late 1910 its members had embarked on a systematic study of Galton's *Inquiries into Human Faculty*.[49]

But although some Fabians were prepared to flirt with eugenics, few, if any, of the Fabian leaders went any further than that. Bernard Shaw gave an address to the central branch of the Eugenics Society in 1910, where his tongue-in-cheek commendation of the lethal chamber and the methods of the stud farm caused a memorable scandal – the officers of the Society felt it necessary formally to dissociate themselves from these views.[50] But on this and other occasions Shaw's main point was that the only way to secure the eugenist's goal of racial improvement was to institute complete equality of incomes; this would ensure that men and women chose their sexual partners by following their instincts (which was Nature's way of promoting eugenics) and not be distracted by biologically irrelevant factors like wealth and social position.[51] In other words, Shaw was saying that eugenists, if they had thought through the full implications of their creed, would be bound to give their support to socialism.

A similar tactical use of eugenics was made by Webb in his pronouncements on the declining birth-rate and in his call for an 'Endowment of Motherhood' to prevent the United Kingdom being over-run by the Irish, Jews and the Chinese. The language was indeed the language of eugenics, but the policies that Webb was advocating – 'unlimited provision of medical attendance on the child-bearing mother and her children', free meals on demand for

---

[49] *Ibid.*, July 1909, p. 64; October 1910, pp. 75–6; but the Group collapsed in the course of 1910, one does not know why.
[50] G. R. Searle (note 1), p. 14.
[51] *Ibid.*, p. 58; A. Chappelow, *Shaw – The Chucker Out* (London, 1969), pp. 146–8.

mothers nursing children, educational reform and child allowances payable to the mother – were precisely the kind of policies which most eugenists detested and predicted would cause racial degeneration.[52] It is surely significant that the Fabian scheme for the Endowment of Motherhood met with a very frosty reception from the Eugenics Society.[53] An even more blatant attempt by Webb to palm off environmental social reform as a device for furthering racial progress came when he addressed the Eugenics Society in December 1909 and used all his ingenuity to demonstrate that the Poor Law Minority Report had been 'drawn on strictly eugenic lines'.[54] Once again, the eugenists proper remained unconvinced; in fact, the Society responded to the publication of the two Poor Law Reports by setting up its own enquiry, which predictably proceeded on the assumption that pauperism and destitution were biological, rather than social, conditions.[55]

In any case, Fabianism was characterized by the emphasis it placed on State intervention and by its predilection for theoretical models that stressed environmentalism, rather than genetic endowment. It is surely significant, therefore, that when the Society held an open, propaganda meeting at St James Hall in March 1909 on the subject of 'Socialism and Race Welfare', Hubert Bland, from the chair, specifically dissociated himself from 'the latest nostrum' of eugenics: 'How could the sweated sempstress be expected to refuse to marry a prosperous artisan because his sister had died of consumption? The eugenist will be a voice crying in the wilderness. Socialist principles alone offer a remedy'. Bland was followed by Dr Lawson Dodd, who declared: 'modern science holds that disease is due to environment rather than heredity'; and this was the main theme of the meeting.[56]

If the view that the Fabians were committed to at least a progressive version of eugenics thus seems an exaggeration, it also strains one's sense of credulity to be told that Karl Pearson still retained the Socialist convictions of his youth in the opening decade of of the twentieth century. There are, of course, continuities in Pearson's thinking which make it impossible to divide up his

[52] See Appendix B.
[53] G. R. Searle (note 1), pp. 86–8.
[54] S. Webb, 'Eugenics and the Poor Law: The Minority Report', *Eugenics Review*, ii (1910–11), pp. 233–41, especially p. 240.
[55] G. R. Searle (note 1), pp. 61–2.
[56] *Fabian News*, April 1909, p. 41; also see Appendix B.

career into two neat phases, an early phase as a Socialist and a later phase as a eugenist, but Pearson's defiant claim in 1909 that he was a 'consistent Socialist'[57] seems to have meant little more than that he rejected *laissez-faire* and individualism and looked to the employment of state power directed by a cadre of professional experts for the promotion of racial progress. But far from being a Socialist, Pearson launched ferocious attacks on even the mildest social reforms passed by the pre-war Liberal Government, arguing that they meant a squandering of money on projects which could not possibly produce *'permanent racial* change'. A national insurance scheme, formulated in such a way as to provide for children and motherhood 'according to the fitness of parentage', would have won his approval,[58] but the actual National Insurance Act of 1911 was dismissed as biologically unsound, along with nearly every other measure produced by the Asquith Ministry.

Moreover, Pearson, who never joined the Eugenics Society, was in many ways unrepresentative of the larger body of eugenists in Britain, and a number of his political and scientific theories were openly repudiated by them. That being the case, it may be slightly irrelevant what view we take of Pearson's professions of socialism. On the other hand, it can scarcely be denied that the overwhelming majority of British eugenists inclined to conservatism; indeed, judging from their public utterances, most of them probably supported the Conservative Party, insofar as they could bring themselves to take any interest whatever in party politics. Leading eugenists in the Edwardian period like Montague Crackanthorpe and Sir James Barr openly expressed their hatred for the radical policies of Lloyd George, while denunciations of socialism were common, before 1914 as well as in the inter-war period.[59] Eugenics, therefore, far from complementing Fabianism, can best be seen, especially in the pre-war years, as a frightened response to the Liberal Government's social welfare legislation, and the Webbs themselves acknowledged this to be so when they wrote in 1911 that eugenics was 'just now the most fashionable version of *laissez-faire'.*[60]

[57] K. Pearson, *Social Problems: Their Treatment, Past, Present and Future* (London, 1912), p. 5.
[58] K. Pearson, *The Problem of Practical Eugenics* (London, 1909), pp. 30–1.
[59] E.g., M. Crackanthorpe, 'The Friends and Foes of Eugenics', *Fortnightly Review,* xcii (1912), p. 741.
[60] S. and Beatrice Webb, *The Prevention of Destitution* (London, 1911), p. 46. It is

This dictum of the Webbs invites us to consider what role eugenists thought that the state bureaucracy would play in a society reconstructed in accordance with their theories. Pearson, for one, clearly envisaged that in such a society the state would 'monitor' population changes, and he advocated a Government Statistical Bureau to supervise the work of other departments. He also called for 'the establishment of university laboratories, adequately equipped biologically, medically and statistically, whose sole business (would) be sociological research'.[61] Thus, the State would endow scientific research and would recognize the importance of science to national life by incorporating into the machinery of government a number of professional experts charged with the task of determining what social policies would benefit the race – policies which other experts would then carry out. Perhaps Pearson was a more thoroughgoing technocrat than most of his fellow eugenists; but there are many references in eugenical literature to the necessity for anthropometric surveys to provide accurate data on the mental and physical fitness of the population,[62] and, of course, politicans are repeatedly called upon to take heed of the teaching of biology.

But eugenists were also insistent that race culture would do away with much current philanthropy and, in addition, would on balance restrict, not enlarge, the activities of the State. Revealingly, Major Darwin, in his 1913 Presidential Address, tried to 'cost' the sums of money needed to keep the 'unfit' alive and comfortable, and concluded that £45 million a year was being spent on the administration of justice, the police, poor relief, infirmaries and lunatic asylums, 'all services which would be much less needed if the unfit were eliminated'. Moreover, said Darwin, one million paupers in daily receipt of relief were being looked after by 'a whole army of able-bodied officials and attendants', men who, in a eugenical state, would be 'set free from their economically useless occupations' and

true that the Webbs also imply that these attitudes, however common in eugenical circles, were vulgar errors which had no necessary connection with 'true' eugenics; and, characteristically, they assert that 'many of the keenest supporters of Eugenics are, at the same time, the most zealous workers' for social reform. But, of course, it was precisely these 'errors' which constituted the core of the eugenics creed – as the Webbs must have been well aware.

[61] K. Pearson (note 16), pp. 32, 38–9.
[62] A. F. Tredgold, 'Marriage Regulation and National Family Records', *Eugenics Review*, iv (1912), pp. 74–90.

'employed instead on productive services'.[63] Rates and taxes, most eugenists agreed, could be drastically cut, were it not for the cost of keeping up 'the ever-increasing lunatic asylums, prisons, houses of detention, homes of refuge, and all the rest of it', made necessary by the 'multiplication of the unfit'.[64] This hardly seems to be a line of argument calculated to appeal to large sections of the modern, scientifically educated professional classes.[65]

Surely, therefore, it makes more sense to divide the professional middle classes, not between 'traditional' and 'modern' occupational categories, but between groups which stood to gain from the growth of the state educational and welfare apparatus and those which did not. This is not to make the crude assumption that professional men took up a position for or against eugenics solely on the basis of an assessment of whether or not eugenics would improve their career prospects.[66] However, rational self-interest would have alienated from eugenics such key occupational groups as medical officers, civil servants, local government officials, school-teachers, most kinds of social worker, and also the type of reform-minded professional man who moved freely between the spheres of academia, journalism and party politics – a type especially prom-inent in both the Fabian Society and in 'New Liberal' circles. In objecting to eugenics, such professional men were not the victims of 'false consciousness', nor were they showing an inability to put the long-term interests of their 'class' before short-term sectional advantage. Arguably, they were acting on a very well-founded assessment of the career opportunities likely to be opened up by a welfare state.

Thus, the proposition that eugenics was the ideology of a newly rising salaried middle class scarcely stands up to critical exam-ination. Indeed, if forced to make a sweeping generalization (and all generalizations of this kind are misleading), I would even be

[63] L. Darwin, *The Need for Eugenic Reform* (London, 1926), p. 296.

[64] E. Alec-Tweedie, 'Eugenics', *Fortnightly Review*, xci (1912), p. 854.

[65] Indeed, MacKenzie himself seems to concede this point when he demonstrates the strong affiliation between the atomistic individualism of eugenic thought and many of the traits of 'classical' nineteenth-century Liberalism (see note 4, pp. 502–3). If this is so, how can it be a 'new' ideology fulfilling the role which MacKenzie assigns to it?

[66] Thus, one can find *some* M.O.H.s who were eugenists, e.g., A. Campbell Munro, whose address on 'The Significance of the Declining Birth-Rate' is printed in *Public Health*, xxiii (1910), p. 340.

inclined to reverse MacKenzie's categories and to argue that eugenics appealed less to 'new' professionals than to the type of family which figures in Noel Annan's discussion of the Victorian intellectual elite.[67] This would fit in with the emphasis placed in eugenical propaganda on genealogy, on tracing the pedigrees of 'eminent' families with a long and honourable tradition of professional service.[68]

Now, of course, these were the very families which were shown to be failing to replace their numbers in the early twentieth century. And, significantly, eugenists viewed this demographic trend with dismay. For example, Major Darwin bewailed the fact that 'our professional classes in fact almost certainly form a group which is dying out'.[69] The same train of reasoning led the Oxford philosopher, F. C. S. Schiller, to explain the shortage of army officers on the eve of the First World War as 'largely a biological phenomenon'.[70] Yet, obviously, all the traditional professions, bar the Church, were undergoing rapid expansion in these years, while, in addition, new kinds of scientific and technical experts were coming into existence. But eugenists feared that differential class fertility meant that those occupying these new places were being recruited from the manual working classes: part of a larger process whereby each class, so R. A. Fisher complained, was being 'vulgarized from below'.[71] Thus, eugenists believed that the general standard of competence in professional life was being lowered; Fisher can often be found complaining that the 'new' professional men were 'on the whole, inferior to the professional families of long standing'.[72] Such arguments as these surely confirm MacKenzie's intuition that 'few eugenists could have had working-class parents.'[73] On the other hand, they throw further doubt on the proposition that eugenics was an ideology that represented the rising professional middle class, since such an ideology would surely not have dwelt on the

[67] N. G. Annan, 'The Intellectual Aristocracy' in J. H. Plumb (ed.), *Studies in Social History: A Tribute to G. M. Trevelyan* (London, 1955).
[68] Galton himself, of course, came from one of the families delineated in Annan's article.
[69] Darwin (note 63), p. 323.
[70] F.C.S. Schiller, 'Eugenics and Politics', *Hibbert Journal*, xii (1914), p. 250.
[71] R. A. Fisher, 'Some Hopes of a Eugenist', delivered on 22 November 1912, *Papers of Cambridge University Eugenics Society* (housed in the Eugenics Society Library).
[72] R. A. Fisher, 'Positive Eugenics', *Eugenics Review*, ix (1917), p. 210.
[73] D. MacKenzie (note 4), p. 530, fn. 41.

genetic value of certain 'stocks' in the community, but would either have drawn attention to the superiority of the professional ethic or would have heaped praise on the expertise possessed by professional men.

Clearly, *individuals* from a scatter of middle-class professions responded enthusiastically to the message of eugenics. Presumably, many were attracted by the way in which it appeared to legitimate the existing class structure, giving an 'up-to-date' and scientific-sounding justification for the existence of social inequality and privilege. This appeal was particularly strong in the years 1908–14 when middle-class groups with a strongly conservative outlook were casting around for arguments to deploy against the Radical policies of the Asquith Government.[74] Eugenics also provided a reassuringly conservative explanation of the Great Depression of the 1930s. But, though not unimportant as a counter-revolutionary ideology, eugenics was at no time of *central* importance as a mechanism of social control. Both in the Edwardian period and in the inter-war years there were plenty of alternative middle-class defence groups ready to denounce extravagant social legislation, press for tax cuts and expose the unworthiness of paupers and the unemployed – groups which were bound to attract more support than the Eugenics Society, whose creed was likely to be rejected, because of intellectual disagreement or from moral scruples, by many of the very people who might have derived material profit from its success.

In short, though many eugenists deliberately sought to make their creed a rallying-point for the professional middle classes, it is difficult to see how this could ever have occurred. For eugenics operated from a narrow occupational base and its appeal was principally directed to certain groups of medical men, statisticians, biologists and social scientists: a narrow constituency of scientifically trained men, some of whom apparently thought that power should be handed over to them by virtue of their qualifications without any necessity for involvement in the dirty trade of politics, while others temporarily attached themselves to the Eugenics Society for opportunistic reasons.

More tentatively it might be argued that eugenics expressed the viewpoint of certain 'isolated' intellectual workers, who, whether

[74] G. R. Searle (note 1), pp. 64–6, 113–14.

salaried or not, moved in an environment which replicated that of the 'independent' professional, for example, academics and surgeons. Significantly, however, the Eugenics Society had very few representatives from two professional categories which were enormously important to Fabianism, namely, those involved with the media (journalists, freelance writers, people connected with the stage), and those active in politics, administration and industrial relations (M.P.s, parliamentary candidates, local councillors, civil servants, trade union officials etc).[75] Both of these groups were obviously essential to the Fabian strategy of 'permeation'. Once again, the differences between Fabians and Eugenists turn out to be far more important than the superficial similarities.

Finally, I have dealt elsewhere with the changes that took place in the formulation of eugenics during the 1930s when, under Dr Blacker's guidance, members of the Eugenics Society were discouraged from making sweeping generalizations about social classes and promises of national redemption, while instead attention was focused on specialized psychomedical issues (e.g., the mentally deficient), which, however important in their own right, were recognized to lie on the margins of national politics. This change of direction can be explained in a number of ways – as an adjustment to a new demographic situation, in which differential class fertility was becoming less pronounced; or as an attempt to dissociate the British eugenics movement from the activities of Fascists at home and abroad.

But it is arguable that Blacker may also have sensed that there was no future for eugenics if its advocates continued to employ the class arguments which had featured so prominently in eugenical propaganda up to that date. This transition to what might be called 'medical eugenics' (e.g., genetic counselling) and the concentration on sexual issues like abortion law reform, artificial insemination, voluntary sterilization and the like have enabled the Eugenics Society to survive as a small, but not uninfluential, pressure group.[76] Eugenics has also made its mark on academic life and on social thought by serving as a 'potting shed' for emergent intellectual disciplines, like demography, which have subsequently

[75] E. Hobsbawm (note 44), pp. 257, 268–9. Unfortunately, Hobsbawm's statistics do not indicate what proportion of the men in his groups labelled 'Universities' and 'Teachers' are scientists.
[76] G. R. Searle (note 28).

become strong enough not to require this sort of protection. By contrast, the direct influence of eugenics on politics and government has been slight, and this surely reflects its failure to articulate the class interests of any major group in British society.

## APPENDIX 1. THE PROBLEM OF DEFINITION

Within the last three or four years eugenics has aroused so much interest amongst historians that whenever one picks up a new book or article on politics, social policy or political thought in Edwardian Britain, one is liable to encounter some discussion of the subject. In fact, a bewilderingly variegated list can be compiled of intellectuals and reformers who have recently been shown to have adopted at least some planks in the eugenics programme or to have been influenced in some way or another by eugenical ideas; William Beveridge, Marie Stopes, James Ramsay MacDonald, J. A. Hobson and, of course, the Webbs have all been discussed recently within this context. Indeed, the danger now is that the 'eugenist' label is going to be placed around the neck of nearly every major political and social thinker. To avoid this absurd situation, we need to discriminate more carefully between different kinds and levels of commitment to eugenics.

It might perhaps be useful to divide eugenists into five groups.

(1) Firstly, there are the eugenists proper, the only people who can without hesitation be designated in this way. Let us call them 'strong eugenists'. These were people for whom eugenics provided a total explanation of human history and of social problems and offered the only means of escape from national collapse and decay. Pearson, Major Darwin, Saleeby, Schiller were all eugenists of this sort. 'Strong eugenists' could scarcely conceal their impatience with contemporaries who continued to engage in traditional party polemics or who discussed politics without reference to the all-important biological determinants of social behaviour. In these men's views either one discussed politics in eugenical terms or else one stood condemned for talking unscientific nonsense. Even this group, however, could be still further sub-divided, since those who agreed that only eugenics could save the world disagreed, sometimes violently, about how eugenics was to be defined and what solutions it enjoined – witness the bitter dispute between Pearson and the spokesmen for the Eugenics Education Society.

(2) A second group might be called 'weak eugenists'. These were people who were attracted to eugenics, or to aspects of it, without feeling under any compulsion to abandon the political creed in which they had been brought up. 'Weak eugenists' were content, in other words, to graft eugenics on to one or other of the traditional political creeds. For example, a certain kind of libertarian progressive in the early twentieth century found eugenics irresistibly attractive because it presented itself to his mind as a refreshing departure from bourgeois conventionality; in this con-

figuration of beliefs eugenics became linked to such things as utopian socialism, vegetarianism, sexual experimentation of one kind or another, proposals for 'the abolition of the family', etc. This, of course, is only one kind of 'weak eugenics'; there are many others.

(3) Merging into this group are a third group who can be called 'medical eugenists'. These people were well aware of the fallacies involved in discussing class as though it were genetically determined or in attributing social problems like crime and destitution to some simple biological cause. In fact, 'medical eugenists' did not really see eugenics as a set of *political* beliefs at all. They did, however, take seriously the possibility that, through the newly achieved understanding of the mechanism of heredity in man, society might eradicate, or at least prevent the spread of, certain crippling and distressing diseases and disabilities thought to be hereditary in their transmission. From this perspective, therefore, eugenics was a branch of medicine or of public hygiene which, if supported, guided or subsidized by the government, could significantly reduce human suffering and misery. Dr Blacker, I argue, did a great deal in the 1930s to steer the British eugenics movement in this direction, away from the grandiose political aspirations of the founding fathers.

(4) Then there are those who might be called 'career eugenists': academics who welcomed eugenics because it stimulated interest in the study of heredity and of population problems, with which they were professionally concerned. One would suppose that these scientists must have winced at some of the crude polemics in which enthusiastic laymen often engaged, knowing as they did how premature or politically impossible were many of the policies which 'strong eugenists' favoured. But they sympathized with the underlying objectives of eugenics, and professional interest encouraged them to attach themselves to the movement.

(5) Finally, one encounters another kind of opportunist ready to employ rhetorically certain eugenical phrases and ideas. As I argue in this paper and in Appendix 2, the Webbs seem to fall into my fifth category. I doubt whether it is reasonable to call such people eugenists at all.

## APPENDIX 2. WERE THE FABIANS EUGENISTS?

The Webbs had long been interested in differential fertility (e.g., *Industrial Democracy*, London, 1897, pp. 636–43), and they were also prone to use language about the high fertility of the casual poor, which superficially seems to derive from an eugenical analysis. For example, there is Sidney's reference to the 'breeding of degenerate hordes of a demoralized "residuum" unfit for social life' (*The Difficulties of Individualism*, 1896, Fabian Tract no. 109, p. 6). The crucial issue, however, is whether the Webbs believed that unskilled labourers were *genetically* defective or whether they simply regretted that a disproportionately large number of children were being born to parents whose social circumstances made them unable to rear a family in decency and comfort. Here the Webbs' language loses its customary clarity, but I think it is fairly evident that although they did not entirely discount the possibility that some at least of the casual poor were hereditarily defective in certain respects (e.g., the feeble-minded), their main concern was with the transmission of cultural values. It is notable that in *Industrial Democracy* they follow their observations about differential fertility with suggestions for improving the living conditions of the poorest strata in society; if by collective bargaining or legal enactment, they argue, we could 'lift the London dock-labourers into an economic position equal to that of the railway porters ... in all probability we should in a very few years find an actual diminution in the size of the average family of the class'. This argument is repeated in Chapter 3 of *The Prevention of Destitution* (London, 1911), which also provides the fullest discussion of the Webbs' attitude to eugenics. Here they discuss 'the existence and therefore the social transmission of an environment which injures or corrupts each generation before it is born, and after it is born', and then contend that an improved environment would lead to more responsible social behaviour, hence a curtailment of the birth-rate among those who at present were 'unfit by inheritance or by environment' (pp. 48–52). This unwillingness to choose between environmental and hereditary factors is interesting. It recurs in Beatrice Webb's well-known *New Statesman* article of 11 July 1914, which contains the following sentence: 'In each annual yield of babies there are fewer born – I will not say of good stock, as that raises the disputable question of heredity – but in a decent social environment'.

On the other hand, the Webbs' solutions surely presuppose an environmentalist explanation. No true eugenist believed that an improved environment would 'civilize' the 'degenerate hordes' or modify their behaviour, and certainly no eugenist would have argued, as Webb did, that those worried about the declining birth-rate should press for the community to 'adopt' the 'unfortunate' pauper children, in order 'to make worthy citizens of them' (S. Webb, *The Decline in the Birth Rate*, 1907, Fabian Tract no. 131, p. 18).

This leads to a second crucial issue. Did the Webbs, in their Endowment of Motherhood scheme, attempt to differentiate between those who were and those who were not fit for parentage? Pearson, by whom they were undoubtedly influenced, had unequivocally drawn this distinction, for example, in *The Ethic of Freethought* (London, 1901; 1st edn., 1887), p. 428. The Webbs, however, did not follow Pearson in this matter. They claimed that their proposals would mean that 'the population (would) be recruited from the self-controlled and foreseeing members of each class rather than of those who are reckless and improvident' (*The Decline in the Birth Rate*, p. 18). The fertility of the casual poor would not be stimulated, since it was already at a high level, but their scheme *would* remove the economic disincentives which were causing 'responsible' families to limit their offspring. But, significantly, the Webbs did not advocate that their child allowances be withheld from anyone – except from the feeble-minded, whom the Webbs, along with most informed social workers, wanted to see placed in custodial care (*The Prevention of Destitution*, chap. 3).

H. G. Wells did, admittedly, in some of his writings, inject a definite eugenical content into his propaganda for the endowment of motherhood.

But almost no trace of this appears in the official Fabian Society pamphlet, *The Endowment of Motherhood*, written by H. D. Harben (Fabian Tract no. 149, 1910). The starting point of this pamphlet is the need for the community to prevent the shockingly high infant mortality rate in working-class districts. Harben goes on to state quite explicitly that his proposed 'children's pensions' will be universal and that 'those without homes, casuals, illegitimate cases, etc.,' would be as entitled to the pension as anyone else. Moreover, Harben envisaged a standard pension of ten shillings a week, a sum which might be attractive to working-class and some lower middle-class groups, but which, as he acknowledged, 'would hardly touch the middle classes' proper. In a way the tone and contents of this tract, which embodies the official Fabian Scheme, tell one far more about what the Fabian Society represented in Edwardian Britain than do the occasional pronouncements of the Webbs, Wells and Shaw.

I am not, of course, claiming that there is any theoretical incompatibility between Socialism and eugenics; as Loren R. Graham has shown in his article, 'Science and Values: The Eugenics Movement in Germany and Russia in the 1920s' (*American Historical Review*, 82 (1977), pp. 1133–64), many Marxists have found it possible to synthesize the two creeds. So have a number of British socialists, e.g., Dr Eden Paul, Stella Browne, Herbert Brewer, etc. But to compile such a list establishes my point, since few members of this heterogeneous group can seriously be assigned to the Fabian, bureaucratic school.

Interestingly enough, at about the same time as the Webbs and Wells were advancing their proposals, the doctor and pioneer psychologist, Dr M. D. Eder, a Socialist who frequently contributed articles to the *New Age*, published his pamphlet, *The Endowment of Motherhood* (London, 1907). Eder's scheme does indeed have a genuine eugenical content, though orthodox eugenists would not have favoured its recommendation of the lethal chamber! Eder also envisages a complete break-up of the traditional family system. Needless to say, neither the Fabians nor the Eugenics Society had any time for such 'subversive' Utopian speculations as these.

# 7. Sociobiologies in Competition: the Biometrician–Mendelian Debate

## DONALD MACKENZIE

The years around 1900 witnessed a bitter controversy within British biology. It involved on the one hand the biometricians, or biometric school, led by the statistician and philosopher Karl Pearson (1857–1936) and the zoologist W. F. R. Weldon (1860–1906), and on the other, the early Mendelian geneticists led by William Bateson (1861–1926). The controversy was marked by the shattering of personal friendships, by heated public debate, by suggestions of fraud and by long-lasting divisions within the British scientific community. Historians of biology have rightly identified the episode as an important one in the development of modern genetics and evolutionary theory, and accordingly it has been the object of considerable scholarly attention, particularly in the last decade.[1]

[1] The controversy has been a primary focus of the following: W. B. Provine, *The Origins of Theoretical Population Genetics* (Chicago, 1971); P. Froggatt and N. C. Nevin, 'Galton's "Law of Ancestral Heredity": its Influence on the Early Development of Human Genetics', *History of Science*, x (1971), pp. 1–27; P. Froggatt and N. C. Nevin, 'The "Law of Ancestral Heredity" and the Mendelian-Ancestrian Controversy in England, 1889–1906', *Journal of Medical Genetics*, viii (1971), pp. 1–36; A. G. Cock, 'William Bateson, Mendelism and Biometry', *Journal of the History of Biology*, vi (1973), pp. 1–36; B. J. Norton, 'The Biometric Defense of Darwinism', *Journal of the History of Biology*, vi (1973), pp. 283–316; *idem*, 'Biology and Philosophy: the Methodological Foundations of Biometry', *Journal of the History of Biology*, viii (1975), pp. 85–93; *idem*, 'Metaphysics and Population Genetics: Karl Pearson and the Background to Fisher's Multi-factorial Theory of Inheritance'. *Annals of Science*, xxxii (1975), pp. 537–53; *idem*, 'Karl Pearson and the Galtonian Tradition: Studies in the Rise of Quantitative Social Biology' (University of London PhD thesis, 1978), see chapter 5; R. de Marrais, 'The Double-Edged Effect of Sir Francis Galton: a Search for the Motives in the Biometrician-Mendelian Debate', *Journal of the History of Biology*, vii (1974), pp. 141–74; L. A. Farrall, 'Controversy and Conflict in Science: a Case Study – the English Biometric School and Mendel's Laws', *Social Studies of Science*, v (1975), pp. 269–301; D. J. Kevles, 'Genetics in the United States and Great Britain, 1890–1930: Queries and Speculations', see chapter 5, pp. 193–215; D. MacKenzie and S. B. Barnes, 'Biometriker versus Mendelianer; eine Kontroverse und ihre Erklärung', *Kölner Zeitschrift für Soziologie und Sozialpsychologie*, Sonderheft xviii (1975), pp. 165–96. The present account has its origins in the last of these, but the argument has been redrafted and expanded, and new material added.

My understanding of this episode has been helped by discussion with many people, in particular Barry Barnes, Bernard Norton, Alan Cock, Merriley Borrell and Garland Allen. A grant from the Social Science Research Council made possible much of the archival work drawn on below.

243

My aim here is neither to produce another account of the events of the controversy nor to discuss its long-term significance. Rather it is to ask a somewhat different question from those that have hitherto been raised in the bulk of the literature on the controversy. I shall inquire as to the extent to which the controversy can be seen as sustained by social factors. I shall examine both the role of factors arising from the 'internal' social structure of science and the way in which the controversy was connected to society at large by the 'sociobiological' uses of the theories of genetics and evolution. First, however, it is necessary to discuss the most obvious issue on which the two sides differed: their approaches to the study of heredity.

### GREEN PEAS, YELLOW PEAS AND GREENISH-YELLOW PEAS

In 1900, Mendel's work on heredity was 'rediscovered' by three Continental biologists: Hugo de Vries, Carl Correns and Erich von Tschermak.[2] The Cambridge biologist William Bateson seized eagerly on the new approach. He became the leading British Mendelian, and played a crucial role in developing the new 'paradigm' and extending it into different fields. He coined the term 'genetics',[3] and the new discipline it refers to owed a great deal to his work. Much of the terminology of Mendelian genetics is his, and many early examples of the successful use of Mendelian explanations are to be found in his work and that of his group of co-workers, of whom R. C. Punnett (1875–1967) was the most prominent.[4]

Bateson and the Mendelians operated with a theoretical model of the process of heredity, at the basis of which were discrete, elementary genetic factors. These latter we have come to call 'genes', but that term is somewhat misleading because we tend to

[2] I place the word 'rediscovered' in inverted commas because of the extremely interesting suggestion by Bob Olby that the 'rediscoverers' read into Mendel's work what was not in fact there: a theory of genetic determinants in the modern sense. See R. Olby, 'Mendel no Mendelian?', *History of Science*, xvii (1979), pp. 53–72.

[3] In a letter of 18 April 1905 to Adam Sedgwick, quoted in B. Bateson (ed.), *William Bateson, FRS, Naturalist: his Essays and Addresses, together with a short account of his Life* (Cambridge, 1928), p. 93. I refer to this volume below simply as *WB*.

[4] See the *Reports* by Bateson and others to the Evolution Committee of the Royal Society (London, 1902, 1905, 1906, 1908). Extracts from these are reprinted in R. C. Punnett (ed.), *Scientific Papers of William Bateson*, 2 vols. (Cambridge, 1928), ii.

think of the gene as a physical thing, while at the beginning of the period discussed here the Mendelian factor was a purely theoretical entity. William Bateson, for example, was reluctant to accept the notion of the Mendelian factor as a material particle and, at least initially, doubted the validity of the chromosome theory on which this imputation was based.[5]

Mendelian factors were held to pass unchanged from parent to offspring: pairs of factors underwent segregation and random distribution, but no blending of factors took place. Using elementary probability theory, together with assumptions about, for example, the dominance of one factor over another in the visible manifestation of the factors in the offspring, theoretical accounts of processes of heredity could be produced. These accounts were applied to the inheritance of characteristics such as, classically, the green and yellow colorations, and smooth and wrinkled forms, of pea seeds.

The biometricians, on the other hand, did not use a developed, explicitly theoretical model of heredity.[6] If we were to seek a single exemplar as typical of their approach, it would be the treatment of quantitative, easily measured characteristics such as height. Galton's 'typical laws of heredity' were descriptions of statistical regularities in the relationship between parental and offspring characteristics.[7] Pearson formalized this approach with his operational definition of heredity as the correlation between the characteristics of parents and offspring.[8] The concept of heredity predominant in the work of the biometric school was thus that of the degree of similarity in the observed characteristics of different generations of the same organism.

The biometric approach pre-dated the 'rediscovery' of Mendelism. The reaction of biometricians to the latter was by no means simple, but in its public aspect was primarily one of scep-

[5] See his review of T. H. Morgan, A. H. Sturtevant, H. J. Muller and C. B. Bridges, *The Mechanism of Mendelian Heredity* (New York, 1915), reprinted in R. C. Punnett (note 4), ii, 452–71.

[6] This statement requires some qualification in the light of the unpublished work of W. F. R. Weldon, referred to below in note 17.

[7] F. Galton, 'Typical Laws of Heredity', *Proceedings of the Royal Institution*, viii (1877), pp. 282–301.

[8] K. Pearson, 'Mathematical Contributions to the Theory of Evolution, III: Regression, Heredity and Panmixia', *Philosophical Transactions of the Royal Society of London*, ser. A. clxxxvii (1896), p. 259.

246    DONALD MACKENZIE

ticism and hostility. Their criticisms of Mendelism met with fierce rebuttals from the Mendelian camp, and a vehement debate about the validity of Mendelism began. This reached its public climax at the 1904 meeting of the British Association. Over thirty years later R. C. Punnett remembered the occasion:

We adjourned for lunch[9] and on resuming found the room packed as tight as it could hold. Even the window sills were requisitioned. For the word had got round that there was going to be a fight ... Weldon spoke with voluminous and impassioned eloquence, beads of sweat dripping from his face ...[10]

Even the report in *Nature* could not but catch some of the drama of the occasion.[11] Weldon was quoted as describing the Mendelians' hypothetical mechanism of heredity as 'cumbrous and undemonstrable'. Bateson in reply argued that the Mendelian theory 'had begun to co-ordinate the facts of heredity, until then utterly incoherent and contradictory. The advance made in five years had been enormous ...'. Pearson accused the Mendelians of producing figures 'without making any attempt to show that the figures were consonant with the theory they were supposed to illustrate'. He suggested further investigation rather than mere 'disputation', but remembered the meeting ending with Bateson 'dramatically holding aloft the volumes of this Journal [*Biometrika*] as patent evidence of the folly of the [biometric] school, and refusing the offer of a truce in this time-wasting controversy'.[12]

The sudden death of Weldon in 1906 brought an end to the most open phase of controversy, but by no means an end to disagreement. As late as 1930 Karl Pearson could still describe Mendelism as a largely unproven theory, long after nearly all professional biologists had accepted it.[13] Fundamentally, the two sides in the

[9] As Provine (note 1), p. 87, points out, Punnett's memory was not quite accurate: Weldon had in fact spoken before lunch.
[10] Quoted *ibid.*, p. 86.
[11] 'Zoology at the British Association', *Nature*, lxx (1904), pp. 538–41.
[12] K. Pearson, 'Walter Frank Raphael Weldon, 1860–1906', reprinted in E. S. Pearson and M. G. Kendall (eds.), *Studies in the History of Statistics and Probability* (London, 1970), 311. Again, Pearson's account is not exact: the last speaker was in fact Professor Hickson.
[13] K. Pearson, *The Life, Letters and Labours of Francis Galton*, 3 vols. (Cambridge, 1914–1930), iiiA, p. 288.

debate were operating with different approaches to heredity, approaches which were 'incommensurable'.[14] To put it crudely, they did not agree on the nature of the problem they were trying to solve, and so there was no clear basis for the assessment of the relative merits of different solutions.

The Mendelians believed that the prime aim of the science of heredity should be the development of a theoretical model of the process of heredity – the development of an account of the passage from parent to offspring of the factors that determined the observable characteristics of organisms, of the 'genotypes' that led to the observable 'phenotypes'. The biometricians – especially Pearson – were primarily concerned with detailing and measuring the resemblances of these 'phenotypes'. These goals sound complementary rather than conflicting, but in practice they translated into sharply different judgements. Thus the Mendelians felt that they possessed the key to a theoretical understanding of heredity. Believing that, they saw the vast range of phenomena for which generally acceptable Mendelian explanations had not been found – a range which included at the time we are discussing all but a handful of human characteristics – as simply puzzles awaiting resolution in the future. But the biometricians saw matters quite differently. Their primary goal being the description of phenotypic resemblance, they judged different approaches according to their success in this task. 'Mendelism is only a truth so long as it is an effective description', wrote Pearson.[15] The simplicity of early Mendelism was a point against it, not for it. What appears to be Pearson's earliest discussion of Mendelism[16] considered Mendelism as a description of patterns of resemblances and concluded that it was unlikely to fit all the cases of inheritance of characteristics such

[14] For the concept of 'incommensurability' see P. K. Feyerabend, 'Explanation, Reduction and Empiricism', in H. Feigl and G. Maxwell (eds.), *Scientific Explanation, Space and Time* (Minnesota Studies in the Philosophy of Science, iii, 1962), pp. 28–97; T. S. Kuhn, *The Structure of Scientific Revolutions*, 2nd edn. (Chicago, 1970). This point is noted, though not quite in this form, by Froggatt and Nevin, and especially by Farrall (note 1), pp. 276–8.

[15] K. Pearson (note 13), p. 288.

[16] An undated manuscript entitled 'Mendel's Law', a copy of which was kindly sent to me by Dr M. Merrington of University College London. If Olby's view of Mendel's papers is justified, then Pearson, in considering Mendelism a theory of phenotypic resemblances and not of genetic determinants, was reading them correctly, and the early Mendelians reading them incorrectly!

as eye-colour and coat-colour, much less more complex characteristics. The flexible descriptive apparatus of biometry seemed much
more hopeful as a descriptive tool than the apparently perilously
narrow Mendelian model.[17]

The two sides could not always agree even on the facts that
stood in need of explanation or description. Mendel's experiments
were predicated on the unproblematic classification of peas into
different classes (yellow/green, smooth/wrinkled, etc.). He deliberately used only characteristics that he felt to 'permit of a sharp
and certain separation'.[18] But the biometricians doubted that this
sharp differentiation was possible, even for the characteristics that
Mendel had chosen. Weldon argued that pea seeds did not fall
naturally into Mendel's classes, but shaded gradually from yellow
to green through intermediate tones, and from smooth to wrinkled
by various degrees. He presented photographs of pea seeds to

[17] In seeking to characterize briefly the salient points of divergence between the two
sides I have undoubtedly engaged in oversimplification. For example, Karl Pearson
and W. F. R. Weldon were not in complete agreement on the strategy for a science
of heredity. Weldon, it appears, placed more importance on the construction of a
theoretical model of the process of inheritance than did Pearson. His work on this
was never published in his lifetime, though shortly after his death Pearson summarized and developed some of the main themes of his thinking. See K. Pearson,
'On a Mathematical Theory of Determinantal Inheritance, from Suggestions and
Notes of the late W. F. R. Weldon', Biometrika, vi (1908), pp. 80–93.

Particularly important surviving documents are Weldon's manuscript 'Theory of
Inheritance' and his correspondence with Pearson and Galton (Pearson Papers, 266,
624 and 625 and Galton Papers, 340G-J, University College London). To summarize this large body of tentative and partly worked-out ideas is difficult, but there
appears to be one consistent theme: Weldon's belief that the Mendelian model was
too narrow and his search for a more general and flexible theory that might include
'pure' Mendelism as a special case but was also capable of accounting adequately for
the much more complex situations studied by the biometricians. As Norton ('Karl
Pearson and the Galtonian Tradition', (note 1) pp. 183–4 and 190–3) points out,
Weldon sought at least in part to return to Galton's 'stirp' model of inheritance.
Weldon wrote in the 'Theory of Inheritance' (ch. 2, p. 20): 'Galton's theory of
hereditary transmission has at least this advantage over Mendel's, that it takes all
the known phenomena of inheritance into account, and endeavours to describe them
all in terms of a single process.' Weldon, then, appears to have been more prepared
than Pearson to theorize about heredity, but it would seem that the goal of his
theorizing remained the comprehensive description of phenotypic resemblance. As
he put it at the very start of the 'Theory of Inheritance' (ch. 1, version A, p. 2), his interest
was 'in the bearing of what we actually know concerning the relation between the visible
characters of parents and those of their offspring upon the possible interpretation of
structural changes revealed by minute study of the germcells and of embryonic processes
in general'.

[18] G. Mendel, 'Experiments in Plant-hybridisation', in W. Bateson, Mendel's Principles
of Heredity: A Defence (Cambridge, 1902), p. 45.

prove his point.[19] In reply Bateson argued that Weldon's key cases were 'mongrel' peas, rather than the 'pure' variety needed to manifest Mendelian phenomena unequivocally. But the very notion of the 'purity' of a variety was itself a theoretical Mendelian concept, not a simple empirical description. Further, Bateson argued that even if pure-bred peas were used, anomalous results could be produced by such contingencies as accidental crossing, 'sporting' and environmental factors.[20]

The dispute between the biometricians and the Mendelians could not, to use Kuhn's phrase, 'be unequivocally settled by logic and experiment alone'.[21] There was nothing *illogical* in arguing, as Pearson did, that the best approach to heredity was that which best described the regularities of phenotypic resemblance, nor in placing *a priori* confidence in a theoretical model and being unabashed at its inability, initially, to explain anything other than a small range of observed phenomena, as the Mendelians did. Nor could experimental studies of heredity have resolved the issue, even if the two sides had been able to agree on the interpretation of a given result. An undisputable experimental demonstration of a predicted Mendelian ratio would not have converted Pearson and Weldon to Mendelism: they could simply have pointed to the vast range of phenomena not adequately described by Mendelism. Nor, *a fortiori*, would the failure of Mendelism in a particular case have caused the Mendelians to jettison their basic model. In fact, attempts at 'crucial experiments' did not in any case reach any definite conclusions, but largely degenerated into disputes about the competence and honesty of the experimenters.[22]

The incommensurability of the two positions did lead to difficulties of understanding and communication. 'Mr Bateson and I do not use the same language', wrote Karl Pearson.[23] This was

---

[19] W. F. R. Weldon, 'Mendel's Laws of Alternative Inheritance in Peas', *Biometrika*, i (1902), pp. 228–54. The colour plate illustrating Weldon's article caused much concern because, through technical difficulties in colour reproduction, it at first showed half the pea seeds green, and half yellow, instead of the continuous gradation of colour that Pearson and Weldon felt undermined Mendel's approach. Pearson to Galton, 28 January 1902, Galton Papers, 293E, University College London.

[20] W. Bateson (note 18), especially pp. 129, 188–9.

[21] T. S. Kuhn (note 14), p. 94.

[22] W. B. Provine, (note 1) *The Origins of Theoretical Population Genetics*, pp. 73–80, 87–88.

[23] K. Pearson, 'On the Fundamental Conceptions of Biology', *Biometrika*, i (1902), p. 331.

particularly the case with the different interpretations of Galton's 'law of ancestral heredity'. As Froggatt and Nevin emphasize, disputes over the validity of this 'law' were prominent in the controversy.[24] Galton had primarily intended the law, first pointed to in his 1865 paper on 'Hereditary Talent and Character', to summarize the degree of influence of ancestors of each degree on the height, say, of an individual: 'the influence, pure and simple, of the mid-parent may be taken as $\frac{1}{2}$, of the mid-grandparent $\frac{1}{4}$, of the mid-great-grandparent $\frac{1}{8}$, and so on'. Pearson interpreted the law as one of phenotypic resemblance, and attempted to recast it in terms of the theory of multiple regression: as a linear equation giving the predicted height of an individual, in terms of the deviation from the mean height of that individual's generation, as a function of the heights of that individual's ancestors, in terms of the deviation of their heights from the means of their generations.[25]

At first sight, Mendelism contradicted Galton's law. Once the genetic characteristics of the parents were known, knowledge of distant ancestry was redundant in predicting offspring characteristics. Thus Weldon could write: 'The fundamental mistake which vitiates all work based upon Mendel's method is the neglect of ancestry ... not only the parents themselves, but their race, that is their ancestry, must be taken into account before the result of pairing them can be predicted'. Bateson appeared to agree that a fundamental divergence existed between Mendelism and the 'ancestrian' approach: 'We note at once that the Mendelian conception of heredity effected by *pure* gametes representing definite allelomorphs is quite irreconcilable with Galton's conception in which *every* ancestor is brought to account in reckoning the probable constitution of every descendant'. The two sides were, however, talking about different things. The Mendelians had in mind, not phenotypic resemblance, but genetic structure. It was true that on a Mendelian view, distant ancestry was irrelevant, in the sense that what mattered was the composition of the zygote: all individuals with the same zygote were genetically identical, irrespective of where the particular factors had come from. When, however, it

---

[24] See P. Froggatt and N. C. Nevin (note 1).

[25] F. Galton, 'Hereditary Talent and Character', *Macmillan's Magazine*, xii (1865), p. 326; *idem*, 'Regression towards Mediocrity in Hereditary Stature', *Journal of the Anthropological Institute*, xv (1885), p. 261; K. Pearson, 'Mathematical Contributions to the Theory of Evolution: on the Law of Ancestral Heredity', *Proceedings of the Royal Society of London*, lxii (1898), pp. 386–412; K. Pearson, 'The Law of Ancestral Heredity', *Biometrika*, ii (1903), pp. 211–29.

came to predicting on a statistical and phenotypic basis the characteristics of offspring, then even on a Mendelian view the characteristics of an individual's ancestry *were* relevant, as these helped predict the (unknown) parental genetic make-up. As Pearson was able to demonstrate, a multi-factorial Mendelian model in fact led, at the phenotypic level, to a multiple regression equation similar to the law of ancestral heredity.[26]

This last development illustrates that difficulties of understanding and communication, while they did exist, were surmountable. In spite of their incommensurability – or, rather, *because* of it, because of the fact that the two approaches were on different ontological levels – there was no absolute formal barrier to a synthesis of the two approaches. Sporadic attempts at reconciliation were indeed made from early on.[27] But the major participants in the controversy chose to maintain it as a controversy, to highlight rather than to gloss over or eradicate the differences in their approaches. Logic did not force them to do this – it was a choice they made. And, to a large extent, it was not a choice made in ignorance. Pearson and Weldon, for example, were perfectly capable of understanding Mendelian work; both sides knew of Yule's work. So the incommensurability of the two positions cannot be taken as explaining the controversy – in fact it is itself something to be explained. We must not stop at the demonstration of incommensurability, but seek to explain the initial generation and continued maintenance of divergent positions.

MATHEMATICS AND BIOLOGY

Perhaps the most obvious factor that might account for the differences between the two approaches is to be found in the different sorts of skills employed by the two sides. Thus Bateson

[26] W. F. R. Weldon (note 19); W. Bateson and E. R. Saunders, *Experimental Studies in the Physiology of Heredity* (Reports to the Evolution Committee of the Royal Society, i, 1902), p. 157; K. Pearson, 'Mathematical Contributions to the Theory of Evolution, XII: On a Generalised Theory of Alternative Inheritance, with Special Reference to Mendel's Laws', *Philosophical Transactions of the Royal Society of London*, ser. A, cciii (1904), pp. 53–86; K. Pearson, 'The Theory of Ancestral Contributions in Heredity', *ibid.*, ser. B, lxxxi (1909), pp. 219–24; K. Pearson, 'On the Ancestral Gametic Correlations of a Mendelian Population Mating at Random', *ibid.*, pp. 225–29. See also K. Pearson, 'On a New Theory of Progressive Evolution', *Annals of Eugenics*, iv (1930–31), pp. 1–40.
[27] See most notably G. Udny Yule, 'Mendel's Laws and their Probable Relations to Intra-Racial Heredity', *New Phytologist*, i (1902), pp. 193–207, 222–38.

appears to have felt that the biometricians did not possess (or, in the case of Weldon, were not using) the competences of trained biologists. He lamented the fact that Galton and Pearson 'were not trained in the profession of the naturalist'.[28] The connection between theoretical Mendelian factors and the observed properties of organisms was not such that anyone could immediately 'see' what was going on. A naïve approach, which failed to take account of the complexities of the relationship between theory and the results of particular experiments, could mislead. Even classification of peas into categories – green or yellow, smooth or wrinkled – could not be done mechanically, as Bateson felt the biometricians did it, but was a difficult task requiring experience.[29] The statistical approach of the biometricians was quite inadequate, Bateson told the 1904 meeting of the British Association, in dealing with subtleties of, for example, the creation of new stocks in practical breeding:

> Operating among such phenomena the gross statistical method is a misleading instrument; and, applied to these intricate discriminations, the imposing Correlation Table into which the biometrical Procrustes fits his arrays of unanalysed data is still no substitute for the common sieve of a trained judgment. For nothing but minute analysis of the facts by an observer thoroughly conversant with the particular plant or animal, its habits and properties, checked by the test of crucial experiment, can disentangle the truth.[30]

Conversely, the biometricians, particularly Pearson, felt themselves to be practising a more rigorous form of biology, which employed exact definitions and mathematical argument. Bateson and the 'old school' of biologists operated with 'confused and undefined notions', the biometricians with 'clear and quantitatively definite ideas'. The lack of mathematical training of the majority of biologists was blamed by Pearson for what he saw as their indifferent or hostile response to biometry. In the theory of evolution, and some other fields of biology, 'without mathematics, further progress has become impossible', and 'mathematical knowledge

[28] W. Bateson (note 18), p. xii. Bateson also suggested that Galton had failed to discover Mendelism in part because of his 'mathematical instincts and training', which had 'prompted him to apply statistical treatment rather than qualitative analysis', WB (note 3), p. 303.
[29] See W. Bateson to G. Udny Yule, 28 November 1922, Yule Papers, box 22, Royal Statistical Society.
[30] WB (note 3), p. 240.

will soon be as much a part of the biologist's equipment today as of the physicist's'.[31]

Thus, the participants themselves viewed the controversy as, at least in part, a clash of traditional biological and mathematical skills.[32] How far is it possible to build this insight into an acceptable account of the controversy? One possible approach would be to start with the training individuals receive and their early disciplinary experiences, and to regard these as having a conditioning effect on their future scientific work. This approach is, in effect, that employed by de Marrais. He argues that the mathematical perspective of Galton and the biometricians, in particular their continual use of the normal curve, constrained their perception. It was impossible logically to move from continuous variation to determine a finite number of underlying factors: 'by its very nature the Frequency Law prohibits the discovery of the real (i.e., finite number of) causal agencies determining a trait's distribution pattern or "type"'. By comparison, Bateson, who was a notoriously weak mathematician, was not constrained in this way: 'The non-mathematical basis of William Bateson's (and all the early Mendelians') thought represented not so much a cause of his Mendelism as an absence of the mainstay holding together the bundle of inhibitory relations that held back the biometricians'.[33]

However, the model of the operation of training and early experience implied in arguments such as this seems implausible. To use Wrong's phrase, it would seem to involve an 'oversocialized conception of man'.[34] Without supporting theory or evidence, it is difficult to imagine why individuals should be trapped in this manner by their disciplinary socialization. After all, there are plenty of instances of individuals breaking with the approach of their training: thus both Weldon and Bateson broke, in different ways, from the morphological and embryological approach to biology of their Cambridge training.[35] An individual is not necessarily

[31] K. Pearson (note 23), pp. 321, 344.
[32] The historians of the controversy listed in note 1 above have at least partly followed them in this. See in particular the work of Cock, Farrall and de Marrais.
[33] R. de Marrais (note 1), pp. 154, 169.
[34] D. Wrong, 'The Oversocialized Conception of Man in Modern Sociology', in L. Coser and B. Rosenberg (eds.), *Sociological Theory* (New York, 1976), pp. 104–13.
[35] K. Pearson (note 12); W. Coleman, 'Bateson and Chromosomes: Conservative Thought in Science', *Centaurus*, xv (1970), pp. 228–314.

programmed for life by his or her training. Yet training obviously is important. Can these two points be reconciled?

The internal social structure of science is, as Hagstrom argues, competitive.[36] Prestige and reward follow in part from the recognition, by their fellows, of scientists' work as correct and interesting. In this 'market', the scientists' resources include the skills relevant to the performance of successful scientific work that they possess. No one is all-competent. Individuals' competences are competences to use particular techniques, to work within the framework of particular theories, to handle particular materials. Thus, we can expect there to arise a tendency to evaluate new theoretical developments, new techniques, and so on, in terms of their effects on the value of scientists' existing skills. Other things being equal, we would expect scientists to be favourably inclined to developments that enhance the value of their skills, and hostile to those that devalue them. Training provides individuals with skills, and these skills can affect a scientist's evaluations because of their role as resources in a competitive market for scientific knowledge.[37]

On this view, it is certainly possible to understand the hostility shown by traditional biologists to biometry. If the biometric approach came to dominate biology, as Pearson and Weldon clearly and publicly hoped, then traditional biological skills would be devalued. E. Ray Lankester wrote:

> You can not (it seems to me) reduce natural history, as Prof. Weldon proposes, to an unimaginative statistical form, without either ignoring or abandoning its most interesting problems, and at the same time refusing to employ the universal method by which mankind has gained new knowledge of the phenomena of nature – that, namely, of imaginative hypothesis and consequent experiment.

One of Bateson's favourite bits of advice to young biologists was to 'treasure your exceptions'. But there seemed to be little room in the biometric approach for the skilled attention of the biologist to the

[36] W. O. Hagstrom, *The Scientific Community* (New York, 1965). Dan Kevles's article in the present volume emphasizes the extent of competition for scarce resources within British science and argues that this explains why it was that in Britain 'the temperature of the dispute rose so high' (p. 204).

[37] D. MacKenzie and S. B. Barnes (note 1), pp. 176–8. This view of the relationship of socialization to future behaviour is largely taken from the work of H. S. Becker, 'Notes on the Concept of Commitment', *American Journal of Sociology*, lxvi (1960), pp. 32–40; *idem*, 'Personal Change in Adult Life', *Sociometry*, xxvii (1964), pp. 40–53.

individual case. Biometry would, at least in part, substitute the skills of the mathematician for those of the biologist, and Bateson (along with many of his colleagues) was no mathematician. Bateson publicly admitted that 'his (Pearson's) treatment is in algebraical form and beyond me'.[38]

Conversely, this view helps us to understand the widespread acceptance of Mendelism by the new generation of professional biologists following the rapid development, by T. H. Morgan and others, of the Mendelian chromosome theory in the period 1910–15. This new generation had been trained in an experimental and mechanistic approach to biology. Initially they were sceptical of the Mendelian approach, which they found too speculative. The establishment of the Mendelian chromosome theory, by the use of the fast-breeding *Drosophila* and the development of techniques such as chromosome mapping, changed their attitude completely. The techniques of Morgan's 'fly room' made the problem of heredity experimentally approachable. Mendelism then became the key to extending the scope of experimental biology: it was a theory that enhanced the value of the competences of experimental biologists, by showing that the use of these competences could throw new light on traditional areas of biological investigation.[39]

Thus, it is perhaps useful to see the scientists involved in the controversy as being faced with competing bases of judgement that embodied different technical competences (those of the traditional biologist, of the experimentalist, of the mathematician, etc.). So as to avoid the 'devaluation' of their competences, they typically rejected bases of judgement involving alien competences and adhered to those involving the use of familiar skills. Take, for example, one instance of a particular scientific judgement: that of the adequacy of Mendelian categories such as 'yellow' and 'green', or 'hairy' and 'glabrous' (hairless). Bateson was confident that a skilled biologist could reliably classify plants and animals into categories such as this, even if an untrained observer would find it a difficult or impossible task. His judgement that these Mendelian categories should be used thus rested on the biologist's com-

---

[38] E. Ray Lankester, 'The Utility of Specific Characters', *Nature*, liv (1896), p. 366, see also L. A. Farrall (note 1), pp. 284–5; *WB* (note 3), p. 324; W. Bateson (note 18), p. 110 fn.
[39] G. E. Allen, *Life Science in the Twentieth Century* (New York, 1975), pp. 33–9, 53, 56–65; *idem*, 'Thomas Hunt Morgan and the Problem of Natural Selection', *Journal of the History of Biology*, i (1968), p. 138.

petences. The biometricians, on the other hand, criticized these Mendelian categories as 'ambiguous', as 'leading to the accummulation of records, in which results are massed together in ill-defined categories of variable and uncertain extent'. Rather than use the category 'hairy', say, they argued for the keeping of detailed records of the numbers of hairs per unit area.[40] Should records be kept in this form, the necessity for the use of mathematical and statistical competences would immediately be clear.

In other words, the detailed technical judgements made by the two sides reflect at least in part the social interests of groups of scientific practitioners with differing skills. Is this all they reflect? Before answering that question, it is worth examining another aspect of the controversy that went beyond the issue of the validity of Mendelism.

HEREDITY AND EVOLUTION

The central figures in the two sides of the dispute (Bateson, Weldon and Pearson) were already involved in controversy before the 'rediscovery' of Mendelism provided the debate with its best-known focus. This wider controversy had various manifestations, but a single central thread ran through all the particular disagreements.[41] That thread was the issue of the nature of evolutionary change.

The biometricians (Pearson, Weldon and their co-workers, but not Francis Galton) believed that evolution was a process of gradual change, taking place by the selection of continuous differences. If height conferred a selective advantage, then the mean height of a population would rise gradually from one generation to the next, because each successive generation would be formed by proportionately more offspring of tall parents than of short parents. In this, the biometricians were following Darwin. The orthodox view had never gone unchallenged, even within the community of evolutionists: both T. H. Huxley and Francis Galton had doubted that evolution worked in this way, and had suggested a greater role for discontinuous variations ('sports' or 'saltations'), which differed markedly from the parental generation. Thus, Galton had felt that evolution might not proceed smoothly, but might 'jerk' from one

---

[40] W. F. R. Weldon, 'On the Ambiguity of Mendel's Categories', *Biometrika*, ii (1902), pp. 44–55.
[41] See, especially, W. B. Provine (note 1).

position of 'stability' to another. Those opposed to Darwinism also took up the issue of discontinuous variations, although, unlike Huxley and Galton, they tended to suggest that a 'nonmaterial directive agency' was guiding the production of these variations.[42]

This long-standing thread of opposition to orthodox Darwinian selectionism was given new force in 1894 with the publication of William Bateson's *Materials for the Study of Variation*.[43] The book is indeed mainly a catalogue of a large number of instances of variation. The subtitle, however, conveyed the import of these examples: *Treated with Especial Regard to Discontinuity in the Origin of Species*. Bateson argued that the morphological approach to evolutionary theory (in which he had been trained) had proven to be barren: attention had to shift to the empirical study of variation. This empirical study revealed, he claimed, that large, discontinuous variations did occur in nature. Further, he concluded that it was this type of variation (and not quantitative individual differences) which was of evolutionary significance. Species were discontinuous entities, differing qualitatively from each other: environments, by comparison, shaded continuously one into the other. The source of specific discontinuity could not, therefore, be the environment (whether acting in a direct Lamarckian or indirect selectionist fashion): it had to lie in variation, in the 'raw material' for evolution. Although Bateson said, cautiously, that 'inquiry into the causes of variation is as yet, in my judgment, premature', he did suggest that the source of discontinuity should be sought 'in the living thing itself', and that the key to its understanding lay in the phenomena of pattern: symmetry and merism.[44]

In the following decade, Hugo de Vries published his *Die Mutationstheorie*,[45] which was in part stimulated by Bateson's work.[46] Like Bateson, de Vries thought that large discontinuities were the key to the evolutionary process: 'The object of the present book is to show that species arise by saltation and that the

---

[42] *Ibid.*, p. 24. Huxley's and Galton's views are discussed, *ibid.*, pp. 10–24. For Galton's first presentation of his argument, see F. Galton, *Hereditary Genius* (London, 1869), pp. 367–70, 375–6.

[43] W. Bateson, *Materials for the Study of Variation, Treated with Especial Regard to Discontinuity in the Origin of Species* (London, 1894).

[44] *Ibid.*, p. 78; W. Coleman (note 35) p. 250.

[45] Leipzig, 1901–03.

[46] G. E. Allen, 'Hugo de Vries and the Reception of the *Mutation Theory*', *Journal of the History of Biology*, ii (1969), p. 65.

individual saltations are occurrences which can be observed like any other physiological process'.[47] While Bateson's work had had an impact amongst only those biologists with clear evolutionary concerns, that of de Vries received wide and generally favourable attention.[48]

Thus, overlapping the controversy over the validity of Mendelism was this further dispute over the nature of evolutionary change. The equation of Mendelism with a discontinuous, anti-Darwinian view of evolution was not, it is true, a logically necessary one. For example, Morgan's work from 1910 onwards on mutant *Drosophila* convinced him that mutations could have small phenotypic effects (no greater than the usual limits of continuous variability): he simultaneously upheld Mendelism, a Mendelian mutation theory, and a view of evolution as a gradual process. Conversely, de Vries, although one of the three 'rediscoverers' of Mendelism, denied that progressive mutations obeyed Mendelian laws, and became disenchanted with Mendelism. But, for all this absence of a *necessary* connection, the two issues became closely bound together, especially in Britain.[49]

In one sense, Bateson came to Mendelism as a result of his belief in the role of discontinuities in evolution.[50] In the years following the publication of the *Materials*, he set himself the task of discovering how discontinuous variations might be passed on to successive generations (a key issue in the development of a 'saltationist' theory of evolution). The method he chose was experimental plant hybridization, the crossing of closely related varieties and the examination of the characteristics of sets of offspring of such crosses. Bateson was travelling by train from Cambridge to London, to deliver a lecture on the preliminary results of his investigations, when he first read Mendel's paper on peas; he immediately incorporated the results into his lecture. He had been 'made ready' for reading Mendel by his own work on discontinuous variations and their heredity. He reacted enthusiastically, and interpreted

[47] Quoted *ibid.*, pp. 59–60.
[48] *Ibid.*, 65–9.
[49] G. E. Allen, 'Thomas Hunt Morgan and the Problem of Natural Selection' (note 39); *idem, Thomas Hunt Morgan: Man and his Science* (Princeton, 1978), p. 314; *idem* (note 46), p. 61; W. B. Provine (note 1), p. 68. B. J. Norton, 'Karl Pearson and the Galtonian Tradition' (note 1), p. 186, argues the point of the logical separability of Mendelism and a theory of evolution by large saltations.
[50] For an interesting account of the reasons for Bateson's favourable assessment of Mendelism, see L. Darden, 'William Bateson and the Promise of Mendelism', *Journal of the History of Biology*, x (1977), pp. 87–106.

Mendelism as supporting his own 'saltationist' evolutionary views. He wrote: 'The discovery of Mendelian elements admirably coincided with and at once gave a rationale of these facts'.[51]

Pearson and Weldon also felt there to be a connection between Mendelism and a discontinuous view of evolution: but this, for them, was a reason to reject Mendelism, not to embrace it. Pearson wrote:

> To those who accept the biometric standpoint, that in the main evolution has not taken place by leaps, but by continuous selection of the favourable variation from the distribution of the offspring round the ancestrally fixed type, each selection modifying *pro rata* that type, there must be a manifest want in Mendelian theories of inheritance. Reproduction from this standpoint can only shake the kaleidoscope of existing alternatives; it can bring nothing new into the field. To complete a Mendelian theory we must apparently associate it for the purposes of evolution with some hypothesis of 'mutations'.[52]

Thus, the biometricians' opposition to Mendelism can be seen, at least in part, as an opposition to the saltationism with which they associated it.

So the problem of explaining the biometrician/Mendelian controversy is one of explaining these divergent views of evolution, at least in so far as we wish to explain the prior dispute between the biometricians and Bateson, and its continuance into the latter phase of the controversy over Mendelism proper. These divergent views on evolution did not arise in any simple way from experimental evidence, but rather took the form of basic assumptions. Thus, Bateson separated variation *by definition* into the two classes of 'specific' variations (which were discontinuous and of evolutionary significance) and 'normal' or 'continuous' variations (which *a priori* were not), and criticized Pearson on the grounds that he had not done so.[53] And, as the quotation above indicated,

[51] W. Coleman, (note 35) 250–51; *WB* (note 3), pp. 161–70, 73, 171–80, 223.
[52] K. Pearson (note 12), p. 63.
[53] W. Bateson, 'Heredity, Differentiation, and other Conceptions of Biology: a Consideration of Professor Karl Pearson's paper "On the Principle of Homotyposis"', *Proceedings of the Royal Society of London*, lxix (1901), 193–205. The paper he was criticizing was K. Pearson, A. Lee, E. Warren, A. Fry and C. D. Fawcett, 'Mathematical Contributions to the Theory of Evolution, IX: On the Principle of Homotyposis and its Relation to Heredity, to the Variability of the Individual and to that of the Race. Part I: Homotyposis in the Vegetable Kingdom', *Philosophical Transactions of the Royal Society of London*, ser. A, cxcvii (1901), pp. 285–379.

Pearson took the continuous view of evolution as 'the biometric standpoint', i.e., fundamentally as a presupposition.

Factors internal to the social system of science, such as professional competences, may again be examined as a possible grounding for these different views of evolution. Allen shows how de Vries's mutation theory appeared initially to solve some of the problems that troubled the Darwinian theory.[54] Biologists might then be expected to take up the new theory as a promising area for innovative work. In particular, the mutation theory gave new relevance to experimental work in the form of attempts to demonstrate mutations in plants and animals reared in experimental conditions. Mayr states of the period immediately after 1900: 'I am not aware of a single experimental ... biologist who championed natural selection'.[55] Old-fashioned field naturalists, by comparison, tended, according to Mayr, to remain faithful to orthodox Darwinism.

It would therefore seem plausible to suggest that the assessment of evolutionary theories by experimental biologists was informed by judgements of the relative scope offered by these theories for experimental work, and that it was in part for this reason that they preferred the mutation theory to orthodox Darwinism. An instance of this would appear to be C. B. Davenport.[56] Davenport had introduced Pearsonian biometry to America, but following the 'rediscovery' of Mendelism and the publication of the *Mutationstheorie* he 'defected'. Davenport had considerable experience as an experimentalist, and had introduced the teaching of experimental morphology to Harvard. A 'painfully ambitious' man, he was from 1902 to 1904 engaged in a campaign to persuade the Carnegie Institution to set up a station for the experimental study of evolution. He therefore approached the mutation theory with a strong interest in the experimental studies it made possible. In 1902, he toured Europe, visiting the Marine Biological Stations

---

[54] G. E. Allen (note 46); see also L. Darden, 'Reasoning in Scientific Change: Charles Darwin, Hugo de Vries and the Discovery of Segregation', *Studies in the History and Philosophy of Science*, vii (1976), pp. 127–69.

[55] E. Mayr, 'Essay Review: the Recent Historiography of Genetics', *Journal of the History of Biology*, vi (1973), p. 149.

[56] For studies of Davenport see E. C. MacDowell, 'Charles Benedict Davenport, 1866–1944: a Study of Conflicting Influences', *Bios*, xvii (1946), pp. 3–50; C. E. Rosenberg, 'Charles Benedict Davenport and the Beginning of Human Genetics', *Bulletin of the History of Medicine*, xxxv (1961), pp. 266–76.

there 'to better fit myself for the work of directing the Station for Experiments on Evolution, whenever the Carnegie Institution establishes it'. On his return Davenport wrote:

The most important events relating to the study of variation that have occurred during the past two years have been the establishment of the journal *Biometrika*, the foundation in America of a Society of Plant and Animal Breeding, the completion of the first volume of de Vries's 'Mutationstheorie', and the rediscovery of Mendel's Law of Hybridity. Especially the latter two events have awakened a strong tendency toward the experimental study of evolution.

During the last four months the recorder has visited many of the experimental evolutionists of Europe. While the total work on this subject in Europe is of the greatest importance, it is carried on under conditions that greatly hamper the work and make it impossible to start experiments that require to be carried on for a long period of years. Everywhere the hope was expressed that in America a permanent station for experimental evolution would be founded, and it was believed that the Carnegie Institution would be the proper organisation to initiate and maintain such a station.

Thus, we can claim that for Davenport the mutation theory and Mendelism made it possible to *do* more (within his desired occupational role) than the Darwinism of the biometricians. In 1904 he did indeed achieve his aim of becoming Director of a Laboratory set up by the Carnegie Institution at Cold Spring Harbor, and the work done under his direction was Mendelian and mutationist in tendency. As he wrote, reviewing the work of de Vries: 'The great service of de Vries's work is that, being founded on experimentation, it challenges to experimentation as the only judge of its merits. It will attain its highest usefulness only if it creates a widespread stimulus to the experimental investigation of evolution'. Such an attitude to mutation was incompatible with collaboration with Pearson, and relations between Pearson and Davenport deteriorated rapidly.[57]

Disciplinary skills seem once again to have been important in the

[57] E. C. MacDowell, *ibid.*, p. 19; C. B. Davenport, '[Report of the] Committee on Variation', *Science*, N.S., xvii (1903), p. 46; C. B. Davenport, 'Species and Varieties, their Origin by Mutation, by Hugo de Vries', *Science*, N.S. xxii (1905), p. 369; Davenport Papers, Pearson File, American Philosophical Society.

overall dispute about evolution. However, most of the evidence about their role concerns the relevance of experimental skills (as against those of field naturalists, for example). As far as these are concerned, the two groups most centrally involved in the dispute in Britain do not seem to have differed too radically. For example, both Bateson and Weldon were arguably closer in their skills to the field naturalist than to the new experimentalists. When Bateson finally began to concede some validity to the chromosome theory, he felt that he would have to import the necessary skills in cell biology from outside his group: 'Cytology here [in the United States] is such a commonplace that every one is familiar with it. I wish it were so with us ... we must try to get a cytologist'. And Weldon was described by Pearson as 'essentially a field naturalist' in his 'tastes' and 'emotional nature'. So, again, it is wise not to close the enquiry at this point.[58]

## NATURE AND SOCIETY: BIOMETRY

On the surface, the biometrician–Mendelian dispute was about the correct way of studying and interpreting the processes of heredity and evolution – it was between two different views of nature. Digging a little deeper, we have found reason to suspect that the vested interests of scientists with different types of skill partially sustained this dispute, particularly those aspects of it that concerned method. When we extend our investigation from the micro-politics of science to the macropolitics of the wider society, we begin to find hints of the possible operation of a quite different set of factors.

The study of heredity and evolution in Victorian and Edwardian Britain was an activity loaded with social and political meaning. As the credibility of religion declined, it was increasingly to nature, rather than to God, that people turned to advocate and defend their political views. To argue for a state of society as natural began to become more common than to argue for it as divinely ordained. While scientific fields such as geometry and physics were by no means immune from use for purposes of legitimation,[59] the biologi-

[58] *WB* (note 3), p. 143; K. Pearson (note 12), p. 297.
[59] See J. L. Richards, 'The Reception of a Mathematical Theory: Non-Euclidean Geometry in England, 1868–1883' and B. Wynne, 'Physics and Psychics: Science, Symbolic Action, and Social Control in Late Victorian England', both in B. Barnes and S. Shapin (eds.), *Natural Order: Historical Studies of Scientific Culture* (Beverly Hills and London, 1979), pp. 143–66, 167–86.

cal sciences were the rhetorical resources most often drawn upon. As Young has documented, the result was that no strict boundaries can be drawn between Victorian biological and social thought, especially in the field of evolution.[60] While the motivation of particular key thinkers such as Darwin remains a matter of dispute, there is ample evidence that theorizing about nature was informed by metaphors drawn from the social world, and that disputes about social policy were frequently carried on in the idiom of biology.[61]

It would be surprising, then, if such a major dispute as that between the biometricians and Mendelians – even if it did take place well after the first bitter debates about evolution and its social meaning – was found not to have some wider social significance. Yet this possibility received but little attention from the historians of biology who documented so thoroughly the course of the controversy. It is indeed true that a social message is not always fully explicit. But perhaps one can be 'decoded' – and perhaps evidence can be found to help check the plausibility of this decoding.

Consider biometry, especially as developed by Pearson. In his crucial third 'Mathematical Contribution to the Theory of Evolution' we find the following statement of a typical biometric research task:

> We, therefore, require a generalised investigation of the following kind: Given $p + 1$ normally correlated organs, p out of these organs are selected in the following manner: each organ is selected normally round a given mean, and the p selected organs, pair and pair, are correlated in any arbitrary manner. What will be the nature of the distribution of the remaining $(p + 1)$th organ? ... If the p organs are organs of ancestry – as many as we please – and the $(p + 1)$th organ that of a descendant, we have here the general problem of natural selection modified by inheritance.[62]

'The general problem of natural selection modified by inheritance' was, for the biometricians, that of constructing a descriptive and

[60] R. M. Young, 'Malthus and the Evolutionists: the Common Context of Biological and Social Theory', *Past and Present*, no. 43 (1969), pp. 109–45.
[61] For the debate about Darwin, and some interesting comments on it, see S. Shapin and B. Barnes, 'Darwin and Social Darwinism: Purity and History', in Barnes and Shapin (note 59), pp. 125–42. For one of many examples of the social use of biology, see J. R. Durant, 'Scientific Naturalism and Social Reform in the Thought of Alfred Russel Wallace', *British Journal for the History of Science*, xii (1979), pp. 31–58.
[62] K. Pearson (note 8), p. 298 (emphasis deleted).

predictive model of the process of evolution. In this model, factors such as heredity, and natural and artificial selection, operated in measurable fashion on biological populations to produce definite effects on succeeding generations. The biometricians' key goal, we might say, was the development of techniques to permit the prediction of the overall incidence of characteristics within biological populations. It did not appear to the biometricians that their enterprise was in any particular sense goal-oriented. They identified their goals as simply those of any properly scientific study of heredity and evolution. Yet from another perspective, the biometricians can be seen as oriented to *particular* goals. Their enterprise was, as suggested above, organized round problems of what we would now call phenotypic resemblances. They studied evolution as a mass process involving gradual, measurable changes in the characteristics of successive generations of whole populations. Their statistical techniques were, as Bateson saw, ill-suited to the identification of suddenly-arising new varieties of evolutionary significance; just as Bateson's techniques were inadequate for the study of mass secular change. The biometricians sought to predict population changes by predicting the characteristics of individuals and summing these for the population. Biological populations were thus seen as individualistic and aggregative, and so as subject to Darwinian selection of continuous differences. 'Holistic' views of biological populations, which saw these as having a stability beyond that of the sum of individual characteristics, were explicitly rejected by the biometricians.[63]

Successful prediction and the potential for control are closely linked. Had the biometric enterprise been fully successful, fully reliable techniques for the prediction of the effects of intervention in one generation on the measurable characteristics of subsequent generations would have been produced. This might indeed have helped the plant or animal breeders, especially had they been concerned with slow improvement of the quantitative characteristics of stock, rather than with the rapid formation of qualitatively

[63] Thus they rejected the notion of a fixed species 'centre of regression', arguing that regression took place only to the shifting mean of individual characteristics. Had they accepted the notion of the fixed 'centre of regression', their predictions about individual organisms would then have been based on a characteristic of the species, rather than vice versa. As Provine points out in *The Origins of Theoretical Population Genetics* (note 1), the clash of these two different interpretations of regression was an important aspect of the debate.

new varieties. Particularly it would have helped those eugenists concerned with the planned improvement of whole populations.[64] For there was a strong parallel between the predictive goals of biometry and the interventionist aims of this type of eugenics. The eugenists wanted to alter patterns of reproduction so as to improve the mental and physical characteristics of future generations. Whole human populations were considered, but as aggregates of the individuals composing them. Eugenics was to proceed by identifying 'unfit' individuals, and preventing them reproducing, and/or by identifying 'fit' individuals and encouraging their repro- duction. Through the process of heredity, the aggregate 'pheno- typic' characteristics of future generations would then be improved; attempts to prove this eugenic assumption were based, largely, on demonstrating correlations between the incidence of key character- istics in successive generations. Eugenic intervention was social improvement by artificial selection paralleling almost exactly biological evolution by natural selection as conceived by the biometricians.

This formal parallelism between biometry and eugenics is hardly surprising. In the origins of biometric methods in the work of Galton,[65] and in their subsequent development and institutional- ization by Karl Pearson, eugenic concerns figured large. The ties of the natural to the social within biometry were present from the beginning. *A priori*, it could be argued that the biometricians first

[64] The proviso relating to concern with the planned improvement of whole popu- lations is important. Eugenists without this concern – say those who wished to restrict eugenic attention to sub-populations identified on the basis of qualitatively distinct traits – might well have found Mendelism a more useful approach. It is interesting to speculate whether this may throw some light on the phenomenon of 'Mendelian eugenics' in, for example, the work of Davenport. See C. B. Davenport, *Heredity in Relation to Eugenics* (New York, 1911).

[65] Galton is a complex figure as far as this controversy is concerned. On the one hand he was the originator of the biometric method, and the connection suggested here between biometry and eugenics clearly holds for this aspect of his thought. On the other hand, there are facets of Galton's substantive theorizing, particularly his emphasis on the idea of 'stability' and the related notion that evolution consisted of jerks from one position of stability to another, that are much closer to Bateson's thought. See R. S. Cowan, 'Nature and Nurture: the Interplay of Biology and Politics in the Work of Francis Galton', *Studies in the History of Biology*, i (1977), pp. 133–208.

One is almost tempted to posit two Galtons: a Galton$_1$ who was a eugenist and biometrician and a Galton$_2$ whose biology might be understood in the light of the analysis suggested below for Bateson's. Certainly both sides in the controversy found resources to draw on in Galton's rich and contradictory thinking.

developed their science, and only then saw its social implications –
this, indeed, is doubtless how they would have presented matters.
But the historical record renders this view unlikely.

Take, for example, the issue of whether evolutionary change was
a continuous or discontinuous process. Pearson had chosen sides
on this well before he became involved in biological research:

> ... *no great change ever occurs with a leap*; no great social
> reconstruction, which will permanently benefit any class of the
> community, is ever brought about by a revolution. It is the result
> of a gradual growth, a progressive change, what we term an
> *evolution*. This is as much a law of history as of nature.
>
> Human progress, like Nature, never leaps; this is the most
> certain of all laws deduced from the study of ˙human
> development.[66]

As these quotations make explicit, the context of Pearson's espousal of evolutionary gradualism was political. He was arguing
against insurrection and for a reformism in which the masses would
submit themselves to the leadership and planning of experts and
intellectuals. As he wrote in the introduction to the volume of essays
from which the above quotations are taken: 'There are mighty
forces at work likely to revolutionise social ideas and shake social
stability. It is the duty of those, who have the leisure to investigate,
to show how by *gradual and continuous changes* we can restrain
these forces within safe channels'.[67]

This early social use of biology by Pearson was of course neither
subtle nor original. Nevertheless, his commitment to a gradualist
position in both politics and biology seems to have remained firm.
He did not waver throughout the vogue of discontinuous, mutationist theories of evolution, and his gradualism was a key basis of
his criticism of these theories. Over forty years after he first adopted
this position he was still battling. His biography of Galton makes
clear the distance between his own position and his master's
'mutationist' theory of evolution,[68] while he quotes with evident
approval Galton's avowal (interestingly, in a letter to Bateson) that
a 'steady though slow amelioration of the human breed' is all that
eugenics can seek.[69]

[66] K. Pearson, *The Ethic of Freethought* (London, 1888), pp. 363, 122.
[67] *Ibid.*, p. 7 (emphasis added).
[68] K. Pearson (note 13), especially p. 170.
[69] F. Galton to W. Bateson, 12 June 1904, quoted *ibid.*, pp. 220–1.

The biometric school's detailed arguments against Mendelism yield further evidence of the connections of biometry and eugenics and of the role of social interests in the evaluation of knowledge. One of the most interesting statements of these arguments is to be found in a comment in a work on human albinism. It is worth quoting in full:

The problem of whether philosophical Darwinism is to disappear before a theory which provides nothing but a shuffling of old unit characters varied by the appearance of an unexplained 'fit of mutation' is not the only point at issue in breeding experiments. There is a still graver matter that we face, when we adduce evidence that all characters do not follow Mendelian rules. Mendelism is being applied wholly prematurely to anthropological and social problems in order to deduce rules as to disease and pathological states which have serious social bearing. Thus we are told that mental defect – a wide term which covers more grades even than human albinism – is a 'unit character' and obeys Mendelian rules; and again on the basis of Mendelian theory it is asserted that both normal and abnormal members of insane stocks may without risk to future offspring marry members of healthy stocks. Surely, if science is to be a real help to man in assisting him in a conscious evolution, we must at least avoid spanning the crevasses in our knowledge by such snowbridges of theory. A careful record of facts will last for ages, but theory is ever in the making or the un-making, a mere fashion which describes more or less effectually our experience. To extrapolate from theory beyond experience in nine cases out of ten leads to failure, even to disaster when it touches social problems. In all that relates to the evolution of man and to the problems of race betterment, it is wiser to admit our present limitations than to force our data into Mendelian theory and on the basis of such rules propound sweeping racial theories and inculcate definite rules for social conduct.[70]

That the biometric school's evolutionary theory was designed to be applicable to society as well as nature did not simply constrain the *content* of biology by ruling out theories, such as those referred to

---

[70] K. Pearson, E. Nettleship and C. H. Usher, *A Monograph on Albinism in Man. Part II* (Drapers' Company Research Memoirs, Biometric Series, viii, 1913), p. 491, quoted by E. S. Pearson, 'Karl Pearson: an Appreciation of Some Aspects of His Life and Work', *Biometrika*, xxix (1938), pp. 169–70.

in the first sentence of this quotation, that formulated evolution as a discontinuous and unpredictable process. It also constrained its *form*, as the rest of the quotation indicates. To be credible, social programmes such as eugenics had to be seen as based on sure knowledge, not knowledge that was subject to future retraction and contradiction. This was taken to mean that a theory of evolution and heredity had to be developed from observational data, and from these alone. Knowledge of the 'facts' was stable and a safe basis for social action. Theory which went beyond the facts was, however, subject to 'fashion', to change. Thus, evolutionary biology should be phenomenalist, not theoretical, in its form.

The biometric school claimed that their own approach met this criterion. As outlined above, their notion of heredity was primarily a phenotypic, phenomenalist one. Biometry attempted to 'display' evolution as measurable mass change in population distributions. The mathematical apparatus developed by the biometricians took observational data and analysed it according to multiple regression models.[71] The law of ancestral heredity, according to Pearson, was derived from observational data, and enabled the apparently theory-free prediction of offspring characteristics from ancestral characteristics.[72] The effects of eugenic intervention were predictable without any biological theory of heredity, because the biometric concept of heredity simply summarized what happened in the 'passage' of a characteristic from given individuals in one generation to those in the next. Theory-free control, as well as theory-free prediction, was thus apparently possible.

Early Mendelism, by comparison, was obviously theoretical. A simple exemplar was being imaginatively and sometimes rashly deployed, and was being modified in what often seemed an *ad hoc* fashion. Pearson wrote:

> The simplicity of Mendel's Mendelism has been gradually replaced by a complexity as great as that of any description hitherto suggested of hereditary relationships ... The old categories are, as Weldon indicated, being found insufficient, narrower classifications are being taken, and irregular dominance, imperfect recessiveness, the correlation of attributes, the latency of ancestral characters, and more complex determinantal theories are becoming the order of the day.[73]

[71] For example, K. Pearson (note 8).
[72] K. Pearson (note 25).
[73] K. Pearson (note 12), p. 306.

With hindsight, we can identify this as creative science, as simply the growth of genetic knowledge. But for those who sought in the study of heredity the basis of an applied social science of evolution, this process could have scandalous consequences.

The most serious of these was when Davenport suggested that feeblemindedness was a simple Mendelian recessive, and went on to argue that a whole range of characteristics of eugenic importance were of a similar nature.[74] Davenport drew from this what seemed to Pearson to be not merely a foolish, but an immoral conclusion: 'Weakness in any characteristic must be mated with strength in that characteristic; and strength may be mated with weakness'.[75] A devastating criticism of Davenport's work was produced by the biometrician David Heron, who showed how Davenport's methods were biased towards producing the simple Mendelian results he sought. It concluded: 'The future of the race depends on the strong mating with the strong, and the weak refraining from every form of parenthood. Nothing short of this rule with satisfy the true Eugenist'.[76] In the course of time, Mendelians themselves came to reject Davenport's simplistic analyses. Bateson was always doubtful, although in the 1920s Punnett still assumed that feeble-mindedness was a simple recessive trait.[77] Pearson's point, how-ever, was that unjustified theoretical extrapolations, even if subsequently retracted, could have disastrous anti-eugenic consequences. Eugenics could not be based on a fallible theory: it had to be based on 'hard fact', reliable prediction, and thus unerring control.

Norton has suggested that Pearson's phenomenalism should be seen as a cause of his rejection of Mendelism.[78] It seems to me that he is right to point to the importance of phenomenalism in connection with the biometric school's assessment of Mendelism, but that it is not necessary – and perhaps wrong – to see Pearson's judgements as determined by an abstract philosophical position. For it is easy to point to instances of Pearson making judge-ments (for example about the desirability of underlying-variable

[74] C. B. Davenport, *Eugenics* (New York, 1910); *idem* (note 64).
[75] C. B. Davenport, *Eugenics*, p. 25.
[76] D. Heron, *Mendelism and the Problem of Mental Defect, I: A Criticism of Recent American Work* (Questions of the Day and the Fray, vii, London, 1913), p. 62.
[77] *WB* (note 3), p. 341 fn.; R. C. Punnett, 'As a Biologist sees it', *Nineteenth Century*, xcvii (1925), p. 705.
[78] B. J. Norton, 'Biology and Philosophy' (note 1); *idem*, 'Metaphysics and Population Genetics (note 1).

theories)[79] that scarcely comply with strict phenomenalism. Rather than see phenomenalist philosophy as a kind of straitjacket within which Pearson's mind was confined, it is perhaps better to consider it as a rhetorical resource that he could employ where it was appropriate. Phenomenalism was a useful weapon in general arguments against the anti-naturalist opponents of scientific expertise: phenomenalist criteria could be used to argue that speculative theorizing about the supernatural was *a priori* unsound. Similarly, phenomenalist criteria could be brought to bear to condemn Mendelians who were engaging in rash (and, as Pearson or Heron would put it, anti-eugenic) theorizing. Phenomenalist philosophy legitimated what the biometric school was doing – producing apparently theory-free predictive models of population processes – and, more generally, legitimated the naturalistic scientist's claim to privileged knowledge. But to say that it *legitimated* these is not to imply that it *caused* them.[80]

Thus far I have not attempted to distinguish between the individual positions held by different members of the biometric school. In some cases – for example those of David Heron or the future political theorist H. J. Laski – individual biometricians appear to have been committed eugenists and to have attacked Mendelism in part on the grounds of its eugenic inadequacies.[81] Not all biometricians, however, were eugenists. Nevertheless, my

[79] D. MacKenzie, 'Statistical Theory and Social Interests: a Case-Study', *Social Studies of Science*, viii (1978), pp. 35–83.

[80] Norton suggests another possible cause of Pearson's opposition to Mendelism: his upholding of a *Weltbild* in which it was denied that any two objects were totally alike (as Mendelian factors in a sense were). It seems to me that, to the extent that Pearson held to this, it can best be seen as a generalization from his biological beliefs and experience, rather than as a determinant of them. That is how I would interpret the following, from K. Pearson (note 13), p. 84, fn., which is perhaps his most explicit statement on the matter:

> I must confess to feeling it extremely difficult to accept the view that the population of germ cells belonging to an individual organism are like atoms, identical in character, and have a germinal capacity defined by absolutely the same formula. Such a population of germ cells is, if parasitical, still an organic population, and one continually in a state of reproduction and change. No other organic population that we know of is without variation among its members ...

This interpretation is, I think, supported by Norton's account ('Biology and Philosophy', note 1) of the origins of Pearson's belief in biological variability.

[81] See E. S. Pearson, 'David Heron, 1881–1969', *Journal of the Royal Statistical Society*, ser. A, cxxx, pp. 287–91; D. Heron (note 76); H. J. Laski, 'A Mendelian View of Racial Heredity', *Biometrika*, viii (1912), pp. 424–30; K. Pearson (note 13) iiiB, pp. 606–9.

argument is unaffected by individual lack of commitment to eugenics. For the connections between biometry and eugenics were *institutionalized* connections.

By this I do not mean simply that eugenics in large part provided the financial base for biometry. That is indeed true. Francis Galton funded a Eugenics Laboratory to work in close liaison with Pearson's Biometric Laboratory (the two were in practice largely one organization even before their formal merging in the Department of Applied Statistics of University College London) and left the residue of his estate for the establishment of a 'Galton Professorship of Eugenics' earmarked for Pearson.[82] What is more directly relevant, however, was that it was publicly asserted that there was a special intellectual connection – one of method – between biometry and eugenics. This connection was subscribed to even by biometricians uncommitted to eugenics, at least if the case of the most important of these, W. F. R. Weldon, can be taken as typical.

Weldon's position on the use of biology in political argument is perhaps best summed up in a letter he wrote to Pearson during the Boer War. He is referring to Pearson's major social-imperialist tract, *National Life from the Standpoint of Science*:[83] 'After talking to invalids in Madeira, who will tell one something about the Army, your lecture seems even more necessary than it did before. I hope you will go on doing work of this kind, as you can do it so well'.[84] Weldon was not hostile to Pearson's social use of science: it was 'necessary'. But it was Pearson, not himself, that he felt should engage in it. His own biological work can hardly be seen as a response to the needs of eugenics: he even pointed out that heredity and environment were not separable factors (as the eugenists assumed), and annoyed Galton by doing so.[85] Yet in defending biometry, he was able to draw upon the connection between biometry and eugenics:

> Dr Mercier [a critic of Galton], and those who think with him, object, first of all, that the actuarial [i.e., in this context, biometric] method is faulty, because it does not account for the

[82] K. Pearson (note 13), contains detailed information on the development of the Eugenics Laboratory.
[83] London, 1901.
[84] 21 January 1901, Pearson Papers, 625; University College London.
[85] Weldon to Pearson, 16 October 1904 Pearson Papers, 625; University College London.

phenomena 'of inheritance ... [But] the actuarial method does not pretend to account for anything. It does pretend to describe a large number of complex phenomena with a very fair degree of accuracy, and for this reason it is admirably adapted for the purposes of Eugenic inquirers. As I conceive the matter, the essential object of Eugenics is not to put forward any theory of the causation of hereditary phenomena, but to obtain and diffuse a knowledge of what those phenomena really are.[86]

So, despite the lack of evidence that eugenics was an important factor in Weldon's motivation,[87] the biometry-eugenics link, constructed and sustained by others, was available to him as a resource in argument. The link was more than a private obsession of Pearson's, it was a public aspect of biometry. While some eugenists wished to deny the special connection of biometry and eugenics,[88] they had to fly in the face of the public position of the founder of their movement, Francis Galton.[89]

One major issue remains: that of the social interests that ultimately sustained eugenics. As the paper by Searle in this volume indicates, the claim that those interests are to be located in the situation of the professional middle class within capitalism is a controversial one. Nevertheless it is one that I adhere to. Indeed it is one that I believe holds particularly strongly for the specific version of eugenics advanced by the biometric school.

Much of Searle's work – his emphasis on the contradictory relationship between the professional and the state, his clarification of the complex position of the medical profession on eugenics, etc. –

[86] Contribution to the discussion of Francis Galton's, 'Eugenics: its Definition, Scope and Aims', *Sociological Papers 1904* (London, 1905), p. 56.

[87] Weldon's actual *motives* for opposing Mendelism seem to me most likely to be accountable for in terms of his personal investment in mathematical and statistical method. He wrote to Pearson on 23 June 1902 (Pearson Papers, 625; University College London):

It seems to me, quite apart from my own share in the matter, that the present is a rather interesting and important moment. There is a 'boom' in a quite unstatistical theory of inheritance, which is so simple that everyone can understand it, and is stated so confidently that all sorts of people are getting interested in it. We can make it ridiculous, and I think we must. It is really the first time the unstatistical folk have fairly recognised that there is a fundamental antithesis, and have accepted battle on that issue. The side which can now get a vulgarly dramatic 'score' will have a better hearing presently.

[88] An account of this is to be found in K. Pearson (note 13), pp. 405–9.

[89] F. Galton, *Probability, the Foundation of Eugenics* (London, 1907).

I warmly welcome.[90] My doubts centre on his key assertion that eugenics *failed* to 'articulate the basic class interests of any major group in British society'.[91]

It is impossible to discuss here the wide range of issues raised by this.[92] They are, indeed, as much matters of historiography as of substance – I suspect that Dr Searle and I differ as to what it means to 'articulate ... basic class interests'.[93] Further, the major topic of substance raised is that of the interpretation of environmentalism and of the relations between environmentalism and eugenics. Work on this has hardly begun.[94] In addition, it may well be that the origins of the divergence of views lie in the fact that my starting point is eugenics as a system of knowledge while Searle's is eugenists as a political pressure group.[95] What we take to be typical may thus differ: my concern has chiefly been with those scientists and intellectuals who attempted to develop eugenic

---

[90] One misunderstanding, the result of unclear formulation in my earlier work, should be cleared up. Searle states (p. 236) that if forced to generalize he would 'even be inclined to reverse MacKenzie's categories and to argue that eugenics appealed less to "new professionals" than to the type of family which figures in Noel Annan's discussion of the Victorian intellectual élite'. This runs together two issues: that of élite versus non-élite professionals, and of new, scientific professions versus traditional professions such as the Church. My article ('Eugenics in Britain', *Social Studies of Science*, vi (1976), pp. 499–532) did indeed suggest that eugenics appealed particularly to 'new professionals' in the sense of scientific professionals. But that does not imply anything about the élite/non-élite distinction, and in fact I devoted several pages (pp. 505–9) to discussing the origins of eugenics within the 'intellectual aristocracy'.

[91] G. Searle, this volume, p. 239.

[92] I have attempted to do so in my book, *Statistics in Britain, 1865–1930: the Social Construction of Scientific Knowledge* (Edinburgh University Press, 1981), ch. 2.

[93] For some indication of the range of interpretations possible see B. Barnes, *Interests and the Growth of Knowledge* (London and Henley, 1977), ch. 3.

[94] A lot of the force of Searle's critique rests on the extent to which professional groups found environmentalism an appropriate ideology. If we define eugenics and environmentalism as mutually exclusive and exhaustive alternatives, then it clearly is the case that eugenics was, at most, appropriate only to a part of the professional middle class. Yet, as Werskey hints, eugenics and environmentalism (at least of certain brands) have perhaps more in common than has been noticed. See G. Werskey, *The Visible College* (London, 1978), pp. 28–30. At least two recent studies, from very different perspectives, indicate the insights that might be achieved if the extent and nature of this common ground were to be systematically investigated: J. Harwood, 'Heredity, Environment, and the Legitimation of Social Policy', in B. Barnes and S. Shapin (eds.), *Natural Order* (note 59), pp. 231–51; N. Rose, 'The Psychological Complex: Mental Measurement and Social Administration', *Ideology and Consciousness*, no. 5 (1979), pp. 5–68.

[95] This possibility was suggested to me by Dr Searle himself.

thought most rigorously, while Searle has focused on the Eugenics Education Society. Explanations appropriate for the latter may not apply to the former. The early history of the Eugenics Education Society has indeed, as Searle emphasizes, a lot to do with the fact that 'middle-class groups with a strongly conservative outlook were casting around for arguments to deploy against the Radical policies of the Asquith Government'.[96] On the other hand, eugenics as a system of ideas is, as Freeden's recent article indicates, often to be found in conjunction with viewpoints commonly labelled 'progressive'.[97]

For the purposes of this paper, then, let me focus on the version of eugenics advanced by the biometric school. To borrow a phrase from Jonathan Hodge, this was 'population–genetical engineering' of an extremely thoroughgoing kind.[98] That such a scheme was quite divorced from the practicalities of Edwardian politics we can accept. Pearson himself had no illusions that it could be introduced rapidly. Rather, the points of interest are the view of society that it implied and the role it promised to the eugenic expert.

The view of society involved had a double aspect. Firstly, it was an individualistic, aggregative one. Fundamentally, the way to improve society was to improve the individual characteristics of its members in aggregate. It was sufficient neither to change social forms without attention to individual capacities, nor to improve a few select individuals at the expense of the mass. To quote from Pearson's definition of socialism: 'Individual societies have the strongest interest in educating, training, and organizing the powers of *all their individual* members'.[99] This passage was written before Pearson became committed to eugenics, but his basic perspective on how to improve society remained the same despite the increased attention he gave to breeding as well as educating the individual. Secondly, individuals and their characteristics were seen as prop-

[96] G. Searle, in this volume, p. 237. See also *idem, Eugenics and Politics in Britain, 1900–1914* (Leyden, 1976).
[97] M. Freeden, 'Eugenics and Progressive Thought: a Study in Ideological Affinity', *Historical Journal,* xxii (1979), pp. 645–71.
[98] Quoted by R. C. Olby, 'Introduction to Symposium 8', in E. G. Forbes (ed.), *Human Implications of Scientific Advance: Proceedings of the XVth International Congress of the History of Science, Edinburgh 10–15 August 1977* (Edinburgh, 1978), p. 447.
[99] K. Pearson, *The Grammar of Science* (London, 1892), p. 433 (emphasis added).

erly subject to state control and planning. Pearson's position was no civil-liberties individualism. 'Socialists', he said, 'have to inculcate that spirit which would give offenders against the state short shrift and the nearest lamp-post'.[100] While this is not to be taken quite literally, there can be no doubt that the subordination of the individual to the collective good was central to Pearson's political and ethical thought, and formed the moral justification for eugenic intervention. Interference in as personal and private a matter as human reproduction was fully justified if it contributed to the planned production of an efficient population.

In short, this position combined an aggregative individualism not dissimilar to classical political economy[101] with advocacy of a 'strong state', the theoretical cement being the social-Darwinian view that the locus of selection had changed from the individual to the nation.[102] It was an updating of classical bourgeois thought for the age of imperialism. Yet it was a position that explicitly labelled itself 'socialist'. This, however, is not as paradoxical as it seems. As Hobsbawm explains, in this period the term 'socialist' functioned as the 'mere antonym of *laissez-faire*'.[103] Emphatically, commitment to the labour movement was *not* implied by Pearson's self-styled 'socialism'. Indeed, amongst the tasks he listed for socialism was to 'discipline the powers of labour'.[104]

To whose interests did this position then correspond? In an ultimate sense, one might well answer that it was to those of capital. 'At root', wrote G. K. Chesterton, 'the Eugenist is the Employer'.[105] There may indeed be long-term truth in this. A thoroughgoing programme of eugenic intervention along the lines anticipated by Pearson arguably was in the interests of a reformed, efficient British capitalism: it would, to borrow a phrase used by Pearson in another context, 'make the individual worker an in-

---

[100] K. Pearson, *The Ethic of Freethought*, 2nd edn. (London, 1901), pp. 307–8.

[101] Philip Abrams emphasizes the extent of the continuity between political economy and eugenics in *The Origins of British Sociology, 1834–1914* (Chicago, 1968). Unlike Searle (this volume p. 235, fn. 65) I do not see this continuity as denying a new ideological role for eugenics.

[102] See, e.g., K. Pearson (note 99), pp. 432–3.

[103] E. J. Hobsbawm, *Labouring Men: Studies in the History of Labour* (London, 1968), p. 261.

[104] K. Pearson (note 99), p. 436.

[105] G. K. Chesterton, *Eugenics and Other Evils* (London, 1922), p. 137.

telligent instrument for his allotted task'.[106] But as the subsequent history of the twentieth century has shown us, large-scale reform and efficiency have typically been forced on British capital from without – usually by war. The actual bearers of such modernization plans have more often been intellectuals than capitalists.

It is to this strand in British politics – that of the modernizing professionals – that biometric eugenics surely belongs. The strand begins with the 'intellectual aristocracy' discussed by Annan, continues through the secular, rationalizing reform sponsored by this group in the nineteenth century, takes on one particular manifestation in the Fabian Society (as discussed by Hobsbawm), and reaches its peak with the work of Keynes and Beveridge.[107] The professionals' reformism was not disinterested: they called for meritocracy, and they had supreme confidence that they were the best and should rule. It is not my assertion that they were all eugenists, although it would be interesting to know how seriously to take the hints of eugenic sympathies to be found in, for example, both Keynes and Beveridge.[108] Rather, I am suggesting that biometric eugenics – the most rational,[109] thoroughgoing form of eugenic thought to be found in Britain – is best seen as one version of this general tendency, and as sustained by the same interests as sustained it.[110]

Of course, eugenics was ultimately not the successful form of this tendency. Explicit 'population-genetical engineering' was not part of altered patterns of social relations that emerged in Britain in the 1940s. Environmentalism at least partially triumphed over eugenics. To say why this happened would be dangerously close to recounting the history of twentieth century Britain; Searle's point

---

[106] K. Pearson, 'Prefatory Essay: the Function of Science in the Modern State', *Encyclopaedia Britannica*, 10th edn., xxxii (viii of new vols.), p. xvi.

[107] N. G. Annan, 'The Intellectual Aristocracy', in J. H. Plumb (ed.), *Studies in Social History: a Tribute to G. M. Trevelyan* (London, 1955), pp. 241–87; E. J. Hobsbawm, 'The Fabians Reconsidered', in Hobsbawm (note 103), pp. 250–71. See also H. Perkin, *The Origins of Modern British Society, 1780–1880* (London, 1972).

[108] Keynes was Treasurer of the Cambridge University Eugenics Society, as is revealed by the records of this Society in the Library of the Eugenics Society (C.1.393). For Beveridge, see his 'Eugenic Aspects of Children's Allowances', *Eugenics Review*, xxxiv (1943), pp. 117–23. M. Freeden (note 97) provides an interesting discussion of the position of Keynes and Beveridge.

[109] In Weber's sense of *zweckrational*: see M. Weber, *The Theory of Social and Economic Organization* (New York, 1947), p. 115.

[110] G. Searle's important study, *The Quest for National Efficiency: a Study in British Politics and Political Thought, 1899–1914* (Oxford, 1971), is of particular interest here.

that environmentalism promised greater job opportunities for professionals is one important starting point.[111] One speculation as
regards the future may perhaps be permitted. If the failure of
eugenics ultimately arose from the particular form taken by the
post-1939 settlement between capital and labour in Britain, will it
re-emerge as that settlement comes under increasing pressure in the
1980s?

### NATURE AND SOCIETY: BATESON

It would be foolish to try to attribute a single political colouring to
a theory such as Mendelism, which was to be found in many
different countries and contexts. Nevertheless, the group around
William Bateson – the biometricians' most central opponent – is
well worth investigating from the point of view of the relation of
images of nature to social interests.[112] It is my suggestion that
Batesonian biology carried, in the context we are discussing, a
social message radically different from that carried by biometry and
can perhaps be seen as sustained in part by social interests quite at
odds with those sustaining biometry.

Happily, much of the groundwork of this investigation has
already been carried out, in the form of Coleman's penetrating
study of the thought of William Bateson.[113] While some aspects of
Coleman's account may be open to challenge,[114] the overall picture

[111] *Ibid.* Here my earlier work must stand corrected, although I would emphasize that in
Pearson's eugenic society there were to be power and jobs both for the eugenic experts
and for the environmentalist experts, especially educationalists. See, e.g., K. Pearson
(note 106). There was nothing intrinsically necessary in the use of eugenics as an argument
against the expansion of state activity in the welfare field. Indeed Pearson's vision of a
'strong state' employing both the velvet glove of environmentalism and the iron fist of
eugenics has a considerable – even a frightening – degree of coherence.

[112] I am not clear as to the extent to which Bateson's position was shared by his
collaborators. There is some possibility that R. C. Punnett shared Bateson's
position: he too was a leader of the campaign for the retention of compulsory Greek.
See F. A. E. Crew, 'Reginald Crundall Punnett, 1875–1967', *Biographical Memoirs of
Fellows of the Royal Society*, xiii (1967), p. 315. For further evidence on Punnett's
position, see R. C. Punnett, 'As a Biologist sees it', *Nineteenth Century*, xcvii (1925),
pp. 697–707. But for an indication of the degree to which some British Mendelians
differed from Bateson, see B. J. Norton, 'Karl Pearson and the Galtonian Tradition'
(note 1), pp. 181–3.

[113] W. Coleman (note 35).

[114] See A. G. Cock, 'Bateson and Chromosomes: an Alternative View', *Abstracts of
the XVth International Congress of the History of Science* (Edinburgh, 1977), p. 198.
Judgement on the points of controversy must await the publication of Cock's full
study.

he draws is convincing. His approach is not a sociological one, in that he does not seek to relate the pattern of Bateson's thought to the social factors that might have sustained it. Nevertheless, it is one crying out for sociological interpretation.

Following the usage of the term by Mannheim,[115] Coleman characterizes Bateson's thought as 'conservative'. Here I shall, however, describe it as 'romantic-conservative', as the meaning of 'conservative' in Mannheim's sense is easily mistaken by those for whom it conjures up, for example, the image of the British Conservative Party. Indeed, romantic-conservatism is best seen as an *oppositional* stance. It is a critique of bourgeois society, although not from the point of view of a socialist future, but from that of an idealized past. Its chief characteristics can be defined precisely as the negations of the major tenets of the 'natural-law' style of thought characteristic of a progressive bourgeoisie.

For example, romantic-conservative thinkers typically oppose rationalist individualism (of which utilitarianism would be the best British example). They would elevate being over thinking, the whole over the parts, the particular over the general, the traditional over the progressive. Romantic-conservatism, if Mannheim is correct, is an anti-atomistic style of thinking: holism, organic unity, the qualitative rather than the quantitative, would be romantic-conservative preferences. Because romantic-conservatism is in a sense defined by what it opposes, Mannheim emphasizes that the work of a single romantic-conservative need not be expected to possess all these characteristics – to negate one or two key aspects of natural-law thought may be sufficient to signal opposition to bourgeois society.

Mannheim's original work concerned romantic-conservatism in Germany as it defined itself in opposition to the ideologies associated with the French revolution. Potential analogies in Britain, are, however, easy to suggest: the 'culture and society' tradition identified by Raymond Williams; Perkin's upholders of the 'aristocratic ideal'; the Christian Socialists as discussed, for example, by Levitas.[116] Romantic-conservative opposition to rampant individualism, to the depredations of capitalist industry, to the

[115] K. Mannheim, 'Conservative Thought', in his *Essays in Sociology and Social Psychology* (London, 1953), pp. 74–164.
[116] R. Williams, *Culture and Society, 1780–1850* (London, 1958); H. Perkin, *The Origins of Modern English Society* (note 107), pp. 237–52, 262–64; R. A. Levitas, 'The Social Location of Ideas', *Sociological Review*, xxiv (1976), pp. 545–57.

destruction of patriarchal order and deference – all these are surely to be found in Victorian Britain.

It is, however, perhaps a little surprising to see a leading professional scientist described as a romantic-conservative. Yet it is precisely in this way that Coleman suggests we characterize Bateson's thought. Coleman's argument rests chiefly on the 'style' of Bateson's science, on what he claims to be its emphasis on experiental concreteness and on the aesthetic, on pattern and form and on visual metaphors. Rather than discuss this general characterization, I will concentrate instead on more specific instances of overt connections of the social and the biological in Bateson's work. Before doing this, it is, however, necessary to discuss one immediate and obvious objection to any characterization of Bateson's science as romantic-conservative.

On Mannheim's schema, atomism is a general characteristic of natural-law thought, and not of romantic-conservatism, which typically counterposes holism to atomism. Yet Bateson was a Mendelian, and surely Mendelism is the archetype of reductionist atomism? The interesting point about Bateson, at least on Coleman's analysis, is, however, precisely Bateson's reluctance to accept the chromosome theory which fully developed the atomic metaphor in Mendelism by, in effect, reducing the gene to a material particle. As against this literal atomism, Bateson developed an alternative metaphor which, while still mechanical, emphasized holistic ordering rather than 'billiard ball' materialism. Animals and plants are not matter, wrote Bateson, they are 'systems through which matter is continually passing'. On this view: 'The cell ... is a vortex of chemical and molecular change ... We must press for an answer to the question, How does our vortex spontaneously divide? The study of these vortices is biology, and the place at which we must look for our answer is division'.[117] Coleman makes the interesting suggestion that the source of Bateson's alternative metaphor was the ethereal, non-material vortex atom of the Cambridge physicists. The latter have themselves been analysed by Wynne as exhibiting a romantic-conservative style of thought.[118]

Holism played an important part in Bateson's biological think-

[117] Quoted by W. Coleman (note 35), pp. 274–5.
[118] *Ibid.*, pp. 264–9; B. Wynne, 'C. G. Barkla and the J Phenomenon: a Case-Study in the Sociology of Physics' (University of Edinburgh MSc thesis, 1977); *idem* (note 59).

ing. His son Gregory writes of him: 'In the language of today, we might say that he was groping for those orderly characteristics of living things which illustrate the fact that organisms evolve and develop within cybernetic, organisational and other communicational limitations'.[119] Early letters to his sister Anna, taken together with the *Materials*, reveal William Bateson's early evolutionary thinking as centring round his dissatisfaction with what he saw as the impoverished view of the organism in orthodox Darwinism and his search for an alternative way of conceptualizing the organism as an integrated, patterned whole.[120] Orthodox Darwinism he criticized as a 'utilitarian view of the building up of Species'.[121] The manifest lack of utility of many specific characteristics, such as plumage, and the fact that many useful characteristics could only be useful if perfect (and thus could not have arisen gradually), were for him strong arguments against this 'utilitarian' selectionism.

It would perhaps be too speculative to place much weight simply on Bateson's choice of the term 'utilitarian' to describe what he opposed in accepted evolutionary theory.[122] It is interesting, however, that at precisely the time when Bateson was developing his opposition to orthodox Darwinism he was conducting his major campaign in Cambridge University politics. He was a leader of the opposition to the abolition of the compulsory entrance qualification in classical Greek. It may seem strange that a man who was a scientist and not a classical scholar should choose such an issue to devote his energies to, but for Bateson compulsory Greek was of enormous symbolic importance. At stake was the 'Classical System' as against mere 'Technical Education'. Mathematics was, he felt, compulsory for the wrong reasons: it was useful 'in trade and professions for the making of money'.[123] Greek, by comparison, was a means of social control and enculturation:

In the arid mind of many a common man there is an oasis of reverence which would not have been there if he had never read

---

[119] G. Bateson, *Steps to an Ecology of Mind* (St Albans, 1973), p. 349.
[120] W. Bateson, *Materials for the Study of Variation* (note 43); *WB* (note 3), pp. 39–43.
[121] *Ibid.*, p. 11.
[122] W. Coleman (note 35), p. 295, does suggest that for Bateson 'Darwinism hued all too closely to the blighted atomistic individualism of the utilitarians'.
[123] Quoted by J. G. Crowther, *British Scientists of the Twentieth Century* (London, 1952), p. 252.

Greek. For Society it would be dangerous, and for the common man it would be hard, if he had never stood thus once in the presence of noble and beautiful things.

Those who came to Cambridge from 'the Black Country of the commonplace' had to be exposed to the 'side of life which is not common'.[124] To remove the entrance qualification in Greek would lead to the selection for Cambridge of those who, in the words of his wife, had 'educational aims ... so utilitarian as to be properly placed outside the University pale'.[125]

Bateson's broadsheet on compulsory Greek suggests a conscious connection between his attacks on utilitarianism in education and in biology. He admitted – even boasted – that the Classical System was 'useless'. However: '... from grim analogies in Nature it must be feared that it is in just this "uselessness" that the unique virtue of the [Classical] System lies'. It seems possible that there was a link between Bateson's social defence 'of the things which are beautiful and have no "use"' and his attack on a biological utilitarianism that held that: 'living beings are plastic conglomerates of miscellaneous attributes, and that order of form or Symmetry have been impressed upon this medley by Selection alone'. The link may have been a common concern for the necessary conditions of holistic order and stability, whether social or biological, as against exclusive concern for the 'useful'; for 'physiological co-ordination' rather than 'malignant individualism'.[126]

One expression of Bateson's hostility to orthodox Darwinism was thus his development of a holistic view of the organism which emphasized those aspects of it, the phenomena of pattern and symmetry in particular, that could not be seen as 'useful'. The publicly more prominent aspect was, of course, his championing of discontinuity. Here again, the social and the biological intermingled in his writings. He opposed, both socially and biologically, the biometric view of evolution as an orderly, predictable process based on gradual changes in the aggregate. Real advance came, he felt, from rare and largely unpredictable discontinuities, whether the appearance of a 'sport' in biology or an exceptional 'genius' in society. The 'genius' and the 'sport' were indeed identified:

[124] *WB* (note 3), p. 48.
[125] *Ibid.*, p. 49.
[126] *Ibid.*, pp. 48, 433; W. Bateson (note 43), p. 80; *WB* (note 3) pp. 315, 316, 348.

It is upon mutational novelties, definite favourable variations, that all progress in civilisation and in the control of natural forces must depend.

... we have come to recognise that evolutionary change proceeds not by fluctuations in the characters of the mass, but by the predominance of sporadic and special strains possessing definite characteristics.[127]

Given the crucial role of eugenics in expressing the connection between society and biology in the work of the biometric school, Bateson's position on eugenics takes on particular interest. Bateson was just as much of a hereditarian as any of the eugenists, and quite happy to interpret class differences in genetic terms. He showed no compassion for most of those on whom the practice of negative eugenics was proposed. He wrote of the 'feebleminded': 'The union of such social vermin we should no more permit than we would allow parasites to breed on our own bodies'. Eugenics disquieted him, however. Its reforming nature was alien to his pessimistic conservatism: 'The kind of thing I say on such occasions [talks on eugenics] is what no reformer wants to hear, and the Eugenic ravens are croaking for Reform'. He disliked what he saw as the narrowly middle-class values of the eugenics movement: 'Consistent and portentous selfishness, combined with dullness of imagination are probably just as transmissible as want of self-control, though destitute of the amiable qualities not rarely associated with the genetic composition of persons of unstable mind'. He would 'shudder', he said, when he read Galton's condemnations of 'Bohemianism'. He suggested that Galton had too much respect for 'material success'.

In the eugenic paradise I hope and believe that there will be room for the man who works by fits and starts, though Galton does say that he is a futile person who can no longer earn his living and ought to be abolished. The pressure of the world on the families of unbusinesslike Bohemians, artists, musicians, authors, discoverers and inventors, is serious enough in all conscience ... Broadcloth, bank balances and the other appurtenances of the bay-tree type of righteousness are not really essentials of the eugenic ideal ... I imagine that by the exercise of continuous eugenic caution the world might have lost Beethoven and Keats, perhaps even Francis Bacon, and that a system might find

[127] *WB* (note 3), pp. 353, 354; see also pp. 296, 309.

advocates under which the poet Hayley would be passed and his friends Blake and Cowper rejected.

Bateson, then, was torn. Eugenic measures might well be in the interests of the 'intellectual and professional class' to which he belonged. Yet their success might merely continue the process of the encroachment of utilitarian rationalization and modernization against which he had set himself. Whatever his private motives for opposing eugenics – several of those to whom I talked in seeking information about Bateson told me that his own pedigree was eugenically dubious – the stated grounds for his opposition fit in well with his overall romantic-conservatism.[128]

It is important to state clearly that in describing Bateson as a romantic-conservative I am not saying that he was simply a Tory. That is not the case. In fact in his youth he actively supported a Liberal parliamentary candidate, though later he became disillusioned with party politics. Unlike the fiercely imperialist Pearson and conventional Weldon, Bateson opposed the Boer War and the vulgar commercialism that he felt lay behind British involvement: Bateson 'is a fanatical pro-Boer', wrote Weldon to Pearson.[129] The personal tragedy of the loss of a son in the First World War did not turn him into an anti-German jingo: he bravely upheld scientific internationalism and reserved his scorn for the 'army contractors' and 'newspaper patriots'.[130] Bateson thus shared many of the strands of left-wing opposition to capitalist imperialism.

Yet his distaste for the 'sordid shopkeeper utility'[131] characteristic of capitalism did not make him a socialist. When his sister Anna was thinking of setting up a market garden, he chided her in a letter: 'I think it always a "regrettable incident" when persons whose parents have got clear of trade, relapse into it'.[132] As Cock suggests, he may have been teasing, but the assumption that lay behind the tease – that 'trade' was to be despised – surfaces again and again in Bateson's writing. Industrial capitalism he condemned as socially unnatural – it made too many concessions to egalitarianism – and ecologically doomed in its dependence on fossil fuel.

---

[128] *Ibid.*, pp. 129, 388, 374, 374–5, 377, 387; see also pp. 304–5.

[129] Weldon to Pearson, 16 February 1902, Pearson Papers, 625; University College London.

[130] *WB* (note 3), p. 374.

[131] *Ibid.*, p. 433.

[132] 31 July 1889, quoted by A. G. Cock, 'Anna Bateson of Bashley: Britain's First Professional Woman Gardener', *Hampshire: the County Magazine*, xix (1979), p. 61.

Instead, 'we recognise in the feudal system a nearer approach to the *natural* plan'. 'We have abolished the Middle Age conception of the State as composed of classes permanently graded, with the ladder of lords rising from the *minuti homines* below to the king on his throne, and yet to such stratification, after each successive disturbance, society tends to return'.[133]

Is it possible to give a precise social location for British romantic-conservatism, such as that exemplified by Bateson? In the German situation discussed by Mannheim it seems that, as one might expect, the landed aristocracy formed the ultimate 'market' whose ideological needs were satisfied by romantic-conservative intellectuals. But at least in the period discussed here, the British aristocracy was predominantly in a situation of accommodation with, rather than opposition to, the bourgeoisie.[134] An attack on industrial capitalism was hardly in the interests of late nineteenth-century British landowners, most of whose income depended directly or indirectly on industry.

In any case, Bateson himself cannot realistically be seen as a propagandist for the aristocracy. He held the old aristocracy in high regard, believing it to have been superior to the middle class, but had no illusions in it as a contemporary social force: 'The old aristocracy has largely gone under, not because it had no great qualities, but because those qualities were not of a kind that count for much in the modern world'.[135] Nor was his social background aristocratic, though it certainly was élite. Both his grandfathers were Liverpool businessmen,[136] and his father, W. H. Bateson, was Master of St John's College, Cambridge, and a leading university reformer and Liberal.

If Bateson's romantic-conservatism can be linked to an actual social institution it must in fact surely be Cambridge University. This formed the background of his life from birth – his father had

---

[133] *WB* (note 3), p. 456 (emphasis added); *ibid.*, p. 354.

[134] See, for example, B. Moore, *Social Origins of Dictatorship and Democracy: Lord and Peasant in the Making of the Modern World* (Boston, 1967), pp. 3–39.

[135] *WB* (note 3), pp. 312, 417.

[136] Apparently on this basis, Crowther (note 123), especially pp. 256, 289, suggests that Bateson should be placed among the class of *rentiers*. He puts forward an interesting but quite unsupported hypothesis that Bateson's early break with evolutionary embryology was connected with his rentier background and with the association of comparative embryology with the landed class through the person of F. M. Balfour and through the aristocratic nature of Balfour's College, Trinity. In the absence of any evidence this suggestion is rather difficult to assess.

already been Vice-Chancellor of Cambridge University before William was born – to his forty-ninth year, when he finally left Cambridge for the security and resources provided by the Directorship of the John Innes Horticultural Institution. The political energies of Bateson's prime were to a significant degree channelled into defending Cambridge University's integrity and élite, anti-utilitarian ethos.[137] His defence of traditional Cambridge was in spite of the fact that his personal career in the University was largely unsuccessful. He never reached the prominent position of his father, and for a long time relied on marginal posts (such as the Stewardship of St John's College) in order not to have to seek employment outside the University.

It is clear that several options were open to Bateson. He could, for example, have chosen to press for Cambridge University to 'move with the times', become 'relevant', and so on, and in doing so could have hoped that this would have improved his own insecure position. In adopting an anti-utilitarian, anti-reforming conservatism, he can be seen as making a genuine choice.[138] Nevertheless, it was a choice between options that were themselves formed by the social structure. He was choosing to defend, rather than reform, a given social institution. He was choosing opposition to, rather than furtherance of, a given process of industrialization and modernization. So it makes sense to see his romantic-conservatism as socially conditioned, as one response to a given set of social circumstances, even if not, at the level of Bateson as a concrete individual, socially determined. Although the generality of the conservative response is not crucial to this argument, it is interesting to note that Wynne finds it to be prominent amongst Cambridge dons of Bateson's generation.[139]

---

[137] On one issue Bateson was a 'progressive'. He was in favour of the admission of women to Cambridge degrees. Why he should have felt that this did not violate the Cambridge ethos I do not know; Beatrice Bateson suggests that the reason may lie in his home background, with its acceptance of academic careers for women, *WB* (note 3), pp. 59–60.

[138] Of course, had we more information about his early life, psychological make-up and so on, we might no longer see this choice as free. The point, however, is that it would be mistaken to see Bateson's social background as determining what he as an individual chose to do. See B. J. Norton (note 1), pp. 187–8.

[139] B. Wynne (note 118), pp. 38–89; see also S. Rothblatt, *The Revolution of the Dons* (London, 1968). It is interesting to contrast this response with Pearson's call for Cambridge University to become more technologically-oriented and up-to-date, K. Pearson, 'A Plea for the Establishment of a Technical Laboratory at Cambridge', *The Cambridge University Magazine*, no. 15 (1886), pp. 173–4.

## SOCIOBIOLOGIES IN COMPETITION

In the first part of this paper, I put forward evidence to suggest that the biometrician-Mendelian dispute was partly grounded in the 'internal' social structure of science. Groups of scientists with large investments in particular skills would typically be reluctant, it was suggested, to accept scientific approaches that implied the devaluation of these skills. This may explain, for example, the clash of 'mathematical' and 'traditional biological' methodologies. In the second part of the paper, it was suggested that a further factor of importance was that the theories of heredity and evolution put forward by the two sides carried, in the context of the time, particular social 'messages'.

A few final words about this second facet of the controversy are perhaps in order. Both Pearson and Bateson were following what might be described as a *sociobiological* strategy: both were advocating or defending particular social arrangements as in accord with nature. It was Bateson who commented that 'the knowledge needed for the right direction of social progress must be gained by biological observation and experiment',[140] but there is no evidence that he was uttering anything other than a common-place. Certainly, while one can find participants in the controversy who seem to have been *indifferent* to the sociobiological strategy (Weldon, for example), I have found none that condemned the strategy as *invalid*.[141]

The point of my account is that the lack of clear challenge to the general sociobiological strategy did not extend to agreement on what nature was like or on what social arrangements were actually in accord with nature. Further, this disagreement was patterned. On the one hand, we find in the writings of the biometric school the view of nature as orderly, predictable and in gradual mass progress alongside the advocacy of orderly, predictable and gradual collective social change, particularly through eugenic improvement of the innate characteristics of entire human populations. On the

[140] *WB* (note 3), p. 334.
[141] It is difficult to find a *scientist* of the time who unequivocally opposed the sociobiological strategy. T. H. Huxley's *Evolution and Ethics* (London, 1893), commonly taken as the classic instance of such opposition, has recently been reinterpreted as a contribution to sociobiological argument rather than as a complete rejection of it. See M. S. Helfand, 'T. H. Huxley's *Evolution and Ethics*: the Politics of Evolution and the Evolution of Politics', *Victorian Studies*, xx (1977), pp. 159–77.

other hand, in the writings of Bateson we find the view of biological evolution as the result of the sporadic appearance of qualitatively different varieties alongside the claim that all that is socially worthwhile springs from the unpredictable appearance of genius; the view that the organism is holistically ordered alongside the view that society ought to be similarly ordered; even the view of evolution as loss[142] alongside the condemnation of what the conventional called progress.

It can thus simply be noted that the biometric school and Bateson constructed different biologies and used them in defence of different social arrangements. Sometimes the role of this context of use in the detailed construction and assessment of knowledge is explicit, as in the biometric school's judgement of the eugenic potential of Mendelism. At other times we may find clues – such as Bateson's use of the term 'utilitarian' to describe what he disliked in both biological theorizing and social organization – but at present lack sufficient evidence to make definitive statements. Nevertheless, I feel that on balance there is a good case for the conclusion that the scientific judgements of those involved in the controversy cannot properly be understood in isolation from the sociobiological use of the knowledge they produced.

Further, these two competing sociobiologies have been analysed as expressing the interests of different social groups. Gradual and orderly reform, made predictable by the guidance of experts and exemplified by cautious eugenic intervention was, I have argued, an appropriate programme for the rising class of professional experts. And defence of the individual genius against the mediocre mass, and of the value of stable hierarchy and tradition, was what one would expect from the romantic-conservative critics of bourgeois progress.[143]

As has been argued elsewhere,[144] this is a structural rather than an individual imputation. It is not my claim, for example, that all

---

[142] This latter is an idea with which Bateson toyed. See *WB* (note 3), pp. 212, 285–96.

[143] It is interesting that a recent study of the Velikovsky controversy has suggested broadly similar connections: see R. McAulay, 'Velikovsky and the Infrastructure of Science: the Metaphysics of a Close Encounter', *Theory and Society*, vi (1978), pp. 313–42. Velikovsky and his followers are portrayed by McAulay as romantic-conservative catastrophists and their opponents within the scientific community as progressive uniformitarians of a type similar to Pearson.

[144] B. Barnes, *Interests and the Growth of Knowledge* (London and Henley, 1977), pp. 58–63.

individual biometricians were rising professionals motivated by meritocratic ambitions. All I suggest is that biometry was an appropriate world view for such a professional group, and that it was actually used in furtherance of this group's interests. Similarly, my claim is merely that Bateson's biology was an appropriate account of nature for romantic-conservatives, and that it was used to advocate a form of society congenial to their interests. I do not feel justified in going beyond these claims into the realm of the deterministic explanation of individual behaviour or the imputation of individual motives. Nevertheless, if these claims are true, and if the sociobiological context of use did indeed structure the production and evaluation of knowledge, then we have here an instance of the detailed connection of social interests and scientific knowledge.

# 8. *Psychologists and Class*

## BERNARD NORTON

This paper traces the development of a view of British society which found its most complete expression in the works of the late Sir Cyril Burt (1883–1971). In this view we are all seen as hereditarily endowed with a certain level of 'general intelligence', which, by turn, is seen as a main determinant of social position within the hierarchy of occupational classes. The barest essentials of the view, which, in effect, turns class into a biological phenomenon, will be familiar to all who have encountered Burt's famous table of I.Q.s reproduced in table 1.[1]

Table 1. *Intelligence of parents and children classified according to occupations*

| | Occupational category | Average intelligence quotient | |
| --- | --- | --- | --- |
| | | Children | Adults |
| Class I | Higher professional: administrative | 120.3 | 153.2 |
| Class II | Lower professional: technical | | |
| | executive | 114.6 | 132.4 |
| Class III | Highly skilled: clerical | 109.7 | 117.1 |
| Class IV | Skilled | 104.5 | 108.6 |
| Class V | Semi-skilled | 98.2 | 97.5 |
| Class VI | Unskilled | 92.0 | 86.8 |
| Class VII | Casual | 89.1 | 81.6 |
| Class VIII | Institutional | 67.2 | 57.3 |

There are very solid grounds for supposing that this image of society has had a considerable influence upon society at large. The mass sales of the more popular works of Eysenck[2] and Herrnstein[3] suggest that the Burtian message is well known to the general reader and book-stall browser. On a different plane, we know that

[1] This table appeared in Burt's paper 'Ability and income', *British Journal for Educational Psychology*, xiii (1943), pp. 83–98. Burt discussed the sources of his data on pp. 83–84.
[2] See, for example, the use made of Burt's work in H. Eysenck, *The Inequality of Man* (London, 1973), see especially chap. 4.
[3] See, for example, R. J. Herrnstein, *I.Q. in the Meritocracy* (Boston, 1973).

Burt's views were much solicited by government functionaries. In 1938, for example, the Consultative Committee on Secondary Education put its collective name to the following proposition upon Burt's advice.[4]

Intellectual development during childhood appears to progress as if it were governed by a single central factor, usually known as 'general intelligence', which may be broadly described as innate all-round intellectual ability. It appears to enter into everything which the child attempts to think, or say, or do, and seems on the whole to be the most important factor in determining his work in the classroom.

In later years, when the eleven-plus examination, which was partly (but only partly) based upon this advice, came under attack, the Burtian view could be mobilized in its defence. There was no point in complaining that it sent a lower proportion of lower than of middle-class children to prestigious grammar schools when it had been scientifically shown that talent was more thinly spread among the working than among the middle classes. If anything was unfair, the Burtians could claim, it was the facts of biology, not the policies of middle-class administrators.[5] At the same time, of course, the Burtian view could also be used to argue that the absolute numbers of working-class children gaining admission to universities was lower than it should have been were the Burtian ideal of pure meritocracy to be the order of the day.[6] As we shall see, the two claims were quite compatible.

Something which makes this whole issue particularly interesting is the circumstance that Burt's theories are now known to have rested upon fraudulent data. It appears that, in the Burt theory, we are faced with a scientific fraud which escaped detection by the psychological profession for a very long time (a circumstance not

---

[4] *Report of the Consultative Committee on Secondary Education* (London, H.M.S.O., 1938), pp. 123–4. In the *Report*, the extracts given here were italicized. The pervasive influence of Burt can also be seen in his major contributions to the earlier *Report of the Consultative Committee on Psychological Tests of Educable Capacity and Their Possible Use in the Public System of Education* (London, H.M.S.O., 1924).

[5] See, e.g., H. Eysenck, 'The rise of the mediocracy', in C. B. Cox and A. E. Dyson, (eds.), *Black Paper Two* (London, 1969). In the same volume, we may find Richard Lynn, an Irish psychology professor, claiming that (p. 30): 'slum dwellers are caused principally by low innate intelligence and poor family upbringing'. In writing this, he attempts to counter the view that 'it is the fault of society that slum dwellers are impoverished and their children do badly at school'. Burt's work is cited as evidence for this.

[6] This point was made in C. Burt, 'Ability and Income', *British Journal for Educational Psychology*, xiii (1943), pp. 83–98, especially see p. 98.

less interesting than the fact of fraud itself), and which was widely used to support policies and to orientate the thinking of a large public.[7]

In many ways, of course, the most significant aspect of the whole affair is the question of how much influence was exercised by the Burtians. One day, we will have an answer – an answer which does not assume that whenever a government's actions fall into line with 'expert' advice, it is legitimate to assume that the advice was the cause of the actions (it may be that governments select those experts whose views will merely reinforce already decided policy lines).[8] For the moment however, hoping like Locke's under-labourer to clear the ground for a grander edifice, I will attempt simply to describe, and wherever possible to explain, the growth of this socially significant theory. Overall, I shall wish to suggest that the Burtian perspective originated in the eugenical thought of Charles Darwin's cousin Francis Galton (1822–1911), that, in Galton's formulation the perspective was an ill-grounded fantasy, and that the development from earlier (Galtonian) to later (Burtian) versions of the perspective was largely the work of men who shared Galton's political perspectives and who worked as they did because of these political beliefs.

FRANCIS GALTON AND 'NATURAL ABILITY'

Every social group is prone to develop ideals and virtues which its members have some chance of exhibiting. Nineteenth-century Britain was remarkable for the emergence of a professional middle class which made a great virtue of intellectual merit. Annan[9] has written of the 'Intellectual Aristocracy', and we may discover Trevelyan and Northcote[10] urging that men be selected for high government service on grounds of 'intelligence' as well as grounds of mere attainments.

Amongst this aristocracy was numbered Francis Galton, related by

---

[7] The most complete exposure of Burt's data was made by Leon Kamin in his *Science and Politics of I.Q.* (Potomac, 1974); see also O. Gillie, 'Sir Cyril Burt and the Great I.Q. Fraud', *New Statesman* (24 November 1978), pp. 688–94. An exciting analysis for Burt's data on intelligence and social mobility is given in D. D. Dorfman, 'The Cyril Burt question: further findings', *Science*, cci (1978), pp. 1177–85.
[8] This is Kamin's suggestion. See article on Kamin, in the *Guardian* (6 November 1979).
[9] N. Annan, 'The intellectual aristocracy', in J. H. Plumb (ed.), *Studies in Social History: a Tribute to G. M. Trevelyan* (London, 1955).
[10] This point is discussed in Keith Hope's forthcoming *Political Conception of Merit*.

blood and marriage to some of its grandest families – the Darwins, the Wedgwoods and the Butlers. Galton, influenced by the achievements of his family and friends, by what he took to be the low intellect of African natives and by his cousin's *Origin of Species*, became the father of eugenics, a creed which held that talent and character were hereditarily rather than environmentally determined, and that the chief desire of the good man should be that of procuring the evolutionary advance of his species by selective breeding from the talented.[11] Eugenics, clearly, had a religious aspect for Galton, but, in the search for empirical support for the main testaments of eugenics, he was led into statistical, biological and, importantly, psychological researches. He is, in fact, generally regarded as the father of individual psychology – that branch of psychology which concerns itself with the nature and distribution of differences between persons in respect of intelligence and personality. Cyril Burt was later to write of Galton that he came to differential psychology at a time when it was a subject fit only for the 'quack and charlatan', and left it in a transformed state,[12] as a 'reputable branch of natural science – perhaps for mankind the most important branch there is'.

Galton himself did not speak of 'intelligence', but of vaguer entities, such as 'natural ability' and 'civic worth'. He was, however, in no doubt that these qualities would follow a normal or Gaussian distribution in the population, arguing from analogy with stature, which could be empirically proven to be thus. Equally important, one supposes, was Galton's long devotion to the normal curve, which he saw as the 'supreme law of unreason', as something which the Greeks would have deified had they known of it.[13] What precisely Galton meant by 'natural ability' was never made entirely clear, though it was, in one account, characterized by the trio of zeal, capacity and power of work. Thus, in *Hereditary Genius*, he wrote as follows.[14]

[11] For details of Galton see K. Pearson, *The Life, Letters and Labours of Francis Galton*, 3 vols. (Cambridge, 1914–1930).

[12] C. Burt, 'Francis Galton and his Contributions to Psychology', *British Journal of Statistical Psychology*, xv (1962), pp. 1–49, especially p. 41.

[13] For a discussion of the role of the normal curve in sociobiology, see V. Hilts, 'Statistics and social science' in R. Giere and S. Westfall (eds.), *Foundations of Scientific Method in the Nineteenth Century* (Bloomington, 1973). For Galton's 'reverence' for the normal curve, see F. Galton, *Natural Inheritance* (London, 1889), p. 66.

[14] F. Galton, *Hereditary Genius*, 2nd edn. (London, 1892), p. 33.

By natural ability I mean those qualities of intellect and dispo-
sition, which urge and qualify a man to perform acts that lead to
reputation. I do not mean capacity without zeal, nor zeal without
capacity, nor even a combination of both of them, without an
adequate power of doing a very great deal of very laborious work.
But I mean a nature which, when left to itself, will, urged by an
inherent stimulus, climb the path that leads to eminence, and has
strength to reach the summit – one which, if hindered or
thwarted, will fret and strive until the hindrance is overcome and
it is again free to follow its labour-loving instinct. It is almost a
contradiction in terms, to doubt that such men will generally
become eminent. On the other hand, there is plenty of evidence
in this volume to show that few have won high reputations
without possessing these peculiar gifts. It follows that men who
achieve eminence and those who are naturally capable, are, to a
large extent, identical.

On other occasions, Galton became a little more specific, showing
that his thinking had two tracks – power of sensory discrimination
and 'energy'. Sensory power as a component of natural ability was
discussed in his *Inquiries into Human Faculty* of 1883, where he
argued that the senses were the only sources of information, and,
consequently, that 'the more perceptive the senses are of difference,
the larger is the field upon which our judgement and intelligence
can act'.[15] Idiots, he wrote, had a low discriminatory power,
whereas a former Lord Chancellor had the most amazing power.
With other evidence, this seemed to point to a superior sensory
power on the part of the gifted, and Galton concluded that 'a
delicate power of sense discrimination is an attribute of a high race,
and that it has not the drawback of being necessarily associated
with nervous irritability'.[16] Thoughts on energy appeared in the
same work: it too was described as the attribute of higher races,
and, moreover, was depicted as an outstanding characteristic of
men of science, and of high significance. 'In any scheme of eugenics,
energy is the most important quality to favour; it is, as we have
seen, the basis of living action, and it is eminently transmissible by
descent'.[17] Finally, therefore, it would seem that Galton's idea
of natural ability was one compounded out of notions of energy

[15] F. Galton, *Inquiries into Human Faculty* (London, 1883), p. 19.
[16] *Ibid.*, p. 23.
[17] *Ibid.*, p. 19.

and of fine sensory powers. Unfortunately, he provided no clear account of how the two worked together, and we must conclude that his thoughts on 'natural ability' were painfully vague, albeit highly suggestive. Certainly, it is worth noting that Galton himself, propelled no doubt by the prospects of explicating ability in terms of a refined sensory apparatus, carried out surveys of the keenness of sight and hearing, reaction time, and so on. In this work he was followed by the American psychologist James McKeen Cattell and others, but all of these failed to find any easy connections between sensory powers and intelligence.[18]

As if to compound the confusion surrounding 'natural ability',

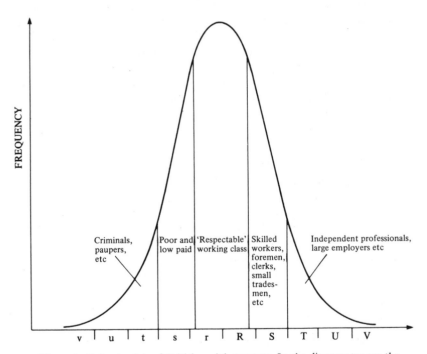

Figure 1. Galton's view of British social structure. In the diagram we see the 'respectable working class' clustered about the mid-point of civic worth. Class V is constituted by the upper fraction of the talented, existing at the frequency of 35 per 10,000 of population. The intervals along the x axis of the graph are multiples of what now is called the 'standard deviation' of the distribution – in this case, of the rather vague 'civic worth'.

[18] For an informative discussion see the chapter on Galton in R. Fancher, *Pioneers of Psychology* (New York, 1979).

Galton introduced another, parallel term, 'civic worth', most notably in his Huxley lecture of 1901 on 'The possible improvement of the human breed under existing conditions of law and sentiment'.[19] Here, Galton expressly identified levels of civic worth – equatable roughly, one supposes, with 'natural ability' – with the different social classes discussed by Charles Booth the statistician and sociologist in his recently produced studies of urban life. The basic features of this identification have been neatly summarized in a diagram due to Don MacKenzie, and this is reproduced in figure 1.[20] Once again we see Galton's commitment to the normal curve of distribution at work.

Galton's views on the sources of talent ran ahead of his times. For, while, in the 1890s, Herbert Spencer was locked with August Weismann over the issue of whether acquired characters might be transmitted in heredity, Galton had long been averring that there was no such inheritance,[21] and, moreover, that in mental and moral characters, what was acquired in heredity could be little changed by environmental means. Indeed, a reading of Galton's works makes it clear that for most of his adult life he was a thoroughgoing genetic Calvinist – seeing all aspects of character and behaviour, and many aspects of social and economic success as determined by the information carried in the mother's egg and the father's sperm. This genetic Calvinism was a sophisticated construction, and nowhere can its sophistication be seen to better effect than in Galton's account of social mobility. By Victorian times, social mobility was a well-established fact of life. Samuel Smiles recorded and lauded it, and, were this insufficient, Galton was brought face to face with a leading example of the process at his Cambridge college, where the master was none other than the formidable Dr William Whewell, risen to great things from a humble background.[22]

The problem which faced Galton was a difficult one. How could

[19] F. Galton, 'The Possible Improvement of the Human Breed', reproduced in F. Galton, *Essays in Eugenics* (London, 1909).

[20] D. MacKenzie, 'Eugenics in Britain', *Social Studies of Science*, vi (1976), pp. 499–532.

[21] This matter is discussed in Pearson's biography (note 11); Galton's views on heredity seem to have been decided by the time he wrote his 'Hereditary talent and character', *MacMillan's Magazine*, xii (1865), pp. 157–77, 318–27.

[22] Galton's feelings for Whewell were recorded in F. Galton, *Memories of my Life* (London, 1908), p. 60.

one reconcile the supposed hereditary determination of social success with the observable facts of social mobility? In practice, dealing with this was simple. For, early in his career Galton had discovered the phenomenon of regression – finding, for example, that in the matter of human stature, sons showed just two-thirds (on the average) of the deviation of their mid-parents (a sort of mother and father average height). Thus, for example, Galton found that mothers and fathers deviating from the average stature of the nation by, say, $+9$ in would yield a set of sons deviating, *on the average*, by only $\frac{2}{3} \times 9 = 6$ in. Obviously, not all the sons showed a deviation of exactly 6 in, and Galton was able to show that these sons would be normally distributed about this point with a calculable variance or 'spread'. In the case of parents deviating by $-9$ in, the set of sons produced would centre on a mean of 6 in deviation in the negative sense.

All of this may be seen clearly in Galton's famous correlation table (see table 2) for the inheritance of stature – a table in which he recorded the offspring produced by parentages of different heights.[23] Statisticians will note that the distribution is approximately bivariate normal.

The same model, applied to talent, Galton considered, would both explain social mobility and show the limits to inter-generational social mobility set by the facts of social biology. The full application of the biological model to class and social mobility can be seen in another of Galton's tables reproduced in table 3.[24] In the table, which relates back to Galton's 'normal' curve of society, class V corresponds to the upper fraction of the middle classes, with only thirty-five out of every 10,000 members of the population falling into that band of talent. These thirty-five, by regression, would produce only six offspring of equivalent talent, and we see the numbers of class V being made up in the next generation by ten promotions from parentages of class U and by a further ten from class T. Yet, to provide these twenty promotions, 851 parentages of grades U and T are required. Quite generally, it was Galton's view that regression ensured that the bulk of top class persons would come from less than top-class origins, but, the lower down the scale one went, the lower was the *relative frequency* of promotions. One cannot be certain to what extent

[23] Taken from F. Galton, *Natural Inheritance* (London, 1889), p. 208.
[24] Taken from F. Galton (note 19), p. 14.

Table 2. *Number of adult children of various statures born of 205 mid-parents of various statures (all female heights have been multiplied by 1.08)*

| Height of the mid-parents in inches | Heights of the adult children | | | | | | | | | | | | | | Total number of | | Medians or values of M |
|---|---|---|---|---|---|---|---|---|---|---|---|---|---|---|---|---|---|
| | Below | 62·2 | 63·2 | 64·2 | 65·2 | 66·2 | 67·2 | 68·2 | 69·2 | 70·2 | 71·2 | 72·2 | 73·2 | Above | Adult children | Mid-parents | |
| Above 72·5 | — | — | — | — | — | — | — | — | — | — | 1 | 3 | — | — | 4 | 5[a] | — |
| 72·5 | — | — | — | — | — | — | 1 | 2 | 1 | 2 | 7 | 2 | 4 | — | 19 | 6 | 72·2 |
| 71·5 | — | — | — | 1 | 3 | 4 | 3 | 5 | 10 | 4 | 9 | 2 | 2 | — | 43 | 11 | 69·9 |
| 70·5 | 1 | — | 1 | 1 | — | 1 | 3 | 12 | 18 | 14 | 7 | 4 | 3 | 3 | 68 | 22 | 69·5 |
| 69·5 | — | 1 | 16 | 4 | 17 | 27 | 20 | 33 | 25 | 20 | 11 | 4 | 5 | — | 183 | 41 | 68·9 |
| 68·5 | 1 | 7 | 11 | 16 | 25 | 31 | 34 | 48 | 21 | 18 | 4 | 3 | — | — | 219 | 49 | 68·2 |
| 67·5 | — | 3 | 5 | 14 | 15 | 36 | 38 | 28 | 38 | 19 | 11 | 4 | 3 | — | 211 | 33 | 67·6 |
| 66·5 | 1 | 3 | 3 | 5 | 2 | 17 | 17 | 14 | 13 | 4 | — | — | — | — | 78 | 20 | 67·2 |
| 65·5 | 1 | 3 | 9 | 5 | 7 | 11 | 11 | 7 | 7 | 5 | 2 | — | — | — | 66 | 12 | 66·7 |
| 64·5 | 1 | 1 | 4 | 4 | 1 | 5 | 5 | 2 | 2 | — | — | 1 | — | — | 23 | 5 | 65·8 |
| Below 64·5 | — | 2 | 2 | 4 | 1 | 2 | 2 | 1 | 1 | — | — | — | — | — | 14 | 1 | — |
| Totals | 5 | 7 | 32 | 59 | 48 | 117 | 138 | 120 | 167 | 99 | 64 | 41 | 17 | 14 | 928 | 205 | |
| Medians | — | 66·3 | 67·8 | 67·9 | 67·7 | 67·9 | 68·3 | 68·5 | 69·0 | 69·0 | 70·0 | — | — | — | | | |

Note. In calculating the medians, the entries have been taken as referring to the middle of the squares in which they stand. The reason why the headings run 62·2, 63·2, etc., instead of 62·5, 63·5, etc., is that the observations are unequally distributed between 62 and 63, 63 and 64, etc., there being a strong bias in favour of integral inches. After careful consideration, I concluded that the headings, as adopted, best satisfied the conditions. This inequality was not apparent in the case of the mid-parents.

[a] I have reprinted this Table without alteration from that published in the *Proc. Roy. Soc.*, notwithstanding a small blunder since discovered in sorting the entries between the first and second lines. It is obvious that four children cannot have five mid-parents. The first line is not considered at all, on account of the paucity of the numbers it contains. The bottom line, which looks suspicious, is correct.

Table 3. *Descent of qualities in a population (the difference between the sexes only affects the value of the unit of the scale of distribution)*

| | Fathers/Mothers of class | v | u | t | s | r | R | S | T | U | V | Totals |
|---|---|---|---|---|---|---|---|---|---|---|---|---|
| **Per 100 father (or mothers)** | | | 2 | 7 | 16 | 25 | 25 | 16 | 7 | 2 | | 100 |
| **Per 10,000 fathers or mothers** | | 35 | 180 | 671 | 1614 | 2500 | 2500 | 1614 | 671 | 180 | 35 | 10,000 |
| **Names of classes** | | v | u | t | s | r | R | S | T | U | V | Sons (or daughters) |
| Sons of class — V | 35 | | | | | | 1 | 6 | 12 | 10 | 6 | 35 |
| U | 180 | | | | | 4 | 20 | 52 | 61 | 33 | 10 | 180 |
| T | 671 | | | | 7 | 44 | 150 | 234 | 170 | 57 | 10 | 672 |
| S | 1614 | | | 6 | 57 | 253 | 512 | 509 | 224 | 47 | 5 | 1613 |
| R | 2500 | | 3 | 42 | 248 | 678 | 860 | 510 | 140 | 18 | 3 | 2502 |
| Daughters of class — r | 2500 | 3 | 18 | 140 | 510 | 860 | 678 | 248 | 42 | 3 | | 2502 |
| s | 1614 | 5 | 47 | 224 | 509 | 512 | 253 | 57 | 6 | | | 1613 |
| t | 671 | 10 | 57 | 170 | 234 | 150 | 44 | 7 | | | | 672 |
| u | 180 | 10 | 33 | 61 | 52 | 20 | 4 | | | | | 180 |
| v | 35 | 6 | 10 | 12 | 6 | 1 | | | | | | 35 |
| **Total 10,000 Fathers (or Mothers)** | | 34 | 168 | 655 | 1623 | 2522 | 2522 | 1623 | 655 | 168 | 34 | 10004 |
| **Total 100 Fathers (or Mothers)** | | | 2 | 7 | 16 | 25 | 25 | 16 | 7 | 2 | | |

Conditions (1) parents to be always alike in class, (2) statistics of population to continue unchanged, and (3) normal law of frequency to be applicable throughout.

Note, the agreement in distribution between fathers (or mothers) and sons (or daughters) is exact to the nearest whole percentage. The slight discrepancy in the ten-thousandths is mainly due to the classes being too few and too wide; theoretically they should be extremely numerous and narrow.

Galton thought of his table as descriptive of social reality in Victorian times and to what extent he was describing the course of events in a pure meritocracy. But, judging from the text of the 1901 essay and from Galton's apparent satisfaction with much of the social *status quo*,[25] it seems reasonable to suppose that he saw his table as at least an approximately correct representation of Victorian society.

Here, in the phenomenon of regression and its putative application to social mobility, we have the dual aspect of Galton's thinking. On the one hand, there is its radical aspect – for it insists that, in a meritocracy, the sons of the gifted must expect to sink on occasions. On the other hand, there is a conservative aspect – for the model insists upon the biological impossibility of anything like full social mobility; on the impossibility, that is, of there being no correlation between fathers' and sons' social classes. In the field of education, to take a particular example, the model insists that even under the best of educational circumstances, only a very few children of the manual working classes, relatively speaking, could hope for advancement to high places in the occupational hierarchy.

This then, was the model of society and of social mobility which Galton offered, sometimes, admittedly, without distinguishing too carefully between the world he saw and the world he desired. We see easily that it was based on the most insecure of foundations, for Galton lacked a number of crucial items. He had no evidence for supposing any clear-cut relation between class and ability: he had no clear account of intelligence, 'natural ability' or 'civic worth': he had no satisfactory theory of inheritance, no reason to suppose that the regression observed in stature would be paralleled by intelligence, nor, in fact, did he have any very solid grounds for supposing ability to be the product of nature rather than of nurture. Yet, over the fifty years following on Galton's death, a range of very distinguished scientists set to work to remedy these faulty timbers and to refloat the Galtonian view as the Burtian view. The remainder of this paper will reflect upon this long drawn out act of refurbishment, analysing some of the most important moves and seeking the motivations of the men involved.

[25] The quotation indicated by note 14 is a clear indication of this tendency in Galton's thoughts.

'INTELLIGENCE' DEFINED AND MEASURED

In the absence of any clear theory of intelligence, Galton's view of society remained painfully vague. It is well known that the first modern schemes for the scientific *measurement* of intelligence came upon the scene in the early twentieth century, emerging not from the laboratories of Galton's immediate followers – who tended to pursue the grail of simple sensory tests of intelligence – but from the work of the Frenchmen Binet and Simon,[26] who laboured in order to provide the French authorities with a proper way of making allocations to special schools. These tests, presented from 1904 to 1911, sampled the child's abilities in a range of 'practical' situations and gave birth to ideas of 'chronological' and 'mental' age, and, thereby to their quotient, the famous I.Q. In the writings of Binet and Simon the question of what it was that the tests measured was not answered with any rigour and, by default, the answer had to come from elsewhere – in practice, from the work of the English psychologist Charles Spearman (1863–1945), whose paper on 'General intelligence objectively determined' appeared in 1904.[27]

In this paper, Spearman used statistical methods developed by Galton and his follower Karl Pearson in the production of a theory of human intelligence which insisted that all mental acts involved the thinker in the deployment of a 'general factor' of intelligence, which was the same for every mental act and also a 'specific ability' which, naturally, was specific to the type of act occurring.[28] Different mental tasks, Spearman claimed, depended upon the general factor to differing degrees, with intellectual pursuits – e.g., mathematics – having the highest dependence on the central or general factor. Such a theory, he claimed, would explain the results obtained when experimental subjects were asked to perform a number of tasks – for it seemed that their results on the different tasks were not independent of one another. His overall

[26] R. D. Tuddenham, 'The nature and measurement of intelligence' in L. Postman (ed.), *Psychology in the Making* (New York, 1966). See also the historical sections in the 1924 Report (note 4); K. Young, 'The history of mental testing', *Pedagogical Seminary*, xxxi (1923) pp. 1–48.
[27] C. Spearman,' "General intelligence" objectively determined and measured', *American Journal of Psychology*, xv (1904), pp. 201–92.
[28] B. Norton, 'Charles Spearman and the general factor in intelligence: Genesis and interpretation in the light of socio-personal considerations', *Journal of the History of the Behavioural Sciences*, xv (1979), pp. 142–54.

conclusion was that: 'all branches of intellectual activity have in common one fundamental function ... whereas the remaining or specific elements of the activity seem in every case different from that in all the others'.[29] Spearman considered that his 'second line' of investigation, undertaken in independence from that of the Frenchmen, answered the problem raised by Simon's remark that the Binet scale 'measures intelligence as a whole without analysing it'.

The answer reached by this second line of investigation is simple, but of wide ranging consequence. It says that the intelligence employed in any mental performance must be analysed into two factors. The one is different for every different kind of performance or test: it seems to be identifiable with the neural structure in the brain specifically subserving that particular performance. But besides this specific factor, there is also a general one, always the same whatever the performance; this general factor in ability seems to be represented physiologically by the free energy of the whole cortex of the brain, or some still wider neural region ... This result, gained wholly independently of the work of MM. Simon and Binet, nevertheless fits it like a glove. An explanation is at once supplied for the success of their extraordinary procedure in casting all the old basal powers to the winds, and, instead, pooling together tests of the most miscellaneous description. For if every performance depends on two factors, the one always varying randomly, while the other is constantly the same, it is clear that in the average the random variations will tend to neutralise one another, leaving the other, or constant factor, alone dominant.

... Great has been the value of the Simon–Binet tests, even when worked in theoretical darkness, their efficiency will be multiplied a thousandfold when employed with a full light upon their essential nature and mechanism.[30]

I have discussed the full details of Spearman's work elsewhere,[31] and, for the moment, would just point out that though Spearman clothed his work in statistics, giving the appearance of having

---

[29] C. Spearman (note 27), p. 284. In the original version, the extract here given was italicized.
[30] This was discussed in C. Spearman, 'The measurement of intelligence', *Eugenics Review*, vi (1914–1915), pp. 312–13. The extract is taken from p. 313.
[31] B. Norton (note 28).

produced an abstract, mathematical definition of intelligence – sometimes referred to, for example, by the bare symbol '$g$' – he tended also to interpret this bleak symbolism in the Galtonian language of 'energy', as may be seen above. This is hardly surprising, as we know Spearman to have been incited[32] to his work by reading Galton's *Inquiries into Human Faculty*, and because energeticist models of the mind were in any case rife at the time, as readers of the early works of Freud will be aware.[33] The main point here, however, is that one could accept Spearman's claims to have shown the existence of a 'central factor of general intelligence', pervading all mental acts and present in different people in different degrees, without accepting the sorts of neurological identities hinted at above in the reply to Simon. As we have seen, the language of the two-factor theory was soon to feature in official government publications. Spearman, in short, offered an attractive and apparently coherent alternative to the Galtonian 'natural ability'. Shortly, we will see something of its uses.

INTELLIGENCE AND SOCIAL CLASS

In the discussion so far, I have omitted to mention that the early twentieth century in Britain was marked by the establishment of an influential eugenics movement, dedicated to changing and 'improving' the imperial race by selective breeding from its 'fittest' members.[34] Not a few scientists linked themselves to the movement, though it seems reasonable to suppose that these scientists were characterized by widely differing levels of eugenic zeal.[35] Spearman was a member of the Eugenics Education Society (one of the main eugenic organizations), and did not hesitate to point a finger to any possible eugenical significance of his work. But, for all this, it would be unwise to suppose that eugenics was the directing force in

[32] Details of Spearman's relations with Galton are given in his autobiographical piece in C. Murchison (ed.), *A History of Psychology in Autobiography* (Worcester, Mass., 1930), i, p. 322.

[33] See, for example 'First Model of the Mind "Project for a scientific psychology"' in R. Fancher, *Psychoanalytic Psychology. The Development of Freud's Psychology* (New York, 1973), chap. 3.

[34] For details, see G. Searle, *Eugenics and Politics in Britain 1900–1914* (Leyden, 1976).

[35] As an example of the low-intensity eugenist, one might take the geneticist R. H. Lock (1879–1915), whose *Recent Progress in the Study of Variation, Heredity, and Evolution*, 5th edn. (London, 1920), contained a moderate discussion of eugenics.

Spearman's researches. All that we know of him suggests that his first interest was with the giving of a coherent account of the principles of cognition, an account in which his theory of intelligence would play a role.[36] Other scientists, however, do seem to have allowed their eugenic zeals to direct their researches. Men like R. A. Fisher, for example (of whom more below), do seem to have pursued problems simply because they were of eugenic importance.

Among this second group of scientists, none is more important the Karl Pearson (1857–1936), a professor of mathematics and Galton's leading disciple,[37] who was able to take up a chair of eugenics at University College, London, funded by Galton. At University College, Pearson superintended a eugenics laboratory, directed towards the 'scientific' resolution of eugenic problems. Some of the work performed here was of great significance in the growth of the Burtian analysis of society, and no single item more important than David Heron's (1906) 'Study in national deterioration', whose central feature (see table 4) was a table of relative fertilities encountered in various London boroughs,[38] which seemed to indicate that the inhabitants of middle-class areas were reproducing themselves at a much lower rate than the inhabitants of working-class areas. To Heron, it showed a state of eugenic crisis, a situation in which the worst elements in society rather than the best were producing each new generation. In the view of Heron and Pearson, this indicated a continuing genetic erosion of the national stock. Evolution had gone into reverse, and had been placed there by environmental improvements on the one hand, and by Malthusian practices amongst the middle classes on the other.[39]

This conclusion, of course, hinged upon an assumption taken directly from Galton, namely that lower-classedness and a dearth

[36] In some productions, e.g., his 'Heredity of abilities', *Eugenics Review*, vi (1914), pp. 219–37, Spearman seems an enthusiastic eugenist. But, it is clear that the bulk of his work was *not* motivated by a desire to resolve social issues. See, for example, his typical *The Nature of 'Intelligence' and the Principles of Cognition* (London, 1923). This, I think, shows that, at root, Spearman was only really concerned with problems of cognition.

[37] For an account of Pearson, see E. S. Pearson, *Karl Pearson. An Appreciation of some Aspects of his Work and Life* (Cambridge, 1938).

[38] D. Heron, *The Relation of Fertility in Man to Social Status* (London, 1906).

[39] The whole thrust of Heron's report was to the effect that, unless something was done very quickly, galloping genetic erosion would bring the British race to its knees.

Table 4. *Typical statistics from Heron's 1906 Study in national deterioration (for the year 1901).*

| Metropolitan borough | Legitimate births per 100 wives aged 15–54 | Legitimate births per 100 wives aged 20 and upwards | Professional men per 1000 occupied males | Female domestic servants per 100 females | Female domestic servants per 100 families | General labourers per 1000 occupied males | Pawnbrokers, general dealers, etc., per 1000 occupied males |
|---|---|---|---|---|---|---|---|
| Battersea | 17.39 | 15.54 | 32.63 | 7.90 | 12.51 | 5.77 | 6.67 |
| Bermondsey | 21.86 | 19.26 | 9.85 | 4.18 | 6.44 | 9.05 | 6.78 |
| Bethnal Green | 22.74 | 20.37 | 6.78 | 3.56 | 5.59 | 4.69 | 9.27 |
| Camberwell | 17.76 | 15.55 | 33.21 | 8.73 | 14.96 | 3.32 | 6.68 |
| Chelsea | 14.97 | 12.95 | 38.92 | 25.36 | 47.46 | 6.19 | 6.89 |
| Deptford and Greenwich | 18.79 | 16.53 | 26.13 | 11.52 | 19.20 | 8.79 | 5.94 |
| Finsbury | 23.10 | 20.89 | 13.59 | 5.28 | 7.87 | 4.33 | 7.28 |
| Fulham | 18.27 | 16.69 | 34.73 | 10.93 | 17.44 | 5.37 | 5.60 |
| Hackney | 17.87 | 15.57 | 33.19 | 9.98 | 17.76 | 3.03 | 5.67 |
| Hammersmith | 16.69 | 14.66 | 37.35 | 10.96 | 18.68 | 6.90 | 6.23 |
| Hampstead | 13.52 | 11.71 | 82.94 | 33.08 | 79.88 | 2.29 | 3.18 |
| Holborn | 19.52 | 17.44 | 58.03 | 12.16 | 20.70 | 6.72 | 7.47 |
| Islington | 16.90 | 14.89 | 30.40 | 9.24 | 15.26 | 3.40 | 5.86 |
| Kensington | 14.64 | 12.67 | 67.04 | 32.66 | 74.92 | 5.11 | 7.28 |
| Lambeth | 18.05 | 15.80 | 35.60 | 10.65 | 17.63 | 4.69 | 7.09 |
| Lewisham | 16.46 | 14.34 | 52.22 | 18.59 | 35.77 | 4.29 | 3.42 |
| Paddington | 15.31 | 13.34 | 53.26 | 24.00 | 46.65 | 2.89 | 4.30 |
| Poplar | 21.85 | 19.34 | 10.26 | 4.90 | 7.96 | 10.54 | 6.45 |
| St Marylebone | 17.62 | 15.52 | 51.15 | 23.99 | 46.02 | 4.45 | 5.80 |
| St Pancras | 16.32 | 14.41 | 32.35 | 10.10 | 15.90 | 3.24 | 7.01 |
| Shoreditch | 21.26 | 19.04 | 6.44 | 3.55 | 5.50 | 4.78 | 9.40 |
| Southwark | 19.91 | 18.00 | 14.25 | 4.88 | 7.33 | 7.62 | 10.65 |
| Stepney | 23.99 | 21.73 | 11.99 | 5.31 | 8.60 | 7.08 | 9.00 |
| Stoke Newington | 14.25 | 12.14 | 46.48 | 14.56 | 27.58 | 1.28 | 4.45 |
| Wandsworth | 16.57 | 14.53 | 56.32 | 17.84 | 34.44 | 4.38 | 5.18 |
| Westminster | 12.55 | 11.04 | 43.25 | 27.28 | 53.36 | 3.38 | 5.38 |
| Woolwich | 18.20 | 16.25 | 14.63 | 9.02 | 14.12 | 10.25 | 3.36 |

of innate intelligence went hand in hand. Such an assumption was easily made by the British eugenists who seem uniformly to have come from good upper class backgrounds. Yet, easy or not, it was just an assumption, and some eugenists had the wit to perceive this. Numbered amongst these was the psychologist William McDougall, who, in the early years of the century, lectured at Oxford and University College, London.[40] Among his Oxford students was the young Cyril Burt, whose father had been an 'ardent Darwinian' and had introduced Burt to Galton whilst Burt was still a boy. Burt was impressed by Galton from the be-

[40] For details of McDougall, see the C. Murchison volume (note 32), containing McDougall's autobiographical essay. For McDougall's eugenic concerns, see his 'Psychology in the service of eugenics', *Eugenics Review*, v (1913), pp. 295–308.

| Children aged 10–14 employed per 100 children aged 10–14 | Number per 100 of total population living more than 2 in a room | Infants under 1 year dying per 1000 births | Mean age of wives aged 15–54 | Deaths from phthisis per 100,000 | Deaths from cancer per 100,000 | Male deaths from cancer per 100,000 males | Female deaths from cancer per 100,000 females | Children aged 2–4 per 100 wives aged 15–54 | Children and 5–14 per 100 wives aged 15–54 | Children aged 13–15 per 100 wives aged 15–54 |
|---|---|---|---|---|---|---|---|---|---|---|
| 10.68 | 10.88 | 163 | 36.91 | 147 | 81 | 59.9 | 101.0 | 56.03 | 126 | 36.7 |
| 14.92 | 19.67 | 169 | 36.64 | 176 | 67 | 64.5 | 70.9 | 64.68 | 145 | 40.6 |
| 16.55 | 29.62 | 153 | 36.28 | 216 | 86 | 71.0 | 99.5 | 68.50 | 146 | 40.6 |
| 9.91 | 9.64 | 142 | 37.19 | 146 | 97 | 69.9 | 121.8 | 57.82 | 135 | 39.5 |
| 8.61 | 14.43 | 138 | 37.51 | 168 | 91 | 70.1 | 107.3 | 48.04 | 112 | 33.1 |
| 8.85 | 8.69 | 138 | 36.96 | 118 | 75 | 72.1 | 80.1 | 59.30 | 135 | 39.5 |
| 15.13 | 35.21 | 142 | 36.60 | 223 | 78 | 58.1 | 97.0 | 58.73 | 130 | 38.4 |
| 8.93 | 10.85 | 152 | 36.36 | 137 | 88 | 71.2 | 104.6 | 57.87 | 118 | 32.0 |
| 12.06 | 10.18 | 135 | 36.94 | 148 | 80 | 66.2 | 92.3 | 56.19 | 128 | 37.6 |
| 8.90 | 11.75 | 168 | 36.89 | 140 | 84 | 66.4 | 100.8 | 53.65 | 121 | 34.7 |
| 7.92 | 6.36 | 104 | 37.61 | 94 | 96 | 97.8 | 95.6 | 46.76 | 113 | 35.7 |
| 13.96 | 25.04 | 124 | 36.60 | 277 | 100 | 98.3 | 100.1 | 43.42 | 101 | 32.2 |
| 12.44 | 17.00 | 140 | 36.83 | 152 | 91 | 68.4 | 112.1 | 52.26 | 116 | 33.8 |
| 10.44 | 14.84 | 163 | 37.79 | 137 | 112 | 79.6 | 133.0 | 47.10 | 109 | 33.8 |
| 9.98 | 12.22 | 139 | 36.92 | 166 | 99 | 77.9 | 116.3 | 52.62 | 119 | 34.6 |
| 8.00 | 2.68 | 129 | 37.24 | 90 | 95 | 59.9 | 124.4 | 54.21 | 124 | 37.2 |
| 9.55 | 13.57 | 136 | 37.33 | 110 | 103 | 84.4 | 117.8 | 46.78 | 105 | 31.8 |
| 12.00 | 16.41 | 165 | 36.77 | 180 | 73 | 62.5 | 83.3 | 63.53 | 143 | 41.0 |
| 11.73 | 21.12 | 107 | 37.19 | 182 | 104 | 15.7 | 94.2 | 46.05 | 102 | 32.5 |
| 11.80 | 23.98 | 154 | 36.75 | 184 | 88 | 74.4 | 100.8 | 50.50 | 115 | 33.4 |
| 16.22 | 29.95 | 197 | 36.48 | 215 | 81 | 77.4 | 84.3 | 61.63 | 134 | 38.7 |
| 13.01 | 22.35 | 168 | 36.37 | 248 | 86 | 80.4 | 92.3 | 57.78 | 126 | 36.2 |
| 12.10 | 33.21 | 163 | 35.82 | 210 | 73 | 65.7 | 81.1 | 67.64 | 141 | 38.5 |
| 9.85 | 5.53 | 115 | 37.36 | 134 | 92 | 44.2 | 129.3 | 47.97 | 109 | 34.4 |
| 8.51 | 4.45 | 132 | 37.14 | 115 | 89 | 63.6 | 111.5 | 54.18 | 122 | 35.6 |
| 12.27 | 13.04 | 135 | 37.37 | 187 | 83 | 78.9 | 85.7 | 40.52 | 93 | 29.9 |
| 10.27 | 6.59 | 129 | 36.47 | 175 | 71 | 49.0 | 94.8 | 56.75 | 126 | 36.7 |

ginning,[41] describing him as 'one of the most distinguished-looking people I have ever known – tall, slim, neatly dressed, with a forehead like the dome of St Paul's', and, under McDougall's tutelage, Burt was encouraged to follow up and clarify the psychological bases of Galton's eugenic claims. At the time, McDougall was much concerned with the question of the relationship between social class and innate intelligence, a question, Burt later recalled, that was brought forcibly to his attention by the publication of Heron's report. This, by turn, had an important influence on the line of work that Burt was encouraged to take up. Burt himself wrote as follows:

[41] This is detailed in C. Burt (note 12), p. 1.

One of Karl Pearson's fellow workers, David Heron, had recently published considerable evidence demonstrating that the birth-rate differed widely with differences of social level, that of the professional classes being less than half that of the so-called working classes. It was therefore arranged that two groups of children representing these two contrasted social classes, should be examined. Complete age-groups (12.0–13.0 years) were chosen (i) from a well-known preparatory school (the Dragon School), where the pupils were sons of men eminent in the intellectual professions (bishops, professors, scientists, civil servants, etc.), and (ii) from an elementary school, where the parents were local tradespeople and working men, not so ill-paid, however, as to lead to serious handicaps from poverty or poor health.[42] The upshot of this was Burt's career-establishing paper[43] of 1909 'Experimental tests of general intelligence', in which he reviewed and confirmed Spearman's theoretical perspectives and went on to examine the intelligences of the two sets of boys. As the Binet scale had not then been adapted to English conditions, Burt devised a series of fairly simple sensory-motor tests which, when pooled, gave a ranking of the boys which correlated highly with headmasterly estimates of their intelligences. Finding that the upper-class boys received scores in these tests which were higher than those of the lower-class boys, Burt concluded that 'wherever there are correlations with intelligence, there (so far as we can discover) boys of superior parentage are themselves superior. Moreover, at the sound, tapping, memory, mirror, alphabet and dotting tests, the preparatory boys are superior even to the cleverest sections of the elementary boys'[44], and, in consequence, that: 'We may conclude that the superior proficiency at intelligence tests on the part of boys of superior parentage, was inborn. And thus we seem to have proved marked inheritability in the case of a mental character of the highest "civic worth".'[45] Intelligence, Burt maintained, had been shown to be 'inherited to a degree which few psychologists have hitherto legitimately ventured to maintain'.

[42] C. Burt, *Intelligence and Fertility* (London, 1946), p. 7.
[43] See C. Burt, 'Experimental tests of general intelligence', *British Journal of Psychology*, iii (1909), pp. 94–177. Burt, in fact, claimed that tests of sensation and memory 'embodied group factors over and above g', so he was not simply agreeing with Spearman.
[44] *Ibid.*, p. 173.
[45] *Ibid.*, p. 176.

From a very early stage in his career, Burt was a keen follower of Galton's ideas. He was a member of the Eugenics Education Society and anxious to find the governing hand of heredity in social phenomena. The 1909 paper is a powerful example of this, for its conclusions grossly exceed in an hereditarian direction that which is licensed in logic by the data.[46] But, for all of this, the paper must have had a good reception, for Burt was appointed to the position of educational psychologist by the London County Council in 1912, and thereafter found himself 'able to put into execution many of the plans that Galton had long ago proposed', doing work that resulted in his books *The Distribution and Relations of Educational Abilities* (1917), *Mental and Scholastic Tests* (1921), *The Young Delinquent* (1925), and *The Backward Child* (1937).[47] During his L.C.C. phase, he was able to defend the Galtonian thesis that ability was normally distributed, to work on the British revision of the new Binet tests and to develop the testing techniques which, by 1926, yielded the data seen in table 1.[48] These data, along with others, have recently been criticized by Kamin, Gillie and Dorfman.[49] So recent, however, is the exposure of Burt, that, for many years, he was known as the man who had replaced Galton's ideas about civic worth and social class with new ideas about intelligence and social class. To complete the 'modern' version of Galton's view, it was necessary only to provide a satisfactory theory of inheritance, which, if possible, would explain and legitimate the Galtonian theory of limited social mobility via regression.

## CLASS, MOBILITY AND GENETICS

To re-establish the Galtonian model for social mobility, Burt had to prove that intelligence, as measured by I.Q. tests, followed the

[46] To be more precise: it is not at all clear what is the significance of there being a difference between the absolute scores of two sets of boys on a set of tests, when all that is known about the tests is that they give rankings of boys corresponding well with rankings given by their teachers.

[47] C. Burt (note 12), p. 40.

[48] Burt claimed that the data for this table were 'obtained during surveys carried out for the London County Council and the National Institute of Industrial Psychology'. Some indication of the ways in which the data were gathered may be gleaned from his 'Principles of vocational guidance', *British Journal of Psychology*, xiv (1924), pp. 336–52.

[49] See note 7.

same general pattern of hereditary regression as did stature, and to show that this was a genuine biological phenomenon, not a socially induced effect. Galton, of course, had no real means of doing this and, in fact, no such means was available until, in 1918, R. A. Fisher published his famous paper on 'The correlation between relatives on the supposition of Mendelian inheritance', which showed that a multifactorial Mendelian model could account for the existence of normally distributed characters and also for the existence of regression relations between relatives in respect of such characters.[50] Additionally, Fisher showed in the paper how one might set about the partitioning of observed variance into environmental and hereditary components – in effect producing the modern notion of 'heritability'. Without doubt, Fisher did this work for eugenic purposes and saw his new methods as a way of finally stopping the mouths of environmentalists, who could support their case by citing an apparently endless list of factors that might environmentally determine a person's development.[51] This becomes quite clear when we read Fisher's earliest papers, given to the Cambridge University Undergraduate Eugenics Society in 1911 and 1912, and when one reads the most recent biography of Fisher, which reveals the extent of his searching after the 'eugenic life'.[52]

For all his long-continued eugenic enthusiasms, however, Fisher did not enter into the realm of psychometric measurements, possibly, but only possibly, because the applicability of his methods to human data was strongly attacked by Lancelot Hogben in 1932.[53] The task was left up to Burt himself, and he did not do this until he was well into the period which even his most generous biographer has recognized as a fraudulent period.[54] Burt may have learned of Fisher's methods from their author when they worked together on

[50] R. A. Fisher, 'The correlation between relatives on the supposition of Mendelian inheritance', *Transactions of the Royal Society of Edinburgh*, lii (1918), pp. 399–433.
[51] I have discussed this matter in B. Norton, 'Fisher and the neo-Darwinian synthesis', in E. G. Forbes (ed.), *The Human Implications of Scientific Advance* (Edinburgh, 1978). See also R. A. Fisher, 'The causes of human variability', *Eugenics Review*, x (1918), pp. 213–20.
[52] J. F. Box, *R. A. Fisher. The Life of a Scientist* (New York, 1979), see, e.g., p. 39.
[53] L. Hogben, 'The limits of applicability of correlation technique in human genetics', *Journal of Genetics*, xxvi (1932), pp. 379–406.
[54] See L. S. Hearnshaw, *Cyril Burt: Psychologist* (London, 1979). Hearnshaw sees Burt's fraudulent period as beginning only late on in his life, in essence, after the Second World War. See, for example, chapter 12 'Posthumous controversies'. There is not universal agreement that Hearnshaw is correct in this respect, though all commentators are agreed upon the excellence of the biography as a whole.

the Research Committee of the Eugenics Education Society or, possibly, from the works of Mather.[55] Whatever his route, by the mid 1950s, Burt felt able to show that a Fisherian model fitted well with the data he had 'collected', in respect of I.Q., on regression between various pairs of relatives.

As a consequence of this work,[56] Burt felt able to claim that there was regression between relatives in respect of intelligence, and that the regression coefficients were of such sizes as to strongly support the view that they were measures of a biological rather than of a social process. Burt's twin studies were on hand to uphold the same view.[57]

Once he had gone this far, Burt did not take long to move to complete his modernized version of Galton's view of society and social mobility. The final statement of this came in Burt's famous paper of 1961 on intelligence and social mobility, whose data have recently been shown to be fraudulent.[58]

In his constructions, Burt moved from an eight class social analysis to a six class social analysis, following the system first described by Carr-Saunders and Caradog Jones in their *Social Structure in England and Wales*. What he did, in effect, was to construct a modern version of Galton's table. In order to do this, Burt had to use two tables, because unlike Galton, he did not simply assume a one-to-one correspondence between class and ability, but offered instead an empirical account of the relationship. We see this in table 5 below, which gives evidence of a good deal of spread or variance about the mean I.Q. for each different social level. The table is equivalent to the column headed 'names of classes' in Galton's table for social mobility.

Burt's second table (see table 6) enables us to read off the types of children produced by the adults of table 5 through the workings of the Fisher-guaranteed process of regression. The resemblance to

[55] K. Mather, *Biometrical Genetics* (London, 1949).
[56] C. Burt and M. Howard, 'The multifactorial theory of inheritance and its application to intelligence', *British Journal of Statistical Psychology*, viii (1956), pp. 95–131. Recently, of course, doubt has been thrown upon the existence of Howard. But, whether Margaret Howard really existed or not, Burt's claims to be able to fit observed correlations with the Fisherian model have been widely taken up, as is made clear in Kamin (note 7).
[57] For a discussion of these, see L. Kamin (note 7).
[58] See C. Burt, 'Intelligence and social mobility', *British Journal of Statistical Psychology*, xiv (1961), pp. 3–24. The most complete exposition of the data of this paper is that due to D. D. Dorfman (note 7).

Table 5. *Distribution of intelligence according to occupational class: adults**

| | 50–60 | 60–70 | 70–80 | 80–90 | 90–100 | 100–110 | 110–20 | 120–30 | 130–40 | 140+ | Total | Mean I.Q. |
|---|---|---|---|---|---|---|---|---|---|---|---|---|
| I Higher Professional | | | | | | | | | 2 | 1 | 3 | 139.7 |
| II. Lower Professional | | | | | | | 2 | 13 | 15 | 1 | 31 | 130.6 |
| III. Clerical | | | | 1 | 8 | 16 | 56 | 38 | 3 | | 122 | 115.9 |
| IV. Skilled | | | 2 | 11 | 51 | 101 | 78 | 14 | 1 | | 258 | 108.2 |
| V. Semiskilled | | 5 | 15 | 31 | 135 | 120 | 17 | 2 | | | 325 | 97.8 |
| VI. Unskilled | 1 | 18 | 52 | 117 | 53 | 11 | 9 | | | | 261 | 84.9 |
| Total | 1 | 23 | 69 | 160 | 247 | 248 | 162 | 67 | 21 | 2 | 1000 | 100.0 |

Table 6. *Distribution of intelligence according to occupational class: children**

| | 50–60 | 60–70 | 70–80 | 80–90 | 90–100 | 100–110 | 110–20 | 120–30 | 130–40 | 140+ | Total | Mean I.Q. |
|---|---|---|---|---|---|---|---|---|---|---|---|---|
| I. Higher Professional | | | | | | 1 | | 1 | 1 | | 3 | 120.8 |
| II. Lower Professional | | | | 1 | 2 | 6 | 12 | 8 | 2 | | 31 | 114.7 |
| III. Clerical | | | 3 | 8 | 21 | 31 | 35 | 18 | 6 | | 122 | 107.8 |
| IV. Skilled | | 1 | 12 | 33 | 53 | 70 | 59 | 22 | 7 | 1 | 258 | 104.6 |
| V. Semiskilled | 1 | 6 | 23 | 55 | 99 | 85 | 38 | 13 | 5 | | 325 | 98.9 |
| VI. Unskilled | 1 | 15 | 32 | 62 | 75 | 54 | 16 | 6 | | | 261 | 92.6 |
| Total | 2 | 22 | 70 | 159 | 250 | 247 | 160 | 68 | 21 | 1 | 1000 | 100.0 |

*Tables 5 and 6 are Burt's tables for social class, I.Q. and social mobility from his paper 'Intelligence and social mobility (see note 58).

Galton's model is immediately perceivable. We can see that the children of top élites are, on the whole, somewhat down in intelligence, whereas the children of the poorest members of society have risen somewhat. Clearly, if I.Q. determined social class, and the class/I.Q. relationship was stable, then social mobility would have to occur, with a new élite recruited largely from below (but from only slightly below) and a new lower class recruited from above (but from only slightly above).

For Galton, it was the 'natural' restoration (within a competitive society) of this talent/class relationship that caused special mobility. Burt now came to essentially the same conclusion: 'Of the various causal factors affecting the individual's rise or fall in occupational status differences in intelligence and motivation appear to be the most influential. Differences in home background and in education seem to exercise a secondary or supplementary influence, but without the basis of the first two they are of little effect'.[59] Here, finally, we have the modern, Burtian version of the old Galtonian view of British society: civic worth has become I.Q., seen as measuring a 'central factor'; regression has become a biologically certified process, and the simple assumption of a class/ability tie up is replaced by an empirical account of the class/I.Q. relationship. Once again, social mobility is seen as necessary to maintain this last relationship and, once again, the pattern of social mobility is said to be dictated by the processes of genetics – which determine that only a very few children of the lower classes will ever 'make it' to élite positions and that the new élite in each generation will be drawn largely from slightly below. Once again, we have the same mixture of radicalism and conservatism. A certain level of mobility is seen to be expected, given the facts of biology, but anything like perfect social mobility is ruled out of court.

CONCLUSION

Given the aims of the paper, basically expository and chronological, conclusions must be relatively few. In fact, there seem to be two main points. First, there is a remarkable coincidence between Burt's and Galton's tables for social mobility. Dorfman has

[58] C. Burt (note 58), p. 23.

recently exposed Burt's tables as frauds, and so remarkable is the resemblance that it is tempting to see Burt's frauds as attempts to re-float Galton's obviously unsatisfactory account of social mobility.[60] Second, there is the matter of the beliefs of the authors of the new perspective. For, when we analyse their views, it seems that Burt, Pearson, McDougall, Fisher and others had strong emotional commitments to eugenics, or, at least, to hereditarianism.[61] When one reads their works, one can see that they saw the establishment of an hereditarian interpretation of ability and social status almost as the triumph of good over evil.

Like other reforming zealots, they were not overscrupulous in their reasonings. Heron and Pearson were happy to equate poverty and stupidity when it suited their book: Fisher, the searcher after the 'eugenic life' was not careful when applying his methods to human data: Burt, in the first early years was prepared to bend and twist logic to establish the hereditarian point and, later on, this extended to the fabrication of data – data much used by Eysenck and Herrnstein and Jensen in their various anti-environmentalist sheets, and by the authors of Britain's *Black Papers* intent upon discrediting 'progressive' trends in education.[62] Why these scientists should have had such commitments is a matter of considerable interest, of an interest which grows when one realizes that their position on the inheritance of ability was more sophisticated than is sometimes supposed – in that regression and its social consequences loomed large.[63] It all means that these scientists cannot be simply written off as straightforward agents of the ruling classes – for, presumably, it is not in the interest of such persons to believe that their offspring will be unsuited to a high station. In practice, on the other hand, the scientists did not play

[60] I have no direct evidence of this, but the similarities are remarkable.

[61] When one reads the works of these men, or, at least, those of their works which attempt to ground social phenomena in biological factors, one constantly encounters the triumph of prejudice over reason. Burt's 1909 paper, I have argued, is an example of such a process, as is his later, criticized work. Persons following up this claim will profit by reading the sociobiological chapters of R. A. Fisher, *Genetical Theory of Natural Selection* (Oxford, 1930); W. McDougall, *National Welfare and National Decay* (London, 1921) and Karl Pearson's eugenic tracts – detailed in G. M. Morant, *Bibliography of Karl Pearson's Statistical and Other Writings* (Cambridge, 1939).

[62] See note 5.

[63] Regression in monetary inheritance, for example, would not gain many votes among the rich.

up this aspect of their work. Burt did not demand any significant redistribution of income when he wrote on ability and income,[64] and Fisher too was polite to the well off.[65] In so far as Britain has been the setting for a continued class war, the basic allegiances of the scientists involved in the re-development of the Galtonian paradigm were never much in doubt: they were suspicious of the lower classes, deferential towards the very rich and powerful, and enthusiastic for the professional middle class.[65]

[64] Burt's paper on 'Ability and Income' (note 1) includes an almost unbelievable train of contorted arguments intended to show that a normal distribution of ability might reasonably be expected to give rise to the distinctly non-normal curve of income distribution.

[65] In this context, see D. MacKenzie's analysis of eugenists (note 20).

# 9. Measuring Intelligence: English Local Education Authorities and Mental Testing 1919–1939

GILLIAN SUTHERLAND

The appeal to science as the embodiment of certainty, the insistence that his particular specialism conforms to a model derived from the 'hardest' physical science, is a familiar, even a commonplace, phenomenon among nineteenth- and twentieth-century social scientists. The new specialism of the psychology of individual differences, emerging from the turn of the century, was no exception to this, nor was its principal field of application, education. The proponents of mental measurement, or psychometrics, as some of them chose to call it, offered it to teachers and educational administrators as the new technology which would at last enable the theory and practice of education to attain scientific status.[1] This essay

The bulk of the work upon which this essay is based was funded by the Social Science Research Council and I am glad to acknowledge their generous support. In particular, their grant enabled Dr Stephen Sharp, now of the Godfrey Thomson Unit, University of Edinburgh, to work with me for two years and I am grateful for his help in collecting and analysing some of the data here discussed. A version of this was first presented at a conference in Aberdeen on The Scientific Movement in Educational Research, 15–17 September 1979, sponsored by the S.S.R.C. and the Scottish History of Education Society; and its substance is being published also by Aberdeen University Press in the proceedings of that conference under the title *The Meritocratic Intellect*, edited by David Hamilton and J.V. Smith.

I am indebted to the Comptroller of Her Majesty's Stationery Office for permission to cite Crown Copyright material and to the librarians, archivists and other officers of The National Union of Teachers, the Isle of Wight Record Office, the Langham Library, Sunderland Polytechnic, the Kent Archives Office, the Wiltshire Record Office, the Burnley Borough Council, the Trustees of the Godfrey Thomson Unit for Educational Research (*Moray House Archives*), the Northumberland Record Office, the Norfolk County Council, and the Buckinghamshire Record Office for permission to cite material in their charge.

Finally, I am indebted to Alister Sutherland for patient and thorough criticism of successive drafts.

[1] For a fuller discussion of this, see Gillian Sutherland and S. Sharp, '"The Fust Official Psychologist in the Wurrld": Aspects of the Professionalization of Psychology in early Twentieth-century Britain', *History of Science*, xvii (1980), pp. 181–208. Cf. C. Spearman's presidential address to the Psychology Section of the British Association, reported in *Education* (4 September 1925), p. 228.

examines some aspects of the reception of this technology, with its claim to certainty and precision, in England between the two World Wars. It focuses not on the academic discussion but on the recognition this received and the resonances it evoked among those who actually ran the schools in the period, the teachers, the local authority members and their officers. It includes some account of the use of this technology and a discussion of an explanatory framework for the peculiarities of this.

The Scottish and American experiences encourage one to expect teachers, politicians and administrators to take the technology of mental measurement very seriously indeed. The Scottish Council for Research into Education was established in 1930 and the first Scottish National Survey was carried out in 1932. Clarence Karier has written of the 'quasi-public bureaucracy of boards, compacts, councils and Commissions which serve to shape policy by giving and withholding both public and private funds at key points in the [American educational] system',[2] and he instances, in particular, the American Council on Education, the Carnegie Foundation and the creation of the Education Testing Service.

The two obvious areas of applicability for the new technology in England were first, the identification of the subnormal and second, the classification of the normal. Individual Binet tests were already in use in England for the identification of mentally defective children by the outbreak of the first World War. This forms a relatively self-contained subject for investigation, which I have discussed elsewhere.[3] Classification of the normal may mean simply 'tracking' or 'streaming' within the school. Alternatively, or in addition, it may mean the segregation of children into different schools at given ages. Such segregation was taking place in English education in the first half of the twentieth century. Between the ages of ten and twelve a tiny minority of children were chosen to proceed to secondary schools, where they could stay until the age of eighteen; the majority remained in elementary schools, which they left at fourteen. This process of choice is the obvious place at which to start looking for the large-scale impact of the new

[2] C. Karier 'Testing for Order and Control in the Corporate Liberal State', reprinted in N. Block and G. Dworkin (eds.), *The IQ Controversy* (London, 1977), p. 361.
[3] See Gillian Sutherland, 'The Magic of Measurement: Mental Testing and English Education 1900–1940', *Transactions of the Royal Historical Society*, 5th ser., xxvii (1977), pp. 135–53.

technology in England. And indeed, the standard text, Olive Banks'
*Parity and Prestige in English Secondary Education*, declares that
'By the outbreak of War in 1939 the use of intelligence tests and
standardized tests of English and Arithmetic with appropriate age
allowances had been adopted by almost every local authority in an
attempt to ensure the maximum efficiency in the selection of
children for the places available'.[4]

She gives no source for this statement and it is simply not true.
Only sixty-eight out of the 128 Local Education Authorities with
responsibility for secondary education in England are now known
to have used some type of group intelligence test, for some purpose
in secondary selection, at some point between 1919 and 1940.[5]
That is to say, only just over half of them used something they
called an intelligence test – and perhaps only once – in what came
to be known as the '11+' examination. Far fewer used standardized English and arithmetic tests. Indeed, the use of these seems to
have been primarily a function of the decision to use Moray House
intelligence tests and the subsequent discovery that, conveniently,
Moray House provided English and arithmetic tests as well; I don't
propose to discuss these any further now. The symbol of the new
technology was the group intelligence or mental test – the terms
were used interchangeably in this period; and it seems the English
were markedly less enthusiastic about it than either the Americans
or the Scots.[6]

How to begin to explain the peculiarities of the English? There is

[4] Olive Banks, *Parity and Prestige in English Secondary Education* (London, 1955), p.
129.

[5] These figures supersede the *interim* figures given in 'The magic of measurement'
(note 3), p. 146. For details of their provenance and the problems of the sources, see
Gillian Sutherland, 'Mental testing and education in England and Wales 1880–
1940', Applications and Reports to the SSRC, grant HR 4204/2 (January 1976,
January 1977, May 1977, May 1978 and December 1978). It should be stressed that
mention of the use of a particular method of selection by a particular authority at
any given time does not necessarily mean that that method was employed by the
authority for the rest or even a large part of the period 1919–39. Authorities
sometimes altered their arrangements with almost bewildering frequency and I find
it surprising that the NUT did not attempt to orchestrate a general call for some
continuity and stability, for the sake of elementary school teachers and pupils.

[6] Comparisons with the American and Scots situations are implicit in the discussion
that follows. As I know very much less about the educational structures and
ideologies of these two societies than I do about those of England, they must remain
tentative. But the discussion at the Aberdeen conference was most helpful in
confirming my sense of the main points of contrast and in indicating areas for future
work, most notably the differing status and training of teachers.

space to present only part of the discussion now.[7] I shall concentrate here on the personnel involved in taking the crucial decisions, the information about testing to which they had access, their attitudes and the social and political structures they represent. These, of course, interact and reinforce each other and any attempt to disentangle them must be an artificial device, purely for explanatory purposes. The process is further complicated by the fact that although there was a national debate, the effective decisions were taken at a local level.

It is important to be clear at the outset that the English educational public was not notably ill-informed about the notion of intelligence and its attendant, burgeoning technology. Cyril Burt claimed that the term 'intelligence' in its modern sense was first used by Herbert Spencer. But Keith Hope has shown its wide currency during the nineteenth century, stretching back at least to writers of the Scottish Enlightenment at the end of the eighteenth century.[8] As early as 1913 *The Times Educational Supplement* reported that Surrey County Council was conducting a secondary school selection examination, in the final oral examination of which: 'the candidates are marked for general intelligence'.[9] By the mid 1920s, 'general intelligence' was as much a part of the stock-in-trade of public discussion as, say, 'national efficiency' had been twenty years earlier. In June 1926 the President, Alderman George Cadbury, explained to the Annual Conference of the Association for Education in Industry and Commerce the problems of balancing quantitative and qualitative considerations in chocolate making, and he summed up: 'general intelligence is of the utmost value in promoting efficiency'.[10] In June 1927 an advertisement for the

---

[7] It was begun in a paper to the Royal Historical Society in 1976. Stephen Sharp and I continued it subsequently, looking in particular – but mostly in vain – for possible correlations between test use and type of authority, geographical location, density of population, etc. We have not been able, so far, to get adequate figures to explore the most interesting possible correlation, that between test use and the number of secondary school places per head of the relevant age group in each Local Education Authority's area. The discussion so far can be followed in detail in 'The magic of measurement' (note 3) and SSRC HR 4204/2 (note 5). The full version will be presented in Gillian Sutherland with Stephen Sharp, *Ability, Merit and Measurement* (to be published by Oxford University Press).
[8] K. Hope, *The Political Conception of Merit* (to be published by Russell Sage), ch. 15. I am most grateful to Dr Hope for allowing me to see and refer to this important work.
[9] *The Times Educational Supplement* (7 October 1913), p. 155.
[10] G. Cadbury, *Education* (25 June 1926), p. 677, Cf. also with Sir D. Milne Watson speaking to the same body, *ibid.* (8 July 1927), p. 38.

Singer Sewing Machine in the weekly journal *Education* quoted an un-named headmistress as declaring: '"The Needlework Lesson now seems to develop general intelligence, too!"'[11]

This kind of cant use was hardly technically precise! But use of a word or catch-phrase like this usually follows on from a more technically informed discussion and this case was no exception. The educational journals regularly reviewed books and reported discussions on intelligence and mental measurement. In 1919: 'in response to a number of inquiries', *The Times Educational Supplement* provided a reading list on the subject. In 1920 they gave a very long and careful review to Burt's *The Distribution of Mental Abilities*. The following year they reviewed recent American group tests, pointing out that many of them were really attainments tests.[12]

Perhaps typical of the many lengthily reported conference discussions was the session on 'Psychological Tests' at the Imperial Education Conference in 1927, at which:

Dr *Ballard* said that too often 'intelligent' means 'interested in the things that interest me'. The psychologist applies a different interpretation: to him intelligence is independent of training, of knowledge, of culture, even of interest. He is looking, not for performance but for promise. The usual verbal tests need to be supplemented by other tests in order to test intelligence in the true psychological sense.[13]

[11] Anon., *Ibid.* (10 June 1927), p. 679.

[12] 'Tests of Intelligence', *The Times Educational Supplement* (24 July 1919), p. 375; 'Local Authorities as Innovators', *ibid.* (30 September 1920), p. 521; 'National Intelligence Tests', *ibid.* (24 December 1921), p. 575. See also a review of the Stanford-Binet Tests, *ibid.* (26 June 1919), p. 319; 'Intelligence Tests in Practice', *ibid.* (3 July 1919), p. 333; a review of Brown and Thompson, *The Essentials of Mental Measurement*, *ibid.* (7 April 1921), p. 157; 'New Work in Mental Tests', *ibid.* (28 January 1922), p. 37; P. B. Ballard, 'The New Examiner', *ibid.* (23 December 1922), p. 557; comments on use of intelligence tests in British Columbia in *Education* (20 November 1925), p. 501.

[13] *Ibid.* (22 July 1927), p. 92. Also cf. report of British Association meeting, section L, *The Times Educational Supplement* (2 September 1920), p. 480; report of the A.G.M. of the Association of Headmistresses, *Education* (24 June 1921), p. 18; reports of British Association meetings, *ibid.* (16 September 1921), pp. 169–70, and *The Times Educational Supplement* (17 September 1921), p. 415; report of a public debate between Ballard and a member of the British Phrenological Society, *ibid.* (31 December 1921), p. 582; report of a meeting of the Child Study Society, *ibid.* (14 January 1922), p. 21; report of the North of England Education Conference, *Education* (11 January 1924), p. 23; report of British Association meetings, *ibid.* (11 September 1925), p. 244; report of the North of England Education Conference, *ibid.* (10 January 1930), pp. 50, 52.

Ballard matched Burt as one of the most popular, or, at least, most frequently heard, lecturer on the rationale and technology of testing.[14] But the professionals in general seem to have devoted considerable time and energy to the work of propaganda. In 1919, with great public fanfare, the British Psychological Society opened its meetings to practising teachers, no longer confining them to accredited research workers.[15] By 1926 the National Institute of Industrial Psychology was advertising a set of five lecture-demonstrations for teachers on intelligence tests, which could be hired by any Local Education Authority in the country.[16]

The debate and discussion was not all one-sided. Ballard's colleague in the London County Council inspectorate, F. H. Hayward, the licensed clown of the educational world in the early 1920s, barracked constantly from the side-lines, stigmatizing intelligence tests as merely 'tests of cleverness'.[17] Others, such as Professor John Adams of University College, London; Professor J. A. Green of Sheffield; Frank Watts, Lecturer in Psychology at Manchester; Professor T. H. Pear of Manchester and Professor E. H. Campagnac of Liverpool, took and developed more seriously Hayward's basic point, the difficulty of separating intelligence from the universe in which it had to operate, the problems with which it had to deal. They discussed questions of motivation, of particular aptitudes and the whole issue of culture loading.[18]

Elsewhere, I have discussed, briefly, the contribution of the Board of Education and its inspectorate to this discussion and said

[14] Besides the references given above in note 13, also see: report of lecture programmes in West Riding and in London, *The Times Educational Supplement* (27 August 1921), p. 388; report of programme of the Notts and District Education Study Society, *ibid.* (15 October 1921), p. 458; report of lecture to the Education Guild, *Education* (28 October 1921), p. 242; report of the programme of the Bingley Summer School for Teachers, *The Times Educational Supplement* (12 August 1922), p. 376; report of the proceedings of the Brighton Summer School in Psychology, *ibid.* (19 August 1922); report of British Association meetings, *Education* (9 September 1927), p. 243.
[15] 'The British Psychological Society', *The Times Educational Supplement* (24 April 1919), p. 193.
[16] *Education* (12 February 1926), p. 180.
[17] 'Dr Hayward and Intelligence Tests', *ibid.* (3 November 1922), p. 260; also *The Times Educational Supplement* (28 October 1922), p. 474 and (25 November 1922), p. 511. On Hayward in general, see his extraordinary autobiography, F. H. Hayward, *An Educational Failure* (London, 1938), also *A First Book of School Celebrations* and *A Second Book of School Celebrations* (both London, 1920).
[18] J. Adams, *Education* (30 January 1920), pp. 82–3; F. Watts, *The Times Educational Supplement* (24 March 1921), p. 132; J. A. Green, *ibid.* (19 November 1921), p. 518; T. H. Pear, *ibid.* (7 January 1922), p. 10; E. H. Campagnac, *Education* (14 January 1927), pp. 38–40.

a little also about the impotence of the central authority in this period.[19] The Local Education Authorities, as both sides were aware, called the tune. One of the principal motives in the planning for reconstruction after the second World War begun by the higher officials of the Board of Education as early as November 1940, was the wish to regain the initiative from the L.E.A.s.[20] To understand the reponse in English schools between the Wars to the kind of discussion outlined above, we have to look in detail at these local authorities and their employees, both officials and teachers, and prepare ourselves in advance for considerable diversity and the likelihood of no tidy patterning.

We can make the transition from national to local most easily if we start looking, not just at discussions of intelligence and mental testing, but at discussions of examinations and notions of measurement more generally. Measurement was, in certain crucial senses, still a dirty word in English education. It was so because of payment by results, the system whereby from 1863 to 1890 the bulk of the government grant to a school (almost half its income) depended upon the performance of each child, each year in examinations, written and oral, conducted by Her Majesty's Inspector.[21] The habits engendered by this Procrustean system lasted longer than the system itself; and indeed there were still teachers in the schools in the 1920s who had trained and begun to teach under it. The battle against payment by results had been the National Union of Teachers' first big battle and their eventual emancipation from its trammels was regarded as a crucial stage in the fight for professional status.[22]

But the efficiency of any mechanism of competitive examination depends to a considerable extent on having a sufficiently large and representative population of examinees. Thus the Northumberland Education Committee had decreed that all the children of the appropriate age group should be examined by Godfrey Thomson in 1921.[23] By 1924 the Middlesex Education Committee had determined to subject all its elementary schools to what were called 'efficiency tests': 'designed to determine the number of their pupils

[19] G. Sutherland (note 3), pp. 141–3, 146–7.
[20] P. H. J. H. Gosden, *Education in the Second World War* (London, 1976), pp. 238–41.
[21] See Gillian Sutherland, *Policy-Making in Elementary Education 1870–95* (London, 1973), esp. pp. 6–9 and chapters 7, 8, 9.
[22] See A. Tropp, *The School Teachers* (London, 1957), esp. chapters 7 and 8.
[23] See G. Sutherland (note 3), p. 144; but cf. also *ibid.* p. 151.

likely to profit by a secondary school course'.[24] They were promptly denounced by the N.U.T., whose conference in 1925 deplored any 'reversion to the individual examination system' and protested 'emphatically against the tendency observable in some areas to use the examination for scholarships to secondary schools as a test of the efficiency of primary schools, instead of what it should be – a test of the child's natural ability'.[25] The Association of Education Committees, the L.E.A. trade union, added fuel to the flames by defending the rights of its member authorities to assess the efficiency of the schools for which they were responsible. Indeed, they encouraged them to do so and a major slanging match ensued.[26] Eventually both sides nominated representatives to a specially formed committee, which then spent nearly four years producing a report so qualified and anodyne as to make no impact at all.[27]

Mass examinations were thus an extremely sensitive subject in elementary schools in the inter-war period. I have discussed elsewhere the possible challenge posed by group intelligence tests in particular to these teachers' hard-won but still precarious social and intellectual authority.[28] The net effect was to make the reactions of elementary school teachers to any such proposals very unpredictable indeed. Nationally the N.U.T. kept a very low profile on intelligence tests and its own Examining Board, significantly, never attempted to experiment with them.[29] Locally, the reaction might depend very much on whose idea it was and how diplomatically it was done. For example, while the teachers in the Isle of Wight seem to have co-operated fully in some very sophisticated uses of Moray House Tests throughout the 1930s,[30] those in the

[24] *Education* (15 February 1924), p. 103.
[25] *Ibid.* (24 April 1925), p. 380.
[26] AEC debate 'Examinations in Public Elementary Schools', *ibid.* 18 June 1926 pp. 650, 652, 654, 656; 'Authorities – the Schools – and the Children', *ibid.* (25 June 1926), pp. 671–2; 'An Individual Examination', *ibid.* (3 September 1926), (pp. 199–200; NUT Conference, Presidential Address, *ibid.* (22 April 1926), p. 450; F. F. Potter's speech to the Association of Directors and Secretaries of Education, *ibid.* (28 January 1927), pp. 116–19.
[27] 'School Examinations: A More Hopeful Outlook', *ibid.* (2 March 1928), p. 237; 'Examinations in Public Elementary Schools', *ibid.* (18 July 1930) pp. 59–69; 'Examinations: Their Uses and Abuses', *ibid.* (12 December 1930), pp. 555–6. Even in 1939 the whole thing seemed to be flaring up again over a proposal in Leamington to examine all elementary school leavers – *ibid.* (10 February 1939), p. 179.
[28] G. Sutherland (note 3), pp. 149–51.
[29] *Minute Books of the NUT Examinations Board*, National Union of Teachers' Library, Hamilton House, Mabledon Place, London W.C.1.
[30] *Minutes of the Isle of Wight Examinations Board* (1932–39) *passim*, Isle of Wight Record Office, Newport.

North Riding of Yorkshire were up in arms in 1931 about the 'intelligence test' paper sprung on them in that year's Junior Scholarship Examination.[31] In Leicestershire, one of the earliest users of group intelligence tests, W. R. Brockington, the Director of Education worried continually about teachers coaching for them.[32]

The teachers in the elementary schools were not, of course, the only teachers upon whom selective examinations for secondary schools impinged. There were also the secondary teachers. One's first thought is that they surely had everything to gain by an 'efficient' selection process. Certainly they did not share the collective sensitivity of the elementary school teachers about the examination process; and some, indeed, took to the new technology in an enthusiastic and well-informed way. In 1922, at the request of the Sunderland County Borough Council Higher Education Sub-Committee, the head teachers of the Bede Collegiate Schools prepared a most lucid and well-illustrated report, beginning 'Intelligence Tests are an attempt to measure *intellectual ability* apart from *scholastic attainment*. The questions must therefore require thought and ordinary general knowledge but no *special knowledge*'.[33]

After trials and consultation with H. M. Inspectorate, they were by 1927 using a standard group test – the Otis – as a check upon the English and arithmetic marks in the selection examination; that is to say, they did not lump the test score in with the rest, but compared it with the total mark for the attainments tests and followed up any major discrepancies.[34] In Halifax secondary and elementary heads seem to have made the pace between 1927 and 1936 in bringing about a selection system dependent primarily upon group intelligence tests (Moray House) and standardized elementary school record cards. H.M. Inspectors found themselves in the somewhat unusual position of having to reassure members of the Education Committee that this was a good system.[35]

But examples like these are somewhat exceptional. Far more often mention of a test of 'general intelligence' in the selection

[31] *Education* (4 September 1931), p. 208.
[32] *Ibid.* (23 November 1923), p. 267; *ibid.* (22 July 1927), p. 92; *ibid.* (17 April 1931), p. 460.
[33] *Minutes of Sunderland County Borough Council Higher Education Sub-Committee* (17 May 1922), Langham Library, Sunderland Polytechnic, Sunderland; see also *ibid.* (13 October 1921).
[34] *Ibid.* (17 May 1922, 18 October 1927); Public Record Office, Ed 77/40.
[35] Public Record Office, Ed 77/126, /127, /128 and 110/84. Cf. also 'Substitute for Examinations', *Education* (5 September 1930), p. 22.

process turns out, on further investigation, to mean that there is an interview or oral examination conducted by one or more secondary head teachers at which questions either made up by them or chosen at random from some of the better known group tests are asked.[36] Handled skilfully and systematically, such interviews might approach the rigour of an individual Binet. But there is an instructive correspondence in *The Times Educational Supplement* in 1921, started by 'Secondary Headmaster' who wrote as follows:

> To each of thirty-five candidates, the most highly recommended out of ninety, from the elementary schools of my neighbourhood I gave as an oral test in a free place examination last week this question which they read in print from a paper:
> 'Captain Cook made three voyages to the South Seas.
> On one of these voyages he was killed. On which one?'
> Only six of the thirty-five candidates could answer this question correctly. The candidates were aged between ten and twelve years. Which is wrong – the test or the intelligence of the children?[37]

The majority of the heads among his respondents took him perfectly seriously; and it was left to the indefatigable Ballard to try to explain that *proper* intelligence tests were *not* conducted like that.[38]

There is a television quiz game element in this kind of thing which one hopes the poor victims were not too terrified to appreciate. But such interviews were surely intended also to demonstrate and enhance the authority of the interviewer. The rationale of playing God like this was set out at its grandest in a paper read by J. L. Paton, High Master of Manchester Grammar School, to the North of England Education Conference in 1920. He considered the extended interviews he conducted infinitely superior to any intelligence test, describing types of questions which ranged

---

[36] E.g., *Minutes Norfolk County Council Education Committee*, 14 Jan. 1922, minute 13, esp. (c), County Hall, Martineau Lane, Norwich; *Minutes Buckinghamshire County Council Scholarship and General Purposes Sub-Committee* (20 June 1929, 15 December 1932), Buckinghamshire Record Office, Aylesbury; Public Record Office, Ed 77/21 (Isle of Ely, 1924), Ed 110/5 (Cheshire, 1933), Ed 77/45 (Gloucestershire, 1928), Ed 77/51 (Herefordshire, 1927 – where HMIs *recommend* that the oral conducted by the secondary school head teachers should include questions of this type), Ed 77/60 (Bury, 1928), Ed 77/87 and Ed 77/88 (Bath, 1924 and 1932), Ed 77/117 (Worcester, 1929) and Ed 77/124 (Dewsbury, 1927). Some of the external examiners employed also conducted their oral examinations in similar fashion – see, for example, Public Record Office, Ed 77/23 (Cheshire, 1923), Ed 77/26 (Stockport, 1928), Ed 77/118 (E. Riding of Yorkshire, 1925) and Ed 77/119 (Hull, 1924).
[37] *The Times Educational Supplement* (28 May 1921), p. 240.
[38] *Ibid.* (4 June 1921), p. 252; (11 June 1921), p. 264; (18 June 1921), p. 280.

from asking for a summary of passages from Addison and Macaulay to sums about the accommodation of motor cars in garages. He ended:

> While you are discussing this ... and whatever may arise out of it, you are gauging from that boy's replies, and specially from the way he speaks and the set of his lips, what his will power is. This is, perhaps, the most important thing of all. What has this boy set himself to be? That more than anything else will determine his future ... This is where Simon-Binet fails us. Your boy may have a first-rate capacity for knowledge, but all he may want to know is all about the Carpentier-Beckett fight. The all-important thing about him is what sort of knowledge does he hunger for? And is his desire for it steadfast? Is it what economists call 'effective demand'? Will it be strong enough to resist the infections of the street with its posters and its newspaper placards? Will he have a soul that refuses to be fed on these things? Will he know the higher from the lower? The temporary from the abiding? And will he choose the better and eschew the worse? Has he his soul, as Plato would say, turned towards the light? If so, he is the lad your school was meant to help and he will help it as much as it helps him.[39]

Thus the final selection of the *crème de la crème* for Manchester Grammar School. But secondary school heads throughout the country clung on hard to any and all discretions given them in the selection process.[40] Part of this is explicable in terms of a whole

[39] *Education* (6 February 1920), pp. 102–3.

[40] For example 'Secondary School Notes', *The Times Educational Supplement* (12 February 1920), p. 92; R. B. Henderson, 'Some aspects of the scholarship system', *Education* (10 April 1925), pp. 346–7; 'Secondary School Notes, *ibid.* (23 December 1927), p. 609; 'Notes from the Association of Assistant Mistresses', *ibid.* (28 April 1933), p. 486; 'School Examinations', *ibid.* (29 June 1934), pp. 747–8; 'Report of the Joint Advisory Committee of the Association of Education Committees and the Four Secondary Associations' *ibid.* (19 November 1937), pp. 534–7, especially p. 535, terms of reference (c). For examples of the extensive involvement of secondary school head teachers and staffs in the selection process see Public Record Office, Ed 77/28 (Cornwall, 1925), Ed 77/29 (Cumberland, 1928), Ed 77/30 (Carlisle, 1924), Ed 77/33 (Devon, 1925), Ed 77/34 (Exeter, 1924), Ed 77/38 (Gateshead, 1929), Ed 77/40 (Sunderland, 1927), Ed 77/41 (West Hartlepool, 1927), Ed 77/48 (Portsmouth, 1924), Ed 77/49 (Southampton, 1932), Ed 77/50 (Isle of Wight, 1927), Ed 77/54 (Lancashire, 1927), Ed 77/58 (Bolton, 1929), Ed 77/61 (Liverpool, 1923), Ed 77/65 (Preston, 1926), Ed 77/66 (Rochdale, 1928), Ed 77/68 (Southport, 1928), Ed 77/74 (Lincolnshire, Kesteven, 1923), Ed 77/75 (Lincolnshire, Kesteven, 1934), Ed 77/91 (Tynemouth, 1924), Ed 77/99 (Staffordshire, 1929), Ed 77/100 (Stoke on Trent, 1928), Ed 77/102 (Wolverhampton, 1923), Ed 77/137 (Isle of Man, 1935) and Ed 110/110 (Smethwick, 1934).

framework of belief, not confined to secondary school heads, to which I shall return below. But some of it seems rooted in a peculiar combination and interaction of two factors, the graduate status of secondary school heads and the buyer's market in which they operated. Their graduate status distanced them from the lowly elementary school teacher, even college-trained, and placed them within the ranks of the local professional élite. But it also meant that their formal training in education was *nil.* They were much less likely than elementary school teachers to have a sustained and formal encounter with considerations of teaching and examining techniques and of mental and psychological testing as it, too, found its way into training college curricula.[41] By a buyer's market I mean that competition for places was such that secondary school head-masters could usually pick and choose. In the selection process, particularly if it included an interview, was a considerable amount of patronage, the exercise of which some of them plainly enjoyed.

The remaining occupational group heavily involved with secondary school selection were the local education officials. Again, one's first thought is that the attraction of the new examination technology, with all its claims to objectivity and precision must have been powerful. Yet again, the reality was more complex and reactions much more mixed. Their occupation had, effectively, been created by the Education Act of 1902 when it created authorities large enough to need full-time professional administrative support. They promptly formed not one but two professional associations; but by 1919 had managed to amalgamate them.[42] By the end of 1937 they had secured the agreement of the AEC and the County Councils Association to a standard job definition and terms of service.[43]

But the terms of this job description reflected perfectly some continuing tensions within the formal grouping. It declared: 'administrative ability and experience are essential while technical knowledge, such as can best be acquired by actual teaching experience in some type or types of school is very desirable. Such officers should, of course, have received a sound general education

[41] Cf. Annie Lloyd-Evans, 'Psychology in the Training of Teachers', *Education* (13 December 1935), pp. 580–2 (paper presented to the British Association).
[42] *Ibid.* (30 July 1926), p. 116.
[43] *Ibid.* (20 March 1936), pp. 348–50; *ibid.* (12 February 1937), pp. 190, 194–5; *ibid.* (9 July 1937), pp. 35–6; *ibid.* (10 September 1937), p. 252; *ibid.* (3 December 1937), p. 584; *ibid.* (4 November 1938), p. 479.

and the possession of a good university degree is most expedient'.[44]
The Association of Directors and Secretaries of Education contained two distinct groups: on the one hand, the older breed of lower
middle-class, upwardly socially mobile, ex-elementary school
teachers, ex-N.U.T. officials, ex-school board clerks, if graduates,
mature students and often London external students; on the other,
slightly younger middle-class graduates of the more conventional
kind, with perhaps some token years of teaching experience, who,
fifty years earlier, might have become public schoolmasters, brief-
less barristers, or even, immediately after 1870, H.M. Inspectors of
Schools.[45] Among the former could be counted Thomas Walling at
Newcastle-upon-Tyne, Spurley Hey at Manchester, Thomas Boyce
at Bradford, Percival Sharp at Sheffield and A. R. Pickles at
Burnley.[46] Among the latter were Salter Davies in Kent, Keith
Innes in Wiltshire, W. R. Brockington in Leicestershire, G. H.
Gater in Lancashire and then at the L.C.C., and, by election, Henry
Morris in Cambridgeshire.[47]

This second group – career local civil servants, if you like –
included some of the earliest and most committed exponents of
mental testing, notably Brockington and Salter Davies; and its
introduction in Wiltshire seems to have coincided with Innes'
arrival.[48] Pickles, on the other hand, provides an exceptionally
interesting example of the reactions of an experienced ex-teacher to
the new technology. Some of it he found acceptable, some not. At

[44] *Ibid.* (4 November 1938), p. 479.
[45] G. Sutherland (note 21), chapter 3.
[46] For Hey see: *Education* (21 November 1924), pp. 369–70; Sharp: *ibid.* (13
February 1925), pp. 158–9; Pickles: *ibid.* (30 July 1926), p. 116; Boyce: *ibid.* (30
January 1931), pp. 132–3; Walling: *ibid.* (8 January 1932), pp. 32–3.
[47] For Gater see: *ibid.* (17 July 1925), pp. 74–5; M. Seaborne, 'William Brockington,
Director of Education for Leicestershire 1903–47' in B. Simon (ed.), *Education in
Leicestershire 1540–1940* (Leicester, 1968), pp. 195–226; and for Innes, Davies and
Morris see: T. Weaver, 'Education: Retrospect and Prospect', *Cambridge Journal of
Education* ix (1979), pp. 3–4, 6–7; H. Rée, *Educator Extraordinary: The Life and
Achievements of Henry Morris 1889–1961* (London, 1973), especially pp. 7–11.
[48] For Leicestershire, see M. Seaborne (note 48); for Kent, see Public Record Office,
Ed 77/53 and Kent Archives Office, County Hall, Maidstone, C/E 10/14, C/E 10/15,
also *The Kent Education Gazette* (February 1934), pp. 157–60, (March 1934), pp.
182–3, (January 1935), pp. 133–6. For Wiltshire, see *Minutes General Education
Committee* (25 November 1932), minute 809 and (28 July 1933), minutes 365 and
366; *Minutes Pupil Records Sub-Committee*, notes of meeting 28 April 1934 and
*interim* Report 16 June 1934, Wiltshire Record Office, County Hall, Trowbridge;
I.M. Slocombe, Wiltshire Education Department to the author 12 May 1975 – in
response to a nationally distributed questionnaire about test use (G.SQ 1975).

the North of England Conference on Education in 1931, he discussed at length the theory about the relationship between general and specific abilities, concluding, 'it is therefore likely that selection for further education at the age of eleven will remain based on range of central capacity rather than type of special ability'. Then he went on:

There is great scope for experiment and research into the methods of transfer from junior schools. No course of senior grade can be properly planned without knowledge of the basis of attainment and capacity reached in the fundamental subjects of the curriculum, and the question of what the normal pupil can or cannot be expected to do assumes a new significance. It will be necessary to know what a pupil can actually do as well as what he is capable of doing. As internal examinations are 'tightened up' the school record will become increasingly valuable; but some form and measure of standardisation will still be desirable. Intelligence tests are still on their trial. Whilst attainment may possibly be tested apart from capacity, it is certain that capacity cannot be ascertained apart from attainment. It is yet doubtful whether intelligence tests measure real capacity; they rather tend to show up sharpness and quickness of reaction, to be by way of puzzles rather than problems. '*If your grandfather's only child was your uncle, draw a square, if not draw a circle.*' Whilst there may be a permanent place for intelligence tests in the educational scheme, it is probable that a good examination can test intelligence and capacity quite as well as these artificial aids. But the sponsors of intelligence tests are undoubtedly showing how examinations can be reformed.[49]

His authority, Burnley, appears to have flirted only once – in March 1922 – with a group test.[50] But the fit is not perfect. The ex-elementary teachers Walling and Boyce, at Newcastle-upon-Tyne and Bradford respectively, presided over selection systems where mental testing was used.[51] By contrast, the London County

[49] *Education* (16 January 1931), pp. 62, 64.
[50] *Minutes Burnley County Borough Council Higher Education Sub-Committee* (March 1922) and *Minutes Burnley CBC Schools Sub-Committee* (25 February 1925), Town Hall, Burnley. Cf. also the Burnley entry in Sir Philip Hartog and Gladys Roberts, *A Conspectus of Examinations in Great Britain and Northern Ireland* (London, International Institute Examinations Enquiry, 1937) sect.1A.
[51] For Bradford, see Public Record Office, Ed 77/123. For Newcastle, see *Moray House Archives*, Index to users of Moray House group intelligence tests (M.H.Ts), and Newcastle-upon-Tyne Education Department reply to GSQ 1975, Edinburgh University Library.

Council did not use mental testing in the Junior County Scholarship Examination either in the time of Gater, or that of his successor, Edmund Rich.[52] Once again, the tidy pattern eludes us.

The last group involved with selection for secondary education is the one which it is most difficult to characterize, and yet the one which made the decisions – the councillors and aldermen who sat on the Education Committees. At the simplest level, they are difficult to characterize because they share no occupational description. However committed and informed they might become about their chosen specialism, their local government work remained ultimately voluntary and part-time. These difficulties are compounded by major problems of evidence. Anyone who has worked on twentieth-century local government records will know how frighteningly incomplete and uninformative they mostly are. Thus it is difficult enough to discover the grounds given for something new, e.g., the decision to try an intelligence test. By definition, hardly anyone bothers to explain carrying on as before.

It is, however, possible to say a little about the general social standing of these people. County and county borough councillors and aldermen were firmly part of the local élite. The reform of English local government at the end of the nineteenth century had brought about no social revolution. The county councils, at least up to 1974, remained remarkably aristocratic bodies. In industrial and the more heavily urbanized areas business and professional men gradually elbowed out the old squirearchy, but without necessarily bringing much change of style.[53] Among the most prominent and active members of the Association of Education Committees in the inter-war years were men like the substantial textile manufacturer Alderman Sir Percy Jackson, Chairman of the West Riding Education Committee from 1917 to 1937, the local solicitor, Alderman Lieutenant-Colonel W. E. Raley, Chairman of the Barnsley Education Committee from 1904 to the end of the 1920s and Councillor W. Byng Kenrick, nephew of Joseph Chamberlain and director of the family hardware firm, who suc-

---

[52] For a fuller discussion of London, see G. Sutherland (note 3), pp. 150–1 and G. Sutherland and S. Sharp (note 1).

[53] B. Keith-Lucas, *English Local Government in the Nineteenth and Twentieth Centuries* (London, The Historical Association, 1977) p. 23. For detailed studies of particular localities see J. M. Lee, *Social Leaders and Public Persons. A study of county government in Cheshire since 1888* (Oxford, 1963); G. W. Jones, *Borough Politics: A Study of the Wolverhampton Town Council 1884–1964* (London, 1969).

ceeded another uncle as Chariman of the Birmingham Education Committee in 1921.[54] Among this company, even the self-made men are rare and I have so far identified only two, Alderman E. G. Rowlinson, the railway trade union official, Chairman of the Sheffield Education Committee from 1926,[55] and George Tomlinson, the Lancashire weaver and union official, a member of the Lancashire Education Committee from 1930[56] who was, of course, to succeed Ellen Wilkinson as Minister of Education in the Labour Government in 1947.

Rowlinson, like Tomlinson, was a solid Labour man. But there has emerged no simple or necessary correlation between progressive politics – or, indeed, any other sort – and a predilection for the new technology in education. Rowlinson's fellow-alderman from Sheffield, H. W. Jackson, indeed embarrassed him badly when he launched a thorough-going attack on psychologists in general, and child guidance clinics in particular, at the A.E.C. meetings in 1938 and 1939.[57] One thinks again of the Halifax Education Committee seeking reassurance from H.M. Inspectorate that the system of selection by standardized school record cards and group tests, so enthusiastically developed by their local teachers and officials, was a good one.[58] But there were 'sports' if you like, testing enthusiasts among L.E.A. members. It was Dr Andrew Messer who, single-handed, persuaded Northumberland to employ Godfrey Thomson in 1921.[59] The Bradford authority, for at least

[54] For Jackson see: P. H. J. H. Gosden and P. R. Sharp, *The Development of an Education Service: The West Riding 1889–1974* (Oxford, 1979) pp. 23–4; Raley: *Education* (24 April 1925), pp. 388–9; Kenrick: *ibid.* (23 January 1925), pp. 92–3.

[55] *Ibid.* (17 June 1932), p. 697. For the working coalition formed between Rowlinson, Sir Percy Jackson, Brockington, Lady Simon and R. H. Tawney on the Consultative Committee of the Board of Education in the 1930s, see Joan Simon, 'The Shaping of the Spens Report on Secondary Education 1933–38: An Inside View', *British Journal of Education Studies* xxv (1977) pp. 63–80, 170–85.

[56] *Education* (9 June 1939), pp. 706–7.

[57] *Ibid* (24 June 1938), p. 825; *ibid.* (23 June 1939), pp. 807, 809, 811. Cf. also *ibid.* (10 January 1936), p. 27.

[58] See above, p. 323.

[59] *The Times Educational Supplement* (3 February 1921), p. 54; *Minutes of the Scholarship and Exhibitions Sub-Committee* 27 January 1921, minute 2, Northumberland Record Office, Melton Park, North Gosforth, Newcastle-upon-Tyne; Notes from 1956 and 1957 for lectures on selection procedures by G. Bosomworth, formerly Examinations Officer for Northumberland Education Committee and kindly made available to the author by Mr Bosomworth and the Director of Education for Northumberland in response to GSQ 1975.

four years running, accepted advice and help from 'the Intelligence Tests Committee, an unofficial body of persons interested in such tests and willing to co-operate in investigating their possibilities in Bradford'[60] – about whom I would give a good deal to know more. And of course any Director or Chief Education Officer worth his salt, the Brockingtons and Daviesses, or indeed, the Wallings and Boyces, could carry his Committee with him at least part of the way when he wanted to do something very much.

This brings us full circle. If some officials, authorities – and teachers – considered intelligence tests the most 'efficient' way of selecting for secondary education, why did others not? I have tried to sketch the complexity of the social and political structure within which decisions were taken and through which information about the new technology was mediated. But to sum this up simply as vested interests and their rationalizations seems too crude – unless one is going to dismiss all ideas, all ideologies as epiphenomena of this kind. These networks of interests and the associated attitudes seem, ultimately, to require a broader frame of reference, some consideration of the role of educational selection in the society as a whole and a discussion of a notion of meritocracy which is peculiarly English.

Central to the concept of meritocracy is the equation of ability with merit, of talent with virtue, as Clarence Karier has called it.[61] This equation can be seen as a very tight, close relationship, possession of one guaranteeing and automatically bringing the other. On this interpretation, the related notion of equality of opportunity becomes quite a strong one, with at least an aura of democracy. But the English, from Macaulay and the Whig–Liberal reformers of the civil service onwards, have tended to see what is simultaneously a much looser and more complex relationship between the two. At the centre is a notion of merit which has social and cultural as well as more narrowly intellectual aspects; gradually, the possession of ability comes to be seen as *a* principal, but not invariably *the* principal, means of achieving this condition. Money, parental culture and aspiration may also make a contribution. It is perhaps hardly surprising to find this in a society with a class structure as well articulated as that of nineteenth-century England; and some members of that society recognized it clearly.

[60] Public Record Office, Ed. 77/123.
[61] Karier (note 2), p. 346.

The influential Royal Commission, the Taunton Commission, which reviewed the state of secondary education in the 1860s, presented the class stratification of English education as a *fait accompli*, which no act of policy could change. Type and duration of education were determined for the child by the finances and ambition of his parent. The Commissioners argued only for the re-modelling of old endowments to provide scholarships in order that 'real ability shall find its proper opening.'[62]

The dominant late nineteenth-century English version of merit-ocracy was thus both a weak and unashamedly socially élitist one. This is the context in which the first state-funded secondary schools were created after 1902. The ladder of scholarships of the kind recommended by the Taunton Commissioners, which linked public elementary schools to private and endowed secondary schools, had grown slowly since 1870. In 1907 the government made a first direct contribution to this. The Free Place Regulations of that year increased grants to secondary schools but made it a condition of the receipt of the full grant that a minimum of 25 per cent of the school's places should be free and open only to children from public elementary schools. The remainder of the schools' intake paid fees and could come from any preparatory school, public or private. *The Times Educational Supplement*, in one of its earliest issues in 1910, approved the principle but struck a warning note:

> to insist all at once upon so large a proportion as 25% of 'free-placers' *ex hypothesi* boys or girls from working-class homes, in an average secondary school to which middle-class parents send their children, is, under present conditions of English life, to say the least of it, 'a large order' ... In an old country like England, where lines of social distinction are sharply drawn, they cannot be ignored or set aside in practice, however anxious we may be to open the best educational advantages to everyone. Most secondary school headmasters would welcome a contingent of capable working class boys to be absorbed into the life of the school and profit by its tone and teaching. But many of them are alarmed lest, if it be known or surmised that the numbers thus

[62] *Report of the Schools Inquiry Commission* P. P. (1867–8), xxvii, p. 95. For a more extended discussion see Gillian Sutherland, 'Secondary Education: The Education of the Middle Classes' in Gillian Sutherland (ed.), *Government and Society in Nineteenth-Century Britain: Commentaries on British Parliamentary Papers: Education* (Dublin, 1977) pp. 137–66. Cf. also Hope (note 8).

coming up from below are large enough to affect the tone and character of the school, the parents of paying pupils will hold aloof and the finances of the school become disorganized. Our administrators and reformers should be careful in the matter not to force the pace.[63]

This remains a theme well into the inter-war period. In 1925 Dr Terry Thomas, the new headmaster of Leeds Grammar School – who was to remain there until the middle 1950s – moved and carried at the Headmasters' Conference a resolution to the effect that a substantial extension of the free place system in existing schools would be unwise: 'They must be careful that their schools were not swamped. They had a great body of boys from middle-class homes who might not be scholars but who were very valuable in building up a right tone in the school.'[64] This is the voice of social privilege. But the argument about 'tone' could and did transmute itself quite easily into an argument for high culture in the strictest Arnoldian sense. If you recall J. L. Paton's account of the interviews he gave to scholarship candidates for Manchester Grammar School, he laboured the distinction between a thirst for knowledge and the kind of knowledge sought. He wanted to discover the strength of a boy's determination and his motivation.[65]

Secondary school heads were, naturally enough, among the leading and most vocal exponents of this kind of highly structured élitism. But they were not the only ones. The economic crisis in 1931 led the government to propose the replacement of 'free places' by 'special places', entailing a means test to discover if the parent could pay part, or even all, of the fee. A handful of local authorities responded to this by declaring all their secondary school places special places and selecting for them by a uniform method; and this, indeed, was what the A.E.C. Executive recommended.[66] But many more did not and continued to subject would-be fee-payers to a qualifying examination rather less stringent than the rigorous

[63] 'The New Secondary Education', *The Times Educational Supplement* (16 September 1910), p. 19.
[64] *Education* (2 January 1925), p. 7.
[65] Is this, incidentally, very different from the objectives some of us have – and occasionally articulate – when interviewing prospective university entrants?
[66] 'Special Places in Secondary Schools', *Education* (18 March 1938), pp. 332–4 especially, p. 332. By this time thirty-six LEAs were offering 100 per cent special places.

competition conducted for special places. Even those accepting the logic of a uniform method of selection were not necessarily convinced that a means test for fees was inegalitarian. When Alderman Rowlinson of Sheffield tried to move a resolution for free secondary education at the A.E.C. annual conference in 1936, he got a somewhat warm reaction. Councillor W. M. Hyman (West Riding) 'deduced from the general argument by Alderman Rowlinson that the children of well-to-do parents who could pay were in the main of lower intelligence than the children of those who required help with the fees. The parent without a bean should be able to produce the children of the highest intelligence and mental capacity!' On a card vote, the motion was lost by 248 to 181.[67]

It might have been expected that considerations of post-war economic reconstruction would have altered the terms of the debate somewhat. Certainly between 1915 and 1920 *The Times Educational Supplement* had declared at regular intervals that in future the nation could not afford to waste its 'child capital'.[68] But after 1920, statements of this kind largely disappeared. In so far as people adverted to the interests of the state in secondary education at all after 1920, they were as likely as not to suggest that the state was at risk from over-education. It was put very elegantly during the debate on the 1922 Education Estimates by Sir Martin Conway, Conservative M.P. for the Combined English Universities:

> It is not, in fact, a ladder that we want from the lowest slum to the highest university honour, what we want is a sieve, so that we may be quite sure that not a grain is kept above the sieve that can get through it, and that not a grain large enough to remain in the top of the sieve gets lost. We want to sift the millions of children born in this country to discover, to isolate, to bring out, to help in every way, all the finest ability in the country, and allow none of it to escape. If you succeed in getting that, you really get all that is required, because the number of really able and most highly developed and educated people that are wanted will never be many.[69]

---

[67] *Ibid.* (19 June 1936), pp. 807, 808, 810, 812, 814, 816, 818; Councillor Hyman's comment is quoted on p. 812; cf. also the remarks of Councillor Tuck of Lincoln on p. 814 and the dispute at Brighton described in the reference in note 66 above.
[68] A Necessary Revolution', *The Times Educational Supplement* (5 October 1915), p. 119; 'The Ways and Means of Revolution', *ibid.*, (2 November 1915), p. 131; 'Some National Aspects of Childhood', *ibid.* (13 December 1917), p. 481; 'Education during the War', *ibid.* (14 November 1918), p. 489; 'Two Steps in Secondary Education', *ibid.* (28 October), p. 575.
[69] Quoted in *Education* (12 May 1922), p. 282.

As economic depression deepened and unemployment increased, comments about the 'saturation' of professions and black-coated occupations became more explicit.[70]

In all the wrangling about special places the argument that ultimately the state would lose from the contraction of investment in education was heard only in a very weak form. Typical was the A.E.C. Memorandum of 1932, which declared:

It is desired – apart altogether from the enunciation of the simplest principles of justice – to emphasize that it is merely an elementary part of economic, social and political prudence to provide that the places in secondary schools maintained or aided by the nation should be allocated to children on an equal basis of merit. This is an ideal in secondary education which should not be forgone even in times of gravest national difficulty.[71]

When Alderman Rowlinson move for free secondary education in 1936, he centred his argument not around national need but around the proposition 'that ability to take full advantage of higher education should be the criterion as to whether or not a child should go forward to this branch of education'.[72]

Thus in trying to explain why the reception given to the new technology of measurement in education in England in 1919–1939 was so lukewarm, we have first to recognize the decentralization of the decision-making process. Then we have to explore a complex social and political network, recognizing ultimately that we are dealing with a society whose educational system is highly and unashamedly elitist, whose version of meritocracy is a somewhat idiosyncratic one. We are dealing also with the society which was first to industrialize, from a relatively low educational base. This particular piece of historical experience made it extremely difficult for the English before the second World War to perceive the force of the argument for spending on mass education as a form of investment for economic growth, thereby reinforcing the élitism.

[70] J. F. Duff to the Eugenics Education Society, *ibid.* (8 January 1926), p. 24; R. B. Henderson, 'Some Reflections on the Scholarship System', *ibid.* (5 October 1928), p. 290; Dr C. Norwood to the British Association, *ibid.* (14 September 1934), p. 228; cf. also 'Local Authority Notes', *ibid.* (3 December 1937), p. 585.

[71] 'Selection for and Tuition Fees in Secondary Schools', *ibid.* (21 October 1932), pp. 378–80. Cf. also some of the comments of P. Sharp, Secretary of the A.E.C. to the North of England Conference, *ibid.* (13 January 1933), p. 41; an extract of Alderman Rowlinson's presidential address to the A.E.C. A.G.M., and the arguments at Brighton, *ibid.* (18 March 1938), p. 332.

[72] *Ibid.* (19 June 1936), p. 807.

# Index